Decolonizing the Stage

Decolonizing the Stage

Theatrical Syncretism and Post-Colonial Drama

CHRISTOPHER B. BALME

CLARENDON PRESS · OXFORD
1999

Oxford University Press, Great Clarendon Street, Oxford OX2 6DP

Oxford New York

Athens Auckland Bangkok Bogotá Buenos Aires Calcutta
Cape Town Chennai Dar es Salaam Delhi Florence Hong Kong Istanbul
Karachi Kuala Lumpur Madrid Melbourne Mexico City Mumbai
Nairobi Paris São Paulo Singapore Taipei Tokyo Toronto Warsaw
and associated companies in
Berlin Ibadan

Oxford is a registered trademark of Oxford University Press

Published in the United States
by Oxford University Press Inc., New York

British Library Cataloguing in Publication Data
Data available

Library of Congress Cataloging in Publication Data
Balme, Christopher B.
Decolonizing the stage: theatrical syncretism and
post-colonial drama/Christopher B. Balme.
Includes bibliographical references and index.
1. Drama–History and criticism.   2. Theater–Developing
countries.   3. Literature and society–Developing countries.
I. Title.
PN1643.B37   1998   809.2'04–dc21   98-36573

ISBN 0-19-818444-1

1 3 5 7 9 10 8 6 4 2

Typeset by J&L Composition Ltd, Filey, North Yorkshire
Printed in Great Britain
on acid-free paper by
Biddles Ltd, Guildford and King's Lynn

Preface

THE first impulse for this book goes back at least ten years. In 1985, during a tenure as post-doctoral student at the University of Munich, I received a letter from the Maori poet Hone Tuwhare containing information about his first play, *On Ilkla Moor B'aht'at (In the Wilderness without a Hat)*, which had just been produced in New Zealand. This was followed by a copy of the script, which, on reading, I realized represented a new departure for drama and theatre in New Zealand. Not only was it a major play by the country's foremost Maori poet (at the time I erroneously thought it to be the first Maori play, full stop), but it contained an astonishing mixture of dramatic and theatrical styles. 'Western' naturalistic dialogue, a lot of which was in Maori, blended with the ritual intricacy and power of a *tangi*, a Maori funeral.

A year later I took up a position with responsibility for drama at another German university; it was suggested that this should include 'Commonwealth drama'. As I began preparing for these courses, I realized that, in terms of its integration of indigenous performance forms, Tuwhare's play was by no means unique, but was consistent with similar experiments throughout the post-colonial world. Tuwhare had, however, written his play independently and without knowledge of his post-colonial precursors such as Wole Soyinka or Derek Walcott, Ola Rotimi or Dennis Scott.

When it came to teaching these plays to German students, it became evident that the techniques of dramatic and theatrical analysis that had been developed for works from the Euro-American tradition had serious shortcomings when applied to post-colonial drama. It was not just a problem of historical and cultural background knowledge—many of the plays employed indigenous performance idioms which were entirely alien to their own experience, but which appeared in many cases to be central for grasping the works themselves. Neither the traditional approaches focusing on plot, character, and social-political criticism, or the more innovative thematic analysis coming from feminist and materialist schools of thought, offered ways of looking at the performative dimension. These plays reminded me of the religious syncretism characteristic of Maori churches I remembered from my childhood, and which I re-encountered academically when I began to study anthropology at Auckland University in the mid-1970s. I invented for myself the term 'syncretic theatre' as a label for these post-colonial experiments and began to consider ways of thinking about culturally disparate works on a comparative level. This project has metamorphosed through various stages including conference papers on particular regional manifestations, a weighty post-doctoral thesis in German, and now, finally, a somewhat more streamlined book.

Looking back over the past decade, the most striking change is the radically altered context for such a study. In 1985 the term 'post-colonial' was by no means on everybody's lips and still less a section on major publishers' stock lists. At the time I felt my project was to negotiate a scholarly no person's land between literary criticism, on the one hand, whose relevant branch, the New Literatures in English, appeared to be almost exclusively interested in prose fiction, and theatre studies, on the other, which was exceptionally Eurocentric in its field of vision. The discipline that has now come to be known as post-colonial criticism was, in the late 1980s, still the preserve of a network of scholars working in Europe and those countries which had had the somewhat dubious distinction of falling under British rule at one time or another. This cooperative venture was for the most part a productive one. The 'colonies' contributed writers (most of whom were still alive and could be invited to a bar for further interrogation), and scholars with invaluable local knowledge. The European scholars created conference frameworks which enabled all kinds of interesting cross-cultural connections to be made. The research carried out was very writer-centred and involved for the most part close textual exegesis of particular works.

Two developments since the mid-1980s have decisively altered the scholarly context for the present study. The first is the 'discovery' of post-colonialism in the United States. This came about through a combination of factors, such as the highly politicized multiculturalism debate, the recognition of literary and artistic heterogeneity on its own doorstep, the application of deconstruction and feminist theoretical concerns to the 'old' texts, resulting in a forefronting of these texts within a new theoretical discourse. The other significant development is the metamorphosis of the term 'post-colonial' from a

general epithet with temporal and spatial coordinates, however ill
defined they may be, into the 'invention' of a critical approach or
methodology. It is now possible to undertake a post-colonial reading
of Shakespeare, a critical practice anticipated by some twenty or
thirty years by writers such as Aimé Césaire. The shift from cultural
and artistic location to critical methodology has, however, important
consequences for the context in which this book will be received.
Post-colonialism as a critical method has been decisively influenced
by the work of Edward Said, Homi Bhabha, and Gayatri Spivak—the
'Holy Trinity', as Robert Young has termed them.[1]

Among the many impulses that these critics have brought to the
field, perhaps the most important—and this is true mainly of Said and
Bhabha—is the temporal extension of the field of research into the
colonial and imperial past. Their work has decisively influenced the
now-growing field of colonial discourse analysis, which recognizes
that discursive practices do not allow themselves to be neatly demarcated by declarations of independence or similar symbolic acts. This
extension of the post-colonial continuum into the colonial period is
reflected in this study by detailed discussions of Rabindranath Tagore
and the Zulu dramatist and theorist H. I. E. Dhlomo. Neither of these
writers features prominently in other discussions of post-colonial
theatre, yet both their dramatic and their theoretical works anticipate
by several decades the strategy of syncretization which in many ways
has become the hallmark of post-colonial theatre since the 1960s.

The second important factor which has emerged since this study
was first envisaged is the recent publication of two books on post-
colonial theatre and drama: Brian Crow with Chris Banfield, *An
Introduction to Post-Colonial Theatre* (1996) and Helen Gilbert
and Joanne Tompkins, *Post-Colonial Drama Theory, Practice, Politics*
(1996).[2] Although very different in their approaches—Crow and
Banfield provide sketches of important dramatists, while Gilbert
and Tompkins stake out an exceptionally varied theoretical and thematic territory for their term 'post-colonial drama'—they intersect at

[1] Robert J. C. Young, *Colonial Desire: Hybridity in Theory, Culture and Race* (London: Routledge, 1995), p. 163.
[2] Brian Crow with Chris Banfield, *An Introduction to Post-Colonial Theatre* (Cambridge: Cambridge University Press, 1996); Helen Gilbert and Joanne Tompkins, *Post-Colonial Drama: Theory, Practice, Politics* (London: Routledge, 1996). Both studies appeared too late for their observations to be included in any detail. However, where appropriate I have tried to include in the notes important cross-references.

various points, both with each other and with this book, to reveal significant common ground. Both highlight the previous dearth of comparative work on post-colonial theatre and drama compared to the extensive research which has been focused on prose writing. Both emphasize the importance of the performative aspect of the texts under consideration, although in practice Crow and Banfield remain almost entirely text-based in their analyses. Both centre their understanding of 'post-colonial' on notions of oppression and subjugation, and analyse theatre and drama as a medium of resistance to them. This means that post-colonial theatre is always implicitly and very often explicitly political. Perhaps the other important common denominator of all three studies is the significance they attach to indigenous performance forms for the creation of a new theatre aesthetic in post-colonial countries. While Crow and Banfield acknowledge it and Gilbert and Tompkins even examine it within similar parameters to mine, my own book focuses exclusively on this aspect of post-colonial theatre. The appearance of these three studies within a short period reveals the exceptional importance of post-colonial theatre as a development of international significance. Through their common ground they demonstrate that a large number of comparative perspectives are emerging which offer points of access to scholars and students of theatre and literature outside the countries of origin of the plays and productions themselves.

While not forgetting the importance of the cultural specificity that underpins much post-colonial theatre (and all the works examined in this book), this study is predicated on the idea that the theatrical elements of the stage offer modes of comparison across cultures. Whatever the cultural provenance of the author or theatre group, all have to find expressive idioms for texts conveyed by voice, body, and space. This book is thus addressed both to students of theatre, who may never have encountered a play by Wole Soyinka, and to scholars of post-colonial literature for whom the performative component of dramatic texts has posed a problem. The concept of syncretic theatre proposes that even theatrical texts incorporating little-known cultural forms can be profitably studied via their performance dynamics. So it is in the spirit of greater interdisciplinary and intercultural dialogue that this book is offered.

C. B. B.
Munich

Acknowledgements

A STUDY of this nature would not have been possible without the cooperation and generosity of scholars and artists from a great number of countries. In New Zealand I was able to profit from two sojourns at the Victoria University of Wellington, where in the Department of Theatre and Film I was welcomed and assisted by David Carnegie and Phil Mann and in the English Department encouraged by Vincent O'Sullivan. At the University of Western Australia, Perth, I was given similar assistance and encouragement by Dennis Haskell and Bruce Bennett (now in Canberra). At the University of the West Indies, Mona, Jamaica, Mervyn Morris extended his renowned hospitality and Eddie Baugh shared with me the riches of his file on Walcott; Harclyde Walcott provided me with invaluable photographs; thanks also to Michael Cooke for introducing me to Caribbean drama and theatre in the first place. At the University of Hawaii, Manoa, I was warmly received and ably guided by Professor James Brandon; the Hamilton Library there is everything a visiting scholar dreams of. My research in Canada would have been exceedingly less productive without the help of Jennifer Preston, then a research assistant at the University of Guelph and later manager of the Native Earth Performing Arts in Toronto.

A number of directors and dramatists also gave generously of their time and ideas. I would like to mention Andrew Ross and Richard Walley, Australia; John Broughton, Roma Potiki, and Hone Tuwhare, New Zealand/Aotearoa (kia ora ka pai!); Tomson Highway, Canada; and Malcolm Purkey, South Africa.

I would also like to thank those photographers who supplied me with their work and gave permission for it to be reproduced here. Every effort has been made to obtain permission for the photographs reproduced in this book. Any omissions will be rectified in future editions. Thanks also to Christoph for redrawing the diagrams.

Jack Davis's play *No Sugar* is published by Currency Press, Sydney, 1986.

Contents

Plates

Figures

Introduction

In his recent monumental study *Culture and Imperialism* (1993) Edward Said maps out the two-way traffic of cultural exchange generated by the imperial system. Imperialism is, he argues, perhaps the single most important historical factor determining contemporary experience and political problems. Said sets up an ideological dilemma: the aesthetics of colonial and post-colonial art are unthinkable without the less than salutary effects of this experience. Thus, for better or for worse, the experience of Empire has permanently altered the perceptions of the West towards its former colonies and vice versa. A view of this perceptual map is offered both by writings about the Empire and the colonized peoples, and by the response of writers and artists in these countries to the experience and the discourses purporting to represent them. This response is encapsulated in Salman Rushdie's now-famous phrase 'The Empire Writes Back'.

It is within this wider historical context that this book is situated. It is intended as a contribution to the understanding of what may be called the 'theatrical' or 'performative' response to imperialism. The works and performances examined here are fundamentally influenced by the triad of imperialism, colonization, and decolonization. It advances the argument that the 'decolonization' of the stage can be examined through a number of formal strategies which involve the combination and amalgamation of indigenous performance forms within the framework of the Western notion of theatre. The process whereby culturally heterogeneous signs and codes are merged together can be termed 'theatrical syncretism'. This development is one of the most striking aspects of the theatrical cultures that we commonly term 'post-colonial'. Although the prevalence of syncretic elements in some post-colonial countries has often been remarked upon,[1] it has

---

[1] The work of Wole Soyinka in particular has led critics to use the term 'syncretism' as an epithet: Wiveca Sotto refers to Soyinka's 'syncretic work material' in her study *The Rounded Rite: A Study of Wole Soyinka's Play 'The Bacchae of Euripides'* (Lund: C. W. K. Gleerup, 1985), 103; see also the article by P. J. Conradie, 'Syncretism in Wole Soyinka's Play *The Bacchae of Euripides*', *South African Theatre Journal*, 4/1 (1990), 61–74.

never been systematically studied; nor has there been any attempt to formulate a coherent theory to account for this phenomenon.

The term 'syncretism' is borrowed from the discipline of comparative religion and denotes the process whereby elements of two or more religions are merged and absorbed into one another. While syncretism has always been a feature of religious change, it has been particularly noticeable and well documented during the period of colonial contact. In contrast to religious syncretism, which is usually an extended process brought about by friction and interchange between cultures, theatrical syncretism is in most cases a conscious, programmatic strategy to fashion a new form of theatre in the light of colonial or post-colonial experience. It is very often written and performed in a europhone language, but almost always manifests varying degrees of bi- or multilingualism. Syncretic theatre is one of the most effective means of decolonizing the stage, because it utilizes the performance forms of both European and indigenous cultures in a creative recombination of their respective elements, without slavish adherence to one tradition or the other.

Although syncretic theatrical experiments thus defined can be found in most post-colonial societies, the scope of this study is limited to those countries which have produced a substantial body of work. In order to map out the full range of responses and strategies encompassed by the term 'syncretic theatre', it is necessary to set wide geographical parameters. Syncretic theatre in this sense is a widespread phenomenon in Africa, the Caribbean, and India, and is increasing in strength in 'Fourth World'[2] or aboriginal cultures in New Zealand, Australia, and North America.[3] Theatrical texts from

[2] For the notion of Fourth World cultures, see Nelson Graburn's definition: 'the collective name for all aboriginal or native peoples whose lands fall within the national boundaries and techno-bureaucratic administrations of the countries of the First, Second, and Third Worlds. As such, they are peoples without countries of their own, peoples who are usually in the minority and without the power to direct the course of their collective lives.' Introduction to Nelson H. H. Graburn (ed.), *Tourist and Ethnic Arts: Cultural Expressions from the Fourth World* (Berkeley and Los Angeles: University of California Press, 1976), 1.

[3] Although the United States, and concretely the arts of the Native American peoples, are not usually included under the rubric 'post-colonial', this is solely a by-product of the origins of post-colonial studies within the parameters of Commonwealth Literatures. From the perspective of theatre studies, however, there is no good reason for making any kind of substantive distinction between the development and strategies of the Native American theatres in the United States and Canada. For a general outline of this discussion, see Bill Ashcroft, Gareth Griffiths, and Helen Tiffin, *The Empire Writes Back: Theory and Practice in Post-Colonial Literatures* (London: Routledge, 1989), 2, who argue for including the United States in the category post-colonial.

these areas form the focus of analysis in this book. Although the number of texts mentioned is large, the body of theatrical activity that they represent is even larger. I have tried to find a balance between discussing representative works by better-known writers such as Wole Soyinka, Ola Rotimi, and Derek Walcott and introducing texts from lesser-known artists and ensembles. The innovative theatrical experiments of the dramatists and theatre-makers in post-colonial societies have, with a few notable exceptions, been largely ignored by the critics and the theatregoing public of the First World. Most activity receives only local attention for obvious reasons of cultural, social, and linguistic specificity; even scholarly interest tends to be either heavily writer- or country-orientated. It is the aim of this book to provide an international perspective by focusing not on just one artistic form and genre—drama and theatre—but also on a single, unifying development observable within the theatrical cultures of practically all post-colonial societies which have some kind of tradition of dramatic enactment. This broad geocultural focus means that there will be no attempt to provide an encyclopaedic survey of the countries, artists, and ensembles working in the syncretic mode. In order to illustrate the complex nature of syncretic dramaturgical strategies a smaller representative number of works have been chosen for more detailed readings.

A central aim of this study is to demonstrate a methodology with which to analyse these works as theatrical texts and to foreground syncreticity as a central component of their communicative structure. The methodology employed relies on a number of semiotic concepts which I wish to introduce briefly. Syncretic theatre cannot be grasped purely as an aesthetic phenomenon but must be embedded in a concept of cultural interaction and change. Yuri Lotman and his school of cultural semiotics have proposed the notion of cultural text as a heuristic category with which to approach cultural phenomena. According to Lotman's definition a cultural text is 'any carrier of integral ("textual") meaning including ceremonies, works of art, as well as "genres" such as "prayer", "law", "novel", etc.'.[4] This broad

---

[4] This definition was first formulated in the 'Theses on the Semiotic Study of Cultures (as Applied to Slavic Texts)', which were published in English in Jan van der Eng and Mojmír Grygar (eds.), *Structure of Texts and Semiotics of Culture*, (The Hague: Mouton, 1973), 1–28, here p. 6. A detailed commentary can be found in the article by Irene Portis Winner and Thomas Winner, 'The Semiotics of Cultural Texts', *Semiotica*, 18/2 (1976), 101–56.

definition of text indicates a conceptual flexibility which overcomes narrow logocentric focus and includes not only linguistic, but also iconographic and performative, cultural manifestations. Other such criteria include: construction according to definite generative rules; organization according to genre or type; and the ascription of value to and the preservation of a text. A key criterion for a cultural text is that it is only fully comprehensible within the culture that produces and uses it. From the perspective of another culture a text will possibly or probably not be understood; in fact a text may not even be recognized as a cultural text, i.e. as a carrier of meaning, at all. The history of intercultural encounter, although not explicitly cited by Lotman in his original definition, provides countless examples of both intentional and unintentional non-recognition of cultural texts. The encounter between literate and pre-scribal cultures, an integral component of colonial history and experience, particularly resulted in a problematic hierarchization of textual genres with an obvious privileging of Western written texts on the part of the colonial powers. However, the concept of cultural text offers a term which is more or less value-free and does not privilege a priori particular cultural forms. It thus offers a terminological instrument with which to avoid hierarchies of genre and aesthetic forms.

Such hierarchical notions are very evident in the early period of colonial literature and drama. The normative aesthetics of realistic drama were exported intact to the farthest-flung colonies and exerted an unmistakable influence on indigenous dramatists and directors. The polyphonic potential of theatre, particularly the interplay of music, dance, and dialogue found in certain Western theatrical genres, tended to be treated pejoratively in comparison to the realistic dialogue-based model of Shaw and Ibsen. In cultural semiotic terms elements such as songs, dances, masquerades, costuming, and oral stories, which all exist in their own right as cultural texts with their own specific mechanisms of production, transmission, and reception, were initially not considered appropriate for inclusion into the dramatic form. The integration of such cultural texts into the framework of a theatrical text involves a process of cultural and aesthetic semiotic recoding which ultimately questions the basis of normative Western drama.[5]

[5] The term 'recoding' is used here in its semiotic sense to mean the reconstitution of signs in either their syntactic, semantic, or pragmatic functions. In the context of syncretic theatre, or indeed of any form of intercultural performance, recoding will predominantly affect the semantic function.

Apart from this terminological revalorization, the concept of cultural text offers certain hermeneutic advantages. Thus the analysis of a syncretic theatrical text can be approached from the point of view of the functionality and interaction of the cultural texts and not on the basis of conventional interpretative strategies deriving from Western poetics such as plot, character, and theme. Since the dominant feature of syncretic theatre is a particular conjunction of aesthetic and cultural codes, it is clear that the monocultural communication model of traditional theatre semiotics requires substantial revision.

An illustration of these somewhat abstract concepts can be provided if we compare syncretic theatre and theatrical exoticism. Both use indigenous cultural texts, but in quite different ways. The latter, which can be traced back at least as far as the Renaissance, also reveals processes of mixing and adaptation of foreign performance elements into Western theatre. On the superficial level of exterior appearance there seem in fact to be parallels. However, theatrical exoticism, whether it is in the form of baroque decoratism, Enlightenment idealism, or nineteenth-century orientalism, pays no heed to the original textuality of the elements it appropriates, whether they be costumes, masks, dances, or songs. They are arbitrarily recoded and semanticized in an entirely Western aesthetic and ideological frame. Exoticism involves the use of indigenous cultural texts purely for their surface appeal, but with no regard to their original cultural semantics. They mean little else than their alterity; they are no longer texts in the semiotic sense, but merely signs, floating signifiers of otherness.

Syncretic theatre, however, takes precisely the opposite approach. Because the dramatists and directors involved come from indigenous cultures, their processes of adaptation respect the semantics of the cultural texts they use. Although the cultural texts in syncretic theatre also, by definition, undergo a process of recoding, there exists a consciously sought-after creative tension between the meanings engendered by these texts in the traditional performative context and the new function within a Western dramaturgical framework. Put simply, we can say that in the various forms of theatrical exoticism foreign elements are neither used nor perceived as texts in their own right. At best they are seen in terms of interesting but naive folklore. In syncretic theatre, on the other hand, cultural texts retain their integrity as bearers of precisely defined cultural meaning.

6 INTRODUCTION

The special problem of syncretic theatre, semiotically speaking, involves the integration and recoding of cultural texts within the art form theatre. The second key semiotic concept which is applicable here is Roman Jakobson's notion of 'dominant shift'.[6] One of the central characteristics of syncretic theatrical texts is that under the influence of diverse cultural texts substantial shifts in the 'hierarchy of dramatic devices' take place.[7] This hierarchy or arrangement presupposes the existence of 'dominants' or dominant codes which enable the spectator, listener, reader, or whoever is engaged in semiotic activity to organize and structure the plethora of signs being generated in some kind of meaningful way. The semiotic system we know as Western theatre consists of a hierarchy of dominants which is organized principally according to genre and performance codes, i.e. a dialogic dominant for drama or a musical dominant for opera, or a kinesic one for ballet and dance. One of the ways to analyse syncretic drama and theatre is to examine if and when and for what purpose such dominant shifts take place, and how indigenous cultural texts influence this hierarchy of dominants.

Finally, the term 'theatrical text' is itself in need of some explication. The concept of theatrical text has been deliberately chosen because it reflects more precisely the methodological approach of this study than terms such as 'drama' or 'play'. In contradistinction to these, the notion of theatrical text can be seen as the transcription of a conceived performance.[8] In this understanding, the main focus of interest is directed towards the implicit or

<hr/>

[6] Roman Jakobson, 'The Dominant', in Ladislav Matejka and Krystyna Pomorska (eds.), *Readings in Russian Poetics: Formalist and Structuralist Views* (Cambridge, Mass.: MIT Press, 1971), 82–7.

[7] A term coined by the Czech semiotician and theatre director Jiňrich Honzl in the 1930s; see 'The Hierarchy of Dramatic Devices', in Ladislav Matejka and Irwin R. Titunik (eds.), *Semiotics of Art: Prague School Contributions* (Cambridge, Mass.: MIT Press, 1976), 118–27.

[8] This definition refers to the relationship between the dramatic–theatrical text and the stage. The generic term 'drama' is still defined by predominantly literary rather than performative criteria which ignore the constitutive relationship between text and stage. In theatre studies it is generally accepted that the drama be seen as a text to be performed, as an artefact conceived by the author with a *mise-en-scène* in mind. This formulation also avoids the other normative notion that the dramatic text contains embedded in it a specific code for production which the director is more or less obliged to realize.

explicit indicators of stage action contained in the text. In concrete terms this means that, among other textual elements, the didascalia will receive closer attention than is normally the case in dramatic analysis.[9] All the theatrical texts that are discussed in the following pages contain extensive didascalic material, in which the indigenous cultural background is glossed and commented on. This form of additional commentary is such a striking characteristic of these texts that one could almost speak of theatrical texts *sub specie syncretiae*. This textual material goes beyond descriptive stage directions. It encompasses glossaries and forewords, as well as short commentaries on ethnographically relevant material, and thus takes cognizance—at least for the reader—of the problem of cultural strangeness that by definition marks these theatrical texts.[10]

Syncretism(s)

In a review and discussion of the term 'syncretism' the German religious historian Carsten Colpe emphasizes the fundamentally positive valorization of syncretism, especially in its reflection of tolerance and intellectual vigour:

A tolerant attitude to all that is of value in the world is thus a basic condition for the rise of any syncretism, as well as a basic virtue of the human being who is shaped by syncretism and in turn supports it. In addition, however, an enormous intellectual power is required in order to

[9] The term 'didascalia' is not used here simply as a synonym for stage directions. Didascalia encompass everything that is in the written text but which is not spoken by the actors. See Anne Ubersfeld, *L'École du spectateur* (Paris: Éditions Sociales, 1981), 11. For a more precise taxonomy, see Michael Issacharoff, 'Space and Reference in Drama', *Poetics Today*, 2/3 (Spring 1981), 211–24.

[10] This form of self-commentary and glossing provided by the writer has been termed by post-colonial theory 'an ethnography of the writer's own culture'. It is considered to be one of the striking features of these new literatures, where, because of the transcultural communication required, the writer must function as the first exegetist of his or her work: 'The post-colonial writer, whose gaze is turned in two directions, stands already in that position which will come to be occupied by an interpretation, for he/she is not the object of an interpretation, but the first interpreter. Editorial intrusions, such as the footnote, the glossary, and the explanatory preface, where these are made by the author, are a good example of this.' Ashcroft *et al.*, *The Empire Writes Back*, 61.

cement all the elements together into a new type of tradition and, further, to maintain the combination of the erudite and the popular.[11]

While this position today may not seem at all unusual—the terms 'hybridity', 'syncreticity', 'fusion', have almost taken on the status of post-colonial orthodoxy—Colpe is in fact taking issue with a long tradition of Western thought. The central ideological strategy motivating this book involves a comparable revalorization of the world-view implied by the term 'syncretism'. It advances the argument that the dramaturgical strategy of syncretizing indigenous performance elements with the Western theatrico-dramatic tradition is a response to what is perceived as a peculiarly Western tendency to homogenize, to exclude, to strive for a state of 'purity', whether it be racial or stylistic. In the conceptual world of the nineteenth and early twentieth centuries clear cultural boundaries were essential for cementing identity. Furthermore, they expressed notions of difference and even superiority *vis-à-vis* other nations and cultures. In this world-view, which encapsulates the essence of colonialism in both its paternalistic and aggressive, exploitive manifestations, any suggestion of mingling and interchange was synonymous with dilution, deracination, and breakdown.[12] Today, however, we find even in Western discourse a tendency to reassess syncretism as an inventive and creative process.

Any attempt to situate the term 'syncretism' in a cross-cultural context must, as indicated, take cognizance of its fundamentally pejorative intellectual history. Whether it referred to doctrinal confusion, as was the case in the sixteenth and seventeenth centuries, or was used to designate 'hybrid', 'impure' religious phenomena deriving from a combination of religions, as the concept was used by

---

[11] Colpe, 'Syncretism', in Mircea Eliade (ed.), *The Encyclopedia of Religion*, xiv (New York: Macmillan, 1987), 226 f. In another study Colpe argues that the pejorative usage of the term has its roots in Romanticism, with its combination of nationalistic ideology and intellectual élitism, which he terms an 'Aristokratismus des Geistes'. For this intellectual tradition syncretism is synonymous with 'decay, decadence, decline, yes, one can say that for such aristocrats of science, the syncretism concept is only applicable as a category of historical wrong. [. . .] This aristocratism is romantic and has its roots in Romanticism.' 'Die Vereinbarkeit historischer und struktureller Bestimmungen des Synkretismus', in Albert Dietrich (ed.), *Synkretismus im syrisch-persischen Kulturgebiet. Bericht über ein Symposion in Reinhausen bei Göttingen in der Zeit vom 4. bis 8. Oktober 1971* (Göttingen: Vandenhoeck & Ruprecht, 1975), 29.

[12] For a discussion of 19th-century English attitudes to cultural and racial mixing, and in particular the concept of hybridity as it shifts from a biological to a cultural paradigm, see Young, *Colonial Desire*.

historians of religion in the nineteenth century, it invariably implied a state of decadence and reflected the inability of certain religions to exist 'dans le rigueur de leurs formes constitutives'.[13]

However, with the establishment in the 1920s and 1930s of the new discipline of comparative religion and a phenomenological approach to religious studies, 'syncretism' was expanded to cover such phenomena as voodoo, the popular religion of Haiti, as well as many other cult practices in the Caribbean which were beginning to attract the interest of ethnographers. Syncretism was compared and contrasted with 'conversion' as one of the dynamic forms of religious contact, but, unlike conversion, which in its apostolic and missionary zeal tends to downgrade the values of the encountered belief systems, syncretism is based on mutual respect and reciprocal exchange of values and beliefs.

Colpe's notion of syncretism as intellectual reshaping cited above shows that the term has application far beyond the borders of comparative religion. In 1956 the American cultural anthropologist Melville Herskovits defined syncretism value-free as a specific form of cultural reinterpretation which is 'the process by which old meanings are ascribed to new elements or by which new values change the cultural significance of old forms'.[14] Herskovits, who carried out extensive fieldwork in Haiti, began to question the homeostatic, functionalist models of cultural anthropology that had been established by the previous generation of anthropologists such as Bronislaw Malinowski and E. Evans-Pritchard. He found them inadequate to explain what had happened and was still happening in syncretic societies such as Haiti. The examples of syncretic reinterpretation that Herskovits cites are drawn almost entirely from the realm of religious practices: the New World cults such as voodoo in Haiti, *candomblé* in Brazil, and *shango* in Trinidad.

The revalorization and expanded application of the term 'syncretism' in ethnographic discourse goes hand in hand with a fundamental reassessment of the precepts underpinning the discipline. Most

---

[13] *Encyclopaedia Universalis*, xvii 17, s.v. 'syncrétisme' (Paris: Encyclopaedia Universalis, 1985), 539. Carsten Colpe has documented the pejorative use of syncretism: 'The first application of the term to a situation in the history of religions probably occurred in an anonymous review (of an edition of Minucius Felix) that appeared in *Fraser's Magazine for Town and Country* (London, 1853), vol. 47, p. 294' .'Syncretism', 218.

[14] Melville J. Herskovits, *Man and his Works: The Science of Cultural Anthropology* (New York: Alfred A. Knopf, 1956), 553.

importantly, the very notion of cultural anthropology as a science
with immutable laws has been radically questioned over the past two
decades. This process of radical reassessment which ethnography is
undergoing at present is to a large extent due to demographic and
cultural changes. Particularly the large, multicultural centres of the
Third World are producing new cultural forms which pose very
special problems for ethnographic methodology and practice. In
order to describe this phenomenon, which is a product first of urbanization and then of the 'global flow of meaning', anthropologists
such as James Clifford and Ulf Hannerz operate with the synonymous terms 'syncretism' and 'creolization'. Hannerz points, for
example, to polyglot urban centres in Third World countries and
their involvement in what he calls 'an intercontinental traffic in
meaning'.[15] Here disparate ethnicities and cultures have been drawn
together and have produced new 'creolized' cultural forms. These in
turn are exported around the world in the form of books, music,
fashion, or theatre. James Clifford links syncretism with a notion of
'post-culturalism' which questions the very idea of firm, homogeneous cultural identities: 'With expanded communication and intercultural influence, people interpret others, and themselves, in a
bewildering diversity of idioms—a global condition of what Mikhail
Bakhtin called "heteroglossia." This ambiguous, multivocal world
makes it increasingly hard to conceive of human diversity as inscribed
in bounded independent cultures. Difference is an effect of inventive
syncretism.'[16]

   In this statement Clifford articulates the essence of what he terms
the 'predicament of culture'. Clear lines of demarcation between
cultures, which existed when the discipline of ethnography came
into existence in the nineteenth century, are becoming increasingly
difficult to distinguish in an internationalized world of mass communication and information exchange. Significant for this book is the
final sentence, which expresses the notion of 'inventive syncretism'.
As in religious studies Clifford is undertaking in this formulation a

[15] Ulf Hannerz, 'The World in Creolization', *Africa*, 57/4 (1987), 546–59, here p.
547. Hannerz stresses the movement from a centre to the periphery, from international
metropolitan centres via 'bridgeheads' (national metropolitan centres) to remote rural
villages (p. 549).
[16] James Clifford, *The Predicament of Culture: Twentieth Century Ethnography,
Literature, and Art* (Cambridge, Mass.: Harvard University Press, 1988), 22 f.

similar reassessment and revalorization of the hitherto perjorative usage of the term.[17]

Clifford's collection of essays also provides the connection to syncretism as an artistic concept. In the realm of literature and art, with which Clifford deals extensively in his cultural essays, writers and artists involved in creating and working in syncretic processes are having to refashion meanings from diverse cultural sources to create products which declare their hybridity as a conscious stylistic device. The emergence of post-colonial syncretic art and literature is thus a natural response to situations of cultural multivocalism. The beginnings of the movement in the 1930s, 1940s, and 1950s resulted from the predicament of binary cultural encounter: the interaction between an indigenous and a Western tradition.

Analogous to the new anthropologists, literary theorists working in the area of post-colonial literature have begun operating with the terms 'syncretism' and 'hybridism' in order to provide a comprehensive theoretical model for certain developments in the New Literatures in English, previously known as Commonwealth Literature. In a recent study, *The Empire Writes Back: Theory and Practice in Post-Colonial Literatures*, which is the first attempt both to provide a synthesis of developments and to formulate a body of theory to account for this relatively recent phenomenon, the authors propose four theoretical models. They justify their undertaking by claiming that European theory has been unable to deal adequately with 'the complexities and varied cultural provenance of post-colonial writing'.[18] In roughly chronological order, the authors identify national or regional models; race-based models; comparative studies of two or more post-colonial literatures; and 'more comprehensive comparative

---

[17] It is striking that in recent discussions there is considerable exchange between religious and ethnographical treatments of syncretism. On a theoretical level there is basic agreement between the two disciplines. See here the definition in the religious scholar André Droogers's article 'Syncretism: The Problem of Definition', in which he attempts to define syncretic processes in terms of information theory: 'The change of meaning is almost by definition prominent in situations of contact. The recipient of a message does not necessarily understand that message in the same way as the person sending it meant it to be understood. This alone can mark the start of syncretism. Since communication between cultures and religions takes place in the context of *doubled sets of symbols, patterns, and meanings*, reinterpretation, misunderstanding, and distortion will be the more probable.' 'Syncretism: The Problem of Definition', in Jerald Gort, Hendrik Vroom, Rein Fernhout, and Anton Wessels (eds.), *Dialogue and Syncretism: An Interdisciplinary Approach* (Grand Rapids, Mich.: William B. Eerdmans; Amsterdam: Rodopi, 1989), 19; my italics.   [18] *The Empire Writes Back*, 11.

models which argue for features such as hybridity or syncreticity as constitutive elements of all post-colonial literatures'.[19] Of the four models proposed the syncretic one appears to be the only approach flexible enough to account for the polycultural nature of the literatures to be studied. As in the new anthropology, the term 'syncretism' takes on a positive valorization: 'the strength in post-colonial theory may well lie in its inherently comparative methodology and the hybridized and syncretic view of the modern world which this implies'.[20] It has been particularly West Indian writers, the study argues, such as Wilson Harris and Edward Kamau Brathwaite who have propounded a view of 'creative syncretism' in opposition to monocultural Western theory. They perceive in their own creole societies capacities for renewal and creative regeneration, a potential Harris terms the 'paradox of cultural heterogeneity': 'The paradox of cultural heterogeneity, or cross-cultural capacity, lies in the evolutionary thrust it restores to orders of the imagination, the ceaseless dialogue it inserts between hardened conventions.'[21]

In the discourse of post-colonial literary theory Homi Bhabha is the critic who more than any other has defined hybridity as a concept which challenges certain premises of Western epistemology. He writes: '[The] interstitial passage between fixed identifications opens up the possibility of a cultural hybridity that entertains difference without an assumed or imposed hierarchy.'[22] Bhabha is referring here, on the one hand, to the concrete experience of multiple identities and, on the other, to the wider post-structuralist project of redefining difference as a strategy to deconstruct notions of hierarchy and centring. The concept of hybridity as elaborated by Bhabha leads to a wider political undertaking which he defines as the possibility of eluding 'the politics of polarity' and recognizing the fundamentally hybrid constitution of self and culture.

When one actually considers the cultural provenance of some of the major writers in the post-colonial literary tradition such as V. S. Naipaul, Salman Rushdie, or Michael Ondaatje, then categories of race and 'national' literatures are of little relevance. In light of such biographies, of which there are an ever-increasing number, it

---

[19] *The Empire Writes Back*, 15.   [20] Ibid. 37 f.
[21] Wilson Harris, *The Womb of Space: The Cross-Cultural Imagination* (Westport, Conn.: Greenwood, 1983), p. xviii; cited in Ashcroft *et al.*, *The Empire Writes Back*, 152.
[22] Homi K. Bhabha, *The Location of Culture* (London: Routledge, 1994), 4.

is little wonder that theoretical models utilizing some notion of syncreticity, hybridity, or creolization (the terms seem to be used interchangeably) are gaining increasing support in post-colonial literary criticism.

The concrete application of the term 'syncretic' to theatre, drama, or the performing arts is a very recent phenomenon and in most cases no more than an epithet to designate some form of polycultural performance style. The performance theorist Richard Schechner discerns in the ritual performances of the Yaqui Indians of Arizona and Mexico a 'syncretic mixture of Catholic, Hispanic and Yaqui pre-contact elements'.[23] Schechner is using the term here in its anthropological sense of cultural redefinition. A concrete application of the concept to theatrical products and thus closer to this investigation is suggested by Colin Taylor in a brief article on Wole Soyinka: 'In his visionary projection of this [Yoruba] society, Soyinka has adopted a syncretic style—fusing the disparate elements of Yoruba song and dance, proverbs and mythology, elements from an ancient tradition of mask and folk-operatic drama, interaction with an anthropomorphic pantheon of gods—in the service of a central controlling viewpoint, aimed at shedding light on the dynamics of a society in transition.'[24] Although Taylor enunciates here some of the central tenets of syncretic theatre—fusion of performance styles, incorporation of ritual and mythic elements to find a new way of presenting in theatrical terms a post-colonial society in the process of change—he does not elaborate this insight, being principally concerned with explaining why Soyinka's plays have been neglected in North America.

The most comprehensive attempts to apply the concept of 'syncretism' to the performing arts have come, perhaps not surprisingly, from two studies dealing with black South African music and theatre. In his study of South African township music and performance David Coplan, an ethnomusicologist, applies in a systematic fashion the anthropological concept of syncretism to aesthetic products. He defines 'syncretic' as the 'acculturative blending of performance materials and practices from two or more cultural traditions, producing

[23] Richard Schechner, 'Intercultural Performance', *Drama Review* (T94), 26/2 (Summer 1982), 3. In this editorial Schechner tries to establish links between interculturalism and post-modernism: syncretic practices, borrowing, and 'the making of new cultural stuff' are, he argues, 'the norm of human activity'.
[24] Colin Taylor, 'Seeing Soyinka', *Theatrum: A Theatre Journal*, 10 (1988), 36.

qualitatively new forms'.[25] In this study of township 'performance culture', a concept embracing music, dance, and drama as well as the contexts and occasions of performance, Coplan provides a detailed analysis of the disparate elements which have gone into the formation of this performance culture over the past 100 years. The social prerequisite for the new forms was, Coplan suggests, urbanization, the coming together of different ethnicities, combined with a multi-tude of Western influences via education, church, and the mass media. He argues forcibly that the openness of township artists, musicians, and performers to these 'outside' influences, especially since the 1960s to black American culture, should be seen neither as 'slavish imitation' nor as the rejection of 'a subjugated but pre-cious African heritage': 'It is rather the result of a creative syncretism in which innovative performers combine materials from cultures in contact into qualitatively new forms in response to changing condi-tions, needs, self-images, and aspirations.'[26]

The particular cultural dynamics of South African theatre prompted the theatre scholar Temple Hauptfleisch to elaborate a detailed set of categories to describe the heterogenous performance culture prevailing there.[27] His six categories distinguish between indigenous traditional forms, indigenous contemporary (to which belong such disparate elements as gumboot dances, funerals, church services); three different categories of 'Western theatre'; and finally indigenous 'hybrid' theatre incorporating elements from the other five categories. 'Hybrid theatre' corresponds roughly to Coplan's concept of syncretic performance. When Hauptfleisch writes 'thea-tre', he means in fact a concept of 'performance' as defined by Richard Schechner, which can encompass initiation ceremonies, storytelling and praise songs, as well as the whole gamut of imported Western forms such as drama, ballet, and opera. Following Coplan, he detects already in the indigenous contemporary forms—church and funeral services with their links to political protest—a process of 'hybridization':

The primary factor in all this is the process of hybridization, the mingling and borrowing which created something not quite African, not quite Western, but

[25] David B. Coplan, *In Township Tonight! South Africa's Black City Music and Theatre* (London: Longman, 1985), p. vii.   [26] Ibid. 236 f.
[27] Temple Hauptfleisch, 'Beyond Street Theatre and Festival: The Forms of South African Theatre', *Maske und Kothurn*, 33/1–2 (1987), 175–88.

somewhere in the middle. Church services utilizing African dance and music, traditional communal dancing utilizing American jazz music and Western clothing. And part of the hybridization lies in the radically redefined socio-cultural functions of these new forms, which at times forcefully dictates not only the form but also the content of the performance.[28]

This indigenous, hybrid theatre has become known internationally as township theatre, where 'all the varied strands of convention, tradition, and experimentation somehow seem to get tied together in a hybrid form of performance which is uniquely South African'.[29] The final product is certainly uniquely South African, but the syncretic process underlying the creation of township theatre is an international phenomenon.[30]

Intercultural Theatre

This brief survey has indicated how the concept of syncretism has undergone a complete reversal of meaning. From its connotations of 'impurity' and 'degeneration' as used by historians of religion in the nineteenth century to those of tolerance, reinterpretation, and invention in contemporary ethnographic discourse, the term reflects a fundamental shift in Western thinking about other cultures. The pejorative usage in the nineteenth century mirrors very much that century's concern with national identity and difference, both within the European cultures and in contradistinction to the non-European cultures the European powers were in the process of colonizing. The increase in syncretic phenomena which commentators such as Hannerz and Clifford point to is certainly a reflection of historical post-colonial processes and the decolonization procedures which have become most evident since the Second World War. The interest in syncretism also reflects a change in thinking and in the way cultural phenomena are apprehended. Cultural homogeneity, the notion of it and the search for it, particularly by pre-war anthropologists, appears to be a peculiarly Western conceptual construct and has seldom, if ever, existed. As Richard Schechner has observed: 'There is no culture uninfluenced by foreigners—invaders, evangelists (Moslem, Christian, Buddhist),

---

[28] Ibid. 181.   [29] Ibid. 184.   [30] Ibid.

traders, colonizers.'[31] In this sense then, syncretism as a category in literary and art criticism is a necessary but ultimately transitional concept for describing the relationship between culture and aesthetics. It is necessary because the processes of mixing and recombination are indeed striking, and transitional because in the context of the globalization of culture it will ultimately be superfluous to define the norm of cultural process. Nevertheless, as we are historically still very much in the transitional process—the upsurge in national and ethnic consciousness, particularly in Eastern Europe, shows that notions of cultural and racial purity are far from dead—processes and phenomena of striking cultural interaction still therefore need to be described and analysed.

This requirement finds its best illustration in the phenomenon termed 'intercultural theatre'.[32] The recent theatrical experiments of directors such as Peter Brook and Ariane Mnouchkine have both drawn heavily on Indian and Japanese performance traditions in a number of *mises-en-scène* of the last decade.[33] Of course, the interest of Western directors and playwrights, particularly in the classical forms of oriental theatre, as a means to rejuvenate Western theatrical aesthetics goes back at least to the turn of the century. As a growing number of studies have pointed out, anti-naturalistic theatre-reformers such as Edward Gordon Craig, Georg Fuchs, Adolphe Appia, W. B. Yeats, Vsevolod Meyerhold, Alexander Tairov, Bertolt Brecht, and Antonin Artaud turned repeatedly to the kabuki and Noh theatres, to *kathakaḷi*, to Balinese dance and the Peking opera, as models for a stylized, anti-naturalistic, and non-dialogic form of theatre as a counter-model to the perceived 'exhaustion' of European dialogue-based and psychologically

[31] Richard Schechner, 'Introduction: Towards a Field Theory of Performance', *Drama Review*, 23/2 (June 1979), 2.
[32] The two most illuminating publications on the subject of intercultural theatre are Erika Fischer-Lichte, Michael Gissenwehrer, and Josephine Riley (eds.), *The Dramatic Touch of Difference: Theatre, Own and Foreign* (Tübingen: Narr, 1990), and the collection of essays published by Patrice Pavis, *Theatre at the Crossroads of Culture* (London: Routledge, 1992), and Patrice Pavis (ed.), *The Intercultural Performance Reader* (London: Routledge, 1996). See also the special number on intercultural performance of the *Performing Arts Journal*, 33–4 (1989).
[33] Peter Brook's concern with intercultural theatre pre-dates, of course, his production of the *Mahabharata*. The foundation of the Centre International de Recherches Théâtrales in Paris in 1970 was motivated by a concept of international theatre. Ariane Mnouchkine's intercultural phase begins with her Shakespearean cycle in 1982 and continues through to the production *Les Atrides* (1990–1).

focused drama.[34] This highly selective reception of foreign theatrical traditions as a kind of 'blood transfusion', to use Joachim Fiebach's term,[35] for a moribund theatrical aesthetic has, particularly recently, been repeatedly criticized as just another form of imperialism and cultural appropriation.[36]

Less well studied, however, has been the appropriation of the Western model of theatre and drama by the colonized people themselves. These responses range from a simple replication of Western dramatic form, sometimes in the colonizing language, sometimes in indigenous tongues, to genuine theatrical interculturalism with highly complex processes of mixing and blending of Western and indigenous elements. To help systematize this activity, one should differentiate between three different forms of indigenous intercultural theatre. In analogy to religious syncretism one can posit three responses to situations of conflict and competition in terms of rudimentary system theory:

1. A new theatrico-cultural system is introduced which eclipses and overlies an existing one. Isolated elements of the older system remain present.
2. The existing system remains dominant. The new theatrico-cultural system is visible only in the form of a few identifiable elements.
3. A new equilibrium is established between the old and the new systems with a balanced number of elements from both being utilized.[37]

One can illustrate these somewhat abstract categories with examples from theatrical cultures which have responded to precisely this situation of conflict and competition with the Western theatrical form.

[34] There is a growing amount of research into the reception of Asian theatre by European directors and dramatists in the 20th century. For a general overview, see Leonard C. Pronko, *Theatre East and West* (Berkeley: University of California Press, 1967), and Nicola Savarese *Teatro e spettacolo fra Oriente e Occidente* (Bari: Editori Laterza, 1992); Savarese's study contains the best bibliographical overview of the subject to date.

[35] See Fiebach's article 'Theater as Cultural Performance: Anthropology, Ethnography and Studies in Performing Arts', in Willmar Sauter (ed.), *Nordic Theatre Studies*, Special International Issue (Stockholm: Munksgaard, 1990), 144–51, here p. 145.

[36] See e.g. Rustom Bharucha, *The Theatre and the World: Performance and the Politics of Culture* (London: Routledge, 1993).

[37] These categories are based on a typology suggested by Carsten Colpe for religious syncretism: 'Die Vereinbarkeit und Bestimmungen des Synkretismus', 15–37.

According to this classification the subject of this book and what is termed 'theatrical syncretism' belong to the first category: the theatre forms that emerged as a result of colonization and decolonization. Either the Western system of theatre was introduced to cultures which did not have an equivalent form, as was the case in most African and Fourth World countries, or the newly introduced system tended to eclipse although not totally destroy existing theatrical traditions. The latter situation pertained in India, where the traditions of dance-theatre suffered greatly from competition from Western-influenced forms. In both cases the new theatrico-cultural system was adopted locally and mixed to varying degrees with local cultural texts. Under the first category can be subsumed indigenous europhone theatre as well as new theatre forms performed in local languages. Examples of the latter are the Yoruba Travelling Theatre in Nigeria[38] or the various forms of commercial theatre that emerged in India in the nineteenth century.[39] In both cases the dramaturgical structure has a recognizably Western provenance, but many performance elements such as songs and dances stem from the indigenous culture. These

[38] The alternative term is 'Yoruba Folk Opera'. On the controversy regarding the terms and other questions, see Oyekan Owomoyela, 'Yoruba Folk Opera: A Cross-Cultural Flowering', in Anna Rutherford (ed.), *From Commonwealth to Post-Colonial* (Sydney: Dangaroo Press, 1992), 160–80. The origin of this form of popular theatre in the 1940s has been documented by Ebun Clark in her biography *Herbert Ogunde: The Making of Nigerian Theatre* (Oxford: Oxford University Press, 1979); see also Biodun Jeyifo, *The Popular Yoruba Travelling Theatre* (Lagos: Nigeria Magazine, 1984), and Karin Barber's analysis of a specific work in performance: 'Radical Conservatism in Yoruba Popular Plays', in Eckhard Breitinger (ed.), *Drama and Theatre in Africa* (Bayreuth: Bayreuth African Studies, 1986), 5–32; see also David Kerr, *African Popular Theatre from Pre-colonial Times to the Present Day* (London: James Currey, 1995), ch. 5.
[39] Around the middle of the 19th century there emerged in different regions of India forms of commercial travelling theatre which were far more than mere replicas of British troupes. In Bombay the Parsees, a merchant class of Persian origin, recognized the commercial potential of theatre. They built theatres and performed their plays in Gujarati. Parsee theatre was decidedly eclectic in form, and its dramaturgical method consisted of 'ransacking all possible sources', as the Indian theatre historian R. K. Yajnik writes: 'Persian and Sanskrit mythology and epics, English novels, farces and plays, medieval legends and historical events from divine races, and modern social problems.' *The Indian Theatre: Its Origins and its Later Developments under European Influence with Special Reference to Western India* (1934; New York: Hashel House Reprint, 1970), 90 f. The emphasis on varied action and spectacular scenic effects indicates links to the conventions of 19th-century melodrama, which was familiar to Indian audiences via touring companies and which came to have a permanent influence on the production and receptive codes of commercial Indian theatre. Equivalents of Parsee theatre emerged in other regions, such as Marathi theatre in Maharashtra in the second half of the century and in Karnataka.

elements weigh so heavily that one can without any doubt speak of theatrical syncretism, no matter whether the theatrical text is performed in a European or indigenous language.

However, it should be noted that not every play written by an African or Indian dramatist can thus be considered an example of theatrical syncretism. Under colonial rule there existed a vigorous local dramatic production, often encouraged by colonial educational or religious authorities, but which in formal terms cannot be differentiated from Western models. Whatever virtues these works may have in terms of thematic interest and psychological characterization, they lack the characteristic use of indigenous cultural texts which is the defining feature of syncretic theatre.

Under the second category of indigenous intercultural theatre, in which an existing theatre system remains dominant while selectively incorporating Western elements, can be subsumed genres such as the traditional *apidán* or *alarinjo* theatre of the Yoruba. It emerged in pre-colonial times and still exists today.[40] In addition, there are any number of Asian theatre forms which, although altered by Western influence, have remained structurally intact. The classical Japanese dance-theatre, Peking Opera, as well as Indian dance-theatre genres such as *kathakaḷi* and *yakṣāgana*, can be included in this group. Here it is not possible to speak of theatrical syncretism but rather of a guarded and gradual reception of foreign elements which are less a direct result of colonization than of internal changes within the cultures themselves.[41]

Most of the theatrical forms belonging to the second category cannot be strictly speaking considered examples of intercultural theatre. When, however, a traditional form absorbs foreign elements to such an extent that formal innovation becomes the dominant characteristic, and old and new elements seem to be in equilibrium,

---

[40] The foreign influence on *apidán* is already evident, particularly in the iconographical materials used in the costuming, but certainly not dominant. See Kacke Götrick, *Apidan Theatre and Modern Drama: A Study in a Traditional Yoruba Theatre and its Influence on Modern Drama by Yoruba Playwrights* (Stockholm: Almqvist & Wiksell, 1984).

[41] In Japan, kabuki has been the form most subject to experimentation and 'modernization', but there are also modernized forms of *kyôgen*. In respect to *yakṣāgana* in India Kenneth Rea writes: 'the temptation to modernize was great, and gradually elements inspired by other drama forms and the cinema began to creep into Yakshagana performances.' 'Theatre in India: The Old and the New, Part II', *Theatre Quarterly*, 8/31 (1978), 45–60, here p. 47.

then a third category has to be differentiated. Particularly when a recognizable aesthetic programme motivates this combining of traditions, then one can speak of 'fusion'. This term has been coined to characterize recent widespread experiments in Asian countries to mix traditional forms with the Western theatrical aesthetic. Examples of fusion can be found already in the 1960s in Asia, where there was a conscious strategy to politicize existing forms of folk theatre. The Indian director Habib Tanvir, for example, who works within the conventions of folk theatre indigenous to the province of Madhya Pradesh, pursued, according to his own admission, a Brechtian strategy. The same can be said for the Bengali director and dramatist Utpal Dutt, who has refashioned local *jatra* theatre in a similar fashion.[42]

Syncretic theatre is not only to be found in the former colonies that today bear the epithet 'Third World', but also among the indigenous peoples of the settler societies such as Canada, Australia, and New Zealand. In comparison to the situation in Africa, India, or the Caribbean, the theatre movements of Indians, Aborigines, and Maori in settler societies are the expression of an indigenous minority surrounded and dominated by a European majority. Their colonial experience is the result of different historical circumstances and to some extent continues until the present day.

The term 'Fourth World' permits a necessary further historical and cultural differentiation of post-colonial societies. It was first coined in the context of political and sociological discussions concerning the plight of minority peoples,[43] and has gained currency particularly among anthropologists dealing with artistic expression among indigenous minorities.[44] The ethnologist Nelson Graburn has investi-

[42] On the work of Tanvir, see Vasudha Dalmia-Lüderitz, 'To be More Brechtian is to be More Indian', in Fischer-Lichte *et al.* (eds.), *The Dramatic Touch of Difference*, 221–35; and Kenneth Rea's comments on the work of Utpal Dutt, Bardal Sircar, and Habib Tanvir, for which he gives the collective term 'Theatre of Synthesis': 'Theatre in India: the Old and the New, Part III', *Theatre Quarterly*, 8/32 (1979), 47–66. For a recent discussion of Sircar's approach, see Crow and Banfield, *An Introduction to Post-Colonial Theatre*, ch. 6. These artists have also published programmatic descriptions of their work: see Sircar's book *The Third Theatre* (Calcutta: Bardal Sircar 1978), and Utpal Dutt's *Towards a Revolutionary Theatre* (Calcutta: Sircar & Sons 1982).

[43] See the book by George Manuel and M. Poslums, *The Fourth World: An Indian Reality* (New York: Free Press, 1974), and the reports on minority questions in Ben Whitaker (ed.), *The Fourth World: Eight Reports from the Minority Rights Group* (London: Sidgwick & Jackson, 1972).

[44] See Graburn (ed.), *Tourist and Ethnic Arts*. For a detailed survey of literature, see Nelson H. H. Graburn, '1, 2, 3, 4 . . . Anthropology and the Fourth World', *Culture*, 1/1, (1981), 66–70.

gated the arts and crafts of Fourth World peoples and set out a classificatory schema for describing the processes of aesthetic and cultural change affecting the visual arts and crafts.[45] Graburn distinguishes seven forms of artistic change. These categories range from complete assimilation, to various types of synthesis, to the complete extinction of indigenous forms of expression. According to Graburn's categorization, the new theatre movements in Canada, Australia, and New Zealand could be termed either 'reintegrated arts' or 'assimilated arts'. By 'reintegrated arts' Graburn means the adoption by indigenous artists of themes and techniques introduced by the colonial culture which result in new formal or thematic syntheses. The production and reception of this art remains still very much confined to the indigenous cultural techniques. In the case of 'assimilated arts', however, indigenous artists compete with the majority-culture artists on their own ground and are no longer part of the 'tourist art' culture.

Fourth World syncretic theatre reveals elements of both categories. When applied to theatre and performance Graburn's line of demarcation between these two categories is too rigidly drawn. For one thing, the synthesizing dynamic—the adoption and adaptation of foreign techniques characteristic of the 'reintegrated arts'—is by definition present as soon as theatre in the Western sense is produced. However, these techniques are synthesized or syncretized with indigenous performance forms in varying ways. For another thing, there are clear attempts to 'assimilate' in the sense of competing on the theatrical or entertainment market. Yet only in very few cases do indigenous ensembles adapt totally to the conditions of production and reception pertaining in the majority culture. The artists and ensembles examined here all work without exception predominantly in metropolitan centres and produce their work as part of the overall theatrical market of these cities.[46]

[45] Graburn (ed.), *Tourist and Ethnic Arts.*
[46] This is certainly the case with Aboriginal and Maori theatre, although metropolitan ensembles may undertake tours to rural districts. To my knowledge, there are no ensembles in New Zealand and Australia which work entirely within an indigenous cultural framework. In Canada the situation is somewhat different. Although the focus in this study will be on Tomson Highway and Native Earth Performing Arts, who are based in Toronto, there are a fluctuating number of Indian and Inuit ensembles whose work is focused on the reserves and who are not particularly interested in metropolitan audiences. As Alan Filewod notes: 'Probably no one can say how many there actually are, because most of them operate sporadically or on short-term grants.' 'Averting the Colonial Gaze: Notes on Watching Native Theatre', in Per Brask and William Morgan (eds.), *Aboriginal Voices: Amerindian, Inuit, and Sami Theater* (Baltimore: Johns Hopkins University Press, 1992), 23.

There are several reasons for grouping the writers and ensembles from these three countries under the rubric 'theatre of the Fourth World'. Firstly, there is the common factor of a similar historical colonial experience undergone by minority indigenous peoples and the fact that their present political and cultural situation is broadly comparable. These parallels are pointed out by the Australian Aboriginal writer Colin Johnson (Mudrooroo Narogin), who has used the term 'Fourth World' to describe the particular situation of his people and by extension the predicament of other indigenous writers and artists: 'Australian Aboriginal literature is a literature of the Fourth World, that is, of the indigenous minorities submerged in a surrounding majority and governed by them. It must and does deal with the problems inherent in this position and it must be compared to similar literatures, for example the American Indian, for the correspondences and contradictions to be seen.'[47] Johnson's explicit use of the term 'Fourth World' indicates that a degree of commonality already exists in the minds of some artists and intellectuals.

Another common feature can be found in the tradition of touristic performance for Western audiences which in some cases goes back to the eighteenth and nineteenth centuries.[48] Folkloristic songs, dances, and music can in most cases be seen as decontextualized cultural texts which have been taken from their original performative context and reassembled in various segments catering to Western dramaturgical and entertainment conventions. Certain elements of folkloristic performances are often internationally known. Indian rain-dances, Maori war dances (*haka*), and the didgeridoo music of the Australian Aborigines are to some extent almost synonymous with the culture itself.

A further justification for grouping the theatrical cultures in Canada, Australia, and New Zealand under the one heading is the

[47] Colin Johnson, 'White Forms, in Aboriginal Content', in Jack Davis and Bob Hodge (eds.), *Aboriginal Writing Today* (Canberra: Australian Institute of Aboriginal Studies, 1983), 28.

[48] The field of tourist-orientated folkloristic performance is both widespread and under-researched. It can be seen as the performative analogy to the tourist arts analysed by Graburn, *Tourist and Ethnic Arts*. It is, of course, a phenomenon not just restricted to Fourth World cultures. In the Third and Fourth World context folkloristic performance has the problem of being often the only cultural image generated to a wider international audience. For a discussion of theoretical questions arising from performances for tourists, see Christopher Balme, 'Staging the Pacific: Framing Authenticity in Performances for Tourists at the Polynesian Cultural Center', *Theatre Journal*, 50 (1998), 53–70.

fact that the historical development of their respective theatrical movements also reveals parallels. It is striking that theatrical activity in the Western sense did not begin in all three countries until the early 1970s. In these years theatre is seen and used as an agitatory weapon for the political struggle for greater autonomy and land rights. This specialized function revealed itself in the choice of form of the plays and performances created. These works turned either to the identificatory aesthetic of stage realism in an appeal to the consciences of white audiences; or they sought direct confrontation in the form of agitprop revues, in which the political message was transported with maximum impact and clarity of stance.

As already mentioned, this study will focus exclusively on theatrical texts written primarily in English. The central concern is the way in which indigenous cultural texts are incorporated into and often alter Western dramaturgical conventions. Since it is difficult, if not impossible, to grasp the effect of this strategy in its totality, specific and recurring elements such as ritualization, strategies of language use, the use of the actor's body, masking, dance and music, and finally experiments with theatrical and dramatic space will be analysed in separate chapters. This arrangement of material under systematic headings rather than according to geographical regions or as examinations of individual dramatists reflects the central theoretical emphasis of the book. It is interested in the way in which theatre and drama as interrelated artistic forms have been appropriated and adapted by theatrical artists in geographically and culturally distant regions of the world. The analysis of formal response to decolonization will provide categories of comparison and dialogue which transcend particularities of regional thematic interest. In this way the large amount of fascinating drama and theatre that has emerged in these countries, mainly since the 1950s, can be placed in a much wider context of international scholarly discussion. For it has unfortunately been the case that the discourses of scholarship are determined by the same disproportionate distribution of power that governs the dissemination of goods and services. The peripheries of the former empires are forced to study the artistic and scholarly products of the metropolitan centres, but the inverse is very seldom the case.

In the following chapters I hope to demonstrate that the theatrical response to colonization has been an international phenomenon that has produced not only a large body of dramatic texts but also a theoretical discourse which questions some of the fundamental principles of Western theatrical aesthetics. For both these reasons, syncretic theatre must be judged and assessed as one of the major developments in twentieth-century theatre.

CHAPTER ONE

Indigenous Theories of
Syncretic Theatre

ANY discussion of intercultural theatre quickly leads to a fundamental discussion on the nature of theatre itself and to related questions of theatricality and performance. The response of intellectuals and theatre artists in colonized countries to the Western form of theatre and their attempts to reconcile it on a theoretical level in some way with existing indigenous performance forms marks a tradition of discourse which is at least as old as theatrical and dramatic practice. The programmatic formulation of an indigenous theory of syncretic theatre reveals a struggle against the normative Western discourse of what constitutes 'theatre' and 'drama'. For the practice of syncretic theatre requires the freedom to adapt a wide range of performance forms which may not appear to conform to narrow definitions of dramaturgy.

This chapter provides a historical overview of indigenous theories of theatrical syncretism. Beginning with Rabindranath Tagore's essay 'The Stage' and continuing with an analysis of the black South African H. I. E. Dhlomo's writings on the theatre in the 1930s, the first part of the chapter situates these theories in the context of what is historically speaking very much a colonial discourse. The second part of the chapter surveys the intensive theoretical and programmatic discussion on indigenous theatre which took place amongst African, principally Nigerian, writers in the 1960s and early 1970s. In the same period a vigorous debate developed in the Caribbean on the form a syncretic Caribbean theatre should take, the main exponents being Derek Walcott and Errol Hill. The third and final part of the chapter provides an overview of programmatic writings on syncretic theatre by indigenous theatre artists in Australia, New Zealand, and Canada.

Linking these geographically and temporally diverse writings is, as already mentioned, a common desire to expand the parameters of Western definitions of theatre. In this respect they parallel and in some cases pre-date the comparable Western discourse known as performance theory or cultural performance. This interdisciplinary field of study, which is closely associated with Richard Schechner and Victor Turner, began in the late 1960s as an attempt to find common areas of interest for anthropologists, sociologists, and theatre scholars. For theatre scholars this meant a fundamental reformulation of disciplinary horizons and a radical questioning of their Euro- and logocentric focus. It meant, on the one hand, a shift towards a sociological and anthropological view of performance phenomena, a re-evaluation of research goals encapsulated in Richard Schechner's apodictic statement: 'I reject esthetics.'[1] On the other hand, it has led in many cases towards a much closer examination of the interrelationships between performative phenomena such as song, dance, and ritual enactment in non-Western societies. In this way of thinking, the Western-staged play is by no means a particularly privileged object but just a specific manifestation of the anthropological entity 'performance'. In order to cement such a view, performance theory has needed to look outside the Western sphere of performance and has preoccupied itself intensively with a wide range of non-Western performance forms. In the following survey of theatre theory from the point of view of the colonized the reverse approach pertains. Writers look at Western theatre from a background and understanding of indigenous performance and ask in what way they are similar and how they can be combined in some way to create a new form.

Rabindranath Tagore: 'The Stage'

One of the earliest critiques of Western theatre is the essay by Rabindranath Tagore (1861–1941), 'The Stage', published in 1913 in Calcutta.[2] Tagore's interest in theatre spanned the whole of his literary career, beginning in 1881 and continuing into the 1930s. Although he 'remained aloof from the Bengali stage', as H. Sanyal puts it, meaning here the commercial Bengali theatre,[3] and despite

[1] Richard Schechner, *Environmental Theater* (New York: Hawthorn Books, 1973), p. vii.
[2] Rabindranath Tagore, 'The Stage', tr. from the Bengali by Surendranath Tagore, *Modern Review*, 14/6 (1913), 543–5.
[3] 'The Plays of Rabindranath Tagore', in *Rabindranath Tagore: A Centenary Volume (1861–1961)*, ed. Mahendra Kulastetna (New Delhi: Sahitya Akademi, 1961), 239.

the fact that his plays have been repeatedly criticized for their excessive symbolism and non-dialogic character,[4] by no means can these works be dismissed as closet drama. Most performances were private affairs, staged outside either in the courtyard of his family home or in the context of his Santiniketan school. Nevertheless, owing to Tagore's international reputation, these performances were at the same time 'public' events, reported and reviewed widely in the local press.[5]

Tagore's essay must be read on two interconnected levels. Firstly, he is taking issue with contemporary developments in Bengali theatre in its crass, commercialized form. Because the aesthetics of this type of theatre are primarily Western in origin, his argument can be extended to Western theatre in general. Tagore launches a full-scale assault on the scenographic conventions of realistic Western theatre, which he ascribes to a European need to have truth concrete. In contrast, he posits his own theatrical poetics on the basis of Indian traditions of theatre. Tagore's point of departure is the Sanskrit treatise on theatre and dance, the *Natyaśāstra*, and the most famous Sanskrit play *Śākuntala*, neither of which require actual pictorial scenery. He takes issue with Wagner's notion of the *Gesamtkunstwerk* which seeks to combine the arts in what Tagore terms an 'artistic pageant' and which is 'common or market Art, not of the Royal variety'.[6]

Tagore's reference to the *Natyaśāstra* shows that his critique of Western theatre is situated in Indian culture and that he will argue with its aesthetic categories. It is important to keep this in mind because his arguments seem to reveal all the attributes of a typical *fin-de-siècle* attack on theatrical realism. Like many anti-naturalistic theatre reformers, Tagore argues in favour of the primacy of poetry in drama and theatre. He pleads for a scenography of the imagination, which means a stage without realistic scene decoration, 'this paraphernalia of illusion' as he calls it.[7] In these points his concept of theatre parallels that of Maurice Maeterlinck, whom Tagore admired. The conclusions he arrives at echo in many points the theatre theory of Romanticism and the symbolist theatre of Maurice Maeterlinck

---

[4] See e.g. C. Paul Verghese, *Problems of the Indian Creative Writer in English* (Bombay: Somaiya Publications, 1971), 155 f.

[5] Edward Thompson provides a number of vivid eyewitness accounts of such performances: *Rabindranath Tagore: Poet and Dramatist* (London: Oxford University Press, 1926).   [6] Tagore, 'The Stage', 543.

[7] Ibid. 544.

deriving from it, which propagates a purely 'mental theatre' of poetry and imagination. Tagore, however, brings an Indian perspective to bear on the widespread discussion and plethora of anti-naturalistic reform models that were being formulated at this time in Europe. This intercultural perspective leads to a fundamental critique of Western thinking: theatrical realism is a reflection of the Western desire for the pragmatic and the concrete. The European, so runs Tagore's argument, certainly desires 'imaginative treats', but he wants them in the form of 'exact imitations of actual things'. He is particularly afraid of being deceived and requires therefore 'sworn testimony' that what he sees is indeed real.[8] In other words, Western theatre suffers from an excessive fixation on and desire for perfect iconicity. Of course, this is an insight Tagore shared with Gordon Craig and W. B. Yeats. The intercultural perspective lies in the assertion that the aesthetic predisposition is based on a deeper metaphysical trait: 'the European wants his truth concrete',[9] which suggests implicitly that the aesthetic proclivity is immutable. The subtext of Tagore's treatise is, then, that it is not enough to import, imitate, and appropriate the surface feature of Eastern aesthetics without the basic metaphysical attitude that informs it. In this way the essay can also be read as an attack on both Western realism and the attempts by the anti-naturalistic theatre movement to abolish these conventions.

As if to demonstrate that in India anti-naturalistic theatre is by no means the preserve of the educated élite, Tagore turns his attention to *jatra*, a form of folk theatre in Bengal. Here Tagore finds a congenial relationship between performer and spectator, which is quite the opposite of the confrontational structure created by the Western proscenium stage: 'That is why I like the *Jatra* plays of our country. There is not so much of a gulf separating the stage from the audience. The business of interpretation and enjoyment is carried out by both in hearty co-operation, and the spirit of the play, which is the real thing, is showered from player to spectator and from spectator to player in a very carnival of delight.'[10] This 'carnival of delight' is realized in *jatra* in spatial terms by the use of a form of arena staging, which fosters to performance a lively exchange between actors and audience. Despite a somewhat idealized characterization of the form, Tagore is certainly justified in seeing in it a theatrical aesthetic that was fundamentally opposed to the European stage conventions of the

---

[8] Tagore, 'The Stage', 544.   [9] Ibid.   [10] Ibid.

late nineteenth century. In *jatra* music, dance, and mime play an integral part; the theatrical code governing communication between performers and spectators differs fundamentally from that of theatrical realism.[11]

While *jatra* may be offered as an example of a functioning counter-model to the conventions of theatrical realism, it is not entirely appropriate as a model for theatrical art in a more general sense: it is too closely tied to its specific cultural context. It certainly cannot satisfy the sensibilities of the dramatist and director Tagore. Thus he turns to the tradition of classical Sanskrit theatre as a model of poetic drama. The empty space of Sanskrit theatre enables the dramatist, Tagore argues, to give his imagination free rein without having to consider the problem of scenery and scene changes: 'The stage that is in the Poet's mind has no lack of space or appurtenances. There scenes follow one another at the touch of his magic wand. The play is written for such a stage and such scenes; the artificial platform with its hanging canvas is not worthy of a poet.'[12]

Tagore is concerned to find for himself and for an Indian audience a new and culturally appropriate form of theatre which combines elements of the folk and classical traditions. Although his comments can be related to the European theatre reform discussion, as I have done, they are designed primarily for home consumption. The wider context of the essay is Tagore's own dramatic writing and theatrical practice against the background of commercialized theatre in Calcutta. His critique of theatrical realism culminates in severe criticism of the new theatres that have been erected and run on the commercial European model. This form of 'capitalist' enterprise offers a type of theatre which is far too costly for 'famine-stricken India':

The theatres that we have set up in imitation of the West are too elaborate to be brought to the door of all and sundry. In them the creative richness of poet and player are overshadowed by the wealth of the capitalist. If the Hindu spectator has not been too far infected with the greed for realism and the

[11] James Brandon describes the main features of contemporary *jatra* as follows, whereby it should be remembered that the form has been subjected to continual change since Tagore's time: 'Performance takes place on a simple raised platform placed in the center of the audience, which sits on cushions and rugs; a prompter (who follows the script and calls out lines) and musicians sit along one edge of the stage; performers may rest along other edges; performance lasts three or four hours; exciting entrances and exits are made on rampways through the audience.' *Brandon's Guide to Theater in Asia* (Honolulu: Hawaii University Press, 1976), 46.

[12] Tagore, 'The Stage', 544.

Hindu artist still has any respect for his craft and his skill, the best thing they can do for themselves is to regain their freedom by making a clean sweep of the costly rubbish that has accumulated round about and is clogging the stage.[13]

The expression 'greed for realism' and the equation of a realist aesthetic with capitalism provides a further intercultural perspective on the European discussion concerning the relationship between theatrical form and ideology. This question did not, however, gain wide currency until the 1920s and 1930s in the formalism debate. Tagore thus attacks theatrical realism not just as a reflection of Western metaphysical and aesthetic tradition but also as a manifestation of the capitalist world-view. Read in this way, Tagore's essay is not just an example of a *l'art pour l'art* plea for a Symbolist poetics of drama, but it establishes—possibly for the first time—a connection between the capitalist-driven politics of colonialism and the artistic products accompanying and established by it. Thus Tagore initiates in his essay a discussion which will accompany the development of colonial and post-colonial theatre. The conventions and practices of Western theatre, above all theatrical realism, are an 'inheritance', comparable to the political and administrative structures, that must be appropriated and adapted to local conditions, but not dispensed with entirely.

H. I. E. Dhlomo and the Africanization of Theatre

While Tagore was little concerned to elaborate a theory of theatre— 'The Stage' remained his only longer disquisition on the subject—and his debt to Western theatre is not made explicit in this essay, many of his plays themselves reveal pronounced syncretic characteristics. To some of these works I shall return in later chapters. The first major exponent of a theory of syncretic theatre is the Zulu intellectual, journalist, and playwright Herbert Dhlomo (1903–56). His writings on the theatre appeared in the 1930s and are for a number of reasons remarkable. For one thing, they articulate in considerable detail a theory of theatrical syncretism, in which the merging of European theatre and indigenous performance forms is explicitly propagated. For another, these writings anticipate a number of the central ideas of

[13] Tagore, 'The Stage', 544.

performance theory. Finally, these essays contain some of the earliest analyses of pre-colonial performance forms from an aesthetic rather than ethnographic perspective. In his substantial dramatic *œuvre* Dhlomo attempted to put his theory into practice without, however, being able to see his plays performed.[14]

H. I. E. Dhlomo remained very much a forgotten writer until the late 1970s, when, due to the efforts of two South African scholars, Tim Couzens and Nick Visser, he was 'rediscovered'. Dhlomo's rehabilitation began in 1977 with the publication of his essays on literature and theatre, which were followed in 1985 by a collected edition of his plays, poems, and short stories. Dhlomo's re-entry into the historiographical record is also a reflection of wider methodological shifts within South African literary and theatrical studies. The following evaluation of Dhlomo's importance by the South African scholar Martin Orkin would hardly have been ventured ten to fifteen years earlier: 'The dramatic projects which Herbert Dhlomo undertook in the 1930s and 1940s in South Africa may be said to mark the first significant attempt in drama to challenge the dominance of the imperial and colonialist centre as well as to contest aspects of prevailing ruling class discourse emanating from the white-settler culture.'[15]

Herbert Dhlomo was born and raised in Natal. He trained there as a schoolteacher, but worked mainly as a librarian and editor at the paper *Ilanga Lase Natal* in Johannesburg. Initially, Dhlomo was a so-called 'progressive', which meant he was an exponent of Western ideas. This included writing in the English language, a belief in Western-style education, and, on the immediate political level, opposition to tribalism and the desire for equality with white society for the educated black élite. In the course of his life, however, Dhlomo became increasingly critical of this Eurocentric stance and, parallel to the growing political radicalization of South African Blacks, rejected his earlier 'progressive' ideas.[16] Dhlomo's writings on the theatre and

[14] Dhlomo is supposed to have written twenty-four plays, of which only nine are extant. Only one was actually published in his lifetime. For a comprehensive study of Dhlomo's life and work, see the biography by Tim Couzens, *The New African: A Study of the Life and Work of H. I. E. Dhlomo* (Johannesburg: Raven Press, 1985).

[15] Martin Orkin, *Drama and the South African State* (Manchester: Manchester University Press, 1991), 21. In his study of South African drama Orkin devotes a whole chapter to Dhlomo, which alone points to the renewed interest in this writer.

[16] The background to this development is the increasingly visible racist politics advocated by the National Party. Dhlomo's reaction to this political situation is traced by Martin Orkin, *Drama and South African State*, 37–43.

his most important plays were written in the 1930s, in the course of which he shifted his position from one of adaptation to rejection of many aspects of Western culture.

The central ideas of his theory of theatre and drama are contained in the essay 'Drama and the African', published in 1936.[17] In it Dhlomo provides a theoretical justification for his first play, *The Girl Who Killed to Save*, which was published in the same year.[18] On a more general level the essay engages with the colonial teaching that the 'subject races' lack any developed form of theatre. Dhlomo begins his treatise with an unusual rhetorical gesture: 'Action! Rhythm! Emotion! Gesture! Imitation! Desires! That is what drama was before it developed into an institution for propaganda, the propagation of ideas, or for commercialized entertainment. Action, rhythm and the other histrionic qualities are not foreign to the African—neither is drama. Indeed, there is no race in the world which did not have some kind of tribal dramatic representation.'[19] These first sentences make quite clear that Dhlomo intends to turn the tables on the Western understanding of theatre: it is not the African cultures which lack theatrical forms, but rather Western theatre that has lost the true essence of theatre and degenerated into a purveyor of propaganda or commercial entertainment. In the place of this model, one hardly worthy of emulation, Dhlomo posits a broader concept of theatre with the goal of breaking the limitations of normative dramatic poetics: the purely dialogue-based conventions of the well-made play. In this way an aesthetic framework can be set up in which indigenous performance forms can be made functional. Dhlomo's theatrical concept leads to a shift away from dialogue as the dominant sign system to an emphasis on non-verbal components of theatrical performance. This move to reduce the importance of purely literary aspects of the dramatic text finds its parallel in the European movement of the turn of the century to 'retheatricalize' the theatre. But, like Tagore, Dhlomo arrives at his position on the

[17] H. I. E. Dhlomo, 'Drama and the African', *South African Outlook*, 66 (1 Oct. 1936). This and other essays and articles have been reprinted in a special issue of *English in Africa*, 4/2 (1977), devoted to Dhlomo's critical writings: *Literary Theory and Criticism of H. I. E. Dhlomo*, ed. Nick Visser. All citations from his theoretical writings will be from this reprint.
[18] According to the literary historian O. R. Dathorne, this play can be considered 'the first African play in English'. *The Black Mind: A History of African Literature* (Minneapolis: University of Minnesota Press, 1974), 401.
[19] Dhlomo, *Literary Theory and Criticism*, 3.

basis of his desire to revalorize indigenous performance and is in no way emulating developments and theories in Europe. However, his concept of theatrical syncretism in this first essay is still relatively Eurocentric:

The development of African drama cannot purely be from African roots. It must be grafted in Western drama. It must borrow from, be inspired by, shoot from European dramatic art forms, and be tainted by exotic influences. The African dramatist should not fear being mocked as an 'imitator' of European art. Only, he should write and produce his plays as he feels. His work should be marked by his own soul and individuality [. . .][20]

Of particular interest in this statement is the botanical metaphor with the idea of grafting elements from one culture onto another. In this trope Dhlomo touches on a recurrent aesthetic and ideological dilemma for any theory of syncretic theatre. The model of syncretic theatre that Dhlomo proposes is basically Western. The task for the African dramatist is to take the foreign medium and 'Africanize' it by integrating indigenous cultural forms. The full extent of this indigenization and whether the aim is a genuine dominant shift in favour of African performance forms is not made clear by Dhlomo in this first essay. But seen together with the articles written in 1939, in which he advocates a drama in African languages,[21] it demonstrates that Dhlomo's concept of syncretism is rooted in the idea of indigenizing the Western theatrical model rather than proposing a new model based on African performance forms.

Although he is not opposed in principle to 'literary' drama, Dhlomo is mainly concerned to demonstrate that a new form of autochthonous African theatre must rely heavily on existing gestural-musical codes of traditional performance forms. A central concept for Dhlomo is that of rhythm. It is a characteristic entirely absent from Western theatre, which he defines as a cultural and educational centre, an agency for propaganda, a social institution, and as literature: 'The African can contribute strong fast rhythm (and rhythm is more than physical), expressive of vigorous gesture and action, and a channel of seeing things from a different angle.'[22] The

[20] Ibid. 7.
[21] See e.g. the articles 'Language and National Drama' and 'African Drama and Poetry', both published in 1939, in which language problems of Bantu drama, mainly the question of an appropriate verse language, are discussed. Both are reprinted in Dhlomo, *Literary Theory and Criticism*.
[22] Dhlomo, *Literary Theory and Criticism*, 7.

mere parenthetical remark—'rhythm is more than physical'—in his first essay is developed three years later into a central cultural category. In the article 'African Drama and Poetry'[23] Dhlomo writes:

[R]hythm is essentially African. The tribal African was under the rigid rule of pattern. There were rigid patterns of behaviour, rigid patterns even in architecture (the hut) and in village or kraal planning. This love of pattern certainly had grave disadvantages, but it gave birth to a marked sense and love of rhythm. This sense of rhythm is seen even in the movement of tribal people [. . .] The element is also well-marked in African music and tribal plastic art. The dances, too, are strongly rhythmical. In fact, one may also say that the greatest gift of Africa to the artistic world will be—and has been— Rhythm.[24]

By extending the definition of rhythm to include a general structural code of African culture, Dhlomo anticipates important tenets of *négritude*, a movement which did not receive widespread attention until after the Second World War.[25] In the writings of many exponents of *négritude* rhythm is the quintessential element of a specifically African cultural tradition. For theoreticians such as the Senegalese poet and statesman Léopold Senghor rhythm encompasses far more than just music and dance; it is as it were a metaphysical and aesthetic concept determining the art and the everyday life of 'Negro-Africans', what he calls their 'architecture of being'.[26] Dhlomo's understanding of rhythm as a structural principle inherent in all aspects of African culture has, however, nothing in common with the Western clichés of the African as a kind of homo saltans. By extending the concept of rhythm to include not just music and dance but also everyday kinesics, plastic art, and architecture, Dhlomo is in fact constructing a counter-discourse to combat the widespread

[23] Ibid.; first pub. in *South African Outlook*, 69, 1 Apr. 1939, 88–90.

[24] Dhlomo, *Literary Theory and Criticism*, 16.

[25] It is improbable that Dhlomo was directly acquainted at this time with the term '*négritude*'. It was coined by Aimé Césaire in his poem *Cahier d'un retour au pays natal*, also published in 1939.

[26] See Senghor's famous definition: 'Qu'est-ce que le rhythme? C'est l'architecture de l'être, le dynamisme interne qui lui donne, le système d'ondes qu'il émet à l'adresse des Autres, l'expression pure de la force vitale. Le rhythme, c'est le choc vibratoire, la force qui, à travers les sens, nous saisit à la racine de l'être. Il s'exprime par les moyens les plus matériels, les plus sensuels: lignes, surfaces, couleurs, volumes en architecture, sculpture et peinture; accents en poésie et musique; mouvements dans la danse. Mais, ce faisant, il ordonne tout ce concret vers la lumière de l'esprit.' 'L'Esprit de la civilisation ou les lois de la culture négro-africaine', *Présence africaine*, 8–10 (1956), 60.

deprecatory characterizations of Africans with which he was no doubt all too familiar.[27]

Dhlomo and the exponents of *négritude*, who almost without exception belonged to the francophone cultural élite, share a particular bicultural way of seeing. Dhlomo's theoretical writings show very clearly that he viewed his own 'Bantu' culture from a kind of double perspective. On the one hand, the educated, urbane 'new African' retains a European viewpoint; on the other he is able to illuminate the structures of his own culture from within with particular empathy. Tied to this double perspective is also the special vision of the writer and theatre-reformer. And in the course of his writings it becomes clear that the intensive study of his own cultural background, with its traditions of performance and aesthetic categories, caused him increasingly to question and finally reject the premises of his Western education and aesthetic training.

The basis of this cultural knowledge was formed by his intimate acquaintance with the traditional performance forms of the Zulu. It was his goal to rehabilitate this cultural inheritance and to make it relevant for a new urban black culture. His theoretical writings advocating a mixing of Western and African performance can be seen as a contribution to a development that was already a reality in South Africa in the 1920s. By this time various forms of cultural mixing, particularly in the performing arts, were already visible in the townships. The most syncretic of these cultural forms was that of *marabi* music which grew out of the so-called shebeen culture, the illegal drinking-halls in the townships.[28] However, Dhlomo was probably too much a product of his own élitist education to be seriously interested in 'proletarian' forms such as *marabi*. Although he was doubtlessly familiar with them, they play no role in his

---

[27] The notion of rhythm as an interconnecting principle in African art is not just a romantic idea propagated by the followers of *négritude*. Recent art-ethnographic research has pointed out the interrelationship between music, dance, and sculpture in black Africa. See Robert Farris Thompson, *African Art in Motion: Icon and Act* (Los Angeles and Berkeley: University of California Press, 1974).

[28] David Coplan regards *marabi* as the result of syncretistic processes, which are derived from a modern musical eclecticism as well as other cultural forms: 'In the 1920s, these musicians assimilated elements from every available performance tradition into a single urban African musical style. [. . .] Marabi music drew heavily on the syncretic forms that preceded it, many of which were developed in the city by specific ethnic groups.' Coplan, *In Township Tonight*, 94–5.

theatrical theory. He was much more concerned to contrast African traditional performance culture in its unadulterated form with Western theatrical culture.

In the early essay 'Drama and the African' Dhlomo outlines the central ideas of a model of an African theatre, which he then modifies and in some respects radicalizes in later essays. The most interesting aspect of this theatrical concept is the importance attached to orality. He contrasts orality in African culture with the primacy of writing in Western culture. This has led in the latter to an impoverishment of oral skills. These skills were not only instrumental in refining and transmitting the traditional form of storytelling, but they represent a crucial factor in the modern mass media: 'The theatre, broadcasting, gramophone recording, etc., have all put a premium on vocal power.'[29] By linking a traditional form with a modern medium, Dhlomo not only outflanks the arguments of colonialist ideology, with its insistence on a crude Darwinist view of cultural evolution and blanket privileging of Western progress over non-Western backwardness; he also anticipates by several decades the primacy given to orality by contemporary media theorists in their considerations of the mass media.

A detailed philological examination of orality is undertaken in the essay 'Nature and Variety of Tribal Drama' (1939). Dhlomo is concerned here to identify a form of dramatic structure in the oral performance tradition of the Zulu: 'I submit that the tribal literary forms whose nature and construction have baffled many investigators, are in reality mutilated and distorted remains of primitive tribal, dramatic pieces.'[30] His methodological approach is taken from a development in biblical exegesis, which sees in the story of Job or in the book of Solomon a form of literary-dramatic genre. By drawing on this analogy Dhlomo identifies in the traditional performance forms of the 'Bantu' similar dramatic structures. For example, he divides the *izibongo*, Zulu praise-songs, into speaking parts, although the written form of these songs does not provide for such a structure. With considerable psychological finesse Dhlomo discerns various 'voices' or characters, which were, so he argues, individualized by the singers with the help of gesture and voice. Of particular significance is the fact that praise-

---

[29] Dhlomo, *Literary Theory and Criticism*, 6.   [30] Ibid. 23.

songs do not have just a ritualistic-utilitarian function, but are 'an end in themselves'. According to Dhlomo, this is the mark of a higher developmental stage on the path to genuine drama.[31] Even the children's songs, which are based on a simple dialogic structure, can be seen as 'creations of dramatic poets anxious and struggling to discover a form of dramatic expression'.[32]

Dhlomo applies the same analytical procedure to the Zulu dance form *ingoma*. The aim here is once again to identify a dramatic structure, individual characters involved in an action, and a chorus. Dhlomo designates these performances 'rhythmic, choral-dramatic dances', which are the expression of an intact community: 'The harmonic sense was so highly developed that it was enough for one individual to compose the melody of a tune and then introduce it to his companions, who would instantly learn the given melody, compose parts to it, sing the whole choral song there and then, and dance to it rhythmically.'[33] Although not stated explicitly, it is clear that this model of organic unity is intended as an idealized counter-image to the diversified and fragmented culture of the Europeans.

Of particular interest for Dhlomo's theory of an Afrocentric syncretic theatre is the central section of this essay. Here he brings together in systematic form the theatrical sign systems deriving from African performance culture. The nine points or aspects listed are not only relevant for Dhlomo's theatrical concept, but they anticipate at the same time the future practice of syncretic theatre. For this reason it pays to summarize them in some detail:

1. The performance forms of African culture analogous to Western theatre—its ceremonies and festivals—had, according to Dhlomo, a predominantly magico-religious function and were an organic part of the life of the people. The didactic function constitutive of Western theatre was entirely absent.

2. 'Tribal drama was national'; i.e. theatre is to be understood as a communal enterprise encompassing all classes.

3. Tribal drama offered opportunity to engender creativity in a variety of artistic spheres.

4. These performances fostered particularly the art of acting: 'On

---

[31] 'In the dramatic Izibongo the aim is no longer a practical one. The Izibongo are an end in themselves.' Ibid. 27.   [32] Ibid. 26.
[33] Ibid. 28.

these occasions the people used their powers of mimicry, creative emotion, gesticulation, simulation.'[34]

5. The existence of facial and body decoration is analogous to theatrical make-up and costume: 'Faces bedaubed with ochre, robes of animal skins donned by the bards, decorations such as circlets, necklaces girdles, all played their part.'

6. With regard to the audience, Dhlomo observes in the participatory behaviour of African spectators a sharp contrast to that of Western theatre. This behaviour also transcends a mere desire for entertainment: 'It was a need, an obligation, besides being a diversion.'

7. In place of artificial scenery tribal drama makes use of the natural surroundings. The atmospheric mood of twilight could be consciously employed as a factor in performance. Even the olfactory senses were catered for: 'We have said "aromatic" hours, because the tribal actor appreciated the efficacy of fragrant and stimulating herbs which were used to arouse certain emotions and moods.'

8. On a metaphysical level Dhlomo argues that the totemistic world-view of the African is a central component of his traditional theatre. The belief in the interdependence of all beings, humans as well as animals, imbued the performances of 'tribal man' with a philosophical foundation. This belief system can in no way be dismissed as mere superstition.

9. This belief system has also contributed to the great mysteries of African culture, its secret societies and occultism. It provides the mythopoetic material for the African poet: 'No wonder tribal Africans were such spontaneous, prolific poets. And who shall say whether this power does not lie dormant but ready in the soul of the African to-day . . .'.[35]

This programme or manifesto makes quite clear that Dhlomo expanded the concept of theatre to encompass what today is meant by the idea of performance theory or *cultural performance*. Dhlomo's

---

[34] Dhlomo remarks here parenthetically that the situation of racial discrimination and oppression fostered even more the acting talent of Africans, because they are continually forced to play different roles. This theme is a central element in the play *Sizwe Bansi is Dead* (1973), written by Athol Fugard, John Kani, and Winston Ntshona. Dhlomo also points to the theatricality inherent in African church services, an aspect of performance culture that South African theatre scholars have only recently become interested in; see Temple Hauptfleisch, 'Beyond Street Theatre and Festival', 181.

[35] Dhlomo, *Literary Theory and Criticism*, 32–4.

heterogeneous catalogue embraces such a range of elements that Western definitions of drama-based theatre are quite evidently inadequate. The constitutive elements of 'tribal drama' can in fact only be covered by the concept of cultural text. By extending the definitional parameters for what constitutes theatre and expanding the repertoire of legitimate artistic devices used in it, Dhlomo has already mapped out the strategy of future post-colonial syncretic theatre.

Dhlomo's programme of theatrical reform is not just restricted to formal innovation, but is founded on clearly defined political goals. In his writings in support of the founding of an 'African Dramatic Movement'[36] Dhlomo advocates the use of drama in support of the emancipation of women and as a contribution to harmonizing race relations. Drama and theatre should also be used for the education of the masses. Requirements of this kind find echoes in corresponding theatrical movements in Great Britain and the United States between the world wars, which advocated a socially committed theatre as a counter-model to the theatrical entertainment industry.[37] However, Dhlomo is not concerned simply to imitate international developments, but rather to integrate a specifically African perception into this model of politically motivated mass theatre. Of particular interest here is his advocacy of drama as a vehicle for redefining African history. He suggests, for example, writing historical dramas as a means of rehabilitating Zulu leaders such as Chaka, Dingane, and Cetshwayo, who had been condemned as bloodthirsty savages by European historiography. Dhlomo views them as tragic figures of great historical importance.[38]

[36] In 1932 the Bantu Dramatic Society and the socialist-orientated Bantu People's Players were founded. These were amateur groups, which were strongly reliant on white 'tutelage'. See Orkin, *Drama and South African State*, 24.

[37] 'New Theatre' is the common, although not particularly precise, term for this left-wing movement, which emerged in the 1920s and 1930s. It embraced in the United States the New Playwrights' Theatre of John Dos Passos and the Group Theatre founded by Harold Clurman, Lee Strasberg, and Clifford Odets. The leading group in England was Unity Theatre, founded in 1936. A co-founder of Unity Theatre, the Belgian André Van Gyseghem, worked in the 1930s with the Bantu People's Players. Orkin draws attention to Van Gyseghem's work in South Africa but does not point out his connection to Unity Theatre. Ibid.

[38] In his article 'Why Study Tribal Dramatic Forms' (1939) Dhlomo writes: 'The African has suddenly become proud and intensely interested in the careers of these national heroes and heroines. Today the new African refuses to accept these men and women as savages, murderers, and impostors of the school-room and the textbook.' Dhlomo, *Literary Theory and Criticism*, 42. The majority of Dhlomo's drama deals with the lives of such historical figures.

In this and many other respects Dhlomo proved himself to be something of a prophet. Today, modern South African historiography accords the political achievements of Chaka, Dingane, and Cetshwayo a much more balanced appraisal than they received in Dhlomo's lifetime.

The prophetic character of Dhlomo's writings mainly reveals itself, however, in his ceaseless propagation of a form of theatrical syncretism. There is no comparable theatrical theorist among anglophone African writers until Wole Soyinka's attempts to found a theory of theatre on the basis of Yoruba myth and ritual performance. Particularly where Dhlomo draws attention to the mythopoetic complexity of African thought and postulates this world-view as a basis for a new form of African theatre, he clearly anticipates Soyinka's analysis of Yoruba culture for the same purpose. To find the next substantial body of African theatre theory, we have to move forward to Nigeria of the mid- and late 1960s.

Discourses on Theatre in Nigeria

The 1960s in Nigeria, the years immediately following independence, saw a period of intensive preoccupation on the part of intellectuals and dramatists with their own indigenous traditions of performance. This writing and research links ethnography with theatre studies and forms the basis for a theory and practice of syncretic theatre. On closer inspection it becomes clear that the consciousness of and sensibility for a new type of theatre that was not just an imitation of Western literary models was conditioned primarily by this interest in the theatricality of African, or more precisely, Yoruba culture. The writings discussed below attempt to negotiate between Western conditioned discourses, on the one hand, and an increasingly Afrocentric perspective on the other, which sees the necessity for creating an entirely different kind of discourse to describe the theatrical forms of this culture. Two aspects make this negotiative process particularly clear. Firstly, in the early writings Aristotle forms the obligatory point of departure in order to characterize the relationship between ritual and theatre in African performance as an evolutionary process towards 'drama' or dramatic elements in the Western sense. Secondly, these elements are defined correspondingly in terms of 'action' and 'conflict'.

Opposing this Western-influenced discourse, there are also attempts to isolate fundamental differences in African theatricality which cannot be explained by European models.

Writings in this early discourse tradition can be found in the work of theatre scholars such as Joel Adedeji and M. J. C. Echeruo, and in essays by the playwright-scholars Ola Rotimi and J. P. Clark. All these writers analyse traditional African performance forms within an evolutionary paradigm based on ritual origins. Adedeji, for example, writes that cults of the Yoruba 'yielded evidences of their theatrogenic character like those of ancient Greece'.[39] Echeruo argues along similar lines for Igbo ritual performance, but including a programmatic flourish: 'The Igbo should do what the Greeks did: expand ritual into life and give that life a secular base.'[40] Both Rotimi and Clark are exponents of syncretic theatre, and their 'academic' essays have an implied link to their dramatic writing. Rotimi, in an essay entitled 'Traditional Nigerian Drama' (1971), makes explicit reference to J. G. Frazer's *The Golden Bough* and constructs an evolutionary paradigm to explain the secularization of traditional theatre, not unlike that once posited for medieval English drama, to which Rotimi refers: 'the way was now set for the ritual to move out from confined conclaves, from sacred groves and from hallowed shrines, and meet the masses on the king's special forecourt'.[41] Frazer is also J. P. Clark's source when he states: 'We believe that as the roots of European drama go back to the Egyptian Osiris and the Greek Dionysus so are the origins of Nigerian drama likely to be found in the early religious and magical ceremonies and festivals of the peoples of this country.'[42] All four writers see strong affinities between indigenous African performance and the heavily music- and dance-based idiom of early Greek tragedy. The

[39] J. A. Adedeji, 'The Place of Drama in Yoruba Religious Observance', *Odù: University of Ifẹ Journal of African Studies*, 3/1 (1966), 88.
[40] 'The Dramatic Limits of Igbo Ritual', *Research in African Literature*, 4 (1973), 30. See the sharply formulated reply by Ossie Enekwe: 'There is no need for us to keep talking of evolving Igbo drama when it is flourishing all over Igboland.' 'Myth, Ritual and Drama in Igboland', in Yemi Ogunbiyi (ed.), *Drama and Theatre in Nigeria: A Critical Source Book* (Lagos: Nigeria Magazine, 1981), 162.
[41] Ola Rotimi, 'Traditional Nigerian Drama', in Bruce King (ed.), *Introduction to Nigerian Literature* (Lagos: Lagos University Press, 1971), 39.
[42] J. P. Clark, 'Aspects of Nigerian Drama', in G. D. Killam (ed.), *African Writers on African Writing* (1966; London: Heinemann, 1973), 20.

apparent contiguity of ritualized festivals and the performance framework of Attic tragedy within the Dionysian festivals in particular offered parallels to Yoruba festivals in which myth is re-enacted, or indeed, in the case of *egungun* festivals, reincarnated.[43]

If we turn to Wole Soyinka's famous essay 'The Fourth Stage' (1969) we can see a number of these issues addressed.[44] Although not written in the idiom of an 'academic' essay, 'The Fourth Stage' is clearly the result of substantial scholarship and research into Yoruba culture.[45] Its idiom and intention is rather that of an aesthetic manifesto, not unlike Nietzsche's *The Birth of Tragedy*, to which it owes a great deal. Soyinka undertakes in his essay a very personal reading of Yoruba mythology for his own mythopoetic and dramaturgical purposes. The intricate exegesis of Yoruba creation myths Soyinka provides is certainly not ethnological in intent. Rather, the essay can be situated in the above-mentioned tradition of discourse prevalent in the 1960s in which traditional African performance forms were reinterpreted and located in a paradigm with structural parallels to European writings on the origin of theatre in ritual—either Greek or Christian. Soyinka, too, makes many direct references to Greek mythology in his essay and adapts and expands Nietzsche's dyadic model of Apollonian and Dionysian principles with Yoruba equivalents. This aspect of the essay has

[43] Biodun Jeyifo provides a detailed critique of writing on African theatre in his article 'The Reinvention of Theatrical Tradition: Critical Discourses on Interculturalism in the African Theatre', in Fischer-Lichte *et al.* (eds.). *The Dramatic Touch of Difference*, 239–51. He identifies three distinct historiographical discourses: Western scholastic discourse, an 'Afrocentric' counter-discourse, of which Adedeji and Soyinka are examples, and an interculturally motivated discourse with a particular interest in the ideological and social functions of theatre. Although Jeyifo's well-known ideological stance informs and colours his whole argument, the article is an important first contribution to providing a discourse analysis of this considerable body of writing.

[44] The essay was first published in D. W. Jefferson (ed.), *The Morality of Art: Essays Presented to G. Wilson Knight by his Colleagues and Friends* (London: Routledge & Kegan Paul, 1969). It was subsequently reprinted with minor corrections as an appendix in Wole Soyinka, *Myth, Literature and the African World* (Cambridge: Cambridge University Press, 1976). All quotations are from the revised edition.

[45] This research is partly the fruit of Soyinka's Rockefeller grant in the early 1960s and partly the result of a resurgence of academic and artistic preoccupation with Yoruba culture. This is most clearly reflected in journals such as *Nigeria Magazine*, *Odù: University of Ifẹ Journal of African Studies*, and the literary magazine *Black Orpheus*. All three journals published important articles on traditional Yoruba theatre during the 1960s.

been the subject of considerable commentary and will not be pursued further here.[46]

More important for this study is Soyinka's interest in syncretism,
which recurs in later essays as well, and his comments on the relationship between indigenous African theatrical idioms and modern theatre aesthetics. Soyinka refers, for example, to the deity Obatala as the
'syncretic successor' to Orisa-nla. This process of mythical syncretism, whereby two gods are merged into one, reflects one of the
fundamental precepts of the Yoruba and, by extension, the African
world-view: 'a harmonious will which accommodates every alien
material or abstract phenomenon within its infinitely stressed spirituality'.[47] The idea of 'accommodation' as a syncretic merging and
absorption of alien elements recurs throughout the essays collected in
Myth, Literature and the African World. For example, in the essay
'Ideology and Social Vision (2)' Soyinka postulates the liberative
power of 'authentic images of African reality', particularly those
deriving from the symbols and values of mythology, for the African
writer:

They [the images] are familiar and closest to hand; they are not governed by
rigid orthodoxies such as obtain in Islamic- and Christian-orientated
matrices of symbols; a natural syncretism and the continuing process of
this activity is the reality of African metaphysical systems; the protean nature
of the symbols of African metaphysics, whether expressed in the idiom of
deities, nature events, matter or artifacts, are an obvious boon to the full flow
of the imagination.[48]

This applies equally, of course, to Soyinka's own creative writing and
most particularly to his theatre. Joel Adedeji, for example, makes
explicit reference to this notion of 'natural syncretism' when he
writes of Soyinka's 'new theatre culture [produced] within the matrix
of the traditional'.[49] Soyinka's positive valorization of syncretic mixing as a constituent and integral component of the African world can

[46] Ketu H. Katrak provides an extensive analysis of the 'Fourth Stage' in her study
Wole Soyinka and Modern Tragedy: A Study of Dramatic Theory and Practice, Contributions in Afro-American and African Studies, 96 (Westport, Conn.: Greenwood
Press, 1986), as do Wiveca Sotto, *The Rounded Rite*, and Ann B. Davis, 'Dramatic
Theory of Wole Soyinka', in James Gibbs (ed.), *Critical Perspectives on Wole Soyinka*
(Washington: Three Continents Press, 1981), 139–46.
[47] Soyinka, *Myth, Literature and the African World*, 146 f.   [48] Ibid. 121 f.
[49] J. A. Adedeji, 'Aesthetics of Soyinka's Theatre', in Dapo Adelugba (ed.), *Before
our Very Eyes: Tribute to Wole Soyinka* (Ibadan: Spectrum Books, 1987), 123.

be read as an attempt to provide a philosophical fundament to his syncretic method of dramaturgy. It is possible to see here a concerted effort to oppose an African poetics of syncretism to the actual, or postulated, 'rigid orthodoxies' of Western normative poetics with their emphasis on purism. By extension it is justifiable to view this concept of syncretism as a general principle of post-colonial syncretic theatre. That this is in fact justified can be seen from the following survey of theories of theatrical syncretism in the Caribbean.

Theatre and Carnival in the Caribbean

More or less parallel to developments in Nigeria there emerged in the anglophone Caribbean a significant theatrical movement advocating an indigenous-based West Indian theatre. The 1950s and 1960s were decades of considerable programmatic as well as practical theatrical activity in the Caribbean. As the various islands prepared for and moved into independence, so, too, did the calls for an indigenous Caribbean theatre, free from the taint of colonial influences, gain in number and volume. Although the political idea of federation very quickly proved to be unworkable, the notion of a Caribbean national drama and theatre as a culturally unifying force remained a vital idea at least until the early 1970s. The various plays and programmes aimed at demonstrating and promoting an indigenous West Indian theatre all sought to quarry the rich mine of the expressive 'folk' culture: the musical, dance, storytelling, and processional traditions which contained a pronounced performative component. First the patois and dialects, the Caribbean 'first' languages, were found to be stageworthy, and then by the late 1950s the performance forms themselves began to be co-opted for the new theatre.

In review, it is possible to discern two main lines of development in the process of indigenizing West Indian theatre. The first and most widespread movement can be termed the 'Theatre of Exuberance'. Here the colour and celebrative nature of carnival and the various indigenous masquerade traditions were proposed as a basis for a theatre and drama incorporating and exploiting the *Gesamtkunstwerk* of carnival. The other line of discussion advocated the Caribbean ritual tradition as the basis for an autochthonous theatre and drama.

The most eloquent theorist and practitioner of the 'theatre of exuberance' was, and perhaps still is, Errol Hill.[50] In 1974 Hill outlined
the central points of his programme in the article 'The Emergence of
a National Drama in the West Indies', which he concludes with a
seven-point credo for a national theatre, an idea which Hill had been
propagating since the 1950s. He is eclectic in his choice of folk forms
adaptable for the stage. Referring to his own efforts as a promoter of
a folk-based theatre in the 1950s, Hill writes:

He [Hill] urged theatre artists to seek inspiration from the indigenous theatre
of the folk, not as curiosities but as the fibre from which a national drama is
fashioned: the carnival and calypso, John Canoe and dead-wake ceremonies,
Shango and Pocomania, Tea Meetings, La Rose and Vieux Croix festivals, the
Hosein and other Indian customs, native music and rhythms, dialect as a
serious medium of expression.[51]

While Hill himself tended to favour the exuberance of carnival and
calypso, the theatrical possibilities of wake ceremonies and the hieratic worlds of Caribbean syncretic cults began to exert a fascination
on other dramatists and directors. Hill had already exploited some of
the theatrical potential of the *shango* cult in his musical comedy *Man
Better Man*.[52] In this work, however, the ritualistic acts are depicted
in a comic light and ridiculed as quackery and bush medicine. By the
late 1960s and early 1970s plays were being created which took the
ritualism of such cults very seriously indeed and ushered in a whole
new development in Caribbean theatre.

In his major work on the carnival, *The Trinidad Carnival: Mandate
for a National Theatre* (1972), Hill offers a résumé of his concept.
The main section of the book is a historical account of the phenomenon from its origins in the eighteenth century up until the 1960s.

[50] Errol Hill is a many-faceted *homme de théâtre*. Born in Trinidad, he trained at
RADA acting school in London, returning to the Caribbean in the 1950s. Staff drama
tutor for the University of the West Indies, he travelled throughout the West Indies,
directing and writing plays. In the late 1960s he was appointed professor of speech and
drama at Dartmouth College in the United States. Here he established himself as a
leading historian of black theatre.
[51] Errol Hill, 'The Emergence of a National Drama in the West Indies'. *Caribbean
Quarterly,* 18/4 (1974), 34.
[52] *Man Better Man* was written in 1956 and staged in 1957 in a prose version in
Jamaica. A calypso version was performed in 1965 during the Commonwealth Arts
Festival in London and in 1969 by the Negro Ensemble Company in New York. The
text is published in the anthology Errol Hill (ed.), *Plays for Today* (1974; London:
Longmans Caribbean, 1985).

The final two chapters are devoted to Hill's primary interest. They form a manifesto propagating the adaptation of carnivalesque theatricality as the basis on which to construct a national theatre. The central problem in such an adaptation, according to Hill, lies in the particular aesthetics of carnival. Because of its exuberance and pronounced exhibitive character carnival lacks the ability to appeal to refined sentiment and reason, features inherent in artistic 'legitimate theatre': 'Essential to any art product, these qualities may be identified as order, coherence, and stillness, or silence.'[53] Since the goal of carnival is the reversal of order, it is necessary to ask, Hill argues, whether the art of theatre and that of carnival can in any way be reconciled. While there were certainly attempts in the 1950s and 1960s to 'theatricalize' the Dimanche-Gras-Show by turning it into a kind of revue with a unifying theme or story into which the standard entertainment forms of calypso and dances were integrated, Hill concludes that such experiments cannot be regarded as a model for a genuine national theatre. Despite such problems, which are rooted in fundamental aesthetic differences, Hill remains convinced that carnival offers a reservoir of performance forms for an indigenous art theatre: 'Yet the art theatre, if it is to be indigenous, if it is to be a national theatre, must take cognizance of the materials of the carnival and the forms in which they are expressed.'[54] Hill ends his book by outlining a precise manifesto for a Caribbean national theatre on the basis of Carnival. The common or adaptable features of the two forms are the following:

1. *Rhythm.* Rhythmic sensibility is a common feature of both carnival and Afro-American culture in general.

2. *Verbal delivery.* The metrical and polyrhythmic speech patterns characteristic of calypso and verbal satire should be a central feature of the new theatre as well.

3. *Dance, song, music.* Hill emphasizes the inseparability of speech, song, dance, and music, and calls for the careful orchestration of these forms in a coherent whole. He is particularly concerned to avoid the mere interludal function of songs and dances in the American musical. They should in fact be an integral part of the action.

4. *Performers* should be proficient in the skills of acting, dancing, and singing. In this way the Western fragmentation of theatrical genres could be overcome.

---

[53] Errol Hill, *The Trinidad Carnival: Mandate for a National Theatre* (Austin: University of Texas, 1972), 104.   [54] Ibid. 113.

5. *Language*. Of central importance is the development of a poetic-metaphorical theatrical language on the basis of local dialects and creole languages. Hill draws the oft-cited parallel with J. M. Synge's poetization of English on the basis of Irish dialect.

6. *Masks and masquerades*. These offer the visual counterpart to the metaphorical language of the Caribbean.[55]

Errol Hill's catalogue represents the synthesis of a whole decade of intense debate among artists, dramatists, and scholars over the form and direction an indigenous Caribbean theatre should take. But, as mentioned earlier, Hill advocates primarily one particular source of folk culture. Another source, the practices of ritual possession, finds less support in his theory.

The other important Caribbean exponent of theatrical syncretism as a theorist, dramatist, and director is Derek Walcott, who was awarded the Nobel Prize for literature in 1992. Walcott was born in 1930 on the small island of St Lucia. In the early 1950s he wrote a number of historical and verse plays, most of which, however, did not receive more than a few amateur productions.[56] In 1959 he founded the Trinidad Theatre Workshop in Port of Spain, the capital city of Trinidad and Tobago.[57] The goal of this experimental theatre group was to develop an indigenous Caribbean style of theatre. For seven years Walcott and the group experimented with improvisations in search of a new theatrical language. It was not until 1966 that the first repertory season was presented: Edward Albee's *The Zoo Story* and Walcott's one-act play *The Sea at Dauphin*, which he had written in 1954. Between 1966 and 1970 there followed a period of intense activity. The Workshop

[55] Ibid. 115–18.
[56] Looking back on these early works, Walcott writes: 'At twenty-seven I had written and rejected a great number of plays, most of them too tortured and strange in their stage poetry to work, and the two or three successful-seeming ones had moved out of poetry into the prose of the people, *The Sea at Dauphin* particularly.' 'Derek's Most West Indian Play: *Ti-Jean and his Brothers*', *Sunday Guardian Magazine* (Trinidad), 21 June 1970, 7. Two plays which reached a wider public were the verse drama *Henri Christophe: A Chronicle* (1950), which, apart from amateur productions, was staged in 1952 in London, and the 'epic drama' *Drums and Colours*, staged in 1958 in Trinidad to mark the opening of the first federation parliament. For an analysis of *Drums and Colours*, see Tejumola Olaniyan, 'Dramatizing Postcoloniality: Wole Soyinka and Derek Walcott', *Theatre Journal*, 44 (1992), 485–99.
[57] The group was initially called the Little Carib Theatre Workshop, as it was housed in the Little Carib Theatre. In 1965 the group moved to the basement of Hotel Bretton Hall. For a thorough history of Walcott and the Trinidad Theatre Workshop, see Bruce King, *Derek Walcott and West Indian Drama: 'Not Only a Playwright but a Company': The Trinidad Theatre Workshop* (Oxford: Clarendon Press, 1995).

staged plays such as Soyinka's *The Road*, Genet's *The Blacks*, Caribbean plays, and of course Walcott's own work. The group attained international recognition with their production of Walcott's drama *Dream on Monkey Mountain*. It was first staged in 1967 in Canada, directed by Walcott. There followed in 1971 in New York a successful off-Broadway production by the Negro Ensemble Company. In the early 1970s Walcott cooperated with the *Hair* composer Galt Mac-Dermot with the aim of creating a specifically Caribbean musical theatre. This collaboration resulted in *The Joker of Seville*,[58] an adaptation of Tirso de Molina's *El Burlador de Sevilla*, and *O Babylon!*, a play about the Rastafarian movement in Jamaica.[59] Walcott remained artistic director and house-dramatist of the Trinidad Theatre Workshop until 1977, when, deeply disappointed about the lack of state support for the group, he resigned from this position.[60]

Walcott's major programmatic writings on the theatre were published between 1960 and 1976, the period when he was most closely involved in the Trinidad Theatre Workshop as director, designer, and dramatist. The main forum for his ideas was the local newspaper the *Trinidad Guardian*, where Walcott was employed from 1960 to 1967 as a staff writer in charge of the arts. Walcott propagated his ideas in the form of columns, theatre reviews, and articles, as well as in interviews and in forewords to his books. Any attempt to depict a 'Walcottian' theory of theatre must bear in mind the need to synthesize it from a variety of discursive forms.[61]

[58] It was premièred on 28 Nov. 1974 by the Trinidad Theatre Workshop, Port of Spain, Trinidad. The text is published in Derek Walcott, *The Joker of Seville and O Babylon!* (New York: Farrar, Straus & Giroux, 1978).

[59] It was premièred on 19 Mar. 1976 by the Trinidad Theatre Workshop, Port of Spain, Trinidad. The text is published in Walcott, *The Joker of Seville and O Babylon!*

[60] Walcott shifted his activities to the United States, where he took up a position at Boston University as professor of creative writing. Since the late 1970s Walcott has divided his time between the United States and the Caribbean. The published plays of this period, although dealing with Caribbean locales and issues, are mainly realistic in form and reveal very little evidence of theatrical syncretism. On Walcott's theatrical activities since his move to the United States, see the interview in Edward Baugh, 'Derek Walcott on West Indian Literature and Theatre: An Interview', *Jamaica Journal*, 21/2 (May–July 1988), 50–2.

[61] There is no full bibliography of these writings. A small selection can be found in Robert Hamner, *Derek Walcott* (Boston: Twayne, 1981); the bibliography by Irma E. Goldstraw, *Derek Walcott: An Annotated Bibliography of his Works* (New York: Garland, 1984), provides a good selection of the newspaper writings. A good coverage is also provided in Victor Questel, 'Derek Walcott: Contradiction and Resolution: Paradox, Inconsistency, Ambivalence and their Resolution in Derek Walcott's Writing 1946–1976', University of the West Indies, (St Augustine, Ph.D. thesis) 1979. Walcott published over 400 reviews and articles between 1960 and 1967.

With the exception of the long introductory essay entitled 'What the Twilight Saw: An Overture', which forms the preface to his volume *Dream on Monkey Mountain and Other Plays* (1970),[62] there is no attempt by Walcott himself to summarize his concept of a Caribbean theatre.

Walcott's writings on the theatre must first of all be seen in the wider context of discourses on art, literature and cultural self-definition of the time. The Caribbean creole societies with their amalgams of British, African, Indian, Spanish, French, Portuguese, and Chinese influence, offer countless examples of cultural commixture. While this state of being is in itself a simple fact of life, there has been considerable debate over the cultural values it represents. In the period of the late 1950s and throughout the 1960s there emerged three distinct discourses of cultural criticism within the Caribbean. The Trinidad-born writer V. S. Naipaul coined the term 'mimic men' to describe the supposed lack of originality of Caribbean culture. Naipaul articulated his harsh criticism of the 'borrowed culture' of the Caribbean islands in his travel book *The Middle Passage*, published in 1962.[63] According to Naipaul, Caribbean culture is basically imitative and has nothing comparable to the great artistic achievements of the Old World. A radical counter-position to Naipaul and the Eurocentric ideology he represents emerged in the 1960s in the wake of the black-consciousness movement in the United States, which quickly found followers in the Caribbean. A new Afrocentric cultural ideology grew up which concentrated on and revalorized the retentions of African culture in the Caribbean.[64] In these competing and highly polarized positions Walcott assumes the role of mediator. He makes his position particularly clear in his essay 'Meanings' (1970). He could not claim, Walcott writes, to have been in any way humiliated by the colonial experience: the exposure to colonial educational values, above all to the literary tradition of Virgil and Horace, of Shakespeare and Milton, contributed to a strength of the

---

[62] (New York: Farrar, Straus & Giroux).

[63] The citation reads: 'Living in a borrowed culture, the West Indian, more than most, needs writers to tell him who he is.' V. S. Naipaul, *The Middle Passage: Impressions of Five Societies—British, French and Dutch—in the West Indies and South America* (New York: Vintage Books, 1962), 68.

[64] This counter-aesthetic is documented by the historian and poet Edward Kamau Brathwaite in his essay 'The Love-Axe: Developing a Caribbean Aesthetic', in H. A. Baker (ed.) *Reading Black: Essays in the Criticism of African, Caribbean and Black American Literature* (Ithaca: Cornell University Press, 1976).

West Indian consciousness which is characterized by 'a fusion of formalism with exuberance [. . .] It's the greatest bequest the Empire made.'[65] The keyword here is 'fusion', which for Walcott represents an equilibrium of European cultural values and elements deriving from the folk tradition. He also applies it in a specifically theatrical context to the acting style of his theatre group: 'But in the best actors in the company you can see this astounding fusion ignite their style, this combination of classic discipline inherited through the language, with a strength of physical expression that comes from the folk music.'[66]

The term 'fusion' and related synonyms occur frequently in the critical literature on Walcott's writing to characterize not only his philosophy of theatre but also as a designation for his writing style in a more general sense.[67] The theatre critic Lloyd Coke, for example, terms Walcott 'a fusionist, and the company [the Trinidad Theatre Workshop] has been molded by his Creoleness, his hybrid vigour'.[68] Robert Hamner refers in a positive sense to Walcott's 'Theatre of Assimilation': 'Assimilation denotes not only taking something in and thoroughly comprehending it; the term signifies also the incorporation and conversion processes that occur as foreign matter is absorbed and adapted. Fusion takes place and new energy is released.'[69] The concept of 'assimilation' as defined by Hamner corresponds closely to the notion of syncretism used in this book. Both terms refer to a process whereby culturally heterogeneous material is recombined to produce new forms.

For examples of performance forms within the existing folk culture which could lend themselves to theatricalization, Walcott, like Hill, looks to the carnival tradition. Although Walcott has a very ambivalent attitude towards carnival as a potentially theatrical form, his frequent preoccupation with it offers insights into more general questions of the relationship between indigenous cultural texts and their potential for functionalization within Western theatre and drama. In an early article on carnival in Trinidad Walcott analyses

---

[65] Derek Walcott, 'Meanings', *Savacou*, 2 (1970), 51.   [66] Ibid.

[67] See e.g. the study by Diana Lyn, 'The Concept of Mulatto in Some Works of Derek Walcott', *Caribbean Quarterly*, 26 (1980), 49–69. Lyn uses the term 'mulatto' to describe the creative 'schizophrenia' of the Caribbean artist, which manifests itself, she claims, in all of Walcott's work.

[68] Lloyd Coke, 'Walcott's Mad Innocents', *Savacou*, 5 (June 1971), 121.

[69] Robert Hamner, 'Derek Walcott's Theater of Assimilation', *West Virginia University Philological Papers*, 25 (Feb. 1979), 87.

the theatricality of this folk festival and concludes that it is fundamentally antithetical to 'classic' aesthetic principles. With reference
to diverse sources such as Goethe, Shelley, Chinese art, and T. S.
Eliot, he defines classical aesthetics in terms of stillness, timelessness,
and distance: 'These Greek classic principles are the antithesis of
Carnival. The essential law of Carnival is movement. Restlessness.
It is outward, directionless. Its dictum is, keep going, and it does this
for three days.'[70] Although Walcott does observe a growing tendency
to aestheticize carnival and to create greater visual formality and
coherence, this still cannot neutralize the 'true spirit' of the festival,
which is anarchy. Walcott sees carnival situated on the borders of
many artistic phenomena without corresponding precisely to any of
them. He calls this the 'great almostness' of carnival:

all these elements combine to make the curious force of Carnival its great
almostness, its near-poetry from the calypso, its near-orchestra from the
steel-band, its near-theatre from its bands, its near-sculpture from its crafts-
men. It will remain always as close as that, but no one should look on
Carnival as art. It is an expression of a people with a fantastic, original
genius for the theatrical who may never produce great theatre.[71]

It is above all the last sentence which shows that Walcott is concerned
to establish a clear demarcation line between the theatricality of
carnival and theatre. This is his answer to Errol Hill's somewhat
simplistic call for a carnival-based Caribbean theatre. In the mid-
1960s Walcott and Hill were involved in a debate over this and
related questions.[72] As we have already seen, Hill considers that a
great many elements of carnival and the folk tradition can be adopted
and adapted to art theatre without major problems of transformation. Walcott, on the other hand, repeatedly draws attention to the
wider aesthetic problems involved in the integration of existing cultural texts into the art form theatre.

In the late 1960s indigenous forms of expression, above all carnival, underwent a radical revaluation on the part of many Caribbean
intellectuals. Representative of this movement is the writer and director Marina Maxwell, co-founder in 1968 of Yard theatre in Jamaica.

[70] Derek Walcott, 'Carnival: The Theatre of the Streets', *Sunday Guardian* (Trinidad), 9 Feb. 1964, 4.   [71] Ibid.
[72] See Walcott's criticism of Hill's calypso-based play *Man Better Man* in his review
'Grande Tonight; Broadway Next', *Trinidad Guardian*, 27 Jan. 1965, 5; and Hill's
answer in the same paper, 'Is "Man Better Man" Mr. Walcott?', 3 Feb. 1965, 5.

Like Hill, Maxwell considered carnival to be the 'seedbed' of West Indian theatre. In her programme, which sought, as the name suggests, to set up theatre in the backyards of Kingston ghettos, open to the people and using performance forms familiar to the people, the impulses of decentralized political popular theatre practised by European and American ensembles conjoined with the indigenization process in Caribbean writing and art. In her manifesto 'Towards a Revolution in the Arts' (1970) Maxwell divided the Caribbean artistic community into 'unconscious' (folk, Rasta) and 'schizoid' (Western-influenced) artists. In carnival, however, there exists an art form which can provide a healing synthesis for this rupture: 'I see the drum at the centre, and Carnival informing all the arts in the future. Out of this can come our painting, our sculpture, our theatre, our costuming, everything—and different and more exciting than anything ever produced before. Here is improvisation [. . .] here is surrealistic, naked, mad experiment and I repeat, here is synthesis.'[73] Walcott vehemently opposed this kind of idealization of carnival as the future model for the Caribbean arts, particularly theatre, as it contained within it an implied attack on his own work towards a Caribbean art theatre.[74] In the essay 'What the Twilight Saw: An Overture' Walcott articulates his frustration towards intellectuals who overemphasize the popular tradition at the expense of genuine aesthetic values:

Duty had delineated itself to him [Walcott]—to transform the theatrical into theatre, to qualify the subtlety between a gift and a curse, but this was a society fed on an hysterical hallucination, that believed only the elaborate frenzy now controlled by the State. But Carnival was as meaningless as the art of the actor confined to mimicry. And now the intellectuals, courting and fearing the mass, found values in it they had formerly despised. They apotheosised the folk form, insisting that calypsos were poems.[75]

In this passage a number of important ideas are touched on. On one level Walcott is restating his own concept of syncretic theatre, the refashioning of existing performance forms into art theatre ('to transform the theatrical into theatre'). On another level he is observing and pointing out how cultural and political developments—state support

[73] Marina Maxwell, 'Toward a Revolution in the Arts', *Savacou*, 2 (1970), 28 f.

[74] This critique is not, however, levelled by Maxwell at Walcott. Her article contains a number of positive references to Walcott as both poet and theatre director. Ibid.

[75] Derek Walcott, 'What the Twilight Says: An Overture', in *Dream on Monkey Mountain and Other Plays*, 34 f.

for carnival and other manifestations of touristic culture with foreign-exchange potential, and an undifferentiated, partly Marxist, partly Afrocentric, glorification of popular culture—have led to an increasing marginalization of his own efforts. The polemical assessment of carnival as 'meaningless' must therefore be seen in the biographical context of Walcott's increasing frustration over state indifference to the Trinidad Theatre Workshop, despite its international reputation.

Walcott's somewhat ambivalent attitude towards carnival as a potential formal reservoir for an indigenous Caribbean theatre becomes clearer when one examines his own suggestions on what kind of style a Caribbean theatre of the future could and should take. Although he repeatedly draws attention to indigenous forms of expression as the basis for a syncretic theatre—the African-influenced dance and music of possession cults, the music of calypso, and the vigorous oral tradition—he strongly opposes simply integrating these forms without some kind of aesthetic filtration. Walcott stresses that a new Caribbean theatre will have to discipline the 'exuberance' of the popular performance forms. Therefore, it is little wonder that in his earliest writings on theatrical aesthetics Walcott should draw attention to Japanese theatre. His interest in Asian theatre appears to have been awakened through reading Brecht. In his article 'The Kabuki . . . Something to Give to our Theatre' (1964) Walcott outlines the anti-naturalistic theatrical style of Japanese theatre: dance theatre instead of text-based drama; the use of a narrator and chorus; the importance of musical accompaniment; the use of masks or masklike make-up, as well as a stage without elaborate sets and backdrops. What attracts Walcott most to Kabuki is the highly gestural language of expression formalized into dance, which results in a decrease in the importance of dialogue. He finds a performative link between kabuki and the dance of Caribbean culture in the technique of the *mie*, the stylized frozen pose used in kabuki, a moment of 'arrested gesture' as he calls it: 'The bongo has its moment of arrest that is as dramatic, though not as long held, as the "mie" of the Kabuki actor.'[76] Walcott points out that the Caribbean dance forms *shango* and *kalenda* have such moments which could be extracted and focused like the Japanese *mie*. More importantly, they would also be recognizable to a Caribbean audience:

[76] Derek Walcott, 'The Kabuki . . . Something to Give to our Theatre', *Sunday Guardian* (Trinidad), 16 Feb. 1964, 14.

'It is pointless to freeze these dances into shapes that are alien, since one does not want a Black Kabuki theatre [. . .] but the choreographer and playwright who extract these essentials from the dance will find that the starting points of a West Indian theatre are there.'[77] Using kabuki as a model, Walcott stresses the necessity of a dominant shift towards kinaesthetic communication—'less speech and more gesture'—because the future of Caribbean theatre lies in the development of a strong, gestural, dancelike theatrical language, immediately recognizable to 'village audiences'.

Walcott's article on kabuki highlights the extent to which the adoption of indigenous performance forms necessitates an adaptation and further aesthetic transformation of these cultural texts. In an interview given much later he speaks of the necessity to dilute the 'folk idiom'[78] for reasons of theatrical communicability. The term refers here primarily to language, that is to the dialects and creoles of the Caribbean islands. Besides the kinaesthetic problems outlined above, language questions form the other central element in Walcott's conception of a syncretic Caribbean theatre. He repeatedly refers to the tradition of African orality, in which the narrator is also the performer and where the basis of performance is an intact 'tribal' society. According to Walcott this tradition was still very much alive in St Lucia during his childhood and he drew on it to form the basis of his most popular play, *Ti-Jean and his Brothers*, which he also calls 'my most West Indian play'.[79] In this same article Walcott lists a number of quite obvious influences on the work such as Lorca, Brecht, and Noh theatre.[80] On a deeper level there are also other less obvious cultural elements at work such as African orality and local rituals: 'Other Saint Lucian rituals came out too, branching from the simple roots of the folk-tale such as our Christmas black mass dances of Papa Diable and his imps, the Bolom, or Foetus, and the melodies which they used.'[81] This list is not just of interest for *Ti-*

---

[77] Derek Walcott, 'The Kabuki . . . Something to Give to our Theatre', *Sunday Guardian* (Trinidad), 16 Feb. 1964, 14.

[78] Sharon Ciccarelli, 'Reflections before and after Carnival: Interview with Derek Walcott', in Michael S. Harper and Robert B. Stepto (eds.), *The Chant of Saints: A Gathering of Afro-American Literature, Art, and Scholarship* (Urbana: University of Illinois Press, 1979), 303.   [79] Walcott, 'Derek's Most West Indian Play', 7.

[80] Walcott writes: 'there was Lorca behind it, particularly in the swift but self-arresting meter, and Brecht in its distancing of characters, and through Brecht the Noh Theatre with its use of masks, musicians and the mimetic indications of scenery'. Ibid.

[81] Ibid.

Jean and his Brothers. It can also be seen as the basis for a more general stylistic catalogue to describe Caribbean syncretic theatre. For these elements—rituals, folk tales and orality, dances and autochthonous music—recur again and again in Walcott's programmatic writings on the theatre. To recapitulate: Walcott's concept of a 'theatre of fusion' is based on the idea that the combining of apparently heterogeneous elements—the language of the Western literary tradition with village folk poetry, the rigidly codified physical stylization of kabuki with the improvisatory dance rhythms of *shango* and *bongo*, the collective creativity of carnival with the discipline of the individual theatre artist—can set free enough creative energy to produce a qualitatively new theatrical form.

Native Canadian Theatre

The main phase of theoretical reflection in Nigeria and the Caribbean falls in the decade roughly spanning the years 1965 to 1975. This is also the period of intense practical activity in writing and production. A decade later, at various times throughout the 1970s, we find the beginnings of theatrical movements indigenous to aboriginal peoples in Canada, the United States, Australia, and New Zealand, in what have also been termed Fourth World contexts. It is striking that theatrical activity did not begin in any of the four countries until the early 1970s and did not consolidate into a widespread movement until the 1980s.[82] In these years theatre was seen and used as an

[82] The beginnings of Aboriginal theatre in Australia are documented by Gerry Bostock, 'Black Theatre', in Jack Davis and Bob Hodge (eds.), *Aboriginal Writing Today* (Canberra: Australian Institute of Aboriginal Studies, 1985), 63–73; and in the articles by Gillian Oxford, 'The Purple Everlasting: The Aboriginal Cultural Heritage in Australia', *Theatre Quarterly*, 8/26 (Summer 1977), 88–98, and George Whaley, 'A City's Place of Dreaming: Black Theatre in Sydney', *Theatre Quarterly*, 8/26 (Summer 1977), 98–100. On the theatre of the Canadian Indians, see Jennifer Preston's article on the Toronto-based ensemble Native Earth Performing Arts 'Weesagechak Begins to Dance: Native Earth Performing Arts Inc.', *Drama Review*, 36/1 (T133), (1992), 135–59, as well as Helen Peters, 'The Aboriginal Presence in Canadian Theatre and the Evolution of Being Canadian', *Theatre Research International*, 18/3 (1993), 197–205. See also the special number 'Native Theatre', *Canadian Theatre Review*, 68 (Fall 1991) and *Theatrum: The Theatre Magazine*, 19 (1990). For a wider survey of Amerindian and Inuit theatre, see Brask and Morgan (eds.), *Aboriginal Voices*. Native American theatre in the United States begins in 1972 with the founding of the Native American Theater Ensemble by the Kiowa dramatist and director Hanay Geiogamah; see his 'Indian Theatre in the United States, 1991: An Assessment', *Canadian Theatre Review*, 68 (Fall 1980), 12–14.

agitatory weapon for the political struggle for greater autonomy and land rights. This specialized function revealed itself in the choice of form of the plays and performances created. These works turned either to the identificatory aesthetic of stage realism in an appeal to the consciences of white audiences; or they sought direct confrontation in the form of agitprop revues, in which the political message was transported with maximum impact and clarity of stance. A third approach, namely the adaptation of indigenous performance elements as a basis for a new form of theatre, which imitated neither stage realism nor agitprop, emerged in all three countries towards the end of the 1970s.

In view of this historical development, a speech held by the American Indian Lloyd Kiva New in 1969 was a prophecy of things to come rather than an analysis of an existing theatrical culture:

We believe that an exciting American-Indian theatre can be evolved out of the framework of Indian traditions. We think this evolution must come from the most sensitive approaches imaginable in order not to misuse or cheapen the original nature of Indian forms, most of which are closely tied to religion. [. . .] [Young Indian people] must be led to examine Indian culture for that which is theatrical, and then find ways to interpret these unique aspects for contemporary audiences in true theatre settings. [. . .] [O]ne must acknowledge the fact that no pure traditional form of Indian theatre presently exists—one must be created. New ethnic cultural forms must result from the forces and ideas within the ethnic group itself.[83]

These words contain *in nuce* the essential points of a theory of syncretic theatre. Lloyd Kiva New stresses the elements of *theatricality* present in cultures which lend themselves to adaptation to the Western theatrical form. At the same time he points out that these cultural texts are indissolubly linked to religion and require a circumspect adaptation process. Finally, he makes quite clear that this type of theatre will constitute a new cultural form for American Indians, which cannot be imposed from outside or simply adopted in its entirety. Rather it must be the result of an intracultural creative process. The programme that Lloyd Kiva New outlines here did not,

[83] Cited in Geiogamah, 'Indian Theatre in the United States', 12. Lloyd Kiva New was co-founder of the famous Institute of American Indian Arts, Santa Fe, New Mexico, which played an important role in popularizing and disseminating Amerindian art. Geiogamah can be considered the first Native American dramatist.

however, begin to be put into practice on a wide scale until nearly a decade later.[84]

The basis of any form of theatrical syncretism is, as we have seen, the existence of cultural texts, which, because of their high degree of theatricality, lend themselves to adaptation to the Western dramatic form. Such cultural texts can be found in the cultures of the indigenous peoples dealt with in this study. However great the cultural differences may be between Australian Aborigines, New Zealand Maoris, and American Indians (and they are considerable), the inherent theatricality of many of their performance forms has been repeatedly stressed by anthropologists and the aboriginal peoples themselves.

With reference to Native Canadians Edward Buller speaks of 'traditional Native theatre in Canada'[85] and means the festivals, ritual performances, and healing ceremonies which reveal theatrical elements such as imitation, role-playing, as well as dance, masking, and song. Terminological distinctions between 'theatre' and 'cultural performance' are not attempted by Buller. Nor does Jennifer Preston undertake a differentiation between such terms in her brief characterization of pre-colonial performance forms in Canada: 'Native drama flourished in this country long before the Europeans arrived and many of Canada's indigenous cultures had very complex and elaborate cultural performances. These were primarily religious dramas that used masks, props, lighting, and smoke effects.'[86] Preston is referring here to the widespread shamanistic healing ceremonies such

---

[84] As far as Native American theatre is concerned, the movement in the United States, centred on the dramatist Hanay Geiogamah, pre-dates that in Canada. The three plays collected in his volume *New Native American Drama* represent three styles outlined above. *Body Indian* (1972), a play dealing with the problem of alcoholism, is in the tradition of stage realism which basically adheres to the classical unities. *Foghorn* (1973) is a condensed satirical history of Native American–Anglo relations from 1492 to the present and uses the open agitprop form of short scenes, songs, and dances. The third piece, *49* (1975), can be termed syncretic. It takes as its dramaturgical framework a '49 celebration' and the performance elements of this festival are an integral part of the work. Hanay Geiogamah, *New Native American Drama: Three Plays*, introd. Jeffrey Huntsman (Norman: Oklahoma University Press, 1980).

[85] Edward Buller, *Indigenous Performing and Ceremonial Arts in Canada: A Bibliography* (Toronto: Association for Native Development in the Performing and Visual Arts, 1981), 3.

[86] Preston also points out that from the end of the 19th century many such 'performances' were forbidden by law until as recently as 1951. 'Weesagechak Begins to Dance', 136.

as the 'shaking tent' ritual[87] or sham operations to remove evil spirits.[88] Native dramatists have not, however, turned to these highly spectacular performance forms for inspiration, but rather to the equally vibrant oral tradition. The reason for this is certainly to be found in Lloyd Kiva New's admonition to Native playwrights to be respectful of the religious nature of traditional performance forms.

The vision of a syncretic theatre based on oral tradition is the cornerstone of Tomson Highway's theatrical concept. Highway, a Cree from the Brochet reserve in northern Manitoba, has in his various capacities as director, artistic director, and dramatist, secured for Native theatre and drama in Canada a large metropolitan audience. Since the late 1980s he has articulated in articles and in numerous interviews his concept of Native theatre.[89] For Highway the road to a contemporary Native theatre must take cognizance of indigenous mythology and the oral tradition as the cultural form with which this mythology was transported and which also lends itself to adaptation to the modern stage:

Why the stage? For me, the reason is that this oral tradition translates most easily and most effectively into a three dimensional medium. In a sense, it's like taking the 'stage' that lives inside the mind, the imagination, and transposing it—using words, actors, lights, sound—onto the stage in theatre. For

---

[87] 'Shaking tent' rituals are carried out by shamans to solve various problems. Those concerned gather in a tent in which the shaman sits with bound hands and invokes his guardian spirit. The invocation has the effect of making the tent shake violently and apparently without any form of human intervention. See Buller, *Indigenous Performing Arts*, 5 f.

[88] A well-known description of shamanistic sleight-of-hand tricks can be found in Claude Lévi-Strauss's essay 'Le Magicien et sa magie', in *Anthropologie structurale I* (Paris: Plon, 1958). See also Edward Buller: 'Considerable rehearsal was required to execute a successful performance, and the Shaman had to also be an expert in staging, lighting, the use of props, timing, and sleight of hand'. *Indigenous Performing Arts*, 7.

[89] The central tenets of Highway's concept are laid out in his article 'On Native Mythology' (1987). From 1986 to 1992 Highway was artistic director of the Toronto-based theatre Native Earth Performing Arts (NEPA), Canada's longest-established Native theatre. Tomson Highway, 'On Native Mythology', *Theatrum: A Theatre Journal*, 6 (Spring 1987), 29–31. The name points to a theatrical concept that from its inception in 1982 has emphasized the importance of the performing arts in their totality for Native culture. Although at present NEPA is heavily involved in promoting indigenous drama and dramatists, in the early years there was a strong emphasis on collective productions utilizing music, dance, and masks. In fact the production of Highway's play *The Rez Sisters* in 1986 was the first 'straight play' that NEPA had attempted. Tomson Highway, *The Rez Sisters* (Saskatoon: Fifth House, 1988). For a history of NEPA and an explanation of its organization, see Preston, 'Weesagechak Begins to Dance'.

me, it is really a matter of taking a mythology as extraordinary and as powerful as the human imagination itself and reworking it to fit, snugly and comfortably, the medium of the stage.[90]

Highway suggests further that the dramaturgical process of incorporating and adapting traditional cultural texts for the stage is in many ways analogous to the approach taken by the first generation of Native painters, who in the early 1960s began to translate the traditional mythology into a non-sacred medium. Without in any way questioning its spiritual significance, Highway claims for himself and other theatre artists the right to treat this mythology in a theatrical form.

In Highway's plays theatrical syncretism manifests itself in an often disturbing combination of mythology and Western dramaturgy, which is still accessible to a metropolitan audience.[91] The mythological material is, however, presented in a highly aestheticized form which avoids the risk of any direct appropriation of sacred ceremonies and rituals.

Aboriginal Theatre

A situation comparable to that in Native American culture can be found in Australian Aboriginal theatre. Here too we find ethnographic enthusiasm for the theatricality of traditional performance forms, and here too Aboriginal dramatists are extremely circumspect when it comes to 'exploiting' this reservoir. There exists a comprehensive literature on the rituals and ceremonies of the Aborigine,

[90] Highway, 'On Native Mythology', 29.
[91] Highway has today a somewhat ambivalent standing in the eyes of the white critical establishment. His two plays *The Rez Sisters* and *Dry Lips Oughta Move to Kapuskasing* have between them collected most of the major theatre awards available to a Canadian dramatist. See Diane Debendam, 'Native People in Contemporary Canadian Drama', *Canadian Drama*, 14/2 (1988), 137–58. Referring to *The Rez Sisters* she stresses an 'extraordinary break with all previous portrayals of native people, including the tentative new perspectives being developed by native playwrights', (p. 152). The critic Denis Johnston considers Highway to be 'the most important new Canadian playwright to emerge in the latter half of the 1980s'. Denis W. Johnston, 'Lines and Circles: The "Rez" Plays of Tomson Highway', *Canadian Literature*, 124–5 (1990), 254–64. This success has at the same time led some white critics to question Highway's work. See e.g. Alan Filewod's article in Brask and Morgan, *Aboriginal Voices* (eds.), 23, who claims that 'we [the white audience] are comfortable with the message we hear'.

which have been grouped together under the somewhat imprecise term '*corroboree*'.[92] Terms such as 'dramatic' and 'theatrical' appear frequently in this literature. In Ronald and Catherine Berndt's standard work on traditional Aboriginal culture the area of art and aesthetic expression is subdivided into four categories: 'poetry-song; oral literature; dramatic performance; and visual art such as painting and carving'.[93] The term 'dramatic performance' encompasses various performance forms manifesting *re-enactment* of some kind in which everyday experiences (as opposed to mythic or dream-time stories) are performed in the form of songs and dances for a non-restricted audience.[94] These often include parodistic and satirical depictions of experiences with the white world. Such performances manifest a strong tendency to mimetic imitation and evidence of role-playing.[95]

The pronounced theatricality of both secular and sacred performance traditions was quickly recognized by Aboriginal theatre artists as the basis for an indigenous theatre movement. In his autobiography the dramatist Jack Davis makes clear that in the early 1970s he saw the future of Aboriginal theatre as lying in its ability to draw on a rich performance tradition. At that time Davis, who had been primarily a political activist and editor, discovered theatre as a potential medium for influencing public opinion: 'Theatre offers an opportunity to use all the talents of speech and body-movement present in

---

[92] 'Corroboree' is an etic term coined by early European observers and is probably a corruption of a word stemming from the New South Wales area. There is no emic equivalent in contemporary Aboriginal languages, which differentiate very precisely between different kinds of performative occasions. The term has of course returned to Aboriginal speech via its European corruption and is generally used to designate secular as opposed to ritual ceremonies.

[93] Ronald M. Berndt and Catherine H. Berndt, *The World of the First Australians: Aboriginal Traditional Life, Past and Present* (Canberra: Aboriginal Studies Press, 1988), 367.

[94] The category *poetry-song* refers to myths which are re-enacted using dance, song, and body-painting and where the ritual function is central. Dances and songs are, of course, also performed on their own for purely aesthetic ends: 'it is the dance and the rhythm which count and not the explanation of it'. Ibid. 387.

[95] Berndt and Berndt describe a traditional performance, in which a conflict between Aborigines and the police was re-enacted: 'In one scene a policeman, a "man with chains", was shown trying to bring in "witnesses" for a court case. The actors here were men, representing attractive young women all roped ("chained") together by the neck in a long line. The policeman led the way, dancing slowly around the clearing; but every now and then when he was looking the other way a small raggedy actor, a "bagman" or "swaggie", would come sneaking up from behind and try to take away one of the girls.' *The World of the First Australians*, 385.

Aboriginal oral literature and dance since time began.'[96] The same point is made by the Aboriginal dramatist and actress Justine Saunders in the foreword to the first anthology of Aboriginal plays: 'Aboriginal culture contains all the dramatic elements that Western theatre demands, but since the coming of the white man two hundred years ago, that part of our heritage has been under attack and the tribal way has been eroded. Under the pressure of European culture and arts, merely to be heard we have had to adopt or adapt European art forms.'[97] The list of similar general comments on the inherent theatricality of traditional culture could be continued *ad infinitum*. A more specific theory of syncretic theatre linking traditional performance and Western drama such as that elaborated by Soyinka or Walcott has yet to emerge.

The one writer who has addressed these issues on a more theoretical level is the poet, critic, and novelist Mudrooroo Narogin. Although Narogin has only recently begun to show interest in writing for the stage, he has followed developments in Aboriginal drama for some time.[98] The national and international success of Jack Davis's plays has tended to place drama at the forefront of Aboriginal literature. In a series of reviews and shorter articles Narogin has outlined what he sees as the formal characteristics of Aboriginal theatre. He uses the term 'symbolic realism'[99] or 'Aboriginal realism'[100] to characterize a theatrical style in which the 'simple realist frame' is not broken but made more flexible by means of dance and elements of orality: 'Aboriginal realism expands European realism by taking in certain supernatural aspects, characters and situations found in Aboriginal storytelling.'[101] In his foreword to *Barungin (Smell the Wind)*, the

---

[96] Keith Chesson with Jack Davis, *Jack Davis: A Life-Story* (Melbourne: Dent, 1988) 191.

[97] Justine Saunders (ed.), *Plays from Black Australia* (Sydney: Currency Press, 1989), p. vii.

[98] Mudrooroo made his debut as a dramatist in 1991 with a play which frames a fictive rehearsal of a Heiner Müller play *The Mission (Der Auftrag)*. It bears the somewhat unwieldy title 'The Aboriginal Protestors Confront the Declaration of the Australian Republic on 26 January 2001 with the Production of the Commission by Heiner Müller'. The work was premièred in Jan. 1996 at the Sydney Festival, directed by Noel Tovey. The production subsequently toured Germany in June and July of that year, with successful seasons in Weimar and Munich.

[99] Mudrooroo Narogin, 'Review of Jack Davis' *Kullark/The Dreamers, No Sugar, and The Honey Spot*', *Australasian Drama Studies*, 15–16 (1989–90), 188.

[100] Mudrooroo Narogin, 'Towards a New Black Theatre', *New Theatre Australia* (Mar.–Apr. 1989), 17.   [101] Ibid.

last part of Jack Davis's dramatic trilogy tracing Aboriginal history
in and around Perth, Narogin draws attention to the Eurocentric
practice in Jack Davis's work of setting up oppositions between terms
such as 'realism' and 'symbolism':

Jack Davis's plays are often accepted as merely examples of twentieth century
naturalistic European drama; but I see this as a white reading in that this way
the symbolic aspects are relegated to secondary motifs—attempts to break
free of the format—rather than being of primary importance. I do not see
them as devices to break down the 'realist' frame, but as integral parts
pointing to the polysemic nature of Aboriginal drama.[102]

The term 'polysemic nature' implies that in plays by Aboriginal
authors traces of indigenous culture can be found which cannot be
easily schematized with Western categories based on a dichotomy
between realism and symbolism. This insight is equally applicable to
Tomson Highway's work. Oppositions such as realistic versus symbolic are more or less irrelevant in the work of both dramatists
because the realms of everyday and spiritual–mythological experience
are not phenomenologically separate but, on the contrary, part of a
continuum permitting continual interchange.

Maori Theatre

However complex the internal semiotics of aboriginal drama in Australia and Canada may be, their institutional forms are not substantially different from that of the mainstream theatre of white artists
and dramatists. The institutional situation of Maori theatre in New
Zealand in both theory and practice is quite different. It is the
declared aim of many Maori theatre artists to indigenize the theatre
as an institution and place of encounter. Maori dramatists and
directors are working towards a theatrical concept that is part-reality
and still part-utopia.[103] The striking feature of this concept is less the

---

[102] Mudrooroo Narogin, 'Black Reality', in Jack Davis, *Barungin (Smell the Wind)*
(Sydney: Currency Press, 1989), p. ix.

[103] Maori theatre is still a relatively new movement, which did not establish itself
until the 1980s. For a historical overview of the movement and its background, see
Christopher Balme, 'New Maori Theatre in New Zealand', *Australasian Drama Studies*, 15–16 (1989–90), 149–66, and 'Between Separation and Integration: Contemporary Maori Theatre', *CRNLE Reviews Journal*, 1 (1993), 41–8; see also Shimon
Levy, 'Maori Theatre in Pakeha Masks', in Claude Schumacher and Derek Fogg (eds.),

creation of a new kind of dramatic writing than a new kind of perceptual 'frame', to use Erving Goffman's term, within which this writing is performed and received.[104] Maori theatre artists refer to this phenomenon as *marae*-theatre or theatre-*marae*. Lexically the word *marae* denotes a gathering-place for a specific tribal subgroup or, in a narrower sense, the space in front of a meeting-house of that group. In the latter meaning it refers to the demarcated sacred space where all important rituals and ceremonial gatherings of the tribe take place. In concrete terms this has meant that certain practices associated with theatregoing have been changed. For some performances, particularly in the early experiments, the spectator did not buy a ticket but was asked to give a *koha*, an offering after the performance. The audience is welcomed with a chant, a *pōwhiri* or *karanga*, and thus not perceived as a spectator but, in analogy to ceremonial practice on the *marae*, treated as *manuhiri*, a guest of the hosts, the *tangata whenua*.

In view of the significance of the *marae* as a living cultural form, it is perhaps not surprising that hybrid terms such as *marae*-theatre or theatre-*marae* are not unproblematic for some Maori artists. The director and actor Rangimoana Taylor differentiates between the two terms instead of using them interchangeably. *Marae-theatre* implies for Taylor that the cultural codes of the *marae* override those of the Western theatre form. He, however, is working towards a theatre model with the opposite structure:

I think we need to make a distinction between marae-theatre and theatre-marae, and I think at the moment we are looking at theatre-marae, and by that we mean we're working in a theatre in which we put up the illusion of a marae concept [. . .] Theatre-marae is more obtainable at the moment, and

Small is Beautiful: Small Countries Theatre Conference (Glasgow: Theatre Studies Publications, 1991), 203–12. A Maori perspective is given by Roma Potiki in a number of articles and interviews: 'Introduction', in Simon Garrett (ed.), *He Reo Hou: 5 Plays by Maori Playwrights* (Wellington: Playmarket, 1991), 9–13; 'A Maori Point of View: The Journey from Anxiety to Confidence', *Australasian Drama Studies*, 18 (Apr. 1991), 57–63; 'Confirming Identity and Telling the Stories: A Woman's Perspective on Maori Theatre', in Rosemary Du Plessis (ed.), *Feminist Voices: Woman's Studies Texts for Aotearoa/New Zealand* (Auckland: Oxford University Press, 1992), 153–62; Christopher Balme, 'It is Political if it can be Passed On', Interview with Roma Potiki, *CRNLE Reviews Journal*, 1 (1993), 35–40.

[104] The reference here is to Erving Goffman's book *Frame Analysis: An Essay on the Organisation of Experience* (Cambridge, Mass.: Harvard University Press, 1974). Goffman's theory will be examined in more detail in the next chapter.

it's probably not so frightening for non-Maoris, because they feel they're in a theatre.[105]

Taylor's distinction draws attention to that fact that *marae*-theatre in a literal sense would no longer be theatre in any accepted meaning of the word.

Taylor is also touching on one of the central and recurrent issues in any discussion of a theory or practice of syncretic theatre. The integration into the Western theatre form of cultural texts is a characteristic of all syncretic theatre. In Maori theatre, however, there is an attempt to perform these texts in a framework analogous to an indigenous ceremony. There exists a clear strategy to alter the receptive mindset of the spectator and transcend the so-called confrontational structure between audience and performers pertaining in Western theatre. Of course, this has been one of the central aims of Western theatre-reformers since the turn of the century—what Peter Brook has termed the search for a 'Holy theatre'. However, the Maori concept of *marae*-theatre is not the product of Western ideas, but a model of theatre that has emerged out of autochthonous preconditions and perceived needs.

One of the needs that *marae*-theatre directly addresses is a lack of interest in or even antagonism towards theatregoing on the part of Maori people. Until recently theatre in the Western sense of playgoing played a very minor role in Maori culture.[106] While traditional culture knew no equivalent of the Western *contrât théâtral*, it did and still does possess varied performance forms including a strong tradition of rhetoric, songs, and dances. However, the use of these cultural texts in a new European aesthetic context contains certain dangers. The director and dramatist Roma Potiki points to the danger of overusing such 'traditional symbols', as she calls them:

Maori writers and directors are also trying to ensure that the symbols they use are not stale. We must resist the temptation to pick out something well established in our own culture (and therefore convenient) and say 'That will

---

[105] Debbie Gee, 'Theatre-*marae*: Welcome Change', *On Film* (Wellington), 7/1 (1989), 44.
[106] Perhaps symptomatic of this lack of interest is the fact that in a new Maori dictionary for use in schools there are lexical items for cinema, film, concert, and television, but none for theatre, play, or drama. Although there are certainly neologisms for these terms, they are evidently not considered to be part of the everyday vocabulary. See Bruce Biggs (ed.), *English–Maori Maori–English Dictionary* (Auckland: Auckland University Press, 1990).

do.' To me a play does not automatically acquire deep meaning because it has a haka or a karanga thrown in. A whaikōrero issuing from the paepae does not ensure good theatre.[107]

Potiki argues that Maori theatre—and here it stands for much syncretic theatre—must go beyond simply incorporating indigenous cultural texts as markers of an autochthonous presence. While this may have initial short-term advantages in attracting an indigenous audience, the danger of creating formal stereotypical devices is very real. Instead, the necessary recourse to traditional cultural texts must be informed by innovative direction and dramaturgy which cast the traditional in a new light without stripping it entirely of its place and function in indigenous culture. It is this balancing act between tradition and innovation, between old meanings and new functions, that will be explored in the following chapters.

[107] Roma Potiki, 'Confirming Identity and Telling Stories', 157.

CHAPTER TWO

Ritual Frames and
Liminal Dramaturgy

A CHARACTERISTIC feature of syncretic theatre is the incorporation
of rituals and myth-based material into a theatrico-aesthetic context.
This highly problematic undertaking involves demarcating the blurred
crossover points between theatre and ritual. Although the expropria-
tion of ritual forms for purely aesthetic ends can, on the one hand,
result in substantial conflicts for indigenous dramatists, on the other,
they are able to tap a still-vibrant and intact mythical-ritual tradition.
Syncretic theatre thus often attempts to reinvest theatre with a communal religious spirit, the long-cherished desire of several generations
of Western theatre-reformers, which they very seldom achieved in
practice.

This chapter is divided into three sections which explore different
ritualization strategies. One method of ritualizing the theatre is to
adopt existing ritual forms and adapt them so as to alter the entire
performance frame. This is the strategy adopted by the Maori theatre
movement in New Zealand with its notion of *marae*-theatre, which
was briefly introduced in the last chapter. Here the rituals of encounter of the *marae*, the traditional meeting-place, are employed to frame
the entire theatrical experience. On the level of the dramatic text, the
ritual dramas of Wole Soyinka are examined as examples of how
indigenous ritual forms can be incorporated into a Western dramaturgical frame. It is argued that Soyinka utilizes the moment of
liminality in specific Yoruba rituals, the period in most rites where
normal laws of causality are suspended, in order both to break free of
the Aristotelian unities on a formal level and to explore on a societal
and metaphysical level the implications of just such ritual interruption. Although not a feature of all his plays, ritual interruption is a
central element of his most syncretic works such as *The Strong Breed*,
The Road, and *Death and the King's Horseman*. In the third section
of this chapter a specific form of liminality, possession, is examined.

Possession is a striking feature of Afro-American religious celebration and is particularly important in West African and in Caribbean
syncretic cults such as voodoo, *kumina*, *shango*, and *pocomania*.
Caribbean dramatists such as Derek Walcott and Dennis Scott have
explored possession as a theatrical and dramatic device, but each
drawing on different Caribbean ritual forms.

Framing Ritual

In order to gain an intercultural perspective on the question of ritual
and theatre, it is important to bear in mind that in many cultures the
aesthetic functions performed by the profane activity of theatregoing
are in fact contained and carried out in the sacred actions of ritual
observance, where there is frequently no apparent specialization and
division of labour. For this reason the emphasis on the distinction
between ritual and theatre, which is so characteristic of Western
theatrical theory, must be re-examined for those cultures which do
not evidence such a distinction.[1] The clear demarcation drawn in
contemporary Western theatre does not allow itself to be so sharply
applied in post-colonial contexts. Instead of opposing ritual and
theatre as two phenomenologically mutually exclusive activities, it
may be more useful to see the two phenomena as located on a
performative continuum. In this way it is possible to stress either
the elements common to both phenomena—and there are many—or
those which allow for distinction and differentiation. In view of the
numerous experiments with ritual in post-colonial theatrical culture,
it is sensible to look at the notion of performance as a unifying
concept allowing for interaction rather than exclusion.

Performance theorists such as Richard Schechner and Victor
Turner are interested primarily in those elements and structures
which they perceive as being common to both theatre and ritual.[2]

[1] The genesis of the discussion in Aristotle's famous reference to the dithyramb as
the origin of tragedy implied at least an evolutionary link between ritualized and
dramatic performance. Older theatre historians attempted to establish a similar evolutionary model for the development of medieval drama. For a critique of this model, see
O. B. Hardison's study *Christian Rite and Christian Drama in the Middle Ages*
(Baltimore: Johns Hopkins University Press, 1965).

[2] On the concept of ritual and performance theory, see Richard Schechner's collection of essays *Performance Theory*, 2nd edn. (London: Routledge, 1988), and Victor
Turner's study *From Ritual to Theatre: The Human Seriousness of Play* (New York:

Thus they are less concerned with questions of differentiation than with the identifying analogies and similarities.[3] If there is any differentiation to be made, then it is solely on the level of reception and not in the structure or form of the performed ritual, as Anthony Graham-White argues in reference to African cultures: 'the ultimate distinction lies in the attitudes of the performers and spectators'; a ritual contains 'expectations of consequences beyond itself'.[4] Graham-White means that a ritual is determined primarily by the horizon of expectation brought to it by the participants who expect some kind of efficacy from it. At the same time he points out that this kind of expectation is by no means fixed and immutable, but can move along the performative continuum, changing from sacred to the profane or from the ritualistic to the theatrical.[5] However, even this more flexible reading is still defined by Western dichotomies. The French art ethnographer Jean Laude stresses that the entire scholarly discussion concerning ritual and performance in Africa has been distorted by such Eurocentric misunderstandings and dichotomies. Central among these are Western dualistic notions such as sacred–profane and religious–secular, which do not exist as rigid dichotomies in African cultures.[6]

Performing Arts Journal Publications, 1982). The differences between his own and Schechner's theory are outlined by Turner in his collection *The Anthropology of Performance* (New York: Performing Arts Journal Publications, 1987), 74–6. See also Donald Baker's article 'A Structural Theory of Theatre', *Yale/Theatre*, 8/1 (Fall 1976), 55–61; Baker sees in the anthropological domains of play and ritual 'deep structures' which provide a theoretical basis for establishing supracultural links between traditional performance and avant-garde theatre.

[3] This is the standpoint now widely adopted by scholars dealing with forms of performance in Africa; see Kacke Götrick: 'African scholars (and playwrights) do not speak as much in terms of distinction, as in terms of similarities.' *Apidan Theatre and Modern Drama*, 14. See also Margaret Thompson Drewal's comments on ritual in her review of performance research in Africa 'The State of Research on Performance in Africa', *African Studies Review*, 34/3 (1991), 1–64.

[4] Anthony Graham-White, *The Drama of Black Africa* (New York: Samuel French, 1974), 16 f.

[5] Graham-White cites as an example of such shifts in attitude Marcel Griaule's description of a ritualistic dance festival of the Dogon in Mali: 'The opera presented on the public square is felt in some measure to be a therapy bringing benefit to the society. But little by little, the form prevails over the essence, the theatrical element gains ground; from being attentive to the progression of the rite, the crowd becomes attentive to the unfolding of the spectacle: it sees the colors and the forms, it hears the songs, it submits to the rhythms of the instruments and the bodies.' *Les Masques dogons* (Paris, 1938), in Graham-White, *The Drama of Black Africa*, 19.

[6] Jean Laude, Introd. to the photographic documentation by Michel Huet, *The Dance, Art and Ritual of Africa* (London: Collins, 1978), 13.

Possibly the most influential performance theorist in the field of ritual and performance is the anthropologist Victor Turner. Turner also points out the problems involved in discussing ritual and performance on the basis of Western conceptual categories. One such category is the notion that rituals are by definition rigid, repetitive, and resistant to alteration: 'The prejudice that ritual is always "rigid", "stereotyped", "obsessive", is a peculiarly Western one.'[7] Turner argues that in many cultures ritualized performances are highly flexible, permitting much opportunity for innovation and improvisation. Rather than stressing rigidity and structure, Turner sees in the ritual performances of pre-scribal cultures primarily the impressive polyphonic combination of acoustic, kinesic, and visual sign systems:

Ritual, in tribal society, represents not an obsessional concern with repetitive acts, but an immense orchestration of genres in all available sensory codes: speech, music, singing; the presentation of elaborately worked objects, such as masks, wall-paintings, body-paintings; sculptured forms; complex, many-tiered shrines; costumes; dance forms with complex grammars and vocabularies of bodily movements, gestures and facial expressions.[8]

This notion of ritual, which privileges theatricality in its widest sense, illustrates why post-colonial theatre artists have turned to their ritual traditions in their search for a syncretic theatre form.

However their own ritual traditions are defined, post-colonial dramatists and directors are aware that the Western theatre form implies a distinct perceptual frame on the part of both performers and spectators. The word 'frame' is used here in Erving Goffman's definition, meaning 'principles of organization which govern [social] events and our subjective involvement in them'.[9] According to Goffman's terminology, theatre and ritual in Western culture would be governed by two distinct frames controlling our perception of these events and our behaviour towards them. Of course, these frames do not remain inviolate or immutable; in fact Goffman's book is devoted mainly to showing what happens when frameworks are broken down, transgressed, and redefined. The process whereby the conventions governing one kind of frame are applied to another kind of activity

[7] Turner, *The Anthropology of Performance*, 26. Interestingly, Turner promoted in his earlier works a more conservative view of tribal societies and ritual, which he saw as being resistant to change and innovation; see Drewal,'The State of Research on Performance in Africa', 19.   [8] Turner, *The Anthropology of Performance*, 106.
[9] Goffman, *Frame Analysis*, 10 f.

not normally defined by that frame is called by Goffman 'keying'.[10]
Thus, an attempt to ritualize theatre would involve the performers
and spectators keying the conventions of ritual into theatre.

Maori Theatre and Rituals of Encounter

The only post-colonial theatre movement that has tried consistently
to alter frames in this way is Maori theatre in New Zealand. As
outlined in the previous chapter, Maori theatre artists tried from the
beginning to found a concept of *marae*-theatre as a means of creating
not just new dramatic works, but an entirely different perceptual
framework within which to experience these texts and performances.
Marae-theatre is based around the rituals and protocol of the *hui*, the
ceremonial gathering, which was and still is the traditional framework for performance in Maori culture. A *hui* can range from sacred
occasions such as a *tangihanga* (funeral) to secular gatherings like
weddings, important birthdays, or conferences. Whatever the occasion, the encounter takes place within the sacred space of the *marae*
and meeting-house and, depending on the type and importance of the
hui, is governed by a strict set of 'rituals of encounter'. It is these
rituals which provide the raw material for Maori theatre.

   In her standard work on the *hui* the anthropologist Anne Salmond
makes explicit use of theatrical and dramatic metaphors to describe
the nature of these rituals. Without claiming any evident aesthetic
function for them, she situates the *hui* and its rituals in Goffman's
framework of social behaviour and dramatic form: 'plays for prestige,
spatial behaviour and types of demeanour are investigated as part of
a social drama, played out by actors'.[11] The rituals of the *hui* which
are also used in modern theatrical performance are listed in their
usual order of enactment on a *marae*:

   karanga—wailing call of welcome, performed by the hosts;
   pōwhiri—action chant of welcome, performed by local women;
   wero—the ritual challenge, if a dignitary is present;
   whaikōrero—the oratory, speeches of welcome held (mainly) by men;
   waiata—concluding song/chant.

---

[10] Goffman, *Frame Analysis*, 43 f.
[11] Anne Salmond, *Hui: A Study of Maori Ceremonial Gatherings* (Wellington: Reed
and Methuen 1975), 3. Salmond is referring here to Goffman's earlier book *Interaction
Rituals: Essays on Face-to-Face Behaviour* (New York: Doubleday, 1967).

Although there is a high degree of skill involved in all these rituals, the participants do not greet them with applause, that is, they are not judged on purely dispassionate, performance-orientated criteria independent of the ritualistic context. Salmond notes: 'Applause is only given on the marae for non-traditional performances; and it is unconsciously used as a European form of approbation appropriate to European-influenced activities.'[12] Exceptions to this may occur when a European (pakeha) speaks on the *marae* or when action songs, which are a relative innovation dating from the turn of the twentieth century, are performed. The *whaikōrero*, the oratory of the elders, contains a particularly high degree of innate theatricality and can be easily transposed into the framework of European-style theatre. These speeches invariably deal with the genealogy of the tribe and the importance of the location; they often include humorous anecdotes and frequently make extensive use of gesture, although at no time is there a conscious or unconscious attempt at role enactment. However, Salmond does see in the *whaikōrero* close parallels between *marae* ritual and theatre: 'Here the marae is very like the theatre. Certain actors become famous and widely acclaimed, and whenever they walk onto the stage, it is into an atmosphere of expectation.'[13] The structure of *marae* rituals, and especially the *whaikōrero* as a balanced exchange between locals (*tangata whenua*) and visitors (*manuhiri*) who remain facing each other, spatially divided, throughout the ceremony, also has something inherently dramatic in its oppositional arrangement and is not unlike the patterns of formalized debate found in certain forms of European drama.

Attempts by Maori dramatists and directors to link theatrical performances to *hui* rituals have not been entirely unproblematic. The fact that certain cultural texts are used time and again can lead to overuse and staleness, as was indicated in the previous chapter. Another danger is that specific rituals and beliefs do not lend themselves to being theatricalized. In the eyes of Maori spectators, at least, they do not submit themselves to the general semiotic law of most theatrical cultures whereby anything on stage, whether person or object, can lose its primary cultural referentiality and be transformed into a sign of a sign. In order to illustrate this problem, one can look at the cultural system of *tapu*. In Maori culture there are a number of objects and behaviours which are subject to the laws of *tapu*. For

---

[12] Salmond, *Hui*, 112.   [13] Ibid. 148 f.

example, most, if not all, objects connected with death are considered
to be *tapu* and must be handled with extreme circumspection. Many
Maori refuse to accept the use of such objects on stage, because they
refuse to accept the semiotic transformation of such objects. A *tapu*
means that it must be either avoided or dealt with in a certain way.
The rules of *tapu* are governed by a complicated semiotic system
which is subject to spatial, temporal, and human variables such as
gender.[14] The conflict between Maori ritual and theatrical semiotics
will be discussed with reference to two of the most frequently performed Maori plays: *In the Wilderness without a Hat* (1977) by the
Maori poet Hone Tuwhare and *Te Hokinga Mai* (1988) by the
dramatist John Broughton.

In the Wilderness without a Hat marks a milestone in the development of an autochthonous Maori theatre. Tuwhare wrote the play
in 1977 before the renaissance of new Maori theatre had really
begun.[15] The large and almost entirely Maori cast precluded a production by one of New Zealand's professional theatres. It is also the
first Maori play which attempts to fuse the performance traditions of
European psychological drama with the hieratic world of Maori
mythology in a truly syncretic way. The action revolves around the
opening of a new meeting-house, the interior of which provides the
only setting. The play begins with two members of the central family
putting the finishing touches on the carvings. The turning-point of
the play is provided by the news that the sister of Waimirea (the
matriarch of the family) has died in the South Island and that the
South Island relatives will shortly be arriving with the body. The third
and final act takes the form of a *tangihanga* (funeral) with all its
associated rituals. With the coffin placed downstage middle, the two
families face each other and debate who should rightfully be permitted to bury the body, an integral part of any *tangihanga* and a sign
of reverence for the deceased. The dispute quickly oversteps the

---

[14] For a discussion of the semiotics of *tapu*, see ibid., particularly pp. 12–13 and
46–9.

[15] Two works by Maori dramatists pre-dated Tuwhare's play: *Te Raukura: The
Feathers of the Albatross* by Harry Dansey, a historical drama, first performed in
1972, which deals with the life of the 19th-century Maori prophet Te Ua Haumene.
Harry Dansey, *Te Raukura: The Feathers of the Albatross: A Narrative Play in Two
Acts* (Auckland: Longman Paul, 1974); *Death of the Land* by Rore Hapipi, first
performed in 1976, which addresses the problem of land rights. Rore Hapipi, *Death
of the Land*, in Simon Garrett (ed.), *He Reo Hou: 5 Plays by Maori Playwrights*
(Wellington: Playmarket, 1991).

accepted conventions of *tangihanga* oratory and turns into a physical struggle to take possession of the coffin. At this moment the carved statues come to life. The ancestors intervene physically in the action to solve the problems of their descendants.

The piece was not staged until 1985. The reason for the time lag lies not just in its aesthetically demanding nature and in practical exigencies of staging. Tuwhare also placed the blame for the delay on what he saw as Maori 'superstition', an inability or unwillingness to distinguish between the aesthetic and the ritualistic. The main bone of contention was the use of a coffin in the third act, which for many Maori constituted a clear breach of *tapu*.[16] In this conflict we find manifested an important dilemma of contemporary Maori theatre. Their performances are often located in an intermediary semiotic space between art and ritual. In the minds of many Maori, young and old, the *tapu* object can never forfeit entirely its ritual character and be transformed into a profane theatrical sign. In view of the fact that the scene takes place in a meeting-house and that performances are often staged in real meeting-houses, the antagonism on the part of spectators is understandable. Although Tuwhare's use of the coffin is perhaps an extreme example, which managed to alienate many spectators, it serves to illustrate that Maori theatre frequently aims to derive its special character and effects from precisely this ill-defined area between ritual and theatre. In Goffman's terminology one could say that in Maori theatre, for some spectators at least, the process of keying between the ritual and the theatre frames is not entirely accepted.

The tension between the ritual status of the *hui* and *marae*, on the one hand, and the aesthetic sign system theatre, on the other, contributes to the special impact of the play *Te Hokinga Mai* by John Broughton, first performed in 1988. The play is set during one day in 1970 on the *marae* of the Matthews family, who have lost a son during the Vietnam war. On this day a young man, Martin, arrives to inform the family of the death of their son, John-Junior. It transpires that the two men were close friends. Although Martin is not a Maori, he is welcomed by the family with full *marae* protocol. Another son

---

[16] Tuwhare writes: 'I think the Maori Players backed off from it because I'd put a coffin on stage. This was a stupid "no, no" superstition which I told them would impede the development of Maori theatre. Now that they've jumped that small hurdle, I'm pleased. But it didn't encourage me to go on with writing plays in the 1970's.' Letter to Christopher Balme, 6 May 1985.

performs the traditional ritual challenge, *te wero*, which is normally reserved for dignitaries. The women follow with a welcoming chant, *te karanga*; the father concludes the welcome with a dance, *te powhiri haka*. Once everybody is seated, the father gives a speech (*te whaikorero*), first in Maori, then in English. It is followed by a song of lament (*waiata*). Martin, the visitor, answers with a few Maori phrases learned from John-Junior, then continues his *whaikōrero* in English. His speech deals with his friendship with John-Junior and is presented in the form of a flashback. While Martin is speaking of his dead friend, he appears suddenly:

> [*J-J walks onto the* marae *from the right side of the Meeting House.* MARTIN *does not bat an eyelid, but the family are aghast.*]

KUINI. Aue! Junior.

HUIA. Mum, Oh Mum. It's J-J.

JOHN. You were right Mother, J-J is with us.

> [*Kuini sobs quite loudly.*][17]

This simple, and to some extent sentimental and melodramatic, device attains additional impact in connection with the oratory of the *whaikōrero*, in which the dead are accorded special honour. Through being embedded in *marae* ceremonial, which is depicted here by five separate cultural texts in the Maori language,[18] the flashback attains a special status which combines dramaturgical and ritual functions. Martin's speech dealing with his friendship with the deceased corresponds in the widest sense to the subject-matter of this cultural text. By having a dead family member appear on stage in the memory of those present, as it were, Broughton is simply expanding the parameters of the *whaikōrero*, but not transgressing them. Martin concludes his speech with a *waiata*, and thus completes the ritual. The play ends with a famous action song, 'E Pari Ra', a song of lament for the soldiers who fell during the First World War.

[17] John Broughton, *Te Hokinga Mai (The Return Home)* (Dunedin: Aoraki Productions, 1990), 28 f.

[18] In a production note Broughton draws attention to the special status of these cultural texts and permits the actors to replace these texts with songs and speeches from their own tribes: 'The play contains some very sacred and traditional aspects of Maori. The actors taking these roles do not necessarily have to keep to the actual script for these parts. The actors should feel quite free to use their own karanga, tauparapara [recitation] and whaikorero, especially pertaining to the area where the play is being performed.' *Te Hokinga Mai*, 12.

Although the theme of this short play—a plea for cultural understanding—is not difficult to uncover, and although the emotionality
of the death scene is dangerously close to the stale sentimentality of
innumerable war films, the sentiment is contained and transformed by
the ritual frame of the performance. The author succeeds in translating the potentially clichéd sentimentality of the dying soldier by
framing it within the authenticity of ritualized cultural texts such
as *karanga*, *whaikōrero*, and *waiata*, which provide a different level of
emotional experience for the Maori spectators at least. The effect of
such texts on both cultures is described by a Maori theatre critic,
Reina Whaitiri:

The waiata in 'Te Hokinga Mai' were as familiar as they were stirring and
those old enough would have remembered 'E Pari Ra' as the song written to
farewell the 28th Maori Battalion when they left for that other war. The
story moved from the present to the past, from the dead to the living, with
casual candour and the mainly Maori audience had no trouble following the
spatial and temporal changes. The Maori concept of the spiral of life and
death and the oneness of the past, present and future was represented here
and the waiata, the rituals, the aroha, the whanau were so referenced that
they would immediately be recognized by every Maori and many Pakeha
present.[19]

This comment also addresses an additional complex which goes
beyond the reception of this particular play and concerns the syncretism of Maori theatre in an intercultural context as a whole. That the
performance of a Maori play always takes place on two different
cultural levels is self-evident. The term *marae*-theatre itself implies
that two disparate cultural codes are conjoined here. Maori spectators have two ways of responding to such performances. They can
either reject outright the use of traditional ritual elements such as
pōwhiri and *karanga* in a new (theatrical) context, or these cultural
texts may have precisely the opposite effect by providing the requisite
contextual signals for creating an acceptance of theatrical performance. Non-Maori spectators are in a similar dilemma when confronted with cultural texts which are alien to the conventions of
Western theatre. The encounter with Maori culture, which may
take place already in the foyer of a theatre and outside the fictionally

---

[19] Reina Whaitiri, 'Te Hokinga Mai (The Return Home)', *Stage and Radio Record*,
3 (Summer 1991), 3. The comments refer to a production of the play performed in
Oct. 1991 in Freeman's Bay, Auckland, directed by Rangi Chadwick.

sanctioned frame of the stage before the performance actually starts, can be alienating for both cultures. However, reactions to Maori performances suggest that spectators realize they are witness to a new theatrical code *in statu nascendi* which calls for new critical criteria and new patterns of response. In a review of an early performance by the group Te Ohu Whakaari in 1983[20] called *Nga Paki o te Maui* the white critic and theatre scholar David Carnegie was moved to question his own legitimacy as a critic of this new kind of theatrical product:

As Maori aspirations grow, and as Maori theatre articulates those aspirations within an increasingly Maori context, new critics will be needed. These critics will speak Maori fluently, will be at home with all the complexities of Maoritanga and its tribal ramifications, and will be sensitive to the enormous theatrical potential of the combination of the Maori oratorical tradition with the European dramatic tradition. Only then will groups like Te Ohu Whakaari get the criticism they deserve.[21]

In a certain sense, this kind of cultural and aesthetic reorientation means that the theatre could become a place of experimentation in the Brechtian sense: the intercultural exchange and communication so urgently needed in a bicultural society like New Zealand are presented and tried out in experimental form on stage.

The Drama of Liminality

The attempts by Maori theatre to ritualize the overall frame of theatrical performance are one relatively unique manifestation of the relationship between theatre and ritual in post-colonial societies.

[20] Started in 1983 as a work collective by the actor and director Rangimoana Taylor, this group with initial funding from a Department of Labour work skills programme rapidly established itself as the most important of the groups working on a professional or semi-professional basis.
    [21] David Carnegie, 'Nga Paki o te Maui (Stories of the Maori)', *Dominion*, 15 Oct. 1983. *Nga Paki o te Maui* reflected both in terms of subject-matter and production process the characteristics of new Maori theatre. The piece depicted various aspects of traditional Maori culture and its place in contemporary society by means of short sketches, songs, movement, and dance. The final script was the result of collective creation and, more importantly, the structure of the programme reflected Maori ceremonial. It began with a traditional *mihi* (introductory chant) and ended with a meal after the show, elements integral to the *hui*, the Maori meeting or gathering, but by no means easily accommodated into the 'confrontational' spectator–performer relationship characteristic of European theatre.

More widespread are experiments with what could be called a ritual dramaturgy. In such texts there is seldom, if ever, a genuine attempt to involve the audience as though they were present at a ritual ceremony. Ritual elements are used as integral parts of the dramatic action, but remain contained within the overall fictional frame of theatrical performance.

Although it is difficult to identify common strategies linking texts from quite diverse cultures, the notion of liminality appears to be one structural feature of rituals which interests dramatists from West Africa and the Caribbean. The term goes back to Arnold van Gennep's influential anthropological study of rites of passage, first published in 1908. The liminal phase refers particularly to practices connected with puberty rites, where the novice or initiate is made to enter a realm which is both physically and mentally outside the confines of normal life. During this time initiates are prepared and instructed for their entry into the world of adulthood. This is often a time of extreme duress and includes religious instruction. The term 'liminality' has been adopted and expanded by Victor Turner to refer to most kinds of ritual performance which create a kind of interim space or period outside the bounds of normal social practice and structures, which he terms a 'betwixt-and-between condition'. In his essay 'Liminality and the Performative Genres' Turner differentiates between *individual* and *communal* rites.[22] Individual rites effect the transition of a person from social invisibility to visibility. In this case the rituals of liminality are usually characterized by the concealment and withdrawal of the novices until they are ready for reintegration into society. In communal rites the passage of a whole group from one culturally defined season to another is marked. The most well-known example in Western culture is carnival, which involves the public celebration of the betwixt-and-between condition.

Although these two types of transitional rites are quite different in scale, they do reveal a number of important common elements. One of these is the transformation of exterior appearance. In a secluded

[22] The theoretical linking of the concept of liminality and performance is one of the central concepts in Turner's wider theory of 'social drama' which he has expounded in practically all his writings since the late 1960s. The essay cited here was first published in John J. MacAloon (ed.), *Rite, Drama, Festival, Spectacle: Rehearsals toward a Theory of Cultural Performance*, (Philadelphia: Institute for the Study of Human Issues, 1984), and revised in Victor Turner's collection of essays *The Anthropology of Performance*, as 'Rokujo's Jealousy: Liminality and the Performative Genres'. All quotations are from the revised version.

place initiates are frequently made to undergo changes to their appearance such as masking. Tendencies towards masking and disguise can also be seen in communal rites both on the part of the individual participants as well as in terms of the public spaces used. According to Turner, the decoration and transformation of public places change the quotidian space into what he terms the 'subjunctive mood' of performance.[23] Life and action in the subjunctive mood are no longer subject to conventional value systems, notions of time and space, or codes of behaviour. During the liminal phase of a ritual the structure of a society becomes anti-structure.[24] Such anti-structural phases enable societies and communities to engage in genuine interrogation of their spiritual and symbolic worlds. During this time a community's myths are retold, sung, or staged, and in this relatively free space, opportunities for sociocultural innovation rehearsed: 'In liminality, new ways of acting, new combinations of symbols, are tried out, to be discarded or accepted.'[25] Processes such as the recombining of symbols suggest that there exists a link between liminality and syncretism. Liminality can perhaps be seen as one of the preconditions and as the preparatory phase which favour the creation of syncretic forms.

In the following examination of ritual in syncretic theatrical texts liminality will be viewed as a specific part of ritual sequences. Of particular interest is the way in which dramatists make use of the anti-structural freedom engendered by liminality to break open the rigid temporal and spatial limitations of realistic drama. Seen in this way the rupture created in ritual sequence by a liminal phase corresponds to the dissolution of the Aristotelian model of dramatic structure. Concrete manifestations of this strategy will be explored in the ritual dramas of Wole Soyinka and then in two plays from the Caribbean which exploit ritual possession as a dramaturgical device.

In Wole Soyinka's theoretical statements on the nature of traditional Yoruba ritual, particularly those regarding the festivals in

[23] 'The village greens or squares of the city are not abandoned but rather ritually transformed. It is as though everything is switched into the subjunctive mood for a privileged period of time—the time for example, of Mardi-Gras or the Carnival-Carême.' Turner, *The Anthropology of Performance*, 102.

[24] For a fuller discussion of this concept, see Victor Turner, *The Ritual Process: Structure and Anti-Structure* (Chicago: Aldine, 1969).

[25] Turner, *From Ritual to Theatre*, 85.

honour of Ogun, a number of striking parallels to the concept of liminality can be detected. For example, his famous concept of the 'fourth stage' refers precisely to such a liminal space. According to Soyinka, the fourth stage is an intermediary realm between the three coexisting realms of the unborn, the living, and the dead. In Yoruba mythology the god Ogun led the other gods on their journey to reunite with the living through this fourth, or 'chthonic', realm. Soyinka terms this event a rite of passage: 'Ogun it was who led them, his was the first rite of passage through the chthonic realm.'[26] The realm itself is characterized by chaos, formlessness; it is a dark continuum, in which men and gods are reconstituted for their entry into the next realm. It is, in other words, a place of transition and transformation. The characteristics of the 'fourth stage'—formlessness, disintegration, transition, reconstitution for another stage of existence—correspond to the features of liminality outlined above. This correspondence is made even clearer in Soyinka's characterization of the ritual performer at an Ogun festival. The state of possession engendered by this participation reveals substantial links to the experience of liminality:

The actor in ritual drama [. . .] prepares mentally and physically for his disintegration and re-assembly within the universal womb of origin, experiences the transitional yet inchoate matrix of death and being. Such an actor in the role of the protagonist becomes the unresisting mouthpiece of the god, uttering sounds which he barely comprehends but which are reflections of the awesome glimpse of that transitional gulf.[27]

Soyinka describes here a state of anti-structure which returns to structure and order once the ritual has been completed.

In Soyinka's dramatic œuvre one finds a large number of techniques and strategies for integrating the ritual elements of Yoruba culture into theatrical form. A striking characteristic of those dramas in which rituals play a central role is the premature rupture or suspension of the ritual action. The sequence of steps laid down by tradition are not carried through to their conclusion. One result of such ruptures is that the figures carrying out the ritual remain suspended in a state of liminality or anti-structure. This state of *ritus interruptus*, as it were, provides the author with the opportunity of exploring on stage the psychic 'abyss' caused by suspended

---

[26] Soyinka, *Myth, Literature and the African World*, 27.   [27] Ibid. 30.

liminality.[28] The concept of interrupted or incomplete rituals has a wider relevance than just to provide a pretext to experiment with the theatricality of a particular ritual. *Ritus interruptus* can also be seen as a theatrical metaphor for a social and spiritual state where old traditions are no longer completely intact. This metaphor of interrupted transition is, it would seem, particularly relevant for postcolonial societies which are themselves involved in difficult processes of cultural and social transition. To explore this thesis it is necessary to survey Soyinka's plays in more detail.

With *A Dance of the Forests*, written in 1960 to coincide with the Nigerian independence celebrations, Soyinka effects a complete shift in the dominant structure of dialogue-based drama.[29] The title immediately points to such a dominant shift: to dance, the paramount idiom of expression in traditional Yoruba performance. The choice of a Yoruba *egungun* festival as the dramaturgical framework is an important innovation and signals a significant departure from previous plays by Soyinka himself and other African playwrights.[30] It also throws up a whole series of theoretical and practical dramaturgical questions which remain central for any assessment of syncretic theatre and which repeatedly attract theatre artists from quite different cultures who attempt to refashion the conventions of Western theatre from within the possibilities of their own specific cultural performative idioms. In an interview Soyinka draws attention to the importance of ritual elements in the play and at the same time to the problems involved in transposing such elements to another, in this case theatrical, context: 'In a play like *A Dance of the Forests*, for instance, I tried to use a lot of the rites, a number of religious rites— and there's one of exorcism, for instance, which I tried to use to interpret a theme which is quite completely remote from the source of

---

[28] The term 'psychic abyss' is found frequently in Soyinka's writings on Yoruba ritual performance: 'Tragic feeling in Yoruba drama stems from the sympathetic knowledge of the protagonist's foray into this psychic abyss of the re-creative energies.' Soyinka, *Myth, Literature and the African World*, 30 f.

[29] The dramaturgy of his previous plays *The Swamp Dwellers* (1958), *The Lion and the Jewel* (1959), *The Invention* (1959), and *The Trials of Brother Jero* (1960) was greatly indebted to Western forms.

[30] Recent research suggests that form and theme are indeed structurally interrelated. Deidre L. Badejo, for example, analyses the structural parallels between the *egungun* festival and *A Dance of the Forests*: 'By suggesting the *egungun* festival and reversing its conclusion, Soyinka enhances his appraisal of the historical process. Thus the ancestors, in the cultural sense, become dysfunctional.' 'Unmasking the Gods: Of Egungun and Demagogues in Three Works by Wole Soyinka', *Theatre Journal*, 39/2 (1987), 205 f.

its particular idiom.'[31] Both the immediate critical reaction to the production and subsequent scholarly examinations of the work would suggest that this experiment was by no means an unqualified success. The central question is then how to transpose 'religious rites' and 'rites of exorcism' out of their original functional context into the aesthetic framework of theatre. This is the central question which repeatedly informs Soyinka's dramaturgical method and theoretical writings, but which cannot be considered to be the exclusive key to his conception of theatre. His command of theatrical idioms is far too multifaceted and cosmopolitan to be subsumed under any one single concern of formal structure. The question of 'ritual transposition', for want of a better term, is, however, certainly central for an understanding of such works as *The Strong Breed*, *The Road*, *The Bacchae of Euripides*, *Death and the King's Horseman*, the radio play *Camwood on the Leaves*, and a number of theoretical essays, including 'The Fourth Stage'. It is of minor importance for the comedies, his satirical pieces, his guerrilla theatre, and perhaps his Beckettian play *Madmen and Specialists*.

The problem of transposing this highly elaborate semiotic system and recoding it for other performative contexts is addressed in 'The Ritual Archetype', the first essay of *Myth, Literature and the African World*. Soyinka asks how one can move a performance linked to a shrine, 'a historic spot in the drama of a people's origin', or a harvest celebration, and place it in the 'fenced arena at a Festival of Arts'.

The essential problem is that the emotive progression which leads to a communal ecstasy or catharsis has been destroyed in the process of re-staging. So this leads us intentionally to the perennial question of whether ritual can be called drama, at what moment a religious or mythic celebration can be considered transformed into drama, and whether the ultimate test of these questions does not lie in their capacity to transfer from habitual to alien environments.[32]

In this passage Soyinka moves from the question of touristic arts and aesthetic displacement of cultural texts with a clearly prescribed functional radius to the problem of reworking ritual material into another form. The external structure of the cultural texts remains more or less intact; the cultural performance context is, however,

---

[31] Dennis Duerden and Cosmo Pieterse (eds.), *African Writers Talking: A Collection of Radio Interviews*. (London: Heinemann, 1972), 170.
[32] Soyinka, *Myth, Literature and the African World*, 5 f.

radically different. This necessarily raises questions about his own theatrical practice. Soyinka, however, turns his attention to 'the recent reversion of European and American progressive theatre to ritualism',[33] singling out the Living Theater, Genet, Grotowski, Schechner, Peter Brook, and even Ariane Mnouchkine's *1789* as examples of this trend. Soyinka insists that the search of the Euro-American avant-garde for answers to white bourgeois existentialist crises through re-created rituals is an entirely different situation from that of the African theatre. The question of the 'supposed dividing line between ritual and theatre should not concern us much in Africa, the line being one that was largely drawn by the European analyst'.[34] Soyinka supports this assertion by pointing to the international success of the Ori-Olokun Theatre in Ifẹ and to Duro Ladipo's Yoruba plays as evidence of 'the capability of the drama (or ritual) of the gods to travel as aesthetically and passionately as the gods themselves have, across the Atlantic'[35] and to black American theatre. This statement collapses the distinction between ritual and theatre for African (or black) drama. While Soyinka is certainly correct when he asserts that it is pointless to distinguish between the two in traditional African theatre, the plays of Ola Rotimi, Duro Ladipo, and indeed of Barbara Ann Teer's Harlem Theater enjoy, however, a substantially different ontological status from that of an *egungun* masquerade.

One of the ways Soyinka reworks ritual material into his plays can be seen in the drama *The Strong Breed*, published in 1964. This work is structured around an interrupted ritual which creates a kind of prolonged liminal state for the main protagonist.[36] *The Strong Breed* has a complex temporal structure with constant shifts between past and present. The central rituals of the play have no specified cultural or tribal links, but are some kind of New Year festival.[37] The play dramatizes the fate of the 'Stranger' Eman, who has broken off his initiation and settled in another village as a teacher. In this village a

---

[33] Soyinka, *Myth, Literature and the African World*, 6.   [34] Ibid. 7.
[35] Ibid.
[36] This play was written shortly after *A Dance of the Forests*, but the manuscript was lost. The première took place in 1966 in Ibadan.
[37] James Gibbs suggests that one of the rituals comes from the Delta region of Nigeria. *Wole Soyinka* (London: Macmillan, 1986), 72. He points out parallels between the ritual in Eman's home village and an actual New Year's rite described by Robin Horton: 'New Year in the Delta: A Traditional and a Modern Festival', *Nigeria Magazine*, 67 (1960), 256–97.

special kind of New Year ritual is carried out: at the end of the year a scapegoat, or 'carrier', is chosen, made to undergo ritual preparation, and then driven from the village with curses and blows as a form of communal purification. Eman protests when he learns that a village 'idiot' has been chosen as the carrier, and offers himself instead. While he is being prepared for the ritual, Eman escapes and in the course of his flight he experiences his past in a series of flashbacks. He recalls a similar ritual in his home village in which his family, the 'strong breed' of the title, has the task of symbolically bearing the evil of the village in a kind of vessel and setting it adrift in the river. The play ends with the death of Eman: he is killed in a trap set by the village chief, Jaguna, and the other villagers. Whether one interprets Eman's death as a loss or gain for the community—ritual deaths are usually to be judged in such terms—of interest here is the way ritual is depicted.

The first striking element is the fact that the performative aspect of ritual—the 'immense orchestration of genres in all available sensory codes', as Victor Turner put it—plays practically no role whatsoever: Soyinka uses neither song nor dances, the dominant performance forms of African ritual. There are also no other identifiable cultural texts establishing links to a particular ethnic or cultural group. Dialogue remains the central motor of the action, and the rituals themselves are indicated by means of a few acoustic or visual signs. For example, the ritual of purification which Eman interrupts in order to escape is not shown but rather indicated by a description of Eman's appearance: 'the alert hunted look is still in his eyes which are ringed in a reddish colour. The rest of his body has been whitened with a floury substance. He is naked down to the waist, wears a baggy pair of trousers, calf-length, and around both feet are bangles.'[38] Eman's appearance is intended to establish a visual parallel to the similar, but less brutal ritual, in his home village, where his father assumes the role of 'carrier'. In the next scene we see Eman's father being prepared for the ritual: 'An old man, short and vigorous looking is seated on a stool. He is also wearing calf-length baggy trousers, white. On his head, a white cap. An attendant is engaged in rubbing his body with oil. Round his eyes, two white rings have already been marked.'[39] In this rite

[38] Wole Soyinka, *Collected Plays*, i (Oxford: Oxford University Press, 1973), 131.
[39] Ibid. 132.

Eman's father carries a small boat in the form of a headdress down to a river and sets it afloat as a symbolic act of purifying the sins of the village. Although there are evident parallels between the rituals in the two villages in terms of their intention and the visual appearance of the protagonists, there are major differences in the performance of the ritual. In Eman's home village the ritual is a symbolic act represented by the carrying and setting afloat of the boatlike headdress. In Jaguna's village the ritual results in physical injury, loss of home, and even death. The important linking element of the two rituals is that in both cases the ritual tradition is ruptured. In his home village Eman has broken off his initiation, which means that the communal ritual carried by his family will no longer be continued. In his new village Eman also escapes during the preparatory phase of the ritual and is caught in a kind of liminal state, during which he recalls his past. The fact that he escapes and is then killed means that the ritual is also ruptured and cannot be successfully completed. The necessary rites of reintegration are unable to be carried out. So in a sense both villages have suffered a break with tradition and are potentially faced with destabilization. The depressed mood of the ending of the play certainly suggests that the future is bleak.

While the performative aspects of ritual are of very little importance in *The Strong Breed*, they occupy a central place in Soyinka's next play, *The Road*, premièred in 1965. A central theme of this work is also transgression against ritual order with disastrous results. However, in *The Road* a traditional cultural order is no longer evident, but only remnants of such an order. Instead we find an almost programmatic mixing of the traditional and the new, of indigenous cultural concepts and Western-influenced lifestyle, which determines both thematic and formal aspects of the play. Syncretism is depicted as the norm of Nigerian society: the Yoruba god of iron, Ogun, has now become the patron saint of truck-drivers and their touts, the central characters of the play. Soyinka stages the crass cultural collisions between Christianity and Yoruba cult religion, between three coexisting languages, and traditional and modern world-views. The central ritual of the play is that of the *agemo* cult. It provides a kind of dramaturgical frame for the action. In a prefatory note 'For the Producer' Soyinka glosses the meaning of this cult by referring the reader to the preface poem 'Alagemo' and offering a simple definition: 'Agemo is simply, a religious cult of flesh dissolution.'[40] The performative expression of the cult is a dance in which the dancer, concealed behind high mats wrapped around him, spins around faster and faster until, unnoticed by the spectators, he slips out of the mats, which collapse in a pile.[41] For Soyinka the dance serves as a theatrical metaphor for the stage of transition between life and death: 'The dance is the movement of transition; it is used in the play as a visual suspension of death.'[42] This transitional state between life and death corresponds to the idea of liminality, particularly to the condition of 'betwixt-and-between', as Victor Turner calls it.[43] This is the state in which Murano, the mute, who has been run over by a lorry, finds himself at the beginning of the play, as Soyinka explains in his prefatory note: 'Murano, the mute, is a dramatic embodiment of this suspension. He functions as an arrest of time, or death, since it was in his "agemo" phase that the lorry knocked him down. Agemo, the mere phase, includes the passage of transition from the human to the divine essence (as in the festival of Ogun in this play).'[44]

This explanation makes clear that a central part of the action is subject to the laws of liminality and anti-structure. When the play begins Murano is mute. In the course of a flashback later in the play we learn that Murano was knocked over by the driver Kotonu during a dance festival held by the lorry-drivers in honour of Ogun. Fearing the drivers' revenge, Kotonu put on Murano's bloodstained *egungun* costume and danced into a state of possession and exhaustion. Kotonu then returned to the roadside shack where the action is set, and the shack's owner, the Professor, nursed Murano back to health.

---

[40] Soyinka, *Collected Plays*, i, 149.

[41] In an interview with Ketu Katrak, Soyinka explained his use of the *agemo* dance: 'Some agemo are just like any other egungun masquerade. There are some others who dance within mats rolled around their bodies. The human being, the form is there [inside the mats]. After a while this form dances, dances into a terrific whirl and then it just collapses. There is absolutely nothing inside the mat. So I used it [*agemo*] to symbolize the passage of flesh into nothingness. It is actually a kind of illusion but it's done in the open, in the courtyard, and suddenly one sees that there is nothing, just a fold of mats collapsed. What had body shape, before, has become fibre. So I used agemo in that sense as illusion.' Katrak, *Wole Soyinka and Modern Tragedy*, 68. See also Oyin Ogunba, 'The Agemo Cult', *Nigeria Magazine*, 86 (1965), 176–86.

[42] Soyinka, *Collected Plays*, 149.

[43] See particularly his essay 'Betwixt and Between: The Liminal Period in *Rites de Passage*', in J. Helms (ed.), *Proceedings of the American Ethnological Society for 1964* (Seattle: University of Washington, 1964), 4–20; repr. in Victor Turner, *Forest of Symbols: Aspects of Ndembu Ritual* (Ithaca: Cornell University Press, 1967).

[44] Soyinka, *Collected Plays*, 149.

Since this incident Kotonu, the driver, refuses to work and appears to be in a state of paralysis, as the stage direction indicates: 'Most of the time he is half-asleep, indifferent to what goes on around him.'[45] This psychological state, which has been caused by his accidental encounter with the ancestors, bears the characteristic marks of a liminal condition.[46]

For the Professor, the main protagonist of the play, Murano represents the embodiment of the central metaphysical question he is obsessed with: the meaning of death, or rather its suspension. In the person of Murano, 'frozen' as it were by the accident in a liminal state, the Professor finds concretized how the inexorable can be delayed. The Professor goes even further and has the godlike Murano serve him palm wine in an act analogous to communion: 'for it came to the same thing, that I held a god captive, that his hands held out the day's communion! And should I not hope, with him, to cheat, to anticipate the final confrontation, learning its nature baring its skulking face, why may I not understand . . .'.[47] In the final scene of the play the Professor makes Murano dance once again in his *egungun* costume. In so doing, the Professor is staging a dance with death, an act which is tantamount to blasphemy in the belief system of the Yoruba. The Professor's blasphemous act deeply offends Say Tokyo Kid, who is both lorry-driver and gang-leader, and a traditionalist. After trying in vain to stop the dancing mask, he stabs the Professor and is then himself killed by the dancer. Murano then completes the *agemo* dance until his body has disappeared and only the material of the mask remains: 'The mask still spinning, has continued to sink slowly until it appears to be nothing beyond a heap of cloth and raffia.'[48] Now the interrupted ritual has finally been completed.

As already indicated, liminality is manifest in various ways in *The Road*. Not only has Murano been suspended in a liminal state because of his injury, but in a wider sense the whole of Nigerian society, of which the roadside shack is a kind of microcosm, or *mise-en-abyme*, finds itself in the transitional state characteristic of liminality where nothing is fixed and unusual and new semantic

---

[45] Soyinka, *Collected Plays*, 167.
[46] A similar conclusion is reached by the Nigerian scholar D. S. Izevbaye, who terms Kotonu's loss of will 'a state of limbo' caused by his possession by the god Ogun: 'Language and Meaning in Soyinka's *The Road*', in James Gibbs (ed.), *Critical Perspectives on Wole Soyinka* (Washington: Three Continents Press, 1981), 98.
[47] Soyinka, *Collected Plays*, 223 f.   [48] Ibid. 229.

combinations can arise. This unstable sociocultural situation, which appears to be extremely favourable for the creation of syncretic forms, is illustrated through the contrasting of Western and African sign systems. One example of this is the scene already mentioned where Murano serves the Professor palm wine, the special drink of Ogun worship, while the Professor himself is talking about Palm Sunday in church. Additional acoustic signs are provided by organ music from the nearby church, which is then drowned out by Yoruba music. This scene is typical for the strategical play of cultural signs and performance forms which punctuate the action. These cultural signs and texts are embedded in the larger ritual complex of *agemo*–Ogun–*egungun* which frames the play. This ritual complex is in turn rooted in a tribalistic–agrarian culture where the *agemo* dance or Ogun worship represented a functional and controlled use of liminality. However, in this play the Yoruba culture is depicted as *en route* to a modern society, where such rituals have become increasingly problematic. The collision between a tribalistic ritual culture with an emerging industrial one is symbolized by the accident. When the *egungun* dancer Murano is run over by a lorry, this act represents in a sense the collision of two belief systems. Turner himself advocates the application of the liminality concept to macrostructures of this kind, in which whole societies can be considered as in a state of transition:

when persons, groups, sets of idea, etc. move from one level or style of organization [. . .] to another level, there has to be an interfacial region or, to change the metaphor, an interval, however brief, of *margin* or *limen*, when the past is momentarily negated, suspended, or abrogated, and the future has not yet begun, an instant of pure potentiality when everything, as it were, trembles in the balance.[49]

Formulated in this general way, the liminal state is applicable to many post-colonial societies. It is Soyinka's achievement to have concretized this general state by means of a specific ritual and its performance on stage, which contains metaphysical, social, and theatrical levels of meaning.

Death and the King's Horseman, published in 1975, is the last play by Soyinka in which the dramaturgy of *ritus interruptus* plays a

---

[49] Turner, *From Ritual to Theatre*, 44.

central role.[50] The central event of the action is the ritual suicide of
Elesin Oba, the commander of the Yoruba king's cavalry.[51] According
to ancient custom, on the death of the king his chief horseman
voluntarily follows his ruler into the next world. It is a ritual by
which the death of one individual ensures the well-being of the rest of
the community. In *Death and the King's Horseman* the ritual is
interrupted by the intervention of the British colonial power with
disastrous consequences for the Yoruba people. Based on an event
which took place in 1946, the play was first performed in 1975. It is
thus interesting to ask about the contemporary status of the suicide
ritual. On the one hand, the ritual itself no longer exists: it was finally
abolished, presumably through a combination of colonial interference and changes within Yoruba culture.[52] Thus the performance of
the ritual on stage is, for a contemporary Yoruba audience, presumably no longer blasphemous. Nor does the ritual have any function in
ensuring the well-being of the community. Despite this historiciza-
tion, many of the constitutive cultural texts of the ritual—the music,
dance, rhetoric, possession trance, talking drums—constitute living
and decodable forms of cultural expression to which a Yoruba audience has immediate access. And one of the central thematic strands of
the play—the destructive interference of one culture in the cultural
and religious belief system of another—is still a highly relevant issue.

In terms of its detailed depiction of ritual performance forms

[50] The other play of this period in which ritual is central is *The Bacchae of Euripides*
(1973). This work will not be analysed here. For one thing it is an adaptation or
translation commissioned by and intended for a Western theatre. Thus it is very much
debatable whether it can be considered syncretic theatre in the narrower sense. In
addition, the idea of liminality plays no importance, possibly because the rituals
invoked are culturally eclectic. Soyinka is interested in exploring the structural parallels
between Greek and African ritual forms: the ecstatic trances of the Bacchantes show
very obvious analogies to the possession-based cults of the Yoruba. However, the play
remains in many respects a theatricalized essay on the necessity of ritual experience
without rooting this experience in a particular cultural matrix as Soyinka does in his
other works.

[51] The 'horseman' of the title signifies the equivalent of cavalry general or commander of the royal cavalry. The word 'horseman' also has a religious connotation, for, on
the death of the king, the king's horseman functions as a horse bearing his deceased
master into the next world. The name of the main character, Elesin Oba, means 'king's
horseman'. See the article by Kacke Götrick, 'Soyinka and *Death and the King's
Horseman*; or, How Does our Knowledge—Or Lack of Knowledge—of Yoruba Culture
Affect our Interpretation?', *African Literature Association Bulletin*, 16/1 (1990), 1–9,
particularly 3.

[52] For a detailed discussion of the historical background to the play, see Gibbs, *Wole
Soyinka*, 117 f.

Death and the King's Horseman is unique among Soyinka's ritual dramas. In no other play is Turner's 'orchestration of the sensory codes' of ritual staged with such immediacy and cultural authenticity. Even in *The Road* the elements of music and dance, although crucial for the play, by no means dislodge dialogue as the dramatic dominant. However, in *Death and the King's Horseman*, particularly in the Yoruba scenes (scenes 1 and 3), there takes place a marked dominant shift in favour of non-dialogic modes. In the scene in which the king's horseman, Elesin, brings on a self-induced death trance,[53] the spectator experiences the immediate power of ritual without the mediation and distanciation of flashbacks. The stage directions for this scene provide a carefully orchestrated score of dance, music, and speech. The means by which Elesin induces his trance and moves into a liminal state are carefully laid out by the author. They constitute a cultural text of ritual trance. Before he can carry out the ritual to its final and fatal conclusion, Elesin is stopped by the colonial police. The rest of the play shows Elesin, similarly to Murano and Kotonu in *The Road*, caught in a culturally determined liminal state between life and death. Imprisoned by the British and scorned by his own people for failing in his ritual mission, Elesin resorts to suicide by self-strangulation. This act is without ritual significance and is senseless, as the leader of the market women, Iyaloja, comments: 'He is gone at last into the passage but, oh how late it all is.'[54] The failure to perform the ritual has serious consequences. Soyinka suggests that the state of *ritus interruptus* can be seen as a metaphor for the cultural destabilization of a traditional culture. The Praise-Singer's admonition—'Our world is tumbling in the void of strangers, Elesin'[55]—has a prophetic ring in this context.[56]

Seen together and in the context of the theoretical writings on ritual drama, these three plays demarcate a central emphasis in Soyinka's work. The notion of *ritus interruptus*, whereby a protagonist is caught up in an anti-structural liminal state, provides a multifaceted dramaturgical and theatrical device. On the dramaturgical

---

[53] Wole Soyinka, *Six Plays* (London: Methuen, 1984), 184 f.   [54] Ibid. 219.
[55] Ibid. 218.
[56] That the demise of this cultural system is to be regretted in Soyinka's view is beyond dispute. For a less idealized view of pre-colonial Yoruba culture, see the Marxist reading of Biodon Jeyifo, who terms the Oyo kingdom 'a code built on class entrenchment and class consolidation'. *The Truthful Lie: Essays in a Sociology of African Drama* (London: New Beacon Books, 1985), 34.

level it offers the playwright the opportunity to break open the dramatic unities and to range far in terms of time, space, and consciousness. It also provides a powerful metaphor for the wider transitional state in which post-colonial societies find themselves. On the theatrical level the performance of rituals on stage offers a rich repertoire of scenic devices such as dance, drumming, chant, and song which are not used or presented as folkloric numbers, but attain a more complex level of significance by being integrated into a dramaturgical structure of meaning and action.

The Performance of Possession

In the essay 'Drama and Ritual Archetype' Soyinka refers to 'the capability of the drama (or ritual) of the gods to travel as aesthetically and passionately as the gods themselves have, across the Atlantic'.[57] The reference here is to the establishment of West African, largely Yoruba, cultural forms in the Caribbean and South America. Turning our attention now to the use of ritual in contemporary Caribbean drama, we find a similar interest in the dramaturgical and theatrical potentialities of liminality. Within this wider concept possession is the ritual technique that is particularly striking. Practically every island in the Caribbean has some kind of African-influenced syncretic cult: *shango* in Trinidad, voodoo in Haiti, *kumina* and *pocomania* in Jamaica, *santería* in Cuba, to name just the best known of these, all possess a relatively homogeneous repertoire of cult practices and rituals.[58] Characteristic among these are trance-induced possession, dancing, drumming, and animal sacrifices. That these practices—particularly possession with its

---

[57] Soyinka, *Myth, Literature and the African World*, 7.

[58] See George E. Simpson in his standard study of Caribbean cult religions: 'The Shango cult in Trinidad combines elements of Yoruba traditional religion, Catholicism, and the Baptist faith. In its theology and rituals it bears considerable resemblance to the Afro-Christian cults in the Catholic countries of Haiti (Vodun), Cuba (Santería), and Brazil (Xango). All these syncretistic cults retain the names of prominent African divinities, include animal sacrifices, feature drumming, dancing, and spirit possession, and utilize thunderstones and swords as ritual objects.' *Religious Cults of the Caribbean: Trinidad, Jamaica and Haiti*, 3rd edn. (Rio Piedras: Institute of Caribbean Studies, University of Puerto Rico, 1980), 11. The comparable cults in Jamaica are of protestant origin; however, they differ little in terms of the African ritual forms they use; see ibid. and Edward Seaga, *Revival Cults in Jamaica: Notes towards a Sociology of Religion*, Special Issue of *Jamaica Journal*, 3/2 (June 1969), 3–20 (repr. Kingston: Institute of Jamaica, 1982).

proximity to role-playing—reveal a high degree of theatricality has been frequently remarked in ethnographic research.[59] In the following analysis we shall look more closely at the phenomenon of possession, in terms of both its dramaturgical functions and its performance aesthetics. The texts are Derek Walcott's dream-play *Dream on Monkey Mountain* and the ritual drama *An Echo in the Bone* by the Jamaican dramatist and director Dennis Scott.[60] As a preliminary to a reading of these texts, I shall survey briefly the theatrical aspects and analogies of voodoo ceremony and its 'staging' of possession.[61]

The central experience of Haitian voodoo ritual is possession. Ritual possession corresponds in its main features to Victor Turner's definition of liminality. Possessed devotees withdraw in the course of the ritual from the rules of quotidian life; they move into a realm in which the power of the gods and spirits rather than that of humans determine action, speech, and behaviour. There exists a considerable amount of research on possession states in general[62] and on their

[59] In her essay 'Ritual Dissociation and Possession Belief in Caribbean Negro Religion', in Norman E. Whitten and John F. Szwed (eds.), *Afro-American Anthropology: Contemporary Perspectives* (New York: Free Press, 1970), 87–101, Erika Bourguignon writes of voodoo: 'During the state of dissociation, the individual plays a complex role or roles, indeed often veritable short plays are enacted' (p. 90).

[60] Despite the comprehensive ethnographic research literature dealing with ritual and possession in the Caribbean, the connections to ritual in dramatic theatre have received very little attention. The best work to date can be found in Rawle Gibbons's unpublished and somewhat inaccessible M.Phil. thesis, 'Traditional Enactments of Trinidad—Towards a Third Theatre', University of the West Indies, St Augustine, 1979. Despite its title, Gibbons does not just restrict himself to Trinidad; see ch. 2: 'Body-Possession'.

[61] The plays by no means exhaust examples of Caribbean theatre and drama using ritual elements, but have been selected because of their focus on the aspect of possession. Another important play revolving around ritual is Michael Gilke's *Couvade*, a work I have examined elsewhere; see Christopher Balme, 'The Caribbean Theatre of Ritual', in Anna Rutherford (ed.), *From Commonwealth to Post-Colonial* (Sydney: Dangaroo Press, 1992), 181–96. The Jamaican women's group Sistren has also utilized ritual in a number of their productions. For an excellent discussion of this aspect of the group's work, see Rhonda Cobham, '"Wha Kind a Pen Dis?": The Function of Ritual Frameworks in Sistren's *Bellywoman Bangaran*', *Theatre Research International*, 15/3 (1990), 233–49.

[62] A central text is Raymond Prince (ed.), *Trance and Possession States: Proceedings of the Second Annual Conference of the R. M. Bucke Memorial Society* (Montreal: R. M. Bucke Memorial Society, 1968). On the geographical distribution and basic patterns, see Erika Bourgignon, 'World Distribution and Patterns of Possession States', in Prince (ed.), *Trance and Possession States*, 3–34; on the situation in the Caribbean, see Bourgignon, 'Ritual Dissociation and Possession Belief in Caribbean Negro Religion'. For examples of institutionalized possession in Africa and for a differentiation between possession and medium, see John Beattie and John Middleton (eds.), *Spirit Mediumship and Society in Africa* (London: Routledge & Kegan Paul, 1969).

manifestations in voodoo in particular.[63] A recurrent theme in this literature is the link between possession and theatricality.[64] This latter aspect is of particular interest, even though we need not attempt here any kind of phenomenological distinction between the two, since the possession manifested in the theatre texts in question is purely of a fictional nature.

It is, however, important to realize that possession is a phenomen that occurs in numerous religions, that in many cultures it is recognized and institutionalized as a legitimate form of religious practice, while in others, as, for example, in most forms of Christianity, it is regarded as a pathological state to be treated with the rites of exorcism.[65] From the point of view of theatrical analysis, possession states can only be analysed properly where they occur, like voodoo, in an institutionalized form. For only in such cults do they reveal the pronounced elements of theatricality, which permit analogies to be drawn between ritual and theatre. These analogies can be summarized under the following headings:

Concept of role. In voodoo the devotees are possessed, or 'ridden', by a particular spirit (*loa*). In the state of possession, there emerges a clear distinction between self and body. Whatever the body does or

[63] Apart from the numerous and mostly distorted, sensationalized treatments in pulp fiction and in the cinema there exists a considerable amount of ethnographic literature on voodoo. Important works are Melville J. Herskovits, *Life in a Haitian Valley* (New York: Knopf, 1937); Louis Mars, *La Crise de possessions dans le voudou* (Port-au-Prince: Imprimerie de l'État, 1946); Alfred Métraux, *Voodoo in Haiti* (New York: Oxford University Press, 1959); and Simpson, *Religious Cults of the Caribbean.* Simpson contains a detailed description of the various phases and symptoms of possession (pp. 29–32, 263–9).

[64] On the various manifestations of possession, Erika Bourguignon writes: 'It may be stereotyped as in Bali, or individuated, as in the Haitian voodoo pantheon; it may be traditional and prescribed drama, as in Bali, or *commedia dell'arte* improvisation, as in Haiti. In both these instances we find dramatic performances.' 'World Distribution and Patterns of Possession States', 11. The most thorough discussion is offered by Michel Leiris in his study of the Ethiopian *zâr* cult, *La Possession et ses aspects théâtraux chez les Éthiopiens de Gondar* (1958; Paris: Le Sycomore, 1980). See also the article by Andrew Horn, 'Ritual Drama and the Theatrical: The Case of *Bori* Spirit Mediumship', in Ogunbiyi (ed.), *Drama and Theatre in Nigeria*, 181–202; see the section 'Ritual and Drama: Intersections and Divergences' (pp. 192–7).

[65] See here Bourguignon, who maintains that in the Judaeo-Christian tradition possession is considered to be 'a feared pathological phenomenon which is treated ritually by exorcism'. 'Ritual Dissociation and Possession Belief in Caribbean Negro Religion', 91. This should perhaps be qualified by the specification that the mainstream opposes possession. In both religions there are marginal groups which practise forms of possession.

says during possession is determined by the spirit in question. The identity of the possessing god or spirit is manifested through the gestural and kinaesthetic signs of the possessed person, which are easily identifiable for the initiated. This means that possession is linked to a finite repertoire of spirits or 'roles' who recur again and again.[66]

Body language. Possession produces changes in motor activity which lend to the kinesic signs (proxemics and gesture) a semiotic quality different from that of everyday movement. This movement not only has a mimetic function, aiding the identification of the various spirits, but can also be observed and enjoyed for its own sake as aesthetically interesting movement.

Dance and music. Although they are not absolutely essential for inducing possession, these performative 'aids' are a central component of most forms of institutionalized possession cults and their rituals. The combination of drum rhythms, choric chants, and the appropriate dance steps is regarded as an extremely potent means of inducing a possession state. That these elements, like body language, also have an inherent aesthetic component need not be stressed.

Catharsis. The affective arousal during possession and the relaxation and distention of the possessed person afterwards have been compared with the Aristotelian concept of catharsis.[67] However, the decisive difference compared to the theatre is that the supposed arousal and cleansing of *eleos* and *phobos* in case of possession occurs for the actor and not for the spectator.

The theatricality of possession should not be viewed as an isolated phenomenon but rather must be seen in the performative context of

---

[66] For voodoo Simpson provides detailed descriptions of seventeen *loas* and the psychophysical behaviour of the devotees when possessed. The spirit Legba, for example, who is syncretized with the Catholic saint Anthony, has the appearance of an old man; a devotee possessed by Legba 'acts like a limping grandfather. Carries a cane and walks carefully so that he will not be trampled on.' Simpson, *Religious Cults of the Caribbean*, 249. Comparable repertoires are documented for the *shango* cult in Trinidad (ibid. 18–20), for the *bori* cult in northern Nigeria (Horn,'Ritual Drama and the Theatrical', 190–1), and for the Ethiopian *zâr* cult (Leiris, *La Possession et ses aspects théâtraux chez les Éthiopiens de Gondar*).

[67] For example, Michel Leiris summarizes in his study of the *zâr* cult in Ethiopia the connection between it and the theatre as a kind of cathartic experience (*La Possession et ses aspects théâtraux chez les Éthiopiens de Gondar*). Andrew Horn sees in the performance by the possessed medium of the *bori* cult a cathartic, psychotherapeutic effect for the medium: 'The medium's personal rewards presumably lay in the social control she acquired, the emotional catharsis of role-playing (not unlike that of psychotherapeutic "psycho-drama"), and the physical stimulation of ecstatic frenzy.' Horn, 'Ritual Drama and the Theatrical', 192.

the ritual ceremony necessary for it to be induced. In an essay written in 1950 for Sartre's periodical *Les Temps modernes*, the French ethnographer and surrealist writer Michel Leiris described the pronounced theatricality of voodoo, pointing out the synthesis of elements drawn from the European theatrical tradition with those from Caribbean ritual ceremonial:

On a purely aesthetic level one observes in voodoo ceremonial the coexistence of unmistakably African-type dances with a system of circling movements of welcome, which inevitably evoke the image of European courtly dances of the seventeenth and eighteenth centuries [. . .] The question of the exact origin of these movements remains insoluble; one must however stress in the ceremonies and simple dances associated with the voodoo cult how gripping the balletic character of the ritual is.[68]

The combination of African and French dance forms, of ritual ecstasy with the measured elegance of baroque dance, not only underscores the theatrical nature of this ritual practice, but also demonstrates the all-embracing syncretic nature of voodoo. According to Leiris, it is this phenomenon of natural syncretism in the Caribbean that offers splendid perspectives for aesthetic innovation in the region. Unfortunately, though, voodoo is not the product of fortunate design but still carries the mortgage of its origin in the slave-trade, which is particularly evident in the social ills of poverty and discrimination.

Although foreign ethnologists such as Leiris were pointing out in the early 1950s the theatrical analogies of voodoo, it was not until the 1960s that local writers began to analyse the theatrical possibilities of the cult. The psychiatrist Louis Mars, son of Jean Price-Mars, the first theorist of *négritude avant la lettre*,[69] outlined in 1966 how an autochthonous Haitian drama and theatre could or should be based in voodoo ceremony and its practice of spirit possession. He outlines three central areas in which parallels to Western theatre are visible. Firstly, the voodoo ceremony is inspired by motives of exceptional gravity: it is concerned with illness and death, and with economic and social crises—all those things which 'plunge the human soul into confusion'. Secondly, the various gods are incarnated in

---

[68] Michel Leiris, 'Martinique, Guadeloupe, Haiti', *Les Temps modernes*, 5/52 (1950), 1345; my translation.

[69] The reference is to the book by Jean Price-Mars, *Ainsi parla l'oncle: Essais d'ethnographie* (Port-au-Prince: Imprimerie de Compiègne, 1928), which, as well as rehabilitating voodoo as a serious object of study, also anticipates the central ideas of *négritude*.

their devotees on the basis of a fixed typology transmitted by tradition; in other words, they represent roles or characters. Thirdly, the
divine figures constitute ceremonial procedures whose role is central
to the course of the religious celebration, but here the voodoo devotee
is not satisfied with just playing a role, like a character in ancient
Greek drama; he identifies totally with the god; he is (the) god.[70] The
singing and dancing, the acts of possession, and the fundamentally
religious nature of the ceremony moved the Haitian critic Robert
Bauduy to hail voodoo as a form of 'total theatre', elements of which
could be married into a 'harmonious synthesis which opens the way
to a renewal of our drama'.[71] The catchwords 'Greek drama', 'total
theatre', and 'synthesis', and the idea of replacing psychologistic,
word-based European drama by a new type of theatre rooted in ritual
ceremony—and thus existentially 'vital' in some way to the spectator-
participants—are the leitmotifs of the Caribbean theatre of ritual.[72]
Voodoo represents an important model because it was the first Caribbean cult whose practices were marketed as a tourist attraction: its
ceremonial procedures were recognized to have a performative facet
which could be appreciated on a purely spectative and not participatory level.[73]

Parallel to the developments in francophone Haiti, anglophone
dramatists in the region began to explore the theatrical potential of
Caribbean cult rituals. A central work in this development is Derek
Walcott's play *Dream on Monkey Mountain* (1967). Although
Walcott had been experimenting since the 1950s with elements of
popular culture in his plays, particularly in *Ti-Jean and his Brothers*

[70] Louis Mars, *Témoignages* (Madrid, 1966), 41; cited in Robert Cornevin, *Le
Théâtre haïtien des origines à nos jours* (Montreal: Leméac, 1973), 193.

[71] Robert Bauduy, 'Aux sources du théâtre populaire haïtien', *Conjonction*, 24/3
(1969), 28; cited in Cornevin, *Le Théâtre haïtien des origines à nos jours*, 193.

[72] See e.g. the 'mystery play' *Shango de Ima*, written by the Cuban Pepe Carril,
which is based on the cult practices of *santería*. An English version was performed on 1
Jan. 1970 by La Mama Dance Theatre in New York. The text is reprinted in the
anthology Paul Carter Harrison (ed.), *Totem Voices: Plays from the Black World
Repertory* (New York: Grove, 1989). See also Wole Soyinka's comments on the play
by the Brazilian dramatist Zora Zeljan, *The Story of Oxala*, inspired by the *candomblé*
cult in Bahía. Soyinka, *Myth, Literature and the African World*, 16–18. The text was
published in *Transition*, 47 (1974).

[73] Under the influence of tourism voodoo ritual performance has developed at least
three distinct forms: genuine ritual for Haitian worshippers; a mixed, but secularized,
form for Haitians and tourists; and finally a form performed exclusively for tourists.
See Michelle Anderson, 'Authentic Voodoo is Synthetic', *Drama Review*, 26/2 (1982),
89–110.

(1959), *Dream on Monkey Mountain* is by far his most complex attempt to fuse the ritual culture of syncretic cults with a Western dramaturgical structure, in this case that of the Expressionist dreamplay. It tells the story of the poor charcoal-burner Makak, who is arrested for drunkenness while visiting town. In his cell he is possessed by a spirit, which causes him to have a dream. The events of the dream provide for most of the action of the play. In a prefatory note revealing intertextual references to the foreword of Strindberg's *A Dream Play*, Walcott draws attention to the importance of the dream as a dramaturgical device:

The play is a dream, one that exists as much in the given minds of its principal characters as in that of its writer, and as such, it is illogical, derivative, contradictory. Its source is metaphor and it is best treated as a physical poem with all the subconscious and deliberate borrowings of poetry. Its style should be spare, essential as the details of a dream.[74]

Into this dramaturgical structure Walcott incorporates ritual elements such as possession, faith healing, masks, and dances of the *shango* cult. As already mentioned, the dream itself is induced by a fit of possession, to which Makak is quite prone, as he mentions in the prologue: 'Sirs, I does catch fits. I fall in a frenzy every full-moon night. I does be possessed. And after that, sir, I am not responsible. I responsible only to God who once speak to me in the form of a woman on Monkey Mountain. I am God's warrior.'[75] A short time later, Makak begins to describe and then to act out possession in the prison cell:

> I feel my spine straighten,
> My hand grow strong.
> My blood was boiling
> Like a brown river in flood,
> And in that frenzy,
> I let out a cry,
> I charged the spears about me,
> Grasses and branches,
> I began to dance,
> With the splendour of a lion,
> Faster and faster,
> Faster and faster,
> Then, my body sink,

[74] Walcott, *Dream on Monkey Mountain*, 208.   [75] Ibid. 226.

> My bones betray me
> And I fall on the forest floor,
> Dead, on sweating grass.[76]

The acting-out of these verses is accompanied by frenetic drumming. The kinesic signs represent a state of extreme affective arousal suggesting the practices of *shango* or a similar cult, in which drumming and dancing are used to induce possession. The metaphors and images of movement in the quoted verses correspond closely to ethnographic accounts of the physiological symptoms produced by possession: violent physical convulsions and dancing to the point of exhaustion.[77]

This scene functions on two levels: firstly in terms of its immediate theatrical impact as the act of possession is depicted on stage. The second level is one of dramaturgical and diegetic function: Makak tells his cell-mates and the audience his life story. This framing device is an important means of distancing and filtering the ritual elements. The following action is both a product of the oneiric–liminal realm of possession, a ritual act, and at the same time a dream. Walcott has stated that the dramaturgical device of the dream was necessary in order to mediate the direct force of the ritual acts on stage: 'In *Dream*, the frenzy comes out of a man's relationship to his dream. If this had been realized more heraldically, its power would have been akin to the power of Shango. Yet this might have been impossible, for if the play becomes that powerful, it becomes the ceremony it is imitating.'[78] Walcott is a dramatist and not a *houngan* (voodoo priest); he is more than conscious of the fact that the depiction of ritual acts on stage must obey certain aesthetic laws.[79]

---

[76] Ibid. 229.

[77] The physiological signs are well described by George E. Simpson, *Religious Cults of the Caribbean*, in connection with *shango* (pp. 26–32), with voodoo (pp. 263–9), and with Jamaican cults (pp. 166–7).

[78] Ciccarelli, 'Reflections before and after Carnival: Interview with Derek Walcott', 229.

[79] In this regard Walcott differs from some of the more radical exponents of ritual theatre such as Artaud and the Living Theater. He terms their experiments 'pseudo-barbarous revivals of primitive tragedy [. . .] acts of absolution, gropings for the outline of pure tragedy, rituals of washing in the first darkness'. Walcott, *Dream on Monkey Mountain and Other Plays*, 6. He considers their efforts to be little more than a despairing response of Western theatre artists to the lack of genuine ritual experience in their own societies.

The ritual acts depicted in *Dream on Monkey Mountain* include faith healing in part 1 as well as numerous dances and, as perhaps the most spectacular act, the beheading of the White Goddess by Makak in part 2. While this ceremonial execution and the nightmarish dance scenes are entirely products of Makak's oneiric fantasies and thus cannot be linked to existing Caribbean cultural texts, the faith-healing scene is based on rituals which are drawn from the reality of Caribbean revivalist cults. The stage direction introducing the scene accentuates the highly theatrical nature of the ritual practices of such cults:

White-robed women, members of a sisterhood, bearing torches, swirl onto the stage, which is now a country road. Behind them, carrying a shrouded SICK MAN in a bamboo hammock, are four bearers and a tall frock-coated man in a black silk hat, BASIL, his face halved by white make-up. The SISTERS, shaking their heads, dancing solemnly and singing, form a circle described by their leader. The bearers turn and rest the sick man down. Around him the SISTERS kneel and pray, swaying, trying to exorcise his sickness.[80]

The whole process of the attempted and finally successful healing of the sick person is accompanied by carefully orchestrated drum rhythms, dance, and song. Makak's healing act—he holds hot coals in his hand—corresponds to similar practices in voodoo ceremonies, in which devotees in trance take up dangerous objects such as burning coals without any physical harm.[81] It is also significant that the dance and song elements of the healing scene were borrowed from an existing choreography, which was in turn inspired by folk elements, chiefly drawn from the *shango* cult.[82]

A further problem associated with depicting rituals on stage is the relationship of the audience to the mythology and cosmology underpinning such practices. In this regard Walcott's comments on the

[80] Walcott, *Dream on Monkey Mountain and Other Plays*, 243.

[81] For examples of such ceremonies, see Simpson, *Religious Cults of the Caribbean*, 262.

[82] Walcott drew on the dance 'Spirits', which was choreographed by Beryl MacBurnie for the Trinidad dance troupe Little Carib Company. In a newspaper article entitled 'Patterns to Forget' Walcott praises this dance as a model for Caribbean musical theatre: 'There have been various approaches. One has been through dance, mainly through the pioneering ballets of Beryl McBurnie, of which the most memorable was her "Spirit". [. . .] But even "Spirit", self-contained as it was, suggested a sequence from a longer work, since its dramatic progression was so overwhelming.' 'Patterns to Forget', *Trinidad Guardian*, 13 July 1966, 5. See also Ch. 6.

plays of his African colleague Wole Soyinka illuminate the problem of the Caribbean theatre artist working in the Afro-European syncretic culture. As we have already seen, both Walcott and Soyinka were working parallel as directors and dramatists on the problem of fashioning syncretic theatre out of the double heritage of Western dramaturgy and indigenous performance culture. In 1966 Walcott directed Soyinka's play *The Road* for the Trinidad Theatre Workshop. Very much propelled by the groundswell of the Africanist movement, which was gathering momentum throughout the Caribbean at the time, Walcott and his actors were confronted with the problem of familiarizing themselves with the complex cosmology of the Yoruba belief system. Despite the existence of numerous retentions of West African, and particularly Yoruba, culture in the Caribbean, the group was ultimately dealing with an alien mythology. In his theatrical essay 'What the Twilight Says' Walcott speaks of the problems involved in resurrecting 'dead gods', as he calls them, within the framework of a theatrical performance: 'Ogun was an exotic for us, not a force. We could pretend to enter his power but he would never possess us, for our invocations were not prayer but devices.'[83] Ultimately the Theatre Workshop found itself in the same dilemma as Artaud's epigones on the experimental stages of New York and London.

The ritual practices of a syncretic cult also provide the basis for the play *An Echo in the Bone* (1974) by the Jamaican dramatist, director, and poet Dennis Scott.[84] In this drama we see a ritual, which is an essential part of the spiritual fabric of its society, forming the framework of an entire play. The work is based on a Nine Night ceremony,

---

[83] Soyinka and his play *The Road* are the subject of two articles by Derek Walcott: 'Opening the Road', *Sunday Guardian* (Trinidad), 23 Oct. 1966, 6; 'Soyinka—a Poet not Content with Genius', *Sunday Guardian* (Trinidad), 12 Jan. 1969, 13.

[84] The text is published in the anthology *Plays for Today*, edited by Errol Hill. *An Echo in the Bone* was premièred in Jamaica in 1974 and since then has been performed numerous times throughout the Caribbean and abroad. Despite the unbroken interest in the play on the part of directors and actors, it has attracted very little academic scholarship. A very good general discussion can be found in Errol Hill's introduction to *Plays for Today*, 8–14; see also Gibbons, 'Traditional Enactments of Trinidad—Towards a Third Theatre', 92–6; Victor Questel's searching review 'Unlocking the Gates of History', *Tapia* (Trinidad), 19 Dec. 1976, 12–13, and Renu Juneja, 'Recalling the Dead in Dennis Scott's *An Echo in the Bone*', *Ariel*, 23 (Jan. 1992), 97–114.

a widespread death ritual practised in Jamaica. A wake is held nine nights after the deceased person's death to ensure that the spirit is expedited away and will leave the family in peace. The ceremony consists of singing, dancing, games, and storytelling, and, depending on the denomination or sect performing it, can vary considerably. The social milieu of *An Echo in the Bone*, poor farm labourers, and the ritualistic elements of the ceremony—drumming, spirit possession, rum-drinking, and ganja-smoking—suggest that the participants are followers of a revivalist cult such as *pocomania* or even *kumina*, syncretic cults with a high retention of African culture.[85]

The action takes place in an old barn, nine nights after the disappearance of Crew, a peasant labourer, and the murder of the landowner Mr Charles. Crew is suspected of the murder and his wife Rachel believes him drowned. She decides to hold a wake, a Nine Night, and gathers together her sons Jacko and Son Son, her daughter-in-law Brigit, a mute drummer, and various other friends. The play is structured round this ceremony but is interspersed by a number of historical flashbacks to the slave-trade and ends with the murder. The ritual framework enables the play to range widely in time and space. As Errol Hill comments, through 'the transforming power of ritual ceremony' the 'mundane stage picture becomes a slave ship moored off the African coast, the auctioneer's office, a grocer's shop, a wooded hillside, a Great House, a field, and a room in Rachel's cottage'. The characters themselves also undergo changes and take on a number of roles. 'Here the act of possession, which is the central objective of the ritual, induces a change of persona in the possessed individual without any obvious change in facial makeup or dress.'[86]

Of the plays considered here, *An Echo in the Bone* is perhaps the one which explores to the greatest extent the theatrical possibilities of ritual. In so doing Dennis Scott establishes, or, better perhaps, re-

---

[85] Among Jamaican revivalist cults can be subsumed a number of cults which arose in the wake of the so-called Great Revival religious movement of 1860–1. See Seaga, *Revival Cults in Jamaika*. According to Sylvia Wynter, these syncretistic revivalist cults can be arranged along an Afro-Christian continuum: 'On the more African side *Convince*, *Kumina*; in the middle of the continuum, *Pukkumina* [*pocomania*], and on the more Christian end, *Zion Revival*.' Sylvia Wynter, 'Jonkonnu in Jamaica: Towards the Interpretation of Folk Dance as a Cultural Process'. *Jamaica Journal* (June 1970), 40.

[86] Dennis Scott, *An Echo in the Bone*, in Hill (ed.), *Plays for Today*, 11.

establishes, the link between the aesthetic stage of Western theatre and the transforming power of ritual-based performance. Scott's play comes closest to actual re-enactment on stage: the drumming, rum-drinking, libations, and recital of the dead-wake litany.[87] The act of possession becomes a kind of paradigm, a ritual equivalent, for the modern convention of role-playing on the stage where one actor can assume a multiplicity of roles. The play combines the aesthetic framework of film—the action is structured around a series of flashbacks—yet its belief system is fundamentally Afro-Caribbean. The acceptance of causal links between a family in the present and the slave-ships of 1792 is one that may tend to strain the credibility of spectators. However, for cults such as *pocomania* and especially *kumina*, where strong ties with the ancestors and ancestor-worship are key notions, such causality is an integral part of the belief system and ceremonial practice.[88] It is a characteristic of many non- or semi-literate cultures that the oral tradition functions to a far greater degree than in scribal cultures to keep the memory of past generations very much alive and immediate through frequent invocation of their lives and deeds.[89] The memory of degradation, both racial and personal, is clearly something that cannot be forgotten or erased through political independence and a change in political structures. As the old cannabis-grower P puts it:

> Three hundred years crying into the white man's ground, to make the cane green, and nothing to show. [. . .] Nothing to show! That's what he always said. And then they plough you back into the canes, and nobody remember how strong you was. [. . .]
> RACHEL. I remember. I remember. Thirty years long like three hundred. [*Hums and the others follow.*][90]

---

[87] Ibid. 84.

[88] On ancestor worship amongst the followers of the *kumina* cult, see Maureen Warner Lewis, *The Nkuyu: Spirit Messengers of the Kumina* (Mona: Savacou Publications, 1977).

[89] The anthropologist Melville J. Herskovits cites an example of ritualized 'acting out' of the slave past in a dance performed by a group of negroes (*sic*) in Paramaribo in then Dutch Guiana: 'Spectators who had been sitting joined the ring of dancers, and circled about close behind each other until one of them shouted: "You'll have to get up early tomorrow. There's a lot of work!" The character was that of the "overseer"; the action had thrown back to the time of slavery.' 'Dramatic Expression among Primitive Peoples', *Yale Review*, 33 (1943–4), 693 f.

[90] Scott, *An Echo in the Bone*, 86 f.

On the one hand, the 'echo in the bone' is personal and familial memory kept alive by the oral tradition and ritual ceremonies; on the other, it is deeply ingrained racial memory, transmitted by and located in the collective unconscious of the race or culture. Scott seems to be operating with a concept which is close to C. G. Jung's definition of the collective unconscious as primal images and archetypal symbols which connect all races and form the common psycho-mythical bedrock of all mankind. It is important to remember, as Jung himself stressed, that it is not the images themselves which are transmitted, but the ability to imagine them. Just as Freud explored and deciphered the symbolic language of dreams as a *via regia* to the unconscious of the individual, so too can the act of spirit possession be seen as a means of unlocking the racial memory of a cultural group.

Besides having such wider dramaturgical functions, spirit possession is depicted on stage in exact ethnographic detail. At the commencement of the Nine Night ceremony, before Rachel has consecrated the barn, the peasant farmer Dreamboat is seized by an unexpected fit of possession, brought on by rum being spilled on the floor. The other participants interpret Dreamboat's possession as a sign that the spirit of Crew has returned. Using stage directions, dialogue and production photographs, it is possible to reconstruct the 'dramaturgy' of possession and compare it to accounts in the ethnographic literature.[91]

After the rum is spilled, Dreamboat becomes rigid; he begins to breathe heavily and his whole body gyrates (Plate 1). The drummer, Rattler, accompanies the physical movements with a rhythm.

DREAM in the silence, pants loud and fast. The others watch him motionless. His head begins to swivel on his neck, slowly till the whole body is weaving on the spot. His feet shuffle a little, then . . .

RATTLER crouches over the drum, picks up the beat softly, moaning a little with concentration.[92]

(See Plates 1–4.) According to ethnographic research into Jamaican revivalist cults, impending possession is normally signalled by a temporary loss of consciousness—the possessed person falls to the ground—and by intensive hyperventilation. This rhythmic breathing glides over into an analogous body rhythm supported by

---

[91] The photographs are of a production staged at the Creative Arts Centre of the University of the West Indies, Mona, Jamaica, in Mar. 1990, directed by Earl Warner.
[92] Scott, *An Echo in the Bone*, 80.

drumming.[93] The violence of an attack can throw the possessed person to the ground (see Plate 2), especially when an attack comes unexpectedly, as in this scene. The fact that rum was accidentally spilled before the preparatory ritual could be properly carried out has caused the spirit to return unexpectedly and therefore in a dangerous state. This kind of unprepared possession can even result in death, according to the followers of this cult. As Madam says: 'He [the deceased Crew] inside the boy trying to get out, and the heart will break open if the oil is not put on his head and his mouth soon.'[94] (See Plate 3.) The oil she mentions, which evidently has strong symbolic healing powers, is promptly administered and brings about the desired effect.

> STONE grapples with DREAMBOAT. They lurch together then fall. STONE pins him down, the candle is held close triumphantly. MADAM makes the sign of the cross on the boy's head, then wets his lips with the oil. DREAMBOAT arches onto his shoulders, shuddering, lies quiet.[95]

(See Plate 4.) This scene demonstrates how Christian symbols are reinterpreted in a way typical of syncretic cults. The candles, the sign of the cross, and the anointment are signifiers of the Christian belief system, which, depending on the confession, have a clearly defined referent with, in most cases, symbolic or metaphorical significance. In the context of possession such traditional symbols are redefined and used as directly efficacious and not just as symbolic devices against the dangers of the spirit world.

Comparable syncretisms can be found in the scene immediately following Dreamboat's possession, in which Rachel carries out the proper rites for initiating a Nine Night ceremony. This ceremony is, as already described, a rite in remembrance of the deceased. As with possession, the ritual acts consist of a combination of kinetic, musical,

[93] See particularly Edward Seaga, who compares possession in *pocomania* and Revival Zion. In *pocomania* the possessed person loses consciousness for a short time; when he or she can stand again unaided, the breathing recommences: 'At this point, the behaviour known as "groaning" or overbreathing begins. [. . .] Accompanying this groaning is a genuflecting or a bowing motion, in which the upper half of the body bends forward [. . .] Each bend is accompanied by an exhalation-groan, with the inhalation-groan on the upswing, setting a one-two beat. (This beat sets the rhythm for the accompanying music.) [. . .] The zion possession pattern is usually not abrupt in its onset. Groaning usually precedes the possession, as it seems helpful in stimulating the trance stage, since the sounds attract the spirits. (Physiologically, the repeated deep inhalation and exhalation also inebriates the mind.)' Seaga, *Revival Cults in Jamaika*, 7.
[94] Scott, *An Echo in the Bone*, 81.   [95] Ibid. 81 f.

and verbal signs, whose structure is precisely laid down by the author. Rhythmical genuflection is followed by drumming and a kind of liturgical call-and-response chant, which lead into possession:

RACHEL. My friends. My children.

> [*In turn she goes to each, stands before him a moment, bows dippingly, so that the motion carries through her whole body in a ripple. As she bows,* RATTLER *makes the drum cry in a cie. She seats herself.*]

P. [*waveringly, sings. The others join in, one by one. The drum joins them*].
He was tempted by the devil in de wilderness, [*repeat*]
Forty days and forty nights inna de wilderness, [*repeat*].

> [*The verse becomes a humming, sustained under the litany.*]

MADAM. Who is dead?
RACHEL. A man.
P. What is his name?
RACHEL. Crew.
DREAM. Where him come from?
RACHEL. Darkness.[96]

(See Plate 5.) Rachel's rhythmical genuflections and the supporting percussive rhythms have a clear African provenance, while the call-and-response chant suggests Christian liturgy. However, the antiphonal structure of the chant also has parallels in African call-and-response songs.[97] The combination has once again a trance-inducing effect. Although the text does not explicitly require possession at this point, Plate 5 shows that in Earl Warner's production a state analogous to possession was depicted. By intensifying the action to a state of possession the director was able to highlight the framing function of this scene for the rest of the play. For this scene provides the essential transition into the historical flashbacks and the background to the conflict: the murder of the landowner.

Both ritual acts, Dreamboat's accidental fit of possession and Rachel's litany, represent cultural texts in Lotman's sense. In terms of their functionality, structure, and generic organization, as well as their production and reception within a particular culture, they correspond in all essential aspects to Lotman's definition. Dreamboat's possession follows a recognizable and predictable sequence of events.

---

[96] Scott, *An Echo in the Bone*, 84.
[97] According to Simpson, 'antiphonal singing' as a characteristic feature of the *shango* cult is an example of this cult's reinterpretation of African elements in its ritual procedures. Simpson, *Religious Cults of the Caribbean*, 106.

His actions are 'read' by the others, and even to some extent directed by the drummer, Rattler. Similarly, the antiphonal chant between Rachel and her family follows a clear textual pattern. The signs of this text are not, however, just verbal, but also kinetic and musical. The fact that these cultural texts, which occupy an important place in the fabric of Caribbean religious culture, have both immediate theatrical effect as well as a dramaturgical function, demonstrates that theatrical syncretism can be highly complex indeed. Besides this formal innovation, the use of such cultural texts offers considerable potential for identification. The convergence of the religio-spiritual horizon of the spectator with the ritual practice shown is a necessary ingredient for a more intense theatrical experience which goes beyond a voyeuristic delectation of the rites performed. Although Scott's play comes very close to becoming 'the ceremony it is imitating', to refer back to Walcott's admonition, it manages to fracture the actual ceremonial procedure by the many flashbacks and include a historical and critical dimension which clearly situates the play finally in an aesthetic context.

The examples of ritual-based theatre I have surveyed in this chapter form together an extraordinarily complex set of aesthetic strategies. They range from experiments in ritualizing the whole framework of the theatrical experience—as is the case in Maori theatre in New Zealand—to various attempts to incorporate indigenous ritual elements into the dramaturgy of plays. In the latter cases ritualization leads almost invariably to dramaturgical structures which pay little heed either to the Aristotelian unities or to strictly empirical coordinates of time and space. The oneiric world of rite has its own laws which provide access to other experiential dimensions, the realm of the 'fourth stage', as Soyinka terms it. On the level of theatre aesthetics, the experimentation with ritual devices enables dramatists and directors to utilize the full range of performative idioms. Ritual-based theatre transcends purely dialogic drama and employs language, song, the semiotics of the body, dance, and spatial concepts. In the following chapters these elements will be analysed in more depth as means by which indigenous performance forms are syncretized in various combinations with Western theatre and drama.

CHAPTER THREE
Language and the Post-Colonial Stage

> [W]hen we borrow an alien language to sculpt or paint in, we must begin by co-opting the entire properties in our matrix of thought and expression. We must press such a language, stretch it, impact and compact, fragment and reassemble it with no apology, as required to bear the burden of experiencing and of experiences, be such experiences formulated or not in the conceptual idioms of that language.
>
> (Wole Soyinka, *Art, Dialogue and Outrage*)

OF all the theatrical sign systems language appears to be the most stable. The fact that the dramatic text is fixed by means of a form of notation, which in comparison to the other sign systems is highly developed and standardized, means that the linguistic component of theatrical production should remain relatively constant. But language in general, and dramatic language in particular, is subject to numerous influences which show that the superficial stability conceals in fact a highly labile form of communication. What appear on the printed page of the dramatic text to be stable, even relatively incontrovertible, meanings accumulate in the act of enunciation on stage a range of additional signifiers. These can manifest themselves in the form of accents, intonation, or dialectal colouring, on the one hand, and through the addition of non-linguistic signs such as gesture, on the other. It is well known that alterations to accepted linguistic conventions in the use of stage language such as the introduction of dialect or other language variants have at various times led to highly explosive reactions on the part of audience reception. Such reactions suggest that the conventions of stage language are always subject to shifting factors affecting the communication between characters on stage and between stage and audience.

In the context of syncretic theatre we must add to these structural characteristics a number of important cultural components, which derive almost without exception from the fact that in most post-colonial countries europhone syncretic theatre is situated in a bi- or multilingual context.[1] The problem of multilingualism is the overall framework determining the aspects of stage language that will be examined in this chapter. The first factor is ideological. The choice of the colonial language as the means of dramatic expression is fraught with social and political implications. There is a vigorous debate in progress, especially in Africa and India, on the question of colonial languages as literary languages. Secondly, multilingualism is itself utilized as a stage device. Most play texts under discussion in fact make use of more than one language. Switching languages in specific contexts and from one mode of expression to another is a feature of syncretic theatre. We will examine when and why this takes place. Thirdly, the existence of bi- and multilingual cultures has resulted in experimentation with forms of translation. Many post-colonial dramatists, although they write in English, are concerned to let the rhythms and syntax of their indigenous language manifest themselves in the europhone language. One interesting form of translation is self-translation. Here a dramatist adapts a drama which already exists in one language into a europhone language. This involves not only linguistic transferral but often also the adaptation of dramatic and theatrical conventions. In India in particular there is a strong tradition of self-translation and 'transcreation', as the process is termed there.

Ideology(s)

The choice of the colonial language as primary means of theatrical communication is by no means an uncontroversial one. Particularly in Africa there has been and still is a lively discussion on the question of using colonial languages as an adequate and legitimate

---

[1] This also applies to Caribbean countries, where, alongside the europhone standard languages, creole languages have established themselves as distinct linguistic entities. The status of creole languages is subject to debate. Because of the so-called 'creole continuum' Caribbean countries are termed 'polyglossic' or 'polydialectal' rather than polylingual. This categorization is based on the assumption that creoles are not distinct languages or dialects as much as overlapping ways of speaking, which move along a continuum; see Ashcroft *et al.*, *The Empire Writes Back*, 44–7.

means of literary or theatrical expression. The often extremely polarized positions and strident tone accompanying the debate are understandable in the context of the orgins of europhone drama in Africa. The first generation of African dramatists were members of an educated élite, who appeared to be directing their works at the very same circle and thus excluding the vast majority of the people. Perhaps the best-known exponent of this ideological critique is the Kenyan novelist and dramatist Ngugi wa Thiong'o. After considerable success in the 1960s writing novels and plays in English, Ngugi effected a radical break with this praxis in the mid-1970s and devoted himself to writing and publishing primarily in his mother tongue *Gĩkũyũ*. It is significant that this break went hand in hand with his own political radicalization, which was particularly manifested in his theatre work. In his essay 'The Language of African Theatre' he points out the contradictions inherent in his own early dramas, which required the acceptance of a number of conventions, 'where everybody speaks impeccable English, although it is understood that the characters are actually speaking in an African language. [. . .] There are other contradictions too: these characters speak English but when it comes to singing they quite happily and naturally fall back into their languages.'[2] It is of course understandable that Ngugi wishes to attain for his plays the immediacy of a monolingual situation without having to resort to artificial conventions. One consequence of his position is that he reduces stage language to simple naturalistic mimeticism, thus depriving it of the semiotic flexibility that such conventions imply. For this reason and because of such semiotic potential the anglophone Yoruba dramatist Ola Rotimi has dismissed the ideologically motivated language debate which seeks to restrict the writer to a simple choice between African or European as unproductive and ill suited to African linguistic contexts: 'The real issue should not be *why* an African writer resorts to perpetuating a colonial tongue. Rather, for the debate to be worthwhile, it should bear on *how* the writer uses that tongue to express the conditions and yearnings of his linguistically *diverse* peoples.'[3] The linguistic and cultural complexity of many post-

---

[2] *Decolonizing the Mind: The Politics of Language in African Literature* (London: James Currey and Heinemann, 1986), 43.

[3] Ola Rotimi, 'The Trials of African Literature', lecture given at the University of Benin, Nigeria, 4 May 1978; quoted in Martin Banham, 'Ola Rotimi: "Humanity as my Tribesman"', *Modern Drama*, 32/1 (Mar. 1990), 75.

colonial societies, particularly on the African continent, prevents the reduction of the language debate to a simple dichotomy of African versus colonial.

Finally, a brief glance at the virulent linguistic debate in India over the status of anglophone drama should serve to illustrate that the discussion is a structural one, inherent in the legacy of colonial rule. The positions oscillate between metaphorically intended demands to slaughter anglophone dramatists: 'Butcher them (the Indo-Anglian) playwrights, castrate them, and force them to write in their native Hindi or Urdu or whatever languages their fathers and mothers used to speak,'[4] and more balanced assessments. Yet even the latter, such as the literary scholar K. R. Srinivasa Iyengar provides, see little point in producing English-language drama. He argues that, in a country where English is only in rare cases the mother tongue of the inhabitants, there is little point in writing dialogue in that language: 'the natural medium of conversation with us—excepting with the super-sophisticated who live in the cities and the larger towns, in the Universities or in certain Government offices or business houses—is the mother tongue rather than English'.[5] The underlying assumption of his statement is the one that has dominated the debate over function and status of English-language drama in India. It revolves around the central question whether Indians speaking English dialogue sound 'natural', 'convincing', or 'credible'.[6] However, criteria such as naturalness or credibility are only applicable or paramount within the framework of particular dramatic genres and theatrical conventions. They reflect a conception of theatrical language which is restricted to a simple aesthetic of mimetic reproduction of everyday reality. The irony of this debate is that in India at least the traditional theatrical forms are located in a completely anti-realistic aesthetic. Yet very few critics and scholars or dramatists seem to entertain the

[4] Dnyaneshwar Nadkarni, 'Butcher the Ando-Inglians', *Enact*, 85–6 (Jan.–Feb. 1974), n.p.; quoted in M. K. Naik, *Dimensions of Indian English Literature* (New Delhi: Sterling, 1984), 165.

[5] K. R. Srinivasa Iyengar, *Drama in Modern India and The Writer's Responsibility in a Rapidly Changing World*, Symposia at the Fourth PEN All-India Writer's Conference, Baroda, 1957 (Bombay: PEN All-India Center, 1961), 35.

[6] The most important positions on the literary language debate in general can be found in R. K. Narayan, 'English in India: The Process of Transmutation', and in Mulk Raj Anand, 'Pigeon-Indian: Some Notes on Indian English Writing', both in M. K. Naik (ed.), *Aspects of Indian Writing in English* (Delhi: Macmillan, 1979). See also G. A. Reddy, *Indian Writing in English and its Audience* (Bareilly: Prakash, 1979), esp. ch. 1: 'Language, Sensibility and the Writer' .

notion that English-language theatre could be contained in anything other than the tradition of the well-made play.

The Polyglottal Stage

The debate over the choice of language resulted in some respects in an ideological impasse. One strategy to circumvent this impasse was to ignore the simple choice of either/or and to allow two or more languages to be heard on stage. Rather than covering up linguistic difficulties by means of conventions, bi- and multilingualism began to be explicitly presented. In terms of our definition of syncretic theatre as strategies of integrating cultural texts within the Western theatrical frame, the use of indigenous languages together with or parallel to europhone languages is a theatrico-semiotic process comparable to the recoding of dances, songs, or rituals. The simultaneous presence of several languages on stage is, on the one hand, a simple problem of comprehension and semantics. On the other hand, it also reflects in complex ways the ideological issues outlined above: language in a post-colonial situation is almost always linked to questions of power.[7] In the following examples of plays from Nigeria, South Africa, Canada, and New Zealand I shall examine how the sociolinguistic 'fact' of bi- or multilingualism is turned into a powerful theatrical strategy for reflecting on a particular cultural and political situation.

When Wole Soyinka's *The Road* was premièred on 15 September 1965 in London during the first Commonwealth Arts Festival, British critics recognized immediately that a new 'voice' or 'language' had made itself heard and not just in a metaphorical sense. Although the play is written in English, when enunciated on stage with Nigerian accent and intonation, it deviates substantially from the 'Queen's English' of British theatrical tradition. If one includes the numerous passages spoken in pidgin and the occasional exchange in Yoruba, then the puzzled reaction of the London critical fraternity is understandable:

[7] It is, however, necessary to distinguish between colonial and post-colonial situations; see Ashcroft *et al.*: 'the discussion of postcolonial writing [. . .] is largely a discussion of the process by which the language, with its power, and the writing, with its signification of authority, has been wrested from the dominant European culture'. *The Empire Writes Back*, 7 f.

The Road, in performance, is tough work for local hearing. (Penelope Gilliat, *Observer*, 16 September 1965)

It's a disadvantage for English audiences that some of this poetry's obscure in idiom and imagery—you need a sharp ear and a smattering of West African mythology. (Ronald Bryden, *New Statesman*, 24 September 1965)

The music of pidgin speech and Yoruba exclamation, difficult for a non-Nigerian ear to catch, must reflect both the earthiness and the transfigura-tion. ('Keep off the Road', *The Times Literary Supplement*, 10 June 1965)

Although few of the players came from Nigeria, they reproduced the Nigerian intonation so successfully that it was difficult enough to get the literal meaning of their speeches, far less the finer points of Mr Soyinka's language. [. . .] we cannot blame the Nigerian actors because our unfamiliarity with the tonality of Nigerian English lost us many of their lines. ('Dramatic Curtain-Raiser', *The Times Educational Supplement*, 24 September 1965)

It is interesting to note that the critics cited here all, with one exception, see the play as work written in English pronounced in a difficult accent. Only the critic of *The Times Literary Supplement* points out that Soyinka uses in fact three languages: standard English, pidgin, and Yoruba. It is the performative aspect of language use, in particular the pronounced West African intonation, that renders a clear understanding of the two central linguistic levels, English and pidgin for a non-Nigerian spectator extremely difficult. As far as the variety of pidgin used is concerned, it deviates in terms of grammar and vocabulary so substantially from standard English that linguists consider it to be a distinct language in its own right.[8] If one includes performance criteria such as intonation and accent as well, then pidgin, while perhaps comprehensible on the printed page, is for a non-local theatre spectator almost totally incomprehensible. For this reason *The Road* can certainly be considered a bilingual or, if one includes the Yoruba passages, a multilingual play. The reaction of the London critics illustrates one of the difficulties that syncretic plays can cause when transplanted to another anglophone environment. It also shows that a play such as *The Road*, when performed in Lagos or Ibadan, creates a substantially different performance text than say in

---

[8] See David Decamp on pidgin and creoles: 'These are genuine languages in their own right, not just macaronic blends or interlingual corruptions of standard lan-guages.' 'Introduction: The Study of Pidgin and Creole Languages', in Dell Hymes (ed.), *Pidginization and Creolization of Languages* (Cambridge: Cambridge University Press, 1971), 15.

London, where the numerous linguistic shifts, which are so crucial to the play's meaning, are simply not comprehended.

The linguistic strategies that Soyinka follows in *The Road* work hand in hand with other sign systems in the texts to demonstrate a state of syncreticity which is a formal condition of the text and its performance and also a feature of the society it depicts, a culture in transition. The simultaneous presence of English, pidgin, and Yoruba is a metonymic representation of competing semiotic spheres, which correlate to some extent with different cultural formations in Nigerian society. David Moody, who considers *The Road* to be *the* characteristic example of a post-colonial drama, emphasizes especially the multilingual aspect of the play:

I want to suggest that [. . .] Soyinka, like other post-colonial writers in English, is producing at the margins of the inter-cultural space; that his plays speak with a language which is neither Yoruba nor English, but which, to use Homi Bhabha's term, is a 'hybrid' tongue. This 'hybrid' tongue is difficult, knotty, many-textured; it speaks not just with two discourses, but with many.[9]

According to this reading, the numerous linguistic shifts in the play are not just means of psychological or sociocultural characterization. On a more abstract level they reflect a whole society in a state of cultural transition. The post-colonial state of hybridity that Moody alludes to, in which both Western discourse and the polyethnicity of Nigeria are manifested, finds its linguistic correlation in multilingualism.

The polyethnic and polylingual state of Nigeria is the background to the most recent plays of Ola Rotimi: *If* and *Hopes of the Living Dead*.[10] In these works multilingualism is treated in ways which represent new approaches to the problem of presenting multiple languages on stage. One of these strategies is the explicit use and demonstration of translation processes on stage. In the play *If*, which is set in the backyard of an apartment block and presents a cross-section of urban Nigerian society, four separate linguistic systems are used: apart from standard English, local varieties of English, pidgin, and indigenous languages are spoken. The backyard setting provides the spatial sphere in which these various linguistic codes can interact.

---

[9] 'The Steeple and the Palm-Wine Shack: Wole Soyinka and Crossing the Inter-Cultural Fence', *Kunapipi*, 11/3 (1989), 99.
[10] 1988 is the date of publication; the first performance took place in 1985.

In the following scene three of these linguistic levels, English, pidgin, and the indigenous language Kalabari, are presented contiguously. The Kalabari-speaking fisherman is complaining to the lawyer Banji about the pollution caused by the oil industry. As the lawyer does not understand the fisherman's local language he is aided by the character Mama Rosa, who understands Kalabari, but translates into pidgin:

MAMA ROSA (*introducing Fisherman*). Dis na my broder wey I go bail now-now for Police Station, sah. Dem catch am for fishing-port say e no pay tax. Monday na court. Broder, I no know anybody for dis country. I beg make you helep me.

BANJI. I see. What really happened?

MAMA ROSA (*to Fisherman in Kalabari language*). Mioku, duko o pirii. Ye goyegoye duko o pirii. [*Meaning: Now tell him. Tell him everything.*]

FISHERMAN. Duko o pirii, yeri njibabo.

MAMA ROSA. He say him be fisherman.

FISHERMAN. Tari i da so njibabo.

MAMA ROSA. Him papa na fisherman.

FISHERMAN. Ida so tari njibaboo.

MAMA ROSA. Him papa-papa, na fisherman.

FISHERMAN. Toru me anie wamina dumo doki yee.

MAMA ROSA. No river be dem life.

FISHERMAN. Mioku torume dikibujiri ofori bara ke fi korotee.

MAMA ROSA. Now di river done spoil finish.[11]

With the help of her pidgin translation Mama Rosa is able to establish communication with the lawyer and with the majority of Nigerian spectators. By using a translation strategy of this kind multilingualism is made into an effective theatrical tool. Rotimi is able to maintain a kind of genuine naturalism without having to resort to artificial conventions such as poetical language of the kind that J. P. Clark used for his fishermen in *The Raft*. Rotimi attains in *If* an authenticity of character and situation which is different from the early mythical–historical dramas with their somewhat conventionalized English. The reasons for this change in strategy cannot be examined here, but they are certainly linked to Rotimi's growing political commitment as a result of the ethnic disputes in Nigeria, which are closely tied to issues of language and language status.

A continuation of the language experiments begun in *If* can be

---

[11] Ola Rotimi, *If: A Tragedy of the Ruled* (Ibadan: Heinemann, 1983), 25 f.

found in Rotimi's next play, *Hopes of the Living Dead*, first performed in 1985. The play is based on the life of the leper Ikoli
Harcourt Whyte and his struggle with the colonial authorities in
the 1920s to have the leper colony in Port Harcourt re-established.
Martin Banham points out that the topical relevance of this story is
reflected in the way Rotimi deals with the issue of polylingual diversity: 'The vulnerability amongst the patients that the authorities
hoped to exploit was the diversity in their backgrounds and languages. The unity that Harcourt Whyte demanded meant surmount-
ing the ignorance and prejudice created by these divisions. The
parallel with the political unity of present-day Nigeria is clear.'[12]
According to Rotimi, he uses in his play more than fifteen different
languages. The act of mediating between these languages, which is
demonstrated on stage in a series of translation chains, is not just a
dramaturgical device but is rather an integral part of the political
message of the play that linguistic diversity does not automatically
exclude political unity and cooperation. With this in mind Rotimi's
attitude to the language debate quoted at the beginning of this
chapter becomes clearer. For this African dramatist the primary
question is not whether an author should use the colonial language
or not, but rather how he uses this language on stage to demonstrate
the complex ethnicity characteristic of most African countries:

To ignore the fact of linguistic heterogeneity, is to be hypocritical, because it
is the very multi-linguality of the peoples—or to put it more bluntly—it is the
very *ethnic* promiscuity in the land that, in the first place, necessitated the
adoption of that foreign tongue to serve as a neutral base for communication
among a reasonable cross-section of the people.

The incongruity of a foreign language in an African work can further be
'tempered' by a sensitive intermingling of the foreign language with some
indigenous linguistic representations. This is most feasible in the genre of
drama, and recent experiments by this writer along this line have received
encouraging response from audiences.[13]

According to Rotimi's view the use of the colonial language has
certain advantages in terms of mutual understanding in a linguistically heterogeneous country like Nigeria. These advantages outweigh
the ideological objections when the local languages are granted status
as stage languages. Polylingualism is, for Rotimi, an ethnic fact and
political issue, the artistic and literary reflection of which can be most

[12] Banham, 'Ola Rotimi', 75.   [13] Ibid. 75 f.

effectively dealt with in the theatre. The theatrical strategies he uses—on the one hand, translation chains in which short messages in English are passed on consecutively in a number of indigenous languages; on the other, more complex communications are rendered into English in full—require from an audience both curiosity and patience. Such translation processes represent in a polyethnic state an act of considerable sociopolitical significance. The theatre attains a kind of laboratory function in the Brechtian sense of being an 'experimentelle Vorschau-Bühne'[14] for a better society. Rotimi assumes that spectators are in a situation analogous to that of the stage characters, who are dependent on the mediation and translation of others or where linguistic comprehension is often only fragmentary. It is important to note that Rotimi does not consider this receptive situation and the dramaturgical strategies reflective of it to be a specifically Nigerian problem. These are structures relevant and applicable to numerous African countries with a comparable linguistic situation. In the foreword to *Hopes of the Living Dead* he writes: 'Although specific languages are given to the characters in this play, the producer/director is not bound by these allocations. Any character may be assigned any language, depending on the linguistic varieties which the actors on hand represent. What is important is for the languages spoken to reflect the cultural spread and the linguistic diversity of the nation where it is being produced.'[15] With this 'offer' Rotimi places his text in a wider post-colonial context. The linguistic elements that Rotimi renders in *Hopes of the Living Dead* in all their naturalistic detail can also be regarded as generalized signifiers whose signifieds can be transferred to any structurally comparable situation. Of central importance is that the special semiotic processes inherent in such 'promiscuous' linguistic diversity is made visible by dramatist and director and that this fragmentariness is presented in such a way that the audience can reconstruct meanings.

One of the African countries offering clear linguistic analogies to the Nigerian situation is South Africa. Temple Hauptfleisch has

---

[14] Roughly translated, the phrase means: the stage as an experimental preview of a better society. It is taken from Ernst Bloch, 'Die Schaubühne als paradigmatische Anstalt betrachtet', in *Das Prinzip Hoffnung: E. B. Gesamtausgabe*, v (Frankfurt-on-Main: Suhrkamp, 1959), 485. Bloch is referring here explicitly to Brecht's theatre theory and praxis.

[15] Ola Rotimi, *Hopes of the Living Dead: A Drama of Struggle* (Ibadan: Spectrum Books, 1988), p. vi.

outlined the linguistic environment of South Africa and its transformation into a new set of linguistic conventions in black theatre, into what he calls 'a new poetry of the theatre stage, in a language born of the polyglot environment in and around our cities'.[16] That this new poetry can draw on anything up to eleven 'formally accepted South African languages' plus a variety of urban lingua franca such as Flaaitaal, which are composites of various linguistic elements, is quite rightly seen as 'an immensely rich mine for the playwright'.[17] The multilingual nature of township theatre is the area where the poly-cultural situation in South Africa is most apparent. One of the truly innovative features of this theatre is the fact that multilingualism is not just registered and reflected, for comic purposes for example, but can in a performance situation be implemented as a strategy to include or exclude sections of the audience, make statements about the linguistic nature of the power structures in South African society, and reflect generally on the place of language in a colonial situation.

In practice, however, the language of communication is primarily English. David Coplan has discussed the quite complex reasons for the adoption of English as the theatrical language of township theatre: 'When questioned, playwrights respond that English is the only *lingua franca* understood in townships throughout the country, but their preference for it as a medium of communication has a deeper significance.'[18] He goes on to analyse this 'deeper significance' and finds three main reasons for the use of English. Firstly, the use of an 'African' art form suggests strongly the separate development advocated by apartheid; secondly, the use of English helps overcome the sense of cultural isolation South African artists suffer from; and thirdly, it enables black artists to communicate their message, theoretically at least, to an international audience. Yet township theatre is extraordinarily multilingual. So finally the choice of the European language is motivated by a combination of ideological, pragmatic, and dramaturgical factors.

It should be noted that the use of multilingualism is by no means a preserve of black theatre artists. At the end of the 1970s the director of the Market Theatre in Johannesburg, Barney Simon, recognized that his model of a multiracial theatre in the midst of the apartheid

---

[16] Temple Hauptfleisch, 'Citytalk, Theatretalk: Dialect, Dialogue and Multilingual Theatre in South Africa', *English in Africa*, 16/1 (May 1989), 77.   [17] Ibid. 78.
[18] Coplan, *In Township Tonight*, 214.

state would have to take cognizance of the polyglottal nature of that state. By virtue of the fact that the plays produced in this period were the result of guided improvisations involving actors from various ethnic groups, these works did in fact reflect to some extent the linguistic diversity of the country. However, Simon's experimentation with multilingualism on stage established little more than a conventionalized 'theatrical sign'.[19] With the overwhelmingly white audience of the Market Theatre in mind, very few of whom had any knowledge of black languages, multilingualism had to remain in carefully circumscribed limits. Nevertheless, the spectators were confronted with indigenous languages and required to semanticize them with the help of contextual elements such as gesture.

Compared to the works produced for the Market Theatre, township theatre utilizes multilingualism in a much more complex fashion.[20] This is no doubt a reflection of the sociolinguistic environment of the townships themselves, where multilingualism is a fact of everyday life. In the township plays multilingualism is not reduced to a single function. While it has a *mimetic* function in that it reflects the linguistic reality of the townships, it can, however, also be used as a *dramaturgical strategy* for a variety of political and/or comic effects. In the latter cases African languages are used literally as a 'code', not in its semiotic sense, but in the everyday sense of an esoteric, secret system, to which only the initiated are privy. This device assumes, of course, a community of the initiated and is very much dependent on the performance context and linguistic environment; that is, it is only useful if sufficient numbers in the audience can understand the languages spoken and the dynamics engendered by frequent linguistic code-switching.

---

[19] See here the study by Anne Fuchs: 'Barney Simon's solution appears to be the best adapted to the particular circumstances: a minimum token use of African languages which would not hinder communication with a white audience but at the same time entail a certain effort on their part and so constitute a theatrical "sign".' Fuchs is referring to the two collaborative projects *Black Dog* (1984) and *Born in the RSA* (1985). She also points out that both works were influenced by Simon's experience with the township play *Woza Albert!*, particularly concerning the conscious experimentation with language(s): 'In *Black Dog* language differences were systematized and became part of what Barney himself qualifies as "the different cultures" he attempted to juxtapose on stage.' Anne Fuchs, *Playing the Market: The Market Theatre Johannesburg 1976–1986* (Chur: Harwood, 1990), 70 f.

[20] It should be noted here that there existed and still exists a close relationship between black theatre artists and the Market Theatre. Many of the works termed township theatre have been produced for, or at least performed at the Market.

There are countless situations in these plays where the multilingualism of the black actors–characters and that of the black audience
demonstrates a situation of superiority over white characters, who
may speak only one, at the most two, European languages and
certainly no African language. However, examples of the opposite
dynamic can also be found. The use of language by white authorities
as a vehicle of oppression is most vividly demonstrated in scene 2 of
Asinamali!, a work created by Mbongeni Ngema in collaboration
with the performers. In this scene the young Zulu boy Bheki is tried
and sentenced for a series of unrelated offences. A trilingual situation
is depicted: the judge speaks Afrikaans, which is rendered into English by the court interpreter; the defendant understands neither language particularly well, and so fragments of these exchanges are
translated into Zulu by a Court Orderly. He in turn *selectively*
translates the defendant's responses back to the judge. Each rendering
results in shifts and slants of meaning until the defendant, Bheki, is
struggling like a hapless fish in a net, enmeshed in legal procedures
which are everything else but transparent. In performance this linguistic confusion is further underlined by the fact that these
exchanges actually gain acoustic momentum during the course of
the trial until there is almost Babylonian turmoil.

This example of victimization, where language is used as an instrument of oppression, is more than compensated for by situations in
which multilingualism creates an area of freedom in which revenge
can be exacted and satirical attacks levelled at white society. Certain
exchanges are clearly not intended for white consumption. For example, intertribal jokes are made in African languages. In Percy Mtwa's
play *Bopha!* Naledi sits 'singing to pass the time' and sings in Zulu:
'I'd rather be like Xhosas and Pondons / and carry shit-buckets on my
shoulders.'[21] A similar remark is made by Zulu Boy in *Woza Albert!*:
'Yabhodla ingane yenZule ukuba okungu—MSuthu ngabe kudala
kuzinyele. [There burps the son of a Zulu; if it was a Sotho he would
be shitting.]'[22] Also much sexually explicit language and humour is
spoken in an African language and thus reserved for the African
audience. There is a good deal of cursing in Afrikaans, too, but of

---

[21] Percy Mtwa, *Bopha!*, in Duma Ndlovu (ed.), *Woza Afrika! An Anthology of South African Plays* (New York: Braziller, 1986), 235.
[22] Percy Mtwa, Mbongeni Ngema, and Barney Simon , *Woza Albert!* (first performed 1982; first pub. 1983), in Ndlovu (ed.), *Woza Afrika! An Anthology of South African Plays*, 37.

the non-literal expletive variety, whereas elaborate sexual metaphors and descriptions are probably reserved for the African languages. In *Bopha!* for example, two black policemen speak Zulu in the presence of the white man one of them has arrested: 'Pis in die straat. Angeke ahamba abonisa umthondo wakhe obomyu yonke indawo. [He was pissing in the street, he cannot expose his red penis all over the place.]'[23] The first part of the statement is in Afrikaans, and comprehensible to the culprit and the whole audience; the rest of the comment, however, is reserved for the Zulu-speakers. Of course, the linguistic situation is not always so clearly demarcated. *Bopha!* includes a scene where Naledi's disparaging comment to his brother in Zulu about Captain Van Donder is in fact understood by the recipient:

NAL. Leyatela leburu lena abuti man! [This Boer is obstinate!]
CAP. Hey wie's 'n boer? [Who is a Boer?] Njandini, polisieman of nie polisieman, BOPHA![24]

This dynamic of inclusion and exclusion is also very evident in the extensive use of songs, not one of which is in a European language. The songs have other functions besides. They can serve such diverse purposes as affective arousal, political agitation, and the invoking of cultural and tribal tradition. But of course in all these categories the actual textual message, whether it be important or not, whether it conveys a note of political protest or a joke at the expense of the Whites, for this part of the theatrical performance, black performers and black spectators are communicating directly, while the white audience, for the most part, can only guess at what is being expressed. *Bopha!*, for example, uses throughout the action a well-known protest song, 'Siyayi nyova', in which the audience can and does join in.

Multilingualism is a central element in the most recent productions of the Johannesburg-based theatre group Junction Avenue Theatre Company, founded in 1976. With its programmatic commitment to multiracial theatre at the height of apartheid it occupied an interesting position between white theatre and black township groups during the 1980s and early 1990s. An element it shared with many committed theatre groups in South Africa of this period was the collective production process. Their most successful production

[23] Mtwa, *Bopha!*, 244.   [24] Ibid. 250.

was *Sophiatown!* (1986), which depicts life in the Johannesburg suburb of that name during the 1950s. During these years Sophiatown became synonymous with the multiracial coexistence of an emerging urban culture, and for this reason as much as any other it was literally steamrollered out of existence by the authorities. The multilingual nature of this work—besides English we find Afrikaans, the 'gangster' language Tsotsitaal, as well as a number of African languages being spoken and sung—serves to reflect the sociolinguistic reality of the environment without the use of translation conventions. For example, one scene (Act 1, scene 4) is performed as a language lesson almost entirely in Tsotsitaal. As Temple Hauptfleisch puts it: 'Simply by admitting the *possibility* of a multilingual conversational convention, the "mirroring" of reality is, at this level at least, far more "real" than in most previous plays.'[25] With the exception of the Tsotsitaal scene, however, languages other than English are either kept on a quantitatively manageable level so that monolingual reception is not seriously endangered, or they are present in the form of conventions such as songs which can be apprehended on a musical rather than a linguistic-semantic level.

The language problem receives an entirely different treatment in Junction Avenue's more recent work *Tooth and Nail* (1989). This production signalled a new direction in the group's conception of theatre. The previous works were all concerned with depicting aspects of South Africa's 'hidden history' using a dramaturgy of epic narration. In the new work, however, narrative coherence was abandoned in favour of a fragmentary theatre, heavily influenced by the work of Tadeusz Kantor. *Tooth and Nail* consists of a series of approximately 100 images or fragments, in which ten characters experience what Malcolm Purkey, the group's leader, called 'living in the interregnum',[26] i.e. the fragmentation of South African reality in the liminal state between apartheid and post-apartheid. Multilingualism, recognized as a crucial factor in South African life, is represented by an 'Interpreter' figure. This character mediates between languages and cultures, translating and distorting in turn. Malcolm Purkey points out that this language 'game' is at the same time a reflection of the central issue of language politics: 'It is a game of when which part of

[25] Hauptfleisch,'Citytalk, Theatretalk', 83.
[26] Malcolm Purkey, 'Fighting Tooth and Nail', Paper presented at the conference 'Theatre and Politics in South Africa', Bad Boll, Germany, 13 Dec. 1989.

the audience hears what. What do they say? Is the translation accurate? Is it a commentary? [. . .] So all of that makes sense to audiences in different ways. And then you can play games where you send out messages in one language so the other group can't understand and so on.'[27] As in Ola Rotimi's conception, translation and multilingualism are staged ostensively in order to highlight that discrepancies, misunderstandings, and partial semanticization are endemic to multicultural societies and that any political action must take cognizance of this state of multiple semiosis.

For a final example I shall shift the focus from a multi- to the bilingual situation of Maori theatre in New Zealand. Although Maori is still the language of ceremonial protocol, it is seldom used in everyday contexts and is no longer the first language of the majority of young urban Maori. This means that an increasing number of Maori are, strictly speaking, no longer able to participate in the formal discussions and decision-making processes of *marae* meetings. Against the background of the renaissance of Maori culture and language, to which the theatre movement has in no small way contributed, the language issue is a central one.

The importance of Maori as a language for the new theatrical movement is evident in what is probably the first play written by a Maori, Harry Dansey's *Te Raukura: The Feathers of the Albatross* (1974).[28] This historical play dealing with the life of the Maori prophet Te Ua Haumene, the founder of the *hau hau* cult in the 1860s,[29]

---

[27] Interview with Malcolm Purkey, in Gabriele Grosse Perdekamp, 'Junction Avenue Theatre Company mit Tooth and Nail. Kontrapunkt-Montage als theatrale Momentaufnahme des südafrikanischen Interregnums', University of Munich MA thesis, 1992, 22. In the same interview Purkey points out the political implications of the language situation: 'we are in a very complex situation, with a very complex multilingual political situation. Like many countries we are faced with the dilemma of: Which will be the language of post-Apartheid South Africa? How do we run our processes? [. . .] if you go to any trade union meeting they will speak in English, then in Zulu, then in Tswana, then in Sotho. So translation is very fundamental to our lives. Mistranslation, misunderstanding, language gaps, language problems are fundamental to South African dilemmas.' (Ibid.)

[28] *Te Raukura* was commissioned by the Auckland Festival Society. The première took place in 1972 at the Mercury Theatre, Auckland, directed by John S. Thompson.

[29] *Hau hau* was a syncretic religion, typical of many which emerged in the second half of the 19th century in colonized countries. See the New Zealand historian Keith Sinclair's laconic summation: 'Te Ua founded a new faith, compounded of a little Old Testament morality and Christian doctrine and some primitive Maori religion. He invoked the Holy Trinity, but revived cannibalism.' Keith Sinclair, *A History of New Zealand*, 3rd edn. (Harmondsworth: Penguin, 1980), 140.

was written *ex nihilo*, as it were, as Dansey had no dramatic models in the modern Maori cultural tradition to draw on. Dansey outlines in his foreword to the play that he was primarily concerned to create historical and cultural authenticity. As well as integrating authentic dances, chants, and songs, he sought a means to incorporate the Maori language without causing insurmountable difficulties for a non-Maori audience. To solve the problem he created a special dramatic convention whereby Maori characters would begin an exchange in their own language but continue in English. But this English, according to Dansey, also bore traces of the Maori language:

It might be of interest to note that many parts of the play were written first in Maori and then recast in English. Thus here and there I like to think that something of the feel of the Maori situation has remained like an echo among the English words. I would ask myself the question: 'How would people say this?' And I found this best answered by letting them say it in Maori first. Though I was tempted to leave whole sequences in Maori untranslated, this might have appeared pretentious and was resisted. Nevertheless not all have been translated. I do not think these untranslated passages interfere with understanding the play as a whole. It means a sharper definition here and there, a bonus as it were for those who understand Maori. One effect of this in the Auckland Festival production was that the Maori actors, once the Maori sentences began flowing from their lips, could seldom resist the temptation of carrying on in Maori—departures from the script which were to me occasions of sheer delight.[30]

Dansey's comments highlight a number of aspects applicable to the complex of bilingualism and syncretic theatre in general and not just specific to Maori theatre. It is first of all significant that he wrote down his Maori dialogues in that language with the result that his own translation into English retained relexified traces ('echoes') of the source language.[31] Although these traces are not immediately visible on the printed page, subtle nuances have nevertheless survived the passage from performance to page. A second important aspect is directly related to performance. While Dansey's convention of beginning exchanges in Maori but continuing them in English is a concession to *pakeha* (white) spectators, in the performance situation this convention was subverted by Maori actors who

[30] Dansey, *Te Raukura*, pp. x–xi.
[31] For an explanation of the term 'relexified', see the following section on translation.

retranslated the English text back into Maori. Thirdly, the bilingualism indicated in the text and extensively practised in performance creates a divided receptive situation which favours bilingual (Maori) spectators ('a bonus as it were for those who understood Maori') and partially excludes audience members without knowledge of the indigenous language. As these strategies have already been encountered in other countries and Harry Dansey created his text without knowledge of other post-colonial theatre practices, the devices and responses he outlines can be seen in some respects as structures common to post-colonial theatre in general.

A more radical form of bilingualism is practised by Hone Tuwhare in his play *On Ilkla Moor B'aht'at* (*In the Wilderness without a Hat*), which has already been introduced in the previous chapter. As this work deals primarily with intracultural conflicts, it is not surprising that the Maori language is extensively used. As Tuwhare's use of Maori is quite complex it may be helpful to outline a number of recurrent situations where the indigenous language is used in Maori plays. Maori is spoken by mythological characters; on ceremonial and ritual occasions (*marae* and *hui*); as a means of sociolinguistic characterization ('elders', *kuia* (old women), etc.); in songs and dances.

All four applications can be found in Tuwhare's play. The mythological ancestor figures speak only Maori. As is customary in contemporary Maori culture the funeral ritual (*tangi*) depicted in the third act is conducted entirely in Maori. In addition certain characters speak Maori, indicating either their age or the locality they come from. The play is set in the north of the North Island, where Maori is still spoken in everyday situations. The visitors from the South Island, on the other hand, speak no Maori, not even during the *tangi*, which occasions negative comment by the other characters. Finally, all songs, both traditional *waiata* as well as popular modern melodies, are performed in Maori.

In 1977, when the play was written, Tuwhare was very conscious of the fact that this extensive use of Maori would create major problems for a potential theatre audience, which he at the time rightly assumed would not be a Maori one. Therefore, he suggests in the play text that longer passages in Maori should be translated over a loudspeaker system: 'A P.A. system will [. . .] carry the voices (male and female) of "Interpreters," who must cue in precisely at the end of spoken words in Maori. Their voices must be flat, discreet, confidential'.[32] This rather unusual suggestion has a number of implications for a bicultural theatrical situation, which point up the potential dilemma for a Maori dramatist. Maori is restricted to cultural spheres where translation is not usual and in 1977 theatre was not one of those spheres. In the theatre at that time all linguistic signs, with the exception of song texts, which Tuwhare does not want translated, would have to be subjected to 'europhonization'. Thus the cultural setting of the play requires the extensive use of a language not considered fit for theatrical representation. That Tuwhare advanced the idea of a 'technical' translation as a solution to this dilemma highlights the dichotomy separating the spheres of Maori and Western theatrical culture at the time. The fact that his suggestion has never been put into practice in performance since the play's first production in 1985 demonstrates that in the intervening years between the play's genesis in 1977 and its première in 1985 a broadly based renaissance of Maori culture had begun. In the course of this development a *rapprochement* between the two cultural realms took place: Maori artists discovered the theatre as a sphere in which their cultural texts, and especially their language, retained legitimacy and the possibility of representation without folkloristic compromise; white New Zealanders, on the other hand, had to accept that the Maori language had now established itself in the sphere of theatre.

Translation(s)

> Theatre translation is never where one expects it to be: not in words, but in the gestures, and in the 'social body', not in the letter, but in the spirit of a culture, ineffable but omnipresent.
>
> (Patrice Pavis, *Theatre at the Crossroads of Culture*)

The diverse strategies employed by multilingual dramatic texts are but one form of linguistic mediation found in syncretic theatre. As with the ideological debate on the choice of dramatic language, so too with the issue of translation, which is by no means a simple linguistic or aesthetic issue but is located in a cultural and ideological matrix. While translation for the stage in the Western theatre has

---

[32] Hone Tuwhare, *On Ilkla Moor B'aht'at* (*In the Wilderness without a Hat*), in Simon Garrett (ed.), *He Reo Hou: 5 Plays by Maori Playwrights* (1977; Wellington: Playmarket, 1991), 59.

been dominated by the notion of transforming the foreign language into the indigenous one, post-colonial dramatists by definition work in the opposite direction. In fact they fulfil the requirement articulated in 1917 by the German cultural philosopher Rudolf Pannwitz, who called for translations which would allow the target language to be altered by the source language: 'Our translations, even the best ones, proceed from a wrong premise. They want to turn Hindi, Greek, English into German instead of turning German into Hindi, Greek, English. [. . .] The basic error of the translator is that he preserves the state in which his own language happens to be instead of allowing his language to be powerfully altered by the foreign tongue.'[33] Powerful alteration by the foreign tongue is an apt description of what happens to European languages in syncretic theatre texts. However, the situation is somewhat different from the one envisaged by Pannwitz because in a post-colonial context the translation is done by the author. This somewhat unusual situation has a number of important consequences. Firstly, the union of author and translator in one person means that the frequently articulated problem of power relations, particularly between First and Third World languages, can be addressed inasmuch as the translation is in indigenous hands.[34] Furthermore, the dramatist is in the position to translate adequately and creatively not just words, but also concepts and structures of thought. This means that dramatists are able to indigenize the European target language by their own source language in both a linguistic and theatrical sense. How this is done and to what ends will be demonstrated in the following examples.

A further issue regarding translation for the stage is the one alluded to in the quotation by the French theatre semiotician Patrice

[33] The quotation is from Pannwitz's book *Die Krisis der europaeischen Kultur* (Nürnberg: H. Carl, 1917); cited in Walter Benjamin, 'The Task of the Translator', in *Illuminations*, tr. Harry Zohn (New York: Shocken Books, 1969), 80–1.

[34] See e.g. the anthropologist Talal Asad, who writes: 'To put it crudely: because the languages of Third World societies [. . .] are "weaker" in relation to Western languages (and today, especially to English), they are more likely to submit to forcible transformation in the translation processes than the other way around. The reason for this is, first, that in their political economic relations with Third World countries, Western nations have the greater ability to manipulate the latter. And, secondly, Western languages produce and deploy *desired* knowledge more readily than Third World languages do.' 'The Concept of Cultural Translation in British Social Anthropology', in James Clifford and George E. Marcus (eds.), *Writing Culture: The Poetics and Politics of Ethnography* (Berkeley and Los Angeles: University of California Press, 1986), 157 f.

Pavis, which serves as an epigraph for this chapter. The notion that translation processes on stage are not just purely interlingual but include non-verbal signs as well, simply because the actor's body serves as the vehicle for transmission of the verbal text, has to be born in mind. Pavis writes: 'we cannot simply translate a linguistic text into another; rather we confront and communicate heterogeneous cultures and situations of enunciation that are separated in space and time'.[35]

In 1966 Martin Esslin remarked in a review of early plays by Wole Soyinka and J. P. Clark that these works, although written in English, were actually translations and their problematic character was a result of this implicit translation process. According to Esslin, drama is largely dependent on social contexts and in the case of these plays the context concerned Africans, 'who in reality speak their own language'.[36] The solution to what he sees as a general problem of Africans writing plays in European languages lies in the use of a highly stylized verse language, as used by the authors, because this was the only kind of language which could be adequately translated. In this way the whole problem of rendering sociolinguistic connotation, so crucial for realist drama, could be avoided. Esslin thus sets up a clear dichotomy between two types of dramatic language without, however, suggesting that realistic dialogue and stylized speech might in fact be mixed; they are rather mutually exclusive. In fact, it is, as we shall see, precisely the fusing of these two modes that characterizes writers such as Soyinka and many other post-colonial dramatists.

In the same year, 1966, one of the authors reviewed by Esslin, J. P. Clark, published an essay, 'Aspects of Nigerian Drama', in which he laid out the complex issues affecting dramatic language in his country. Clark replaces Esslin's simple dichotomy of realism versus stylization by a much more differentiated understanding of the linguistic problems affecting African dramatists. It is their task, he says, to find in European languages verbal equivalents for the particularities of the indigenous characters and their languages. The search should not, however, remain on what Clark calls the 'horizontal' plane of 'dialect and stress', but rather on the vertical plane 'of what the schoolmasters call style and register [. . .] this is a matter of rhetoric, the

---

[35] Pavis, *Theatre at the Crossroads of Culture*, 136.
[36] Martin Esslin, 'Two Nigerian Playwrights', in Ulli Beier (ed.), *Introduction to African Literature: An Anthology of Critical Writing*, 2nd edn. (1966; London: Longman, 1979), 282.

artistic use and conscious exploitation of language for purposes of persuasion and pleasure'.[37] Although Clark does not use the word 'translator', preferring to call himself 'a letter-writer for my characters', the process he describes is one of translation. As well as rendering linguistic structures, the dramatist must also pay attention to forms of cultural behaviour which also require transposition. As an example Clark quotes from his play *The Song of the Goat*, set amongst the Ijo people of southern Nigeria. He justifies a certain awkwardness or 'indirection' in his dialogue by drawing attention to the importance of social conventions among the Ijo which forbid important issues being spoken about in a direct manner. It is interesting that Clark considers it necessary to justify his deviations from the norms of realistic English drama. His arguments are directed at Nigerian critics, 'encumbered with conventions and critical theories that pile up good grades in the old English schools'.[38] These Nigerians, he argues, when confronted with new forms, require the aid of programme notes, 'as in Chinese theatre'.

What Clark outlined in this early essay in terms of his dramaturgical praxis anticipates the linguistic strategies now termed 'relexification'. This term was coined to describe linguistic processes widespread in post-colonial societies: the use of europhone vocabulary in combination with indigenous structures and rhythms. While the language remains recognizably English or French, it is changed, often substantially, in its rhythm, grammar, and idioms by the presence of an indigenous language, which is present as a kind of palimpsest beneath the European language. This linguistic definition, first used by the sociolinguist Loreto Todd, has been adapted by the literary scholar Chantal Zabus as a means to analyse strategies of indigenization found in the West African novel.[39] According to Zabus, relexification is a literary device or strategy of writing by means of which African authors have tried to deal with the problem of translating African concepts, thought structures, and linguistic features into a europhone language. For Zabus the artistic process of relexifying language is tied closely to ideological questions. She sees in this strategy the expression

---

[37] J. P. Clark, 'Aspects of Nigerian Drama', in G. D. Killam (ed.), *African Writers on African Writing* (1966; London: Heinemann, 1973), 31.   [38] Ibid. 32.
[39] See Loreto Todd, 'The English Language in West Africa', in R. W. Bailey and M. Görlach (eds.), *English as a World Language* (Ann Arbor: Michigan University Press, 1982), 303 n. 22; cited in Chantal Zabus, *The African Palimpsest: Indigenization of Language in the West African Europhone Novel* (Amsterdam: Rodopi, 1991), 101.

of a subversive intention to deconstruct the (neo-)colonial power structures inherent in the languages they established:[40] 'On the strategic level, relexification seeks to subvert the linguistically codified, to decolonize the language of early, colonial literature and to affirm a revised, non-atavistic orality via the imposed medium.'[41] Relexification is, however, also a form of implicit translation, which distinguishes itself from the normal translation process because it takes place in one and the same language. Because only one subject is active in the process, namely the author, it is difficult to ascertain to what extent translation has actually taken place. The source language is only extant in the form of an indigenous palimpsest, which can certainly be sensed and felt on stage, and even on the page, but is seldom written down and scarcely even consciously carried out by the writer.

Although Zabus exemplifies her theory almost exclusively on the basis of West African prose texts, it is logical to suppose that this indigenization strategy is also relevant for syncretic dramatic texts. However, the process is by no means identical in both genres. Translation for the stage includes rendering not just linguistic signs from a source to a target language, but also the encoding of paralinguistic and non-verbal signs and conventions, including gesture and movement. That speech and movement on stage condition and influence each other is a truism that any actor will confirm. Thus any examination of relexification as a dramaturgical strategy must take into consideration the importance of non-verbal signs.

An early example of dramatic relexification can be found in the play *The Dilemma of a Ghost* (1964) by the Ghanaian writer Ama Ata Aidoo. While this work is largely a product of theatrical realism and shows very few syncretic elements, its use of language is exceedingly complex. In his study of the play Dapo Adelugba ascertained six different linguistic levels. Besides sociolinguistic categories such as 'American English' or 'educated African English' and familiar dramatic conventions such as stylized verse in the prologue, there are also transcriptions from an African language, Fanti, into English, where

---

[40] Chantal Zabus uses the term 'deconstruction' in the post-structuralist sense with the important corollary that she understands decolonization as a process of deconstruction: 'If understood not in terms of destruction but as meaning "to undo", "to analyse" a given order of priorities in language, deconstruction becomes an interesting way of reading and writing West African texts, and of elucidating the motivation or justification for such linguistic experimentation and the indigenization of language-as-system.' *The African Palimpsest*, 10.   [41] Ibid. 107.

the characters are still recognizable as Fanti speakers.[42] In addition to these six discrete linguistic levels, there are also, according to Adelugba, 'transcriptions' between them, kinds of code-switching, for which Ama Ata Aidoo has developed special conventions. Although the presence of African languages behind the English text is palpable and made evident through the use of particular conventionalized signs, which indicates that a type of relexification strategy has been achieved here, it still remains doubtful whether the techniques used in *The Dilemma of a Ghost* manifest the subversive critical dimension that Zabus sees in relexification in its developed form. Whether this is the case or not, Adelugba, an important scholar and critic of African drama and theatre, can still consider the work ten years after its appearance in 1965 to be a model for emulation by dramatists: 'The six levels here identified certainly recommend themselves for efforts in dramatic writing, not only in Ghana but indeed in all other African countries which share this heritage.'[43]

'Transcription' or 'translation' would also be apt terms to describe the approach of the Cree Indian dramatist Tomson Highway. Highway has described his dramaturgical process as a way of translating from his Cree mother tongue into English, in which sometimes a Cree version may emerge as an intermediary form:

My characters speak in Cree, because I write about my home community where the people speak Cree. The older generation, my parents for example, and my older brothers and sisters, my aunts and uncles, don't speak any English at all. So, when I write about them, and I write mostly about them, I have a picture of my cousins, my aunts and uncles, in my head. So my characters talk in Cree. And sometimes whole sections of the first draft will come out in Cree. So what I do, because I am a musician as well, I treat the language as music. I experiment with a form of English writing that attempts to capture the rhythm and the humour of the Cree language. Humour is very much at the centre of the Cree language.[44]

---

[42] 'Although "transcribed" into English by a dexterous dramatist, there is every reason to believe that these speeches are made by characters who speak a Ghanaian language, probably Fanti, and Aidoo (like Synge *vis-à-vis* the Gaelic-speaking characters—as opposed to his English-speaking characters—in his Anglo-Irish plays) wants us to believe so.' Dapo Adelugba, 'Language and Drama: Ama Ata Aidoo', *African Literature Today*, 8 (1976), 72 f.   [43] Ibid. 80.
[44] Christopher Balme, Interview with Tomson Highway, Toronto, 16 Apr. 1991; repr. in Christopher Balme, 'Strategien des synkretischen Theaters. Studien zu einer postkolonialen Theaterform im anglophonen Raum', University of Munich, Habilitation thesis 1993, 395.

The palimpsest of the Cree language manifests itself in the rhythm and tempo of the dialogue, which can cause problems for both actors and spectators. Highway stresses that during rehearsals he is particularly careful to ensure that actors acquire the character-istic rhythm of Cree. This is necessary because the actors stem from different language groups and are by no means fluent in Cree.

Although the palimpsest of Cree is really only fully perceptible in live performance, where culturally specific paralinguistic signs such as accent and intonation are fully developed, Highway's relexification strategy can be illustrated by reference to the published text. This is particularly clear in passages where characters switch between Cree and English and the rhythm of Cree is transposed onto the English text. The following example is taken from Highway's first published play, *The Rez Sisters* (1988). The action revolves around seven women living on the fictional reserve Wasaychigan Hill. Bored and frustrated with their dreary lives on the reserve, they decide to travel to Toronto to take part in the 'Biggest Bingo in the World'. With the help of various fundraising activities they scrape together the neces-sary money. Their activities are observed and often interfered with by the mythological Trickster figure of Nanabush. On the linguistic level it is noticeable that those characters who are aware of Nanabush and can communicate with the mythological world are the ones who can speak Cree. Marie-Adele, who is dying of cancer, objects to the threatening presence of Nanabush appearing this time in the guise of a seagull:

NANABUSH. As-tum. [Come.]
MARIE-ADELE. Neee. Moo-tha ni-gus-kee-tan tu-pi-mi-tha-an. Moo-tha oo-ta-ta-gwu-na n'tay-yan. Chees-kwa. [*Pause*]. Ma-ti poo-ni-mee-see i-goo-ta wee-chi-gi-seagull bird come shit on my fence one more time and you and anybody else look like you cook like stew on my stove. Awus![45]

The shift from one language to another in mid-sentence occurs here under extreme emotional duress. While the translation of the Cree passage into English is comprehensible on a lexical level, the syntax

---

[45] Tomson Highway translates the Cree text as follows: 'MARIE-ADELE. Neee. I can't fly away. I have no wings. Yet. [*Pause*]. Will you stop shitting all over the place you stinking seagull bird.' *The Rez Sisters*, 19.

resembles the holophrastic structure of Cree.[46] By leaving out all punctuation and chaining together conjunctions, a technique which corresponds neither to 'good' style nor to natural English speech rhythms, Highway finds an equivalent in English for what he terms the humorous rhythm of Cree: 'You laugh all the time when you speak it. In spite of the violence on the reserve, the rhythm of the language is funny. It must have something to do with the Trickster being at the centre of it.'[47]

The holophrastic syntax of Cree is used extensively in Highway's most successful play to date, *Dry Lips Oughta Move to Kapuskasing* (1989). This work, termed by the author the 'flip side' to *The Rez Sisters*, features the men related to the women of the previous play. The action of this thematically and structurally very complex play is motivated in part by the decision of the women on the reserve to enter the male domain of ice hockey. On the linguistic level Highway again writes dialogues or monologues which dispense almost entirely with punctuation. When in such passages the somewhat strange, even grotesque-sounding, names of the Cree characters are linked together in sound chains, then, although the text is largely comprehensible on a purely lexical level, the effect of a foreign language being spoken is created. If, as in the following example, the whole speech is spoken in the form of an ice hockey commentary, then such a speech act contains at least three interlocking linguistic codes: lexical items in Cree, sporting jargon, and a rapid-fire syntax which corresponds to Cree speech rhythms and the conventions of a sporting commentary:

BIG JOEY. [. . .] Number Thirty-seven Big Bum Pegahmagabow, defense-woman for the Wasy Wailerettes, stops the puck and passes it to Number Eleven Black Lady Halked, also defense-woman for the Wasy Wailerettes, but Gazelle Nataways, Captain of the Wasy Wailerettes, soogi body check meethew her own team-mate Black Lady Halked woops! She falls, ladies igwa gentlemen, Black Lady Halked hits the boards and Black Lady Halked

---

[46] Cree belongs to the Algonquian family of languages, for which linguists have coined the term 'polysynthetic' or 'holophrastic'. This refers to the great complexity of individual words created by the chains of prefixes and suffixes which have a syntactical as well as lexical function; see Michael K. Foster, 'Canada's First Languages', *Language and Society*, 7 (1982), 7–16; and 'Native People, Languages', in James Marsh (ed.), *The Canadian Encyclopedia* (Edmonton: Hurtig, 1988), 1453–5.

[47] Ray Conologue, 'Mixing Spirits, Bingo and Genius', *Globe and Mail* (Toronto), 21 Nov. 1987, C5.

is singin' the blues, ladies igwa gentlemen, Black Lady Halked sings the blues.[48]

These two examples demonstrate clearly that the strategy of relexification opens up for the indigenous dramatist a greater range of possibilities than a simple choice between the alternatives indigenous versus European. When in addition the situation of stage performance and enunciation is kept in mind, in which signs such as accent, intonation, and the vocal presence of a Native actor combine to increase the linguistic presence of the Cree language behind or beneath the English text, then relexification on stage attains even greater subversive potential than that suggested by Zabus for the novel.

While relexification manifests itself primarily on the level of rhythm, grammar, and vocabulary, other translation strategies in post-colonial drama can be found, which, while related to it, use more complex discursive elements such as proverbs and sayings. As early as 1966 J. P. Clark in his essay 'Aspects of Nigerian Drama' drew attention to the work of the novelist Chinua Achebe as an example of 'a faithful reproduction of the speech habits of one people into another language [. . .] proceeding by technique of the proverb'.[49] In the meantime a considerable amount of research has been carried out into the use of proverbs and other indigenous epigrammatic forms in europhone African prose literature.[50] As far as dramatic writing is concerned, where similar strategies can be observed, the situation is less encouraging. This is all the more remarkable in light of the many parallels between the indigenization strategies used in drama and prose writing.

The concept of 'ethno-text' is used by Chantal Zabus to describe the translation of more complex indigenous linguistic elements in prose literature: 'The Nigerian Igbo-informed novel of English expression is made of discursive elements ranging from rules of address, riddles, praise-names and dirges to the use of proverbs. These constitute the ethno-text which is grafted onto the English-language narrative, in an attempt to recapture traditional speech and atmosphere.'[51] If one were to replace the words 'novel' and 'narrative'

---

[48] Tomson Highway, *Dry Lips Oughta Move to Kapuskasing* (Saskatoon: Fifth House, 1989), 74.   [49] Clark, 'Aspects of Nigerian Drama', 31.
[50] Zabus, *The African Palimpsest*, 133–47.   [51] Ibid. 133.

by drama and action, and 'Igbo' by 'Yoruba', then this definition could be applied unchanged to the dramatic work of Wole Soyinka or Ola Rotimi. Zabus's notion of 'ethno-text' corresponds in some respects to the concept of cultural text which is central to this study. Such ethno-texts can be further differentiated, and the forms characteristic for the Igbo people such as ritually linked prayer formulas, forms of address, invectives, and other culturally determined forms have their correspondences in the language and culture of the Yoruba.

Linguistic cultural texts such as proverbs and oracular divinations are used extensively in Ola Rotimi's Oedipus adaptation *The Gods are not to Blame* (1971). Here they fulfil a number of functions. Their enactment on stage is usually in the context of a ritual act connected with the Yoruba culture, but the intertextual links with the Greek model establish resonances which transcend a simple ethnographic replication. Rotimi's play can in a certain sense be seen as a product of his research into traditional Yoruba performance, in which he explored parallels between Greek theatre and the rituals and festive performances of the Yoruba.[52] In his play he combines fairly precise re-enactments of traditional court culture—its music and dances—with a modern dramaturgical structure utilizing flashbacks and technical devices such as voice-overs. In the prologue, which takes place before an Ogun shrine, the background events leading up to the story are enacted. On the birth of a king's son it was tradition that a Yoruba oracular priest (*ifa* priest) performed a divination ritual. He foretells patricide and incest, whereupon the newborn child is condemned to death. The prologue is written in verse and contains a number of proverbs. This highly formalized language suggests both the rendering of a Greek play and a translation from the Yoruba language. The prophetic riddles that foretell the tragic events to come are drawn not from Greek oracular tradition but from the cult practices of the Yoruba *ifa* priest. In fact the riddles and proverbs in the play are so numerous that Rotimi actually ironizes his own stylistic device:

ODEWALE. What is the matter, fellow, aren't you a Yoruba man? Must proverbs be explained to you after they are said?[53]

---

[52] See the references to Ola Rotimi's theatre theory in Ch. 2.
[53] Ola Rotimi, *The Gods are not to Blame* (Oxford: Oxford University Press, 1971), 32.

Rotimi employs a similar self-reflexive ironical remark in his historical drama *Kurunmi*: 'Your Ifa Oracle jargon kills me.'[54] This remark refers to the prophecy scene in which a 'witch doctor' throws the divination beads in order to divine a course of action. In this scene the enigmatic diction of the proverbs and the hieratic language of the prophetic ritual reveal the same type of formalized foreignness:

> Aruku, Aruku,
> Aruku-gb'oku-roja-mata;
> the corpse that was carried to the market
> did not sell.
> It was thrown into the bush;
> the same was brought back home
> covered in a shroud
> and called 'egungun'.[55]

Since *ifa* divination consists of prescribed, memorized texts, which are determined by the configuration of palm nuts thrown on the ground, it is quite likely that Rotimi has incorporated in his play a genuine cultural text in translation. In both these plays the proverbs and oracular sayings are recognizable cultural texts. Because they manifest structural similarities to a comparable form in ancient Greek culture they fulfil the function of mediating between two cultural worlds.

Following the same strategy, Wole Soyinka goes a step further in his drama *Death and the King's Horseman* (1975). Here the transliteration of proverbs attains a complexity which transcends Rotimi's experiments and in fact tests the limits to which foreign material can be directly translated into another language for stage performance. Even in everyday speech the educated Yoruba utilizes an elaborate idiom of expression, rich in metaphor and wordplay, which is only comprehensible within the referential framework of a generally known repertoire of proverbs. Thus Soyinka's practice of transliterating rather than adapting proverbs in his play could be seen on the one level as a search for linguistic authenticity. However, he uses the discursive element of the ethno-text so extensively in *Death and the King's Horseman* that it transcends the mere necessity to indicate cultural and linguistic setting. The language of the major Yoruba characters (Elesin, Praise-Singer, and Iyaloja) consists in fact largely

---

[54] Ola Rotimi, *Kurunmi* (Ibadan: Ibadan University Press, 1971), 73.
[55] Ibid. 71.

of aphoristic and epigrammatic forms. 'There is hardly a dramatic moment in the dialogue between Yoruba characters which is not expressed by a proverb taken from Yoruba idiom,' concludes David Richards in his study on the use of proverbs in the play.[56] This linguistic dominant shift in the scenes in which the Yoruba culture predominates (scene 1: market and wedding; scene 3: trance dance and ritual suicide) redefines conventional notions of dialogue and creates a new kind of linguistic code. While this code contains dialogic features, it does not correspond to accepted ideas of dramatic dialogue. The spectator not familiar with Yoruba language and culture is confronted with considerable problems because this verselike language is linked mainly to the referential system of Yoruba proverbial culture. The so-called 'closed' world of dialogic drama is repeatedly opened up because the language draws on an external system of reference. While this translated verse language is comprehensible on a metrical and lexical level, the metaphors and tropes derive from a cultural world entirely alien to the traditions of English poetry and literature. An additional difficulty lies in the fact that the artistry of the Yoruba proverb depends often on its laconicism. This means that the meaning of the saying cannot be derived directly from the text iself but is contained in a commentary, the knowledge of which is assumed. In the process of translation, this orally transmitted commentary either is lost or must somehow be integrated into the new text at the cost of the poetic elegance. A further translation problem can be located in the actual act of enunciation. Often a proverb is only partially stated and its completion is expected to be carried out in the mind of the listener. This technique of alluding to a proverb is frequently used in the oral tradition of Yoruba poetry which is based largely on the proverbs and oracular sayings of the *ifa* oracle.[57]

[56] David Richards, 'Òwe l'esin òrò: Proverbs like Horses: Wole Soyinka's *Death and the King's Horseman*', *Journal of Commonwealth Literature*, 19/1 (1984), 91.

[57] Ulli Beier draws attention to the translation problems inherent in rendering Yoruba poetry into European languages: 'Yoruba is a *learned* language, and as such, full of allusions which remain meaningless to the reader who was brought up outside the culture.' Beier provides the following example of a translation, which needs a commentary to complete it: 'Often the translation must complete such phrases if the reader is not to be left completely puzzled. The refrain "the worm is dancing" in a song about the thunder god Shango implies the proverb: "the worm is dancing, but that is merely the way it walks" which in turn implies the meaning: you think Shango is angry with *you*, but in fact he is just a quick-tempered person . . .'. Ulli Beier (comp. and ed.), *Yoruba Poetry: An Anthology of Traditional Poems* (Cambridge: Cambridge University Press, 1970), 16.

As Soyinka tries neither to find English equivalents for Yoruba proverbs nor to explain them by means of implicit or explicit commentary, his translation strategy is one that retains the cultural integrity of the ethno-texts. The English language is forced to accommodate the concepts and linguistic forms of the Yoruba world. However, Soyinka is not engaged in a subversive deconstruction of the colonial language. His primary concern is to communicate features of a complex culture, one of whose chief characteristics is its dense metaphorical language. An example from *Death and the King's Horseman* illustrates his approach. In the third scene Elesin prepares himself for his ritual suicide:

> It promises well; just then I felt my spirit's eagerness. The kite makes for wide spaces and the wind creeps up behind its tail; can the kite say less than—thank you, the quicker the better?[58]

Elesin employs here a familiar proverb about the hawk which receives unexpected help from a tailwind and does not object to or refuse the assistance.[59] In the context of the action the proverb functions as a trope for Elesin's mental and spiritual preparedness to join his ancestors. Without knowledge of the original proverb, this metaphor is hardly comprehensible. The dialogue of the Yoruba characters contains dozens of similes and metaphors of this kind. However, apart from the stated problems of semanticization, it should not be forgotten that this linguistic strategy is one of a number of sign systems that Soyinka deploys in order to convey the notion of an intact culture. This is at least the impression created at the beginning of the play. In the course of events the image of an organic and cohesive cultural system is relativized. Just as the Yoruba world is destabilized by Elesin's failure to carry out the ritual suicide, so too does his language begin to lose coherence and cohesion. The undisputed master of proverbs in the first scenes of the play, Elesin in the final scene, incarcerated in the colonial jail, reveals a clear loss of linguistic proficiency. He even apologizes to Iyaloja and the Praise-Singer for this failure of language: 'It is when the alien hand pollutes the source of will, when a stranger force of

---

[58] Soyinka, *Six Plays*, 181.

[59] According to David Richards, this passage is based on the proverb 'Àwòdi to'o nre Ìbarà, èfùfù ta á n'ídi pá, o ni 'Işẹ́ kúkú yá.' Richards refers to the collection of Yoruba proverbs and sayings collected and edited by Oloye J. O. Ajibola, *Owe Yoruba* (Ibadan: Oxford University Press, 1971). Ajibola renders the proverb as: 'The hawk wishing to go to Ibara, is blown by the wind in that direction and he says, "Now is my chance".' Richards, 'Òwe l'esin òrò: Proverbs like Horses', 97 n. 21.

violence shatters the mind's calm resolution, this is when a man is
made to commit the awful treachery of relief, commit in his thought
the unspeakable blasphemy of seeing the hands of the gods in this
alien rupture of his world.'[60] Elesin's language, formerly rich in
African metaphor, is here abstract and discursive, its tropes revealing no particular ethnic or cultural identity.[61]

The translation of proverbs and their incorporation as ethno-texts
expand the possibilities of relexification, because the presence of
another language is palpable not just on the level of grammar or
individual lexical items, but also as a whole cultural referential system.
This strategy results in the coexistence of two semiotic systems, the
prerequisite for any kind of functioning syncretism. In *Death and the
King's Horseman* this syncretism takes on an additional ideological
facet, because the thematic and formal design of the play is based on
an implicit if not explicit contrasting of two cultures.[62] The concept of
relexification permits a more differentiated perspective on processes
and possibilities of intercultural stage translation as a response to the
state of bi- or multiculturalism characteristic of most post-colonial
societies. In the relexified theatrical text the spectator hears not just
the rhythms and conventions of the indigenous tongue, but also, via
the signifying function of the performer's voice, accent, and intonation, a living demonstration of cultural pluralism.

Self-Translation and 'Transcreation'

As we have already seen, relexification is a form of self-translation.
The dramatists considered here render their texts from an indigenous
language into the signs and conventions of europhone dramaturgy,

---

[60] Soyinka, *Six Plays*, 211 f.

[61] See Richards on this passsage as well: 'Elesin no longer controls his world through
proverbial language, since he has lost the right to utter the linguistic summations of
"the Yoruba mind" which proverbs express.' 'Òwe l'esin òrò: Proverbs like Horses', 95.
Soyinka's thesis that the changes in consciousness wrought by colonization are reflected
in the use of proverbial language is the central question examined by Wolfgang Bender,
*Kolonialismus. Bewusstsein und Literatur in Afrika. Zur Veränderung des Bewusstseins
an der Yoruba in Westnigeria durch den Kolonialismus von 1850 bis heute. Aufgezeigt
an literarischen Dokumenten insbesonders an Beispielen aus der Oralliteratur* (Bremen:
Übersee-Museum, 1980). Bender is concerned primarily with oral literature.

[62] The reference is to Soyinka's oft-cited remark in the preface to his play that *Death and
the King's Horseman* is not about a 'clash of cultures'. Even if Soyinka is primarily
interested in presenting the Yoruba culture, some form of cultural contrasting is inevitable.

usually without the intermediate form of a version written in their own language. Another form of self-translation, practised principally in India, involves translating works written in indigenous languages into a European or another Indian language. This practice is closely linked to strategies of syncretic theatre because it most often implies rendering not just linguistic signs but a whole set of cultural and theatrico-aesthetic conventions into the target language and culture. Since Rabindranath Tagore India has had a strong tradition of 'trans-created' drama, the generic term in India to refer to works translated and adapted by the author from one language and performance tradition to another, usually English. Indian dramatists tend to link performance conventions very closely with language. This has meant that English drama since the nineteenth century has been narrowly epigonic in form. Initially Shakespearean verse drama, and since the 1930s the theatrical realism of Ibsen and Shaw, provided the most important models, in line with prevailing Western fashions and developments. M. K. Naik writes: 'Most Indian verse drama in English is a vast whispering gallery of Shakespearean echoes.'[63] It is only through the process of transcreation in the work of Tagore (and in his wake many other lesser-known dramatists) to be considered below that this performance dichotomy is overcome and a syncretic theatre is realized. The task here will not be to attempt a linguistic comparison of the plays, which is beyond my resources, but rather to consider to what extent the process of linguistic translation also affects the theatrical conventions of the works.

Translation has always been an important activity in Indian culture, a result no doubt of the linguistic diversity of a continent which has nevertheless very strong common religious and cultural roots. For this reason translation was traditionally considered to be an independent creative act and not just an intermediary, interpretative activity. In the words of the Bengali scholar Sujit Mukherjee: 'Until the advent of Western culture in India we had always regarded translation as new writing.'[64] During the colonial period there was widespread 'literary bilingualism',[65] which continued into the post-colonial period and is

[63] Naik, *Dimensions of Indian English Literature*, 159.
[64] Sujit Mukherjee, *Translation as Discovery and Other Essays on Indian Literature in English Translation* (New Dehli: Allied Publishers, 1981); see ch. 6: 'Translation as New Writing', 77.
[65] The term comes from Vilas Sarang, 'Self-Translators', *Journal of South Asian Literature*, 16/2 (1981), 33: 'Literary bilingualism is particularly relevant to the Indian context. To begin with, like most educated Indians, Indian writers are usually bilingual to a greater or lesser extent in their daily life.'

reflected in the everyday bilingualism of the educated classes in India. For the dramatist this state of bilingualism resulted either in two separate literary and theatrical activities or, as was more often the case, in a state of continual and mutual exchange between work in the mother tongue and that in English or often between two Indian languages.

In the special case of dramatic translation, which is by tradition closely tied to the rendering of classic Sanskrit texts, the term 'transcreation' has been introduced. It was coined in 1964 by Purushottan Lal, a publisher and translator from Calcutta, in connection with his English versions of Sanskrit plays.[66] The most comprehensive theoretical justification of the concept can be found in Lal's essay 'On Translating *Shakuntala*'. Although there already exist any number of translations, Lal claims to want to produce an 'actable'—that is, a stageable—version of the classic text. According to Lal, the crucial problem is not one of translating the language itself, but rather of rendering value systems, cultural conventions, and forms comprehensible to a Western audience. This means that it is not possible to make a simple separation of form and content: problems of comprehension linked to the Hindu thinking also manifest themselves in the structure of the play. The circularity of theme and form found in *Sākuntala* is a reflection of Hindu metaphysics, which must create problems of reception in another culture: 'to a mind grooved in a different cultural pattern it [the theme] must surely appear farfetched and abstruse'.[67] In order to counter intercultural misunderstandings, the translator must be entitled to take considerable liberties with the source text. Apart from the lack of cultural knowledge on the part of a Western audience, there are other difficulties arising from the dramaturgical and stage conventions inscribed in the text, which Lal terms the 'technical level':

the play is full of irritating *dei ex machina*; stage divisions are not into acts and scenes but parts and interludes, fluid, interwoven—seven altogether; asides, whispers, soliloquies, and chantable slokas abound [. . .] Then there are naive bits of melodrama. [. . .] Faced by such a variety of material, the translator must edit, reconcile and transmute; his job becomes largely a matter of transcreation.[68]

[66] See P. Lal (ed.), *Great Sanskrit Plays in Modern Translation* (Calcutta: New Direction, 1964). The title-page reads: 'Great Sanskrit Plays in New English Transcreations by P. Lal'. On this coinage see Mukherjee, *Translation as Discovery*, 85.

[67] P. Lal, *Transcreation: Two Essays* (Calcutta: Writers Workshop, 1972), 24.

[68] Ibid. 23.

The solving of these supposed 'technical' problems places the inter-cultural stage translator in a typical dilemma, according to Lal. On the one hand, the translator is free to 'smooth over' stylistic and cultural elements so as to render a foreign text into a form corre-sponding to Western theatrical and dramatic conventions. The other strategy would be to retain consciously such 'technical' difficulties and thus the theatrico-cultural characteristics of the text, and risk alienating a target audience. However, Lal's argument is based on an oversimplified dichotomy because it assumes a much more restrictive Western receptive theatrical code than is in fact the case. Lal posits for Western theatre a degree of homogeneity that in the second half of the twentieth century no longer exists. He presumably wishes to 'transcreate' for the dialogic literary theatre of Shaw or Ibsen. In this supposition he is by no means alone. In the following comments on the translation practices of Rabindranath Tagore it is important to keep in mind the tension between the assumed homogeneity of West-ern theatre, on the one hand, and its actual heterogeneity on the other.

Rabindranath Tagore was an important initiator of the widespread practice in India of self-translation into English, the colonial lan-guage. Throughout his life, he remained primarily a Bengali writer. Apart from a number of essays and lectures, Tagore conceived and wrote his poetry and prose in his mother tongue, which was then rendered into other languages by translators. As far as his plays are concerned, the situation is a little more complicated. Some of the works best known in Europe such as *The Post Office* and *The King of the Dark Chamber* (both 1914) were popularized in translations not done by Tagore himself, while other equally important works were rendered into English by the author. Therefore it is necessary to differentiate, as M. K. Naik suggests, between those plays translated by others and those 'transcreated' by Tagore himself: 'These plays evidently form a significant and autonomous body of writing which must be judged in and for itself.'[69] Naik argues that Tagore consid-ered his 'transcreations' as contributions to Western dramatic litera-ture and that the translation process entailed substantial adaptation,

---

[69] Naik lists thirteen plays translated by Tagore himself out of a total *œuvre* of fifty-three plays and dance-dramas. Of these thirteen he included only seven in his *Collected Poems and Plays* (1936; New York: Macmillan, 1941). Naik, *Dimensions of Indian English Literature*, 167.

condensation, and refashioning of the Bengali original for Western theatrical conventions.

It should be kept in mind that Tagore's position within his own theatrical culture was by no means unproblematic. He remained outside mainstream Bengali theatre, both the popular and the socially committed streams. As one Tagore scholar succinctly put it: 'he remained aloof from the Bengali stage'.[70] His plays have also been criticized for their excess of symbolism, on the one hand, and lack of brisk dialogue, on the other,[71] and although they were by no means conceived as closet dramas, the first productions were largely private affairs.[72]

All this notwithstanding, Tagore was keenly interested in theatre and problems of staging. This is immediately reflected in his translation practices. In the preface to his 'dramatic poem' *Chitra* Tagore indicates that he is very conscious of the fact that translation for the stage implies reworking not just the language but stage conventions as well:[73]

NOTE:.—The dramatic poem 'Chitra' has been performed in India without scenery—the actors being surrounded by the audience. Proposals for its production here having been made to the author, he went through this translation and provided stage directions, but wished these omitted if it were printed as a book.[74]

The 'here' referred to means England and the published version contains no stage directions. Tagore was, however, prepared to provide them for rehearsal purposes so as to allow the text to be adapted to the scenographic and spatial conventions of the picture frame stage. Indirectly Tagore also indicates to what extent his text is

[70] Sanyal, 'The Plays of Rabindranath Tagore', 239.
[71] The following assessment by C. Paul Verghese is fairly representative of a widespread opinion amongst Indian scholars: 'The symbolism of Tagore's plays, for example, often becomes excessive. The main characters of his symbolical plays are not so much persons of flesh and blood as personifications of the poet's subjective experience.' *Problems of the Indian Creative Writer in English*, 155.
[72] They were performed either on the family estate in Calcutta or later at the Santiniketan school. Because of Tagore's regional and international reputation these performances were public theatre in so far as they attracted a large number of spectators and press.
[73] The Bengali original with the title *Chitrangada* was written in 1891, whereas Tagore's English version did not appear until 1914. The plot is based on a story from the *Mahabharata*, which deals with the love between Arjuna and the girl Chitra, who has been raised by her father as a son.
[74] Tagore, *Collected Poems and Plays*, 152.

indebted to traditional Indian theatre. The comment suggests that the
Bengali original contains, perhaps not unlike Shakespearean plays,
chiefly *implied* stagecraft and scenographic conventions which would
have determined the performance text in India. The reader of the
English version has the impression that the actors, who speak a
lyrically heightened but dialogically structured text, are the dominant
sign system. The few didascalia provide no indications of stage
action, nor are there many implied stage directions in the spoken
text. For the opening scene between the eponymous girl Chitra and
the gods Madana and Vasanta there is no spatial specification whatsoever; the scene takes place in a neutral, unlocalized space typical of
traditional Indian dance-theatre.[75] The only deictic signs provided
pertain to the role of Chitra. The story itself points, of course, to its
origin in the *Mahabharata* and hence more indirectly to a link
between Tagore's play and classical Sanskrit theatre, which used the
same sources. This affinity, however, is not immediately evident in the
English version because Tagore pared back what he considered to be
the excessive ornamentation of Bengali language for Western tastes
and removed whole sections of the action and characters which
supposedly distracted from dramatic unity.[76]

A number of the significant changes made by Tagore to the English
version of *Chitra* in the process of 'transcreation' were documented
by Edward Thompson in 1926 in his study of Tagore's work. He
bemoans the excision of long lyrical descriptive passages which were
apparently sacrificed in favour of an emphasis on the action. Another
element which Tagore pared back was the strong erotic and sensual
character of the language, 'in obedience to the laws which forbid in
one language what they permit in another'.[77] Thompson sees also
improvements in the English version compared to the Bengali original, particularly in the simplification of the dramatic dialogue—a

---

[75] Suresh Awasthi, 'The Scenography of the Traditional Theatre of India', *Drama Review*, 18/4 (T-64) (1974), 36–46, here p. 38. For a discussion of the spatial conventions of Indian theatre, see Ch. 7.
[76] 'Frequently the plays emerge from his translations shorn of sub-plots and super-fluous characters making a distinct *advance in dramatic structure* even if they fail to gain in any other aspect' (Sujit Mukherjee, *Passage to America: The Reception of Rabindranath Tagore in the United States 1912–1941* (Calcutta: Bookland, 1964); my italics). Sujit Mukherjee's assessment betrays quite clearly a somewhat Eurocentric notion of dramatic form since he appears to view terms such as 'dramatic structure' in terms of a hierarchy of advancement, rather than as being questionable culturally specific constructs.   [77] Thompson, *Rabindranath Tagore*, 126.

result, he argues, of the 'maturity' of a writer twenty years older. It is interesting to contrast two examples of Tagore's transcreative translation process. In the left column are passages taken from Thompson's translation from the Bengali original, in the right column Tagore's adaptation of these passages:

Tell me, slender lady, the tale of yesterday. I have a desire to know what my loosèd, flowery dart wrought.	I desire to know what happened last night.
As in a song, in the tune of a moment, an endless utterance cries out weeping.[78]	Like an endless meaning in the narrow span of a song.

While the examples selected may seem somewhat crass, they are nevertheless representative of the transcreative process of adapting between two stage languages. Whatever the conventions of Bengali stage language at the turn of the century may have been—and it could be argued that Tagore was working within a self-created genre *sui generis*—it is still evident that the transformation into a text intended for Western performance entailed in the mind of the author substantial linguistic and, as we have seen, dramaturgical adjustments. The norm that Tagore is moving towards but by no means trying to imitate in his English version is the laconicism of realistic drama with its ideology of concentration and exclusion of all linguistic embellishments not immediately necessary for characterization or advancement of dramatic action.[79]

Much of the cultural misunderstanding and criticism that has been directed at Tagore's drama is rooted in this particularly narrow view of what constitutes 'drama'. In his analysis of the play *Phālguni* (*The Cycle of Spring*) (first performed 1916) Thompson praises the use of music, but criticizes the text itself: the play 'falls short of literature [. . .] the residue is not drama'.[80] While Thompson was intimately

---

[78] Ibid. 130.

[79] In a moment of ethnocentric condescension Thompson sees these concessions to another norm as an 'enrichment' for Tagore: 'Rabindranath's exceptionally receptive genius has not come into contact with our Northern thought and life without great enrichment.' Ibid.   [80] Ibid. 250 f.

acquainted with Tagore's dramatic *œuvre*—he was present at many performances of the plays—he appears unable to find the critical language to place the works in the context of Indian theatre aesthetics, or perhaps more accurately within the framework of Tagore's adaptation of these aesthetic principles.[81] This standpoint is by no means unique but rather symptomatic of a negative attitude to Tagore's theatrical texts, which is based on a normative, neo-Aristotelian understanding of theatre and drama. Interestingly enough this attitude was echoed by a number of Indian critics. It is this tradition of Tagore scholarship that M. K. Naik attacks in a more recent reassessment of Tagore's English theatrical texts:

Those who condemn the dialogue as clumsy and awkward, flowery and rhetorical forget not only that it is highly stylized but that this stylization was inevitable in a kind of drama which had so plainly discarded the realist convention and opted for the larger freedom of the imaginative theatre. In a theatre like this, rhetoric and declamation, soliloquy and song, poetry and mystic paradox are the natural idiom and need not be out of place at all.[82]

Naik argues here convincingly for reassessment of the critical parameters with which to view Tagore's translated dramas. Although Tagore at no time voiced any interest in working purely within the realist tradition, the very act of rendering his plays into that language had the effect of placing them entirely within a new theatrical code.

The reception of Tagore's drama in Europe takes place significantly after 1913, the year he was awarded the Nobel Prize, and is an important step in the process of intercultural reception among the anti-naturalistic theatre-reformers. Practically every major theatre-reformer of this time looked to the Asian theatre for inspiration and for a theatrical language to combat the strictures of naturalism, realism, and the well-made play. Tagore's theatre (and here one must include besides the transcreated English dramas also the later dance-plays) is not, however, in the first instance a counter-model to a prevailing tradition. It is rather the attempt to combine Tagore's primary Indian aesthetic sensibility with his interest in and ency-

---

[81] Thompson's credentials as a scholar of Bengali were not uncontested. Tagore's reaction to Thompson's study cited here was extremely unfavourable to say the least. For a discussion of Tagore's somewhat contradictory response to Thompson's work, see Harish Trivedi, *Colonial Transactions: English Literature and India* (Manchester: Manchester University Press, 1995).

[82] Naik, *Dimensions of Indian English Literature*, 178 f.

PLATE 1 *An Echo in the Bone*, by Dennis Scott, directed by Earl Warner; Creative Arts Centre, University of the West Indies, Mona, Jamaica, March 1990. Dreamboat is possessed by the spirit of Crew

PLATE 2 *An Echo in the Bone*, by Dennis Scott, directed by Earl Warner; Creative Arts Centre, University of the West Indies, Mona Jamaica, March 1990. Dreamboat collapses. Madam: 'The spirit on him back. It will tear him.'

PLATE 3 *An Echo in the Bone*, by Dennis Scott, directed by Earl Warner; Creative Arts Centre, University of the West Indies, Mona Jamaica, March 1990. Madam calls for oil to heal Dreamboat

PLATE 4 *An Echo in the Bone*, by Dennis Scott, directed by Earl Warner; Creative Arts Centre, University of the West Indies, Mona Jamaica, March 1990. Dreamboat is anointed

PLATE 5 *An Echo in the Bone*, by Dennis Scott, directed by Earl Warner; Creative Arts Centre, University of the West Indies, Mona Jamaica, March 1990. Transition into possession

PLATE 6 Percy Mtwa and Mbongeni Ngema in *Woza Albert!* by Percy Mtwa, Mbongeni Ngema, and Barney Simon, directed by Barney Simon; Market Theatre, Johannesburg, 1982

PLATE 7 Bakary Sangaré and Mamadou Dioume in *Woza Albert!* by Percy Mtwa, Mbongeni Ngema, and Barney Simon, directed by Peter Brook; Théâtre Bouffes du Nord, Paris, 1989

PLATE 8 *Sarafina!* by Mbongeni Ngema, directed by Mbongeni Ngema; The Committed Artists, 1987. Final Scene: 'Freedom is Coming Tomorrow'

PLATE 9 *Barungin* by Jack Davis, directed by Andrew Ross; The Playhouse, Perth, 1988

PLATE 10 Steven Page as the Mimi spirit in *Murras* by Eva Johnson, directed by Eva Johnson; Adelaide Fringe Festival, 1988

PLATE 11 Billy Merasty as Creature Nataways and Doris Linklater as Nanabush in *Dry Lips Oughta Move to Kapuscasing* by Tomson Highway, directed by Larry Lewis; Royal Alexandra Theatre, Toronto, 1991

PLATE 12 *Bopha!* by Percy Mtwa, directed by Percy Mtwa; Market Theatre, Johannesburg, 1985. Graduation ceremony (scene 1)

PLATE 13 *Bopha!* by Percy Mtwa, directed by Percy Mtwa; Market Theatre, Johannesburg, 1985. Playing the national anthem 'Die Stem van Suid Afrika' (scene 1)

PLATE 14 *Bopha!* by Percy Mtwa, directed by Percy Mtwa; Market Theatre, Johannesburg, 1985. Street demonstration and police attack (scene 13)

PLATE 15 *Death and the King's Horseman* by Wole Soyinka, directed by Phyllida Lloyd; Royal Exchange Theatre, Manchester, 1990. The Market women taunt Amusa (scene 3)

PLATE 16 Billy Merasty as Simon Starblanket and Gary Farmer as Zachary in *Dry Lips Oughta Move to Kapuscasing* by Tomson Highway, directed by Larry Lewis; Theatre Passe Murallie, Toronto, 1989

clopaedic knowledge of Western forms.[83] Through the process of 'transcreation' Tagore arrives at an early form of syncretic theatre, rewriting his plays partly in the linguistic and performance codes of Western theatrical sensibility, yet retaining the unmistakable signature of Indian performance aesthetics.

Even in a monocultural context, theatrical performance or even an unperformed theatrical text is, as we know, a highly complex semiotic system. But syncretic plays, whether composed in English or transcreated from another Indian language, whether mono- or multilingual, have by definition diverse and perhaps even contradictory cultural codes inscribed in them. These codes may work on the level of relexification, as we have seen in Yoruba-influenced drama, where the indigenous is present as a kind of palimpsest beneath the surface of the europhone language; or there may be two or more languages being utilized on stage for linguistically and culturally diverse audiences. In order to read the signs and to appraise the theatrical codes of syncretic theatre, it is necessary to engage in a kind of bicultural receptive strategy in order to assess these works according to their culturally determined dominant structures. Only by a recognition of these dominant structures, which must predetermine and direct the next stage of hermeneutic activity, will outmoded Eurocentric critical methods be able to be overcome and replaced by culturally and aesthetically appropriate strategies.

---

[83] Thompson traces Tagore's interest in and debt to Western theatre: 'From the Elizabethan drama, at first necessarily the only European drama known to him at first hand, Tagore got his rags of convention, rags long gone out of fashion.' He goes on to argue that his prose dramas (post 1900) were 'very much in line with that present day movement which strives to make the drama a synthesis of all the arts—pageant and scenery, dancing and costume and music, being as essential as the words [. . .] It has been an independent development, in the main: but he is well aware of what is happening outside India.' *Rabindranath Tagore*, 287. Sanyal also stresses Tagore's interest in and experimentation with new dramatic techniques: 'taking in his stride nearly all the known "isms" in dramaturgy: naturalism, realism, symbolism, expressionism'. 'The Plays of Rabindranath Tagore', 239.

CHAPTER FOUR
Orality as Performance

'How is it', asks Antonin Artaud in his essay 'Production and Metaphysics', 'Western theatre cannot conceive of theatre under any other aspect than dialogue form?'[1] Artaud's assault on logocentric theatre and his impassioned plea for a new theatrical language is directed at what he sees as the foundation stone of Western theatrical aesthetics: psychological drama based on dialogue. Artaud has received indirect scholarly support for this contention from Peter Szondi in his seminal study *The Theory of Modern Drama* (1956).[2] Szondi sees dramatic dialogue as the paramount communicative mode of the Western dramatic tradition up until the beginning of modernism: 'The sole supremacy of dialogue, that is of people talking to one another in drama, is a reflection of the fact that drama consists purely of this interpersonal frame of reference, that it only knows this sphere.'[3] All the 'crises' of modern drama that Szondi analyses deal formally or thematically with this structural characteristic. Semiotic dramatic theory (as opposed to theatre theory) can only reiterate Szondi's findings. Manfred Pfister introduces his semiotic study of drama as follows: 'the figures' speech, and, above all, their dialogical speech [. . .] constitutes the predominant verbal matrix used in dramatic texts [. . .] In drama [dialogue] is the fundamental mode of presentation.'[4] Of course while both Szondi and Pfister relativize in the course of their respective studies this apodictic premiss, dialogue remains nevertheless, even if it is itself the subject of critique in a dramatic text, the dominant code of the theatrical genre drama. This means that any deviation from this norm—be it in the form of epic theatre, of linguistic critique in the work of Brecht or Pinter, or even in the total meaninglessness of human communication that we find

---

[1] Antonin Artaud, *The Theatre and its Double*, tr. Victor Corti (London: Calder & Boyars, 1970), 27.   [2] Quotations from Szondi's book in my own translation.
[3] Peter Szondi, *Schriften*, i (1956; Frankfurt-on-Main: Suhrkamp, 1978), 17.
[4] Manfred Pfister, *The Theory and Analysis of Drama* (Cambridge: Cambridge University Press, 1988), 6.

suggested in the plays of Ionesco and Beckett—is only an indirect confirmation of this dominant position.

In the context of post-colonial theatre and the experiments of indigenous dramatists with the Western dramatic form, the perceived supremacy of dialogic communication was seen as both a provocation and a challenge. Any attempt to indigenize the Western dramatic form had to take account of dialogue as the dominant generic code. This recognition manifests itself in earlier syncretic theatre theory as a search for dialogic elements in indigenous performance forms. In H. I. E. Dhlomo's theatre theory we find the search for a dialogic structure in traditional Zulu praise-songs (*izibongo*). Similar undertakings are evident in the studies of the Nigerian dramatist Ola Rotimi and his scholar colleague J. A. Adedeji, both of whom link African theatricality with the presence of dialogic elements. The presence of structures analogous to dramatic dialogue becomes thus a definitional premiss for a theory of indigenous theatre. In syncretic theatrical texts we very seldom find a substantial deviation from this norm to the extent that the code dominance of dialogue is completely replaced. There are, however, numerous occasions where dialogue is replaced by other modes of linguistic communication. The most frequent and important of these 'deviations' is *oral performance*, which provides in most cases the performative framework for the others. A second non-dialogic mode is constituted by various forms of *lyric-musical songs or verse*, which are usually integrated into oral performances. In these cases dramatists make use of the formality of song or poetry as a way of approximating the structural features and functions of indigenous cultural texts. A third deviation from dramatic dialogue can be found in the occasional use of *paralinguistic* signs manifested in the form of recognizable culturally specific vocalizations.[5] Such

---

[5] Paralinguistic signs encompass a broad range of phenomena such as voice quality, intonation, vocal noises, vocal reflexes (sneezing, yawning, coughing, etc.), as well as consciously enunciated vocalizations such as laughing, crying, breathing. For the relevance of these linguistic signs for theatre semiotics, see Fischer-Lichte, who stresses the intercorrelation between paralinguistic, linguistic, and kinesic signs, which can increase the semantic potential of paralinguistic signs. Erika Fischer-Lichte, *The Semiotics of Theater*, tr. Jeremy Gaines and Doris L. Jones (Bloomington: Indiana University Press, 1992). For important observations on paralinguistic signs in drama, see also Keir Elam, *The Semiotics of Theater and Drama* (London: Methuen, 1980), 78–83. For a wider definition of paralinguistic signs in the context of oral performance, see Isidore Okpewho, who includes under this term 'all nonverbal accompanying resources'. *African Oral Literature: Backgrounds, Character, and Continuity* (Bloomington: Indiana University Press, 1992), 46.

paralinguistic signs are of interest because they appear to have strong signal functions, particularly as markers of cultural group identity when a non-indigenous language is used by that group. They are inscribed in the theatrical texts and are thus regarded as an important feature of them.

In practically all pre-scribal cultures forms of storytelling and formal rhetoric (which often include a diegetic component) fulfil many functions of theatrical art and entertainment because they are inseparable from performance aesthetics. Forms of orality and oral literature provide thus an additional complex of cultural texts which can be integrated into the Western theatrical form besides the already mentioned songs and dances mostly associated in the popular imagination with pre-scribal cultures.[6] Whether oral performances can actually be considered 'dramatic' in the Western sense of indicating role embodiment, a hotly debated issue in earlier research into the subject,[7] is not really a central concern for syncretic theatre. The integration of oral forms within a syncretic frame implies that existing cultural practices are theatricalized and undergo a process of aesthetic transformation.[8]

This distinction only makes sense if we distinguish between concepts of theatricality, which include a broad range of forms analogous to theatre, and theatre as defined in the narrower sense of Western aesthetics. That oral performance can be highly theatrical in the sense of emphasizing non-verbal, particularly gestural and proxemic, sign

---

[6] In addition to the traditional ethnographic interest in orality as the most important source for the transmission of myths, one must cite Albert B. Lord's study of the Homeric epic, which provided orality research with new impulses: *The Singer of Tales* (Cambridge, Mass.: Harvard University Press, 1960). Lord argues that Homeric epics were the product of an oral creative process, which can still be detected in the 'formulaic technique' of Homeric verse structure. Lord supports his text exegesis with the results of research into the oral poetry of Yugoslavia, where he conducted fieldwork in the 1930s and 1950s. Lord was able to examine the poetological and performative aspects of a living oral tradition. For a contemporary assessment of orality, see Walter Ong, *Orality and Literacy: The Technologizing of the Word* (London: Methuen, 1982).

[7] The theatrico-dramatic aspects of African orality are discussed by Ruth Finnegan in her study of African oral literature; she accords them, however, only scant importance: *Oral Literature in Africa* (London: Clarendon Press, 1970); see esp. the final chapter. Finnegan's definitional criteria are based mainly on the question of whether role enactment takes place in oral literature, for which she finds very little evidence.

[8] As we have seen in Ch. 1, the Zulu dramatist and theatre theorist H. I. E. Dhlomo drew attention to the possibility of integrating traditional oral forms into Western-style theatre. In the 1930s Dhlomo analysed the oral tradition of Zulu praise-songs, the *izibongo*, as a theatrical form. Apart from identifying a 'dramatic' structure in these narrative songs, Dhlomo stressed that the performance style associated with them was highly theatrical.

systems is pointed out by Harold Scheub in his study of the *ntsomi*, the storytelling of the South African Xhosa people:

The 'language' of this artistic performance involves much more, then, than the word. It includes the relationship with the audience, the nuance of the hand, the movement of a hip, the subtlety of the face, the range and variety of human sounds, the rhythmic use of language; it includes physical touch, a sudden and fleeting bit of mime, a dancing-in-place. [. . .] It involves the blending of gesture and word, of dance (body movements) and song, so that they become so closely interwoven that it is impossible to speak of one without treating the other.[9]

What Scheub describes is the interaction of most of the important theatrical codes and signs which are not of a technological nature. The narration, or rather performance, of an *ntsomi* tale corresponds in its basic structure to a theatrical performance in the sense that linguistic, gestural, musical and proxemic signs are combined into an aesthetic form and directed towards a particular receptive situation.[10] What needs to be emphasized, however, is less the problem of phenomenological definition—is oral performance theatre?—than the strength of the analogies between what are culturally and historically distinct forms filling within their societies both similar and different functions. It is the strength of such analogies that has drawn indigenous directors and dramatists to include oral cultural texts into their syncretic plays and productions.

South African Township Theatre

One of the components of *ntsomi* oral performances that Scheub particularly stresses is the musical element.[11] Songs and chants are able in a

---

[9] For an analysis of physical movement in the oral performances of the Xhosa, see Harold Scheub's article, 'Body and Image in Oral Narrative Performance', *New Literary History*, 8/3 (1977), 345–67.

[10] Oral performance does not, however, have to be highly gestural or kinetic, as Isidore Okpewho stresses in reference to Scheub: 'Not every storyteller, of course, goes into all this elaborate histrionic or dramatic activity.' He cites examples of oral performers who command attention by virtue of their stillness. Whatever the style, however, the audience 'is a force to be reckoned with'. *African Oral Literature*, 46, 63.

[11] On the function of songs and chants, Scheub writes: 'Their most potent use is at the height of crises, when the artist seems to have no recourse but to express herself in song. Spoken words alone do not sufficiently communicate the feelings the artist is attempting to project [. . .] Songs and chants recapitulate action, precipitate crises, and reveal extreme emotions [. . .] [They] reveal rather than state emotions and actions.' Harold Scheub, *The Xhosa Ntsomi* (Oxford: Oxford University Press, 1975), 50–4.

sense to transcend linguistic and gestural codes to create a special level of emotional intensity unattainable by other means. It should be kept in mind to what extent Scheub's thesis—that songs and music strengthen the 'theatrical' element of the performance in comparison to the 'epic-narrative' component of the linguistic text—can be accepted as a general principle or structural feature of oral performance. In the following examples taken from South African township theatre, Caribbean, and Australian Aboriginal theatre my focus will be on the performative element of orality and less on the epic-narrative side. It is necessary to examine how indigenous themes and concerns are linked with their formal presentation as oral performances, which enables the integration of indigenous cultural signs. In other words, I am more interested in how the story is told than in the details of the action.

That traditional oral forms are still present in contemporary South African township culture and have been utilized in the plays created there has been emphasized by a number of scholars. David Coplan, for example, has analysed township performance culture as the result of a syncretic mixing of traditional performance forms with the aesthetic conventions of urban culture.[12] On the basis of this analysis traditional oral forms such as *ntsomi* tales or Zulu *izibongo* would only be present and used in the new urban context in a mediated form. What is retained in the urban context is the rhetorical potential and the performance form, although the content will be a different one. The South African director Mark Fleishman has termed orality the basis of performance and communication in township theatre.[13] It is also a central component of the way plays are created in the workshop situation, Fleishman argues. Workshop theatre is essentially an oral form and thus opposed to the hegemony of the literary play promulgated by white theatre. In Fleishman's terms workshop theatre could be considered a form of mediation between oral and scribal (theatrical) cultures. In a similar vein Keyan Tomaselli sees orality as a key to understanding what he terms the 'semiotics' of alternative theatre in South Africa, meaning primarily politically committed black theatre: 'committed theatre grows, expands and is nurtured by the very fact that it is, by and large, oral in tradition, construction and rendition.'[14]

---

[12] Coplan, *In Township Tonight*.
[13] Mark Fleishman, 'Workshop Theatre as Oppositional Form', Paper delivered at the conference 'Theatre and Politics in South Africa', Bad Boll, Germany, 13 Dec. 1989.
[14] Keyan G. Tomaselli, 'The Semiotics of Alternative Theatre in South Africa', *Critical Arts*, 2/1 (1981), 18.

The term 'oral in construction' refers to the genesis of texts by means of improvisation. The importance of improvisation in the creation of texts in township theatre provides an important link between the avant-garde theatrical techniques of the Grotowski school, represented in South Africa above all by Athol Fugard, and the *per definitionem* improvisatory mode of oral performances. In contemporary township theatre the narrative mode plays a central role; in some cases it even equals dialogic communication in importance.

A decisive influence on the development of township theatre in the 1980s was the workshop production *Sizwe Bansi is Dead*, created by Athol Fugard, John Kani, and Winston Ntshona.[15] The first half of the play consists of a monologue in which John Kani, shifting between a number of roles, describes his previous workplace, a Ford factory, and how he has set himself up as a photographer. He imitates the accents and body language of these figures, sings African songs, and utilizes a pronounced pantomimic acting style. The linguistic and gestural score that has been preserved in the published text is mainly a product of John Kani's improvisations, which were then systematized in a second stage of rehearsal as Fugard describes the process: 'we then applied ourselves to disciplining and structuring it so that the gesture, word, or event was capable of controlled repetition'.[16] While Fugard's theoretical statements on his work betray pronounced universalistic tendencies—frames of reference include Greek myth and Jerzy Grotowski—the plays he created in collaboration with Kani and Ntshona demonstrate very clearly the culturally specific experiences of the black actors.[17] However, this referentiality should not be restricted solely to the thematic level of apartheid, the experiential basis of all three 'Statement' plays. Kani and Ntshona decisively influenced the form of these works in terms of performance conventions.[18]

[15] *Sizwe Bansi is Dead* was first performed on 8 Oct. 1972 at The Space in Cape Town. Published in Athol Fugard, John Kani, and Winston Ntshona, *Statements: Two Workshop Productions Devised by Athol Fugard, John Kani, and Winston Ntshona* (Oxford: Oxford University Press, 1974).   [16] Ibid., p. xii.
[17] For a critical view of this cooperation, see Robert Kavanagh (Mshengu): 'Kani and Ntshona's real knowledge and masterful depiction of the life of black people in the Eastern Cape is weakened by their acceptance of Fugard's interpretation of it.' 'Political Theatre in South Africa and the Work of Athol Fugard', *Theatre Research International*, 7/3 (1982), 176.
[18] While this is perhaps difficult to ascertain on the basis of the text alone, independent of a performance situation, other evidence can be used. Fugard describes, for example, a live performance in the black township New Brighton, where the audience reacted to Kani's half-hour monologue in a particularly subtle way; see Fugard, 'Sizwe Bansi is Dead', 26–32.

Sizwe Bansi is Dead was certainly one of the models which influenced Percy Mtwa and Mbongeni Ngema as they were creating their play *Woza Albert!*, perhaps the best-known township production. It is, however, only one of many elements which went into forming a complex structure of African and European components, the cultural provenance of which is often extremely difficult to separate into discrete spheres. Temple Hauptfleisch identifies the following elements: '*Woza Albert!* employs the *commedia dell'arte* style as frame, but emphasizes the narrative element in a way reminiscent of *ntsomi* usage—*but* utilizing two narrators and thus setting up dramatic interchanges in something like vaudeville fashion.'[19] While traces of the oral performance form *ntsomi* are certainly evident, they are manifested in a way characteristic of syncretic theatre: the generic borders between *commedia dell'arte*, *ntsomi*, and vaudeville crisscross to such an extent that the individual components are difficult to discern. While this is true for the overall style of the play, there are also individual segments or scenes which can be isolated in terms of their cultural provenance. An example of oral performance can be found in scene 13 of *Woza Albert!*, in which an old Zulu relates how the Boer leader Piet Retief and his followers were massacred by the Zulu chief Dingane.[20] This story is interesting on a number of levels. In terms of its content the story deals with a historical event told from the perspective of a Zulu who, dwelling on the theme of broken promises, subtly draws analogies between apartheid and Dingane, a Zulu leader not exactly honoured in Boer historiography. Of greater interest for this study, however, is the way in which the old man, played by Mbongeni Ngema, uses gestural and kinaesthetic signs as well as elements of song to communicate the story. In order to analyse the way language, gesture, movement, and song interact, the text is reproduced below in full in the left column. In the right column non-verbal signs are indicated, drawn from an analysis of a performance recorded for a television film.

---

[19] Hauptfleisch, 'Beyond Street Theatre and Festival', 185. See e.g. the article by Anne Fuchs on *Woza Albert!*: 'Re-Creation: One Aspect of Oral Tradition and the Theatre in South Africa', *Commonwealth: Essays and Studies*, 9/2 (Spring 1987), 32–40. Fuchs argues that the action of the play is based on the structure of Zulu 'folk tales'.

[20] On the 6 Feb. 1838 the Boer leader Piet Retief and a group of followers were murdered on the orders of Dingane, when they were negotiating with the Zulu leader in his headquarters. This scene is alluded to, although not depicted, by Dhlomo in his play *Dingane*.

Scene 13

> [*Lights up on Mbongeni enter-*
> *ing as a fragile, toothless old*
> *man. He sits throughout the*
> *following action. He settles on*
> *the boxes, attempts to thread a*
> *needle. His hands tremble but*
> *he perseveres. He succeeds on*
> *the third, laborious attempt*
> *and begins to sew a button on*
> *his coat.*]

MBONGENI [*humming*].
Bamqalokandaba bayimpi
Heya we-bayimpi izwelonke
Ngonyama ye zizwe
Ohlab' izitha
Undaba bamgwazizwe lonke
okazulu
Amambuka nkosi

> [*Mbongeni becomes aware of*
> *the invisible interpreter. Laughs*
> *knowingly.*]

MBONGENI [*speaking*]. Eh? What
would happen to Morena if he
comes to South Africa? What
would happen to Morena is what   Continues sewing.
happened to Piet Retief! Do you
know Piet Retief? The big leader
of the white men long ago,[a] the   [a] Indicates distance with his hand.
leader of the Afrikaners! Ja! He
visited Dingane, the great King
of the Zulus! When Piet Retief
came to Dingane, Dingane was
sitting in his camp with all his
men. And he thought, 'Hey these
white men with their guns are
wizards. They are dangerous!'   [b] Summoning with his arms, which
But he welcomed[b] them with a   he then crosses majestically.

big smile. He said, he said, 'Hello.
Just leave your guns outside[c] and
come inside and eat meat and
drink beer.' Eeeeeii! That is what
will happen to Morena today! The
Prime Minister will say, just leave
your angels outside and the power
of your father outside and come
inside[d] and enjoy the fruits of
apartheid. And then, what will
happen to Morena is what happened to Piet Retief when he got
inside.[e] [*Mimes throat-slitting,
throwing of bodies.*] Suka! That
is what will happen to Morena
here in South Africa. Morena
here? [*Disgusted.*] Eeii! Suka![f]

[c] Alternates dismissive and welcoming hand movements.

[d] Beckoning with his index finger.

[e] Stands up; outstretched hands;
claps his hands; stabbing motion
with his fists; gesture of cutting
throat.

[f] Exits with a threatening gesture.

Out of an everyday situation—an old man trying to sew a button on
his coat—there develops an oral performance combining language,
gesture, and song. This transition from the quotidian to the aesthetic
has been termed by scholars of orality the 'breakthrough into performance'.[21] An oral performance of this kind can arise from any
everyday situation without the necessity of a formal occasion. Far
more important than an occasion for the signalling of such 'breakthroughs' is the use of any number of verbal, musical, or gestural
indicators which show that the shift into oral performance has taken
place. In our example, the breakthrough into performance is marked
by the change from present to past tense as he begins to tell the story
of Piet Retief. At this point the old man begins to use different kinds
of gesture from the preceding segment of the scene. Until this point
his gestures were restricted to concrete acts, mainly the threading of a
needle and sewing. As soon as he begins with the narration, he stops

---

[21] Hymes analyses analogous situations in the storytelling of Native Americans
from the north-west Pacific coast. In the chapter 'Breakthrough into Performance' he
tries to establish criteria for differentiating between everyday linguistic behaviour and
what he calls 'performance in full'. Dell Hymes, '*In vain I tried to tell you*': *Essays in
Native American Ethnopoetics* (Philadelphia: University of Pennsylvania Press, 1981),
84. However, in all his examples Hymes restricts his attention to linguistic signs and
does not consider other signifying systems.

this action and uses henceforth primarily emblematic or indexical gestures, which serve to emphasize, illustrate, or even replace particular verbal sequences in his story. Gesture substitutes language, for example towards the end of the story ('And then, what will happen to Morena . . . '), where the actual massacre of Piet Retief is indicated by gestural signs. The performative aspect of the tale is further underlined by the fact that the old man stands up at this point and acts out the actions kinaesthetically.

What is missing from this performance and its analysis is, of course, audience response, a crucial factor for all forms of oral performance. The Xhosa *ntsomi*, for example, often has audience participation in the form of call-and-response chants built into the structure of the performance. While audience participation of this degree tends to be exceptional in township theatre, many plays appear to permit, or indeed invite, audience response on a musical level. In the context of township theatre one can speak of frame expansion in comparison to Western theatre to encompass a set of conventions from a performance culture where audience participation is the norm. This thesis could also be applied to Mbongeni Ngema's play *Asinamali!*, which, like *Woza Albert!*, is episodic and dispenses entirely with a conventional dramatic structure. The whole play is built around interlocking stories, in which narration and oral performance are not surprisingly the dominant codes. Of central importance in this work are gestural and kinaesthetic signs, which underscore the indigenous cultural signs. The response to this work with its pronounced oral component varied according to the audience. A cast member of *Asinamali!*, Thali Cele, has emphasized the essential difference and participatory nature of township audiences: 'When we played in the townships, it seemed as if the whole hall was on the stage. By the end of the show, you couldn't differentiate. Every hall had become a stage. Everybody was participating—whistling, ululating, singing.'[22] The special theatrical nature of this audience response is engendered by a fusion of political content, familiar musical codes, and the expectation of audience response built into the structure of traditional oral performance.

Less political than perhaps metaphysical is the use of orality in Soyinka's *Death and the King's Horseman*. The tale of the Not-I bird,

---

[22] Quoted in Emil Sher, 'Apartheid on Tour', *Canadian Theatre Review*, 50 (Spring 1987), 59–61, here p. 60.

into which Elesin launches, is a performative *tour de force* communicating equally on a physical, musical, and verbal level in its treatment of the ambivalence of man's attitude when facing death. The following stage direction must be kept in mind throughout Elesin's narration of the story:

ELESIN executes a brief, half-taunting dance. The drummer moves in and draws a rhythm out of his steps. ELESIN dances towards the market-place as he chants the story of the Not-I bird, his voice changing dexterously to mimic his characters. He performs like a born raconteur, infecting his retinue with his humour and energy.[23]

The opening line, 'a brief, half-taunting dance', indicates to what extent and with what subtlety kinesic signs can communicate in African movement aesthetics. It is a physical reply to the admonitions of the Praise-Singer. The participial adjective 'half-taunting' in particular suggests a subjunctive mood which normally one associates only with verbal messages. The reaction of the drummer points to another aesthetic constant in Robert Farris Thompson's categories of African 'art in motion': that of call-and-response, the continual dialogue between kinesic and musical codes and messages. As Thompson points out, the response is itself an active, controlling component in the performance of the caller.

The actual story itself is 'chanted', not told, and incorporates all the verbal, musical and role-playing skills of the traditional *griot*. The status of this 'performance', although a fictional creation of Soyinka, resembles structurally a traditional performance form. Thus it is not in a strict sense a transposed cultural text, but rather an analogous re-creation of one.[24] There are also obvious structural similarities to the narrative segments of Yoruba *alarinjo* theatre, the central element of which is a chanted story with a *bata* accompaniment. In *Death and the King's Horseman* the Praise-Singer and then the women provide the necessary choric voices. Otherwise, the various characters are imitated

---

[23] Soyinka, *Six Plays*, 149.

[24] For an assessment of ballad singers and *griots* in traditional Yoruba society, see J. A. Adedeji, 'Form and Function of Satire in Yoruba Drama', *Odù: University of Ifẹ Journal of African Studies*, 4/1 (1968), 61–72, and Ulli Beier, *Yoruba. Das Überleben einer westafrikanischen Kultur*, Exhibition Catalogue (Bamberg: Historisches Museum, 1991). Beier reports that the oral storytelling tradition among the Yoruba was by the 1950s largely a thing of the past, a victim of other, more powerful Western media; ibid. 123 f.

vocally by the narrator, Elesin. His recital of the story of death with 'humour and energy' is a verbal and gestural equivalent of the celebratory mood with which impending death is dealt.

Storytelling and Caribbean Folk Culture

Orality as a performance form can also be found in Caribbean syncretic theatre. The great importance attached to eloquence and theatrical storytelling are certainly among the 'retentions' of African culture which survived the 'middle passage' and reconstituted themselves in the New World. The ethnographer and folklore researcher Roger D. Abrahams has examined the performative aspects of oral culture in both the United States and the Caribbean. He ascertains in Afro-Caribbean oral culture a deep structure, not only in terms of the content of the tales, but also in respect to the aesthetic organization of the performances accompanying or integral to the stories themselves. Such performances are highly conventionalized, Abrahams argues, and these conventions govern the form, content, and the relations between performers and listeners:

Folklore is constructed of conventional materials, and these conventions organize performance in the areas of form, content, imagined roles and role-relationships, and in relationships between participants in the aesthetic transaction. Because the performance is public and unrecorded, the audience must have a constant sense of orientation; that is, they must be aware at all times at what stage they are in the performance.[25]

If one bears in mind that this organization with its contractual structure is analogous to the *contrât théâtral* of conventional theatre,

---

[25] Roger D. Abrahams coined the term 'men-of-words' as a designation for the verbal skills characteristic of African American culture. He also draws attention to the African roots of the phenomenon; see his essay and the literature listed there: 'Patterns of Performance in the British West-Indies', in Whitten and Szwed (eds.), *Afro-American Anthropology*. Although Abrahams speaks continually of 'performance' in his early research, he has in a more recent study questioned the theatrical analogy, or what he calls the dramatistic metaphor: 'They ["storytelling" and "speech-making"] are performances to be sure, and they do approach theatre—even great theatre—at certain points. But the personae taken by the men-of-words in each case differ from those of stage characters, and the qualities of these enactments differ precisely because they are not theatrical but engage the audience in an entirely different manner.' *The Man-of-Words in the West Indies: Performance and Emergence of Creole Culture* (Baltimore: Johns Hopkins University Press, 1983), p. xxxi.

then it is little wonder that dramatists have made recourse to such structures and incorporated them in their plays.

The adaptive potential of oral performance and its inherent theatricality were recognized by the West Indian dramatist and director Derek Walcott as early as the 1950s. In interviews and articles Walcott repeatedly drew attention to the importance of orality for popular Caribbean culture and for his own personal experience growing up exposed to such a culture. Walcott regards the storyteller in pre-scribal cultures as a 'narrator as performer'. Because of poverty, isolation, and illiteracy this function has remained intact until the present. Walcott further points out that orality in Caribbean culture is closely allied with the percussive rhythms of African drumming, the natural accompaniment to the human voice:

If one begins to develop a theatre in which the drum provides the basic sound, other things will develop around it, such as the use of choral responses and dance. If we add to this the fact that the story-teller dominates all of these, then one is getting nearer to the origins of possibly oral theatre, but certainly African theatre. Oral theatre may be Greek, or Japanese, or West Indian, depending upon the shape percussion takes.[26]

Walcott's adaptation of St Lucia's oral tradition is most evident in his play *Ti-Jean and his Brothers* (1957). It is his first syncretic theatre text, which, according to Walcott's own admission, is deeply influenced by the Afro-Caribbean oral tradition, 'the African art of the story-teller'.[27] This influence is evident in the tripartite structure of the work, which, as Walcott has explained, is indebted to the universal three-part form of the fairy tale. Besides such structural analogies—the plot of *Ti-Jean* is a play within a story, in which animals from the forest gather together and one of them, the frog, tells a story about humans—Walcott works with performative devices of orality. For instance, the prologue introducing the central action begins with the conventionalized verbal sign 'crick-crack', signalling in Caribbean oral culture the

[26] In another interview given in the same year to Edward Hirsch Walcott stresses that the oral tradition in the Caribbean is still vibrant and his use of it can in no way be seen as anachronistic or as literary artificial resuscitation. He sees his dramaturgical use of orality as an attempt to formalize and structure existing elements for the stage: 'I was lucky to be born as a poet in a tradition that uses poetry as demonstration, as theatre [. . .] I am someone who is simply coming out of a tradition and trying to formalize that tradition in terms of the necessity for structure in theatre.' Edward Hirsch, 'An Interview with Derek Walcott', *Contemporary Literature*, 20/3 (1979), 286.   [27] Walcott, 'Derek' s Most West Indian Play', 7.

beginning of a tale. Walcott alters the sign somewhat so as to make ironic reference to the chorus of Aristophanic comedy:[28]

FROG. Greek-croak, Greek-croak.
CRICKET. Greek-croak, Greek-croak.

> [*The others join.*]

FROG [*sneezing*]. Aeschylus me! All that rain and no moon tonight.
CRICKET. The moon always there even fighting the rain.
  Creek-crak, it is cold, but the moon always there
  And Ti-Jean in the moon just like the story.[29]

The first words of the play signal that a folk tale, or, more precisely, an Anansi story featuring usually a Trickster character, will be told.[30] By alluding to an existing cultural form, Walcott can establish connections to genres familiar to a Caribbean audience, and by citing a single verbal sign he can conjure up the expectation of a whole performative context. An audience familiar with the convention brings expectations of a story featuring cleverness and trickery and involving music and dance.[31]

Despite comic elements such stories are coloured by a serious tone as well. The stories deal invariably with matters of life and death. In *Ti-Jean*, for example, the devil issues a challenge to the three brothers Gros-Jean, Mi-Jean, and Ti-Jean: whoever can elicit a human feeling in the devil will be rewarded with riches and peace; failure to do so means death. The other factor leading to a serious tenor derives from the performative context: very frequently such tales are told during

---

[28] This sign, marking the commencement of a story, is responded to by a conventionalized counter-sign. The exclamation 'crick-crack' serves to draw attention to the narrator; see Roger D. Abrahams: 'Commonly, then, the one who began the song leaps up and proclaims "Crick-crack!", to which the others respond "Rockland come!" He or she may have to say "crick-crack" a number of times before the response occurs'. *The Man-of-Words in the West Indies*, 169.

[29] Walcott, *Dream on Monkey Mountain*, 85.

[30] Anansi stories are widespread throughout the Afro-Caribbean world; see Abrahams: 'Like trickster figures everywhere, Nansi is clever with words and with transforming and bewitching performances in general. Although he is small and childlike, he manages to trick those larger and supposedly wiser.' *The Man-of-Words in the West Indies*, 170.

[31] The connection between music, dance, and oral performance in the Caribbean is well documented by Abrahams, *The Man-of-Words in the West Indies*, 168f. That these three elements are normally used in conjunction with one another is made clear by Walcott himself. Ciccarelli, 'Reflections before and after Carnival: Interview with Derek Walcott' in, Michael S. Harper and Robert B. Stepto (eds.), *The Chant of Saints: A Gathering of Afro-American Literature, Art, and Scholarship* (Urbana: University of Illinois, 1979), 297.

funeral ceremonies such as Nine Night rituals to entertain the dead. Thus the recurrent theme of life and death is mirrored in the performance context. The connection with the supernatural is made using verbal formulas whose 'magic power' is made efficacious by a particular performative act. Songs often mark the transition between the different levels of reality. In *Ti-Jean* it is the creole chant of the devils which signals the dramaturgical transition:

> Bai Diable-là manger un'ti mamaille,
> Un, deux, trois 'ti mamaille!
> Bai Diable-là manger un'ti mamaille,
> Un, deux, trois 'ti mamaille![32]

The verses cited above constitute an authentic cultural text deriving from the New Year masquerades performed on St Lucia.[33] Songs such as these are an integral feature of the performative structure of Caribbean oral culture and normally involve a large degree of audience participation.[34]

Orality functions in *Ti-Jean* on a number of levels. On the one hand culturally defined texts and signs are used to signal a specific performative context which in turn influences the receptive code of the audience. On the other hand, the conventions of orality fulfil a dramaturgical function by providing a framework derived from Afro-Caribbean mythology. Thus orality in Walcott's play is not simply a particular segment of the work, but a factor determining content, structure and performance style.

Trustori: Retelling Aboriginal History

In the plays of the Australian Aboriginal dramatist Jack Davis the use of oral performance is one of the chief characteristics of his syncretic

---

[32] Walcott, *Dream on Monkey Mountain*, 131.

[33] According to Rawle Gibbons, this masquerade is known as Bwa Bwa; the song marks the appearance and disappearance of devils. 'Traditional Enactments of Trinidad—Towards a Third Theatre', 207.

[34] Walcott has drawn attention to the African origins of the narrative tradition informing his play: 'What was there too, but was too deep to be acknowledged, was the African art of the story-teller, a tradition which survived in my childhood through the figure of a magical, child enchanting aunt [. . .] and those skin-prickling chants whose words may change, but whose mode goes as far back and even past the tribal memory.' 'Derek's Most West Indian Play', 7.

dramaturgy. Although many stories are told and in different ways, they fulfil two recurrent functions. Firstly, they transmit an Aboriginal view of colonial history, an alternative historiography which has remained alive by means of oral transmission. Secondly, Davis links the act of storytelling to physical performance: they are, in other words, an integral component of Aboriginal performance aesthetics, whether in a traditional or an urban context.

The function of orality in pre-contact culture was always linked to a wider performative situation. Ethnologists refer to orality, there-fore, as 'dramatic art' in which a communicative situation between storyteller and listeners is established that is analogous to theatre. In traditional Aboriginal culture the performance itself utilized a wide range of theatrical elements: 'And in doing so he [the storyteller] has at his command all the local repertoire of gestures, hand and body movements, facial expressions, changes in tone, supplemented per-haps by embellishments of his own. [. . .] the actual words he uses are only a skeleton, a framework upon which the narrative itself is built up and comes to life.'[35] Significant here is the differentiation between a fixed performative code ('local repertoire') and the individual art-ist's own ability to provide variations on the code ('embellishments of his own'). Orality is a highly conventionalized cultural form. Because of this high degree of codification and conventionalization it can be integrated into a dramatic text and recognized as indigenous sign material. It is also important to remember that Aboriginal orality falls into various categories. Besides the sacred stories and myths of the dreamtime, there exists a large repertoire of profane stories. The difference is not so much a question of content—there can be a sacred and a profane version of the same story—as one of performance code. The sacred version of the story will be sung and danced, whereas the profane one is normally narrated in prose. There exists also a genre of profane stories which deal with the encounters and conflicts between Whites and Aborigines. These stories form the basis of an alternative historiography in which Aborigines can rewrite or retell the history of European–Aboriginal relations with their own culturally specific emphasis.[36]

[35] Berndt and Berndt, *The World of the First Australians*, 390.
[36] See Stephen Muecke, 'Ideology Reiterated: The Uses of Aboriginal Oral Narra-tive', *Southern Review* (Adelaide), 16 (1983), 86–101. Muecke cites examples of such stories in Aboriginal English, which deal with concrete episodes in Aboriginal–Eur-opean history (pp. 97 ff.).

The latter type of story occurs in Jack Davis's historical play *No Sugar* (1986). Set during the Great Depression, it deals with the infamous internment of Aborigines in the Moore River Settlement. The detribalized Aborigines from south-western Australia who were relocated there encountered for the first time more traditional Aborigines from the north. Davis shows how cultural exchange between the two groups takes place during a *corroboree*, in which dances are performed, body-painting is explained, and stories are told. One of these stories is performed by Billy, a black tracker from the north, who tells how his tribe was massacred.

> [*He* [Billy] *sits in silence. They watch him intently.* JOE *puts wood on the fire. He speaks slowly.*]

BILLY. *Kuliyah*.[a] [*Miming pulling a trigger, grunting*] *Gudeeah*[b] bin kill'em. Finish kill'em. Big mob, 1926, kill'em big mob my country.

[*Long pause.*]   5

SAM. *Nietjuk?*[c]

BILLY. I bin stop Liveringa station and my brother, he bin run from Oombulgarri. [*Holding up four fingers.*] That many days. Night time too. He bin tell me 'bout them *gudeeah*. They bin two, three stock-man *gudeeah*. Bin stop along that place, Juada Station, and this one   10 *gudeeah* Midja George, he was ridin' and he come to this river and he see these two old womans, *koories*, there in the water hole. He says, what you doin' here? They say they gettin' *gugja*.[d] [*He mimes pulling lily roots and eating.*] Midja George say, where the mans? They over by that tree sleepin', and Midja George, he get off his horse, and he   15 bin belt that old man with the stockwhip. He bin flog'em, flog'em, till that *gudeeah*, he get tired. Then he break the bottle glass spear, and he break the *chubel* spear. [*He grunts and mimes this.*] And that old man, he was bleedin', bleedin' from the eyes, and he get up and he pick up that one *chubel* spear, and he spear that one *Midja George*.   20 [*He demonstrates violently.*] And that *gudeeah*, he get on his horse, he go little bit way and he fall off . . . finish . . . dead.

JIMMY. Serve the bastard right.

BILLY. No, no, no bad for my mob. Real bad. That old man and his two *koories*, they do this next day. [*He indicates running away.*] Two   25 *gudeeah* come looking for Midja George. They bin find him dead. [*Silence.*] [*Holding up a hand.*] Must be that many day. Big mob *gudeeah*. Big mob politjmans, and big mob from stations, and shoot 'em everybody mens, *koories*, little *yumbah*.ᵉ [*He grunts and mimes pulling a trigger.*] They chuck 'em on big fire, chuck 'em in river.   30

[*They sit in silence, mesmerized and shocked by Billy's gruesome story.*]³⁷

ᵃ Yes.
ᵇ European, white man.
ᶜ Why?
ᵈ Water lily roots.
ᵉ Children.

This apparently straightforward narrative contains several levels of discourse that reflect a syncretic mixture of cultural texts manifested in several sign systems. In terms of the linguistic sign system Billy's English is itself a cultural indicator which sets him apart from the southern Aborigines. He speaks what is known as Kimberley English, a linguistic variant that is understood although not necessarily spoken by most Aborigines. According to Stephen Muecke, this language constitutes not so much a deviation from a standardized norm as a 'subversive' code.³⁸ This means that Billy's language represents an independent code which is already part of Aboriginal culture and is not merely a 'poor' version of white culture. Muecke also draws attention to the existence of an oral tradition in this language known as the 'Kimberley stories', to which Billy's story generically belongs. The status of the historical discourse is more difficult to define. On the one hand, it is a true story; on the other hand, the differentiation between fact and fiction, between historical and ahistorical stories, has no equivalent category in traditional Aboriginal oral culture. As has already been pointed out, there is only a distinction between stories from the dreamtime and those which don't belong to this category. With reference to the stories of the Aborigines from the region around Broome in north-west Australia Stephen Muecke concludes that there is no metalinguistic

---

³⁷ Jack Davis, *No Sugar* (Sydney: Currency Press, 1986), 67–8.
³⁸ In keeping with his post-structuralist approach Muecke argues for a de-centring of linguistic hierarchies: 'Aboriginal English, the language of the Kimberley stories, is often taken to be as politically bankrupt as its speakers. What if, instead of being seen as a deviant form of English, it were recognized more as the common language of the Aboriginal people of the mainland and the Torres Strait Islands—the language which in fact made possible their political unification to combat the destructive pressures of White society? What if it were seen as a *subversive* element among the codes of English in Australia?' Muecke, 'Ideology Reiterated', 97.

category 'fiction'. Stories are either true (*trustori*) or of the dreaming. A true story means that the narrator either was there or knows somebody who passed on the story: 'Just as the Broome Aborigines do not recognize a generic category "fiction," so they do not recognize a category "history." There is no specific discourse which produces the truth effects of dominant Western historical discourse with its usual communicative devices of exact chronology, emphasis on the role of important individuals, cross-referencing to "official" sources, and so on.'[39] Billy's story occupies therefore three discursive spaces. It is based on an account he heard from his brother so that in the epistemological framework of traditional orality it would have to be categorized as 'true', a *trustori*. It is, of course, also 'fictional' because it is performed within the framework of Western theatre. Thirdly, Davis is concerned that the historicity of the story in Western terms is also established, which he does in the published text in the form of an annotation.[40] He also takes great pains in the text to ensure that the cultural authenticity of the performance itself is communicated.

This cultural authenticity reveals itself above all in the meticulously recorded gestural and paralinguistic score. Davis specifies several times the paralinguistic sign 'grunts' in connection with the mimed depiction of important actions. This sign has the function of emphasizing particular mimed actions, which themselves reduplicate the verbal signs. But there are other gestural signs which do not reduplicate but rather replace or accompany linguistic descriptions. Such accompanying gestures consist principally of *illustrators*, which have a representational function. According to the classification of Ekman and Friesen most of the gestural signs could be defined as *kinetographs*, that is, as movements which

[39] Muecke, 'Ideology Reiterated', 95.
[40] That Davis himself makes use of Western historical categories is evident. Robert Hodge presents in his foreword to *Barungin* a complex view of the question of historicity in Jack Davis's work. Hodge concedes that the Western historical model based on linearity and causality is alien to traditional Aboriginal thought. But for Jack Davis and many other non-traditional Aborigines Western historiography is alien or questionable not on epistemological grounds but because it has distorted Aboriginal–European history. Thus the oral tradition offers an alternative historiography: 'Linear history is not alien to Aboriginals: on the contrary, oral traditions of many Aboriginal families have tenaciously preserved records that challenge the received versions that have been taught in school text books.' 'The Artist as Hunter', in *Barungin*, pp. xiii f.

depict a physical action.[41] Kinetographs can also contain *picto-graphic* elements. These include signs such as pulling the trigger (lines 3, 28), picking and eating water lily roots (line 13), the actions of breaking and stabbing with a spear (lines 18, 20). *Emblematic* movements are culturally coded gestures, which illustrate, repeat, or replace verbal statements. Emblematic gestures are, for example, the indication of a number (lines 19, 26) or of running away (line 24). Whatever classificatory system one wishes to use, the sheer number of gestural signs that Davis specifies underlines their important performative function.

On the basis of this precise scenic score a number of basic elements of the performative code of orality can be reconstructed. Even if the content of the story is not exactly traditional in the narrower sense, Billy's way of telling reveals, nevertheless, all the key performative elements of the traditional code that has been recorded by ethnographers.[42] There is a high density of gestural, kinaesthetic, and paralinguistic signs. In association with the verbal text these signs constitute a culturally specific performance form which could be termed a cultural text of Aboriginal orality. The example of Billy's story also illustrates how difficult it is to view linguistic and body-related signs separately in the context of oral performance.

Billy's story encapsulates many of the central features of oral performance I have been examining in this chapter. It shows how indigenous themes and concerns are linked with their formal presentation as oral performances, which enables the integration of indigenous cultural signs. It is both an exciting performance and an alternative historiography on the part of the dispossessed. The story illustrates also how out of an everyday situation an oral performance combining language, gesture, and song can emerge. This 'breakthrough into performance' can arise without the necessity of a formal occasion. Far more important than an occasion for the signalling of such 'breakthroughs' is the use of of verbal, musical, or gestural

---

[41] See Paul Ekman and Wallace V. Friesen, 'The Repertoire of Nonverbal Behavior: Categories, Origins, Usage and Coding', *Semiotica*, 1 (1969), 49–98. Ekman and Friesen differentiate between *emblems*, which are strongly codified and not dependent on language, and *illustrators*, which are weakly codified and accompany language. Traditional Aboriginal cultures possess in addition a sophisticated sign language which can replace natural language and is thus an independent semiotic system. Sign language will be analysed in Ch. 6.

[42] See here particularly Berndt and Berndt, *The World of the First Australians*, 387 f.

indicators which show that the shift into oral performance has taken place. Whether in Australia, South Africa, or the Caribbean, the great importance attached to eloquence and theatrical storytelling in these cultures has attracted dramatists and directors to orality as a strategy to indigenize theatre forms. Within the theatre frame orality functions on a number of levels. On the one hand, culturally defined texts and signs are used to signal a specific performative context which in turn influences the receptive code of the audience. In terms of the production of texts, workshop theatre, particularly in the South African context, but not only there, can be regarded as an oral form and thus opposed to the hegemony of the literary play promulgated by white theatre. In such terms workshop theatre could be considered a form of mediation between oral and scribal (theatrical) cultures. Finally, the conventions of orality fulfil a dramaturgical function by providing a framework derived from a mythological or oral historical base. Thus orality is not simply a particular segment of the work, but a factor which can determine content, structure, and performance style.

CHAPTER FIVE

Visualizing the Body

THE great upsurge of interest into the semiotics of the body is one of the striking features of recent trends in theatre studies research. The chief influence here has been Foucault's discourse theory focused through the searching critiques of feminism and gender studies. As the performance theorist Philip Auslander puts it: 'questions of who or what is speaking through the body and in what language, of what discourses are inscribed on/in the body, are clearly questions of power relations of the sort excavated by Michel Foucault'.[1] Auslander sees the performing body as being doubly coded: through the performance itself and through the exterior, socially determined discourses. In this chapter both types of encoding are examined. In the first section questions of the materiality of the body and in particular ethnicity are examined under the heading *le corps sauvage*. This admittedly somewhat problematic term is consciously used to set up a field of associations, some pejorative, some positive. These categories are examined as dramaturgical and theatrical strategies to utilize the performer's body as a cultural and artistic text. The second part of the chapter looks at the question of masking, a characteristic device of syncretic theatre. The use of full-body masks in West African masking traditions such as *egungun* underlines in particular the necessity to view masking as part of a semiotics of the performing body. It is demonstrated that the use of masks and the masked body is also subject to double encoding. On the one hand, dramatists in Africa, the Caribbean, and India can draw on intact indigenous ritual and performance traditions; on the other, there is usually some attempt to tap into the Western tradition of theatrical modernism and its experimentation with masks.

---

[1] Philip Auslander, 'Embodiment: The Politics of Postmodern Dance', *Drama Review*, 32/4 (Winter 1988), 9.

Le Corps Sauvage

The body as a material presence possesses semiotic possibilities, which have always been used in the theatre. These include biological givens such as sex, physical size, and ethnic origin. The way they have been used and to what ends is a subject that has attracted a great deal of scholarly attention. Recent research into the manipulation of sex and gender in particular has demonstrated the range of permutations which supposedly fixed categories such as sexual identity can be subjected to.[2] The play with ethnicity has attracted less attention, although some performance forms such as Black and White Ministrel Shows or theatrical conventions such as 'black' or 'white' Othellos have been examined to show that on stage at least ethnicity is also a malleable semiotic field rather than an immutable given.[3] The examples cited are, however, drawn from mainstream Western theatre. Of interest for this study is the question how indigenous dramatists and directors working in the syncretic mode take up the challenge posed by a theatrical tradition which had relegated or restricted indigenous performance and performers to the realm of folklore. In this context the 'savage body' was presented for the European gaze in its untrammelled 'naturalness'. The visual codes of folkloristic performance, which is almost always touristic performance, and its presentational form even today are still predicated on associations with and expectations of the 'noble savage'. The performer's body is presented in a state which is, if possible, 'untainted' by Western signs and thus timeless.[4] In both the Third and Fourth Worlds, but particularly the latter, touristic performances were for decades the only theatrical medium of expression for indigenous actors, dancers, and singers. And this touristic 'face' was correspondingly influential

[2] A great deal of research on this field has appeared in recent years. See particularly Laurence Senelick (ed.), *Performance in Gender: The Presentation of Difference in the Performing Arts* (Hanover: New England University Press, 1992), which includes several discussions of gender presentation in an intercultural context.

[3] On Shakespearean performance, see Errol Hill, *Shakespeare in Sable: A History of Black Shakespearean Actors* (Amherst: Massachusetts University Press, 1984). On wider questions of body politics in post-colonial drama, see Gilbert and Tompkins, *Post-Colonial Drama*, ch. 5.

[4] For a semiotic discussion of folklorization in the context of European festivals, see Marianne Mesnil, 'The Masked Festival: Disguise or Affirmation?', *Cultures*, 3/2 (1976), 11–29: folklorization means that particular cultural texts, especially with respect to the performance, have been frozen in a certain historical stage of development. Mesnil refers to 'fossilization' (p. 27).

in conditioning non-indigenous audiences. With this background experience in mind, it is little wonder that syncretic dramatists consciously work with the visual semiotics of the body as one of their dramaturgical tools.

Three categories are proposed under which syncretic dramatists and directors use the materiality of the body as theatrical strategies: the ethnicity of the body is either *effaced*, *resemanticized* in a particular way, or *mythologized*. Effacement, understood in the double sense of either erasure or self-effacement, refers to the process by which visual corporeality attains an abstract degree of referentiality. Resemanticization is the opposite process. An example of semanticization in this sense would be the explication of traditional body-painting for a theatre audience. Finally mythologization denotes the frequent use of mythological characters in syncretic plays and the physical appearance of such characters.

The strategy of *effacement* is characteristic of the early South African township productions. These plays created a code in which the neutrality and changeability of the body are paramount. The appearance of the actors Mbongeni Ngema and Percy Mtwa in *Woza Albert!* established the conventions of this code: unclad upper body, grey tracksuit trousers, socks, and running shoes (Plate 6). The photograph (Plate 7) of Peter Brook's Paris production of *Woza Albert!* suggests that this code established itself even outside South Africa. This basic uniform and its consciously intended associations with Grotowski's 'poor' theatre are reused in slightly altered form in other township plays such as *Asinamali!* and *Bopha!* Although this minimalizing effacement of body signs serves to underplay the actors' ethnicity—not the least reason for which being that they play Whites as well—and the acting body as a flexible sign becomes perhaps the most important signifier, ethnic significations do remain ever present because of the political background.

In addition to the significations of this corporeal code outlined above, it can also be read as a counter-discourse to the tradition of presenting the African body in a folkloristic context. South Africa can look back on a long and doubtful tradition of folkloristic theatre troupes presenting to a mainly foreign audience the image of Africans in an eternal state of dancing, singing, and drumming. Apart from the regular performances for foreign tourists and local audiences, troupes have gone on extended and often very successful international tours. That bare-breasted women, for example, were an integral component of such performances was more a reflection of the organizers' undifferentiated cultural projections than a genuine demonstration of particular ethnic practices.[5]

A tactical response to crude conceptions of this kind featuring 'happy' near-naked Blacks on stage is the scene in Mbongeni Ngema's play *Asinamali!* in which the Zulu Bongani relates how he was humiliated during a medical examination. In order to obtain a stamp in his pass which would permit him to reside and work in Johannesburg, Bongani has to undergo an examination for venereal disease:

No one has ever seen my man, except my older wife, maZulu. The other three . . . no way! They can't even touch it. [. . .] fifteen years with my four wives and my twelve children, no one has ever seen my man. But the first day I come to Johannesburg, a white boy commanded me to open my fly and show him my man.[6]

The stage directions indicate that the actors are to reveal their genitals on stage for this scene, which not only underscores the humiliating character of such practices, but presents to a white audience an image alluding to but totally at odds with the clichés established by touristic performances.[7]

Even more complex is Mbongeni Ngema's recourse to folkloristic images in his musical *Sarafina!*, which premièred in 1987. The final scene of this work, which deals with the resistance and determination of the black school children of Soweto, presents an unusual demonstration of folkloric performance. The presentation takes place within the context of a school celebration. Up to this point the pupils were seen in school uniforms; now they appear in traditional costume. The musical ends with a frenetic dance to the song 'Freedom is Coming Tomorrow', a symbolic anticipation of the day when Nelson

[5] For a critique of such productions, see Anthony Akerman's essay 'Why Must these Shows Go On?'. He argues that 'black musicals' such as *Ipi Tombi*, which idealize traditional culture, also reflect apartheid and represent mainly a projection of white directors and choreographers: '*Ipi Tombi* has been a great favourite among white theatre lovers in South Africa. It offers them a glimpse of naked black breasts—presumably passed by the censor because it is "tribal tradition" and not sexually titillating to a white audience—and a view of the black man in his "place".' 'Why Must these Shows Go On? A Critique of Black Musicals Made for White Audiences', *Theatre Quarterly*, 8/28 (Winter 1977–8), 69.

[6] Mbongeni Ngema, *Asinamali!*, in Ndlovu (ed.), *Woza Afrika!*, 207.

[7] This scene was initially banned by the South African censorship authority, then later permitted; see Sher, 'Apartheid on Tour', 62.

Mandela will be released.[8] The striking element in the scene is less the song itself, which is sung several times in the course of the action, than the image of African traditionalism being celebrated (see Plate 8). Although the image is, on the one hand, problematic in that it seems to confirm rather than critique the tradition of folkloristic performance, it is legitimate and coherent within the context of the story. The visual contrast alone of the traditional costumes and the austere school uniforms serves to illustrate the idea of liberation.[9]

How post-apartheid South Africa is to be shaped is not the subject of Ngema's musical. Whether he is advocating a return to the traditionalism that apartheid politics had itself propagated is highly unlikely considering his political position and his artistic endeavours as an exponent of a syncretic theatrical and musical culture.

Although the 'savage' body in *Sarafina!* is deployed in contrast to Western notions of African performance corporeality, one cannot say that a precise semanticization is attained. Concrete semanticization is, however, an important means of countering broad prejudices and misunderstandings. One such example of body semanticization can be seen in the use of body-painting on stage. This device sets up a very complex, ideologically fraught semiotic field. It creates associations with folkloric performance which, as we have seen, can have highly pejorative connotations for many indigenous performing artists. The aesthetics of folkloric performance try by definition to 'fossilize' cultural texts in a particular stage of historical development. In folkloric performance in Third and Fourth World contexts this usually means some state of pre-contact 'primitiveness'. The use of body-painting in particular creates further unfortunate associations with the 'painted savage' of pulp fiction and Hollywood. In post-colonial theatre in general there can be observed a tendency to experiment with a culturally appropriate contextualization of body decoration and to view the body in general as an important performative cultural text.

Aboriginal drama, for example, abounds with dancer-figures clad

[8] Of course, the scene was fortunately overtaken by history. Mandela's release from prison in 1990 happened while the *Sarafina!* troupe was on tour. The ending then became a celebration of this event rather than its anticipation.

[9] That Mbongeni Ngema also uses folkloristic display for its own sake is reinforced by his musical *Magic at 4 am* (1993), where the change to traditional costume and the extended display for dancing and singing no longer have the same dramaturgical justification nor the contrast with the school uniforms.

in loincloths and decorated with body paint. That body-painting as a particular form of textuality can have complex semiotic functions is shown in the *corroboree* scene from Jack Davis's historical play *No Sugar*. In the course of the *corroboree* the textuality of body-painting is shown to have far more than a decorative function—it contains its own sign system. In traditional culture body-painting is an essential component of rites of passage and other rituals. The three important occasions where it is used are circumcision, initiation of a young man into the ritual secrets and objects of his clan, and funerals. The painting is applied to breast and stomach and represents primarily totemistic affiliations. Depicted on the body are also the mythically sanctioned territorial rights of a clan: their part of the dreamtime myths. It is expected that every initiated Aborigine is familiar with the techniques of body-painting.[10]

As has already been mentioned, the *corroboree* depicted in *No Sugar* is of a secular nature.[11] It is an occasion where genuine cultural exchange takes place between groups of Aborigines from different districts and with differing contact to traditional lifestyle. Within the dramaturgy of the play the *corroboree* is shown to be the one moment where the antagonisms between the groups are suspended for the duration of the ceremony. The participants explain to each other tribal differences and the meaning of their songs, dances, and body-painting:

SAM [*pointing to Billy's body paint*]. Eh! Eh! Old man, what's that one?
BILLY. This one *bungarra*, an' he lookin' for berry bush. But he know that fella eagle watchin' him and he know that fella is cunnin' fella. He watchin' and lookin' for that eagle, that way, this way, that way, this way.

[*He rolls over a log, disappearing almost magically.* BLUEY *plays the didgeridoo and* BILLY *appears some distance away by turning quickly so the firelight reveals his painted body. He dances around, then seems to*

[10] There exists a close connection between the iconography of body-painting and the motifs of contemporary Aboriginal Art. On these aspects of body-painting, see Nancy Williams, 'Australian Aboriginal Art at Yirrkala: Introduction and Development of Marketing', in Graburn (ed.), *Tourist and Ethnic Arts*, 266–84, here p. 268. A comprehensive study of the iconography of body-painting as part of a symbolic system is provided by Nancy D. Munn in her book *Walbiri Iconography: Graphic Representation and Cultural Symbolism in a Central Australian Society* (Ithaca: Cornell University Press, 1973).
[11] The secular *corroboree* is a form of entertainment in which past and present concerns are represented; see Oxford, 'The Purple Everlasting', 93 f.; and Berndt and Berndt, *The World of the First Australians*, 381–7.

disappear suddenly. He rolls back over the log and drops down, seated by the fire.][12]

Billy's explication of his body-painting as well as the brief dance, point to different aspects of a particular kind of corporeal semioticization. Billy's explanations show the cartography of the body through painting. The painting depicts the interplay between the goanna (*bungarra*), presumably Billy's totem, a berry bush, and an eagle. As well as having an iconographic function, the painting is part of a performative complex. This performative aspect becomes clear when Billy shifts from explaining the painting to actually dancing the action depicted. The extensive stage direction and above all the allusion to the firelight underline that the aesthetic function of body-painting revolves around the interplay of light, body motion, and darkness. This dynamic aesthetic effect makes clear that the significance of this scene transcends by far a mere ethnographic explication of body-painting for the uninitiated spectator. Rather it is an attempt by Davis to point out the particular aesthetics of traditional Aboriginal theatricality. The important difference in this scene as compared to the use of body-painting in his other plays is that there is no attempt to mythologize the figures. They are part of the material world of the drama. In plays such as *The Dreamers* or *Barungin* (*Smell the Wind*), the decorated dancer-figure appears to stem from a non-localizable past or is a symbol for a lost way of life. In *No Sugar*, on the other hand, the decorated dancers are characters in the play with whom the audience is already familiar. In this way there is a conscious attempt on the part of Davis to demythologize notions of *le corps sauvage*.

Although the notion of a demythologized body can be applied to this one scene at least, there are an equal number of examples in plays from the Fourth World where one can discern the opposite strategy: a mythologized body. What is meant by this is the frequent appearance of figures which belong to the realm of myth. The common factor linking such characters in Maori, Aboriginal, and Native American plays is that they represent the idea that the realms of the mythical and the quotidian are in some way contiguous or coexistent. Although this thematic element indicates an intriguing link between culturally and geographically disparate works, the visual solutions for representing such figures are by no means homogeneous.

[12] Davis, *No Sugar*, 66.

The heterogeneity of visual representation is certainly influenced by the fact that the notion of mythical use here is itself a broad one. Whereas some characters such as the ubiquitous Trickster figure Nanabush or Weesagechak in Canadian Native drama can be classified unequivocally as mythic, other figures represent ancestors occupying an intermediary realm between actual tribal history and mythical time, as is the case in some Maori plays. The enigmatic dancer-figures which populate Aboriginal plays can frequently be linked neither to a specific myth nor to a defined historical period. However, this kind of fixed referentiality is not significant. More important is the visual appearance, as these figures communicate primarily with non-verbal codes. They are both a pure presence, and thus difficult to semioticize, and a corporeal text that wants to be decoded.

Examples of the enigmatic Aboriginal dancer can be found in *The Dreamers* and *Barungin*. In both plays the dancer-figure clad in loin-cloth and decorated with body paint emanates an unsettling presence. The fact that these two plays represent two parts of a larger family drama suggests that there are particular dramaturgical reasons for having the continuity of such a physical presence.[13] It is quite clear that this figure represents a link with the pre-contact or least traditional way of life. In the case of the Aborigines from the area around Perth this culture has been totally destroyed, an omnipresent background to the daily life of the Wallitch family in suburbia.[14] As the dancer in *The Dreamers* always appears in connection with old Worru, he indexes in a way Worru's still partially intact link to traditional life. In both plays the spatial contiguity of a traditional body image and the everyday clothing of the other characters is very

---

[13] There is a slight change in the dancer's appearance, however. In *The Dreamers* the didascalic description preceding the first appearance of the dancer reads: 'an intricately painted DANCER'. Jack Davis, *Kullark (Home)/The Dreamers* (Sydney: Currency Press, 1982), 80. In *Barungin* the direction reads just 'dancer', without further iconographic specification.

[14] The function of the dancer in *The Dreamers* is given the following explanation by Andrew Ross, the first director of all Jack Davis's plays: '[The dancer] was going to serve a number of purposes. It was to find some way of opening the old man's consciousness and exploring his ability to live on a number of levels. That while he was living physically in this very restrictive suburban place that he still had a relationship with the land, the past, with a spirit world, but also with the world of his childhood and his youth which was so radically different to the historical world I suppose.' Andrew Ross, interviewed by Christopher Balme, Perth; 16 Mar. 1991 repr. in Balme, 'Strategien des synkretischen Theaters', 399.

much a question of proxemics, as the photograph from a production of *Barungin* illustrates (Plate 9).

At the end of *The Dreamers* the dancer-figure gains another visual dimension which has little in common with folkloric nostalgia. Shortly before Worru's death the dancer appears in the ceremonial body decoration of a featherfoot—a harbinger of death or ritual executioner in traditional Aboriginal society.

Shafts of cold light fade in revealing THE DANCER as featherfoot at the front of the stage. He is heavily decorated with leaves and carries two short sticks.[15]

After Worru's death the featherfoot reappears and scatters leaves across the stage in a symbolic act that is both culturally appropriate and decodable for a non-Aboriginal audience.

A decorated Aboriginal dancer-figure in the mythological convention also features in Eva Johnson's play *Murras*. This figure is the 'Mimi Spirit', which represents a connecting element between the characters of the present—the action, set in the 1960s and 1970s, is concerned with problems of urbanization—and the traditional way of life. The author outlines the ethnographic background of the figure in a prefatory note:

Mimi is a mythical being that inhabits certain parts of the country. It can be the spirit of a dead ancestor, sometimes friendly, sometimes hostile, and the Mimi dance is very much a part of the traditional dances performed today. Mimi is a very powerful spirit who can generate magic to bring about sickness and death. It is the caretaker of the dead spirit.[16]

In this commentary the figure is related to the dreamtime. As with Jack Davis's dancer-figures the Mimi Spirit moves to the language of dance, accompanied by didgeridoo music and the rhythms of the clapsticks. The visual appearance of the figure differs considerably, however, from Davis's dancers, who appear usually clad only in a loincloth and body paint. In the original Adelaide production of *Murras*, the Mimi Spirit wore close-fitting leotards, on which ceremonial body-painting was applied (see Plate 10).[17]

---

[15] Davis, *Kullark (Home)/The Dreamers*, 130.
[16] Eva Johnson, *Murras*, in *Plays from Black Australia* (Sydney: Currency Press, 1989), 84.
[17] The première took place in Mar. 1988 as part of the Adelaide Fringe Festival. It was directed by the author.

In this solution the *corps sauvage* is consciously stylized through the device of painting onto leotards. Although the dancer is still recognizable as a 'real' Aborigine, the costume signals a convergence with the conventions of theatrical dance and a distancing from associations with folkloric performance. *Le corps sauvage* is incorporated into the code of Western theatre while retaining at the same time its connection with Aboriginal culture. This solution signals that the ethnic materiality of body signs loses significance. The ethnic corporeality is literally covered up and reproduced artistically. In view of this strategy of aestheticization, it is possible even to conceive of a non-Aboriginal performer in this role, something that would hardly be acceptable in the works of Jack Davis. It is doubtful, however, whether this would quite be in keeping with the ideals of the Aboriginal theatre movement, which is rightly concerned that such roles should be performed by Aborigines.

Mythical figures are also a feature of Maori theatre in New Zealand. In one of the earliest works of this movement, Rore Hapipi's court drama dealing with land disputes, *Death of the Land* (first performed 1976), a mythical being, Rongo, makes his presence felt, accompanied by bizarre lighting effects and eerie sounds. The author terms the figure a 'supernatural and omnipotent being. He is the manifestation of the conscience and consciousness of the Maori voices whose thoughts would otherwise be unsaid.'[18] Although not specified by the author, Rongo or Rongomatane, the god of peace in Maori mythology, has an identifiable place in Maori cosmology.

Rongo's appearance in Hapipi's play may have possibly provided a model for Hone Tuwhare's play *In the Wilderness without a Hat*, which was written a year later. Here too mythical figures interfere in worldly events, also accompanied by unusual lighting and sound effects. However, the semiotic function and scenic realization of Tuwhare's figures is more complex. First introduced as wood-carvings, in the course of the action they transform themselves from iconographic signs into living beings. Since their first appearance is in the form of wall-carvings of a family meeting-house, they are initially firmly located in their traditional cultural system. When they comment on or, in the third act, directly influence events in the meeting-house, this corresponds to the accepted notion in the Maori belief system that the ancestors are contiguous with their living descendants,

[18] Hapipi, *Death of the Land*, 16.

an idea that is given form in the wood-carvings. When in the third act the funeral ritual becomes bogged down in dispute, the ancestors, as well as an unnamed statue of a Maori warrior, intervene. This action marks the culmination of a gradual process of reintegration. The ancestral figures undergo a transformation from the static form of wood-carvings, who can speak but not move, to the proxemical level of their physical intervention in the fist fight that has broken out amongst the family members. The only indication of physical appearance that Tuwhare gives is the laconic direction 'skin-tight masks and hair-wigs'.[19] This costume serves to conceal material body signs and to achieve an approximation of the formal characteristics of wood-carving.

Tuwhare's play underlines more than anything else the idea that mythical-ancestral figures are adaptable beings and any attempt to 'stage' them must take into account this characteristic. Adaptability is also the key to understanding the unusual visual forms that mythical figures take on in Canadian Native drama, particularly in the plays of Tomson Highway. In his essay 'On Native Mythology' Highway stresses the tremendous possibilities that such figures offer for visual staging: 'Indian mythology is filled with the most extraordinary events, beings and creatures. These lend themselves so well to visual interpretation, to exciting stage and visual creation. [. . .] Not only are the visuals powerful, the symbolism underlying these extraordinary stories is as basic and as direct as air.'[20] The key figure in Tomson Highway's work is a trickster character known to the Ojibwa as Nanabush and to the Cree, Highway's people, as Weesagechak. The dominant characteristic of this figure is its flexibility. Depending on context, it can appear in any number of human or animal forms. In addition Nanabush can be categorized neither as exclusively male or female nor as predominantly good or evil.[21] These three characteristics provide for Highway the traditional cultural basis on which to shape his visual and dramatic version of the figure. Because of

---

[19] Ibid. 57. [20] Highway, 'On Native Mythology', 30.

[21] For an ethnographic discussion of this creature, see the commentary in Jennifer Brown and Robert Brightman, *'The Orders of the Dreamed': George Nelson on Cree and Northern Ojibwa Religion and Myth 1823* (Winnipeg: Manitoba University Press, 1988), and Richard J. Preston, *Cree Narrative: Expressing the Personal Meanings of Events* (Ottawa: National Museum of Man, 1975). In interviews Tomson Highway has made frequent reference to the figure and invariably stressed the characteristics of adaptability of form and sexual and moral ambivalence. He is primarily concerned to adapt Nanabush for a contemporary theatre public.

Nanabush's proverbial transformability there is no set iconographic tradition for a dramatist or director to work from or react against. Hence, the first striking feature in Highway's plays is the absence of folkloristic elements in Nanabush's depiction. In the first production of *The Rez Sisters* (1988) Nanabush was played by a dancer dressed in jeans and T-shirt. While the conception of Nanabush-as-dancer is Highway's invention—there appears to be no ethnographic evidence for it—it is dramaturgically coherent because in this way the figure is removed from the level of dialogue. Specific kinaesthetic aspects are of less importance, as Highway is not concerned to specify a particular type of dance: 'a male dancer—modern, ballet, or traditional'[22] is the only requirement.[23] Much more important are Nanabush's diverse physical appearances. In accordance with his well-known adaptability, he appears variously as a seagull, a nighthawk, and finally as the master of ceremonies of a bingo game. The effect of these different 'roles', although it is more than debatable whether the term is even applicable here, is to highlight the play's unreal level. The figure of Nanabush in his various guises provides Highway with a means to bring into play a level of experience beyond the empirical and quotidian, which otherwise dominates the seven women's lives on the reservation. The intervention by Nanabush in their lives can be seen as analogous to structural features found in Native oral traditions, where the borders between mythological and empirical worlds are not clearly demarcated. In such stories Nanabush can operate in both worlds.[24] The consciousness that the mythological and the empirical worlds are in some way contiguous can be seen in the hope expressed by the character Pelajia that Nanabush's return will hasten the realization of local development projects: 'and Nanabush will come back to us because he'll have paved roads to dance on'.[25]

Nanabush undergoes even more spectacular metamorphoses in Highway's most successful work to date, *Dry Lips Oughta Move to Kapuskasing* (1989). This play features the men related or connected

[22] Highway, *The Rez Sisters*, p. xi.
[23] In the first production Highway's brother René, a dancer, performed this role by combining traditional Cree and Ojibwa dances with modern dance.
[24] Ethnographic research differentiates between two narrative genres which correspond to an emic category of Cree and Ojibwa orality: *acaðōhkīwin* are stories belonging to a distant mythic past; *acimōwin* are stories which take place in the here and now and can include human beings whom the narrator may even know; see Brown and Brightman, *'The Orders of the Dreamed'*, 125. Nanabush stories belong to both categories.   [25] Highway, *The Rez Sisters*, 59.

to the Rez Sisters living on the same reservation. In accordance with the gender shift, Nanabush now appears in various female forms. To explain this transformation Highway provides a note to the published text. He draws a comparison between the lack of gender specification in Indian languages, which he terms the 'male–female–neuter hierarchy', and the indeterminate gender of the trickster. Indirectly he justifies the 'sex change' that Nanabush undergoes between the two plays. He goes on to explain the significance of such a figure for contemporary Native culture:

So that by this system of thought, the central hero figure from our myth-ology—theology, if you will—is theoretically neither exclusively male nor exclusively female, or is both simultaneously. [. . .] Some say that Nanabush left this continent when the white man came. We believe she/he is still here among us—albeit a little the worse for wear and tear having assumed other guises. Without the continued presence of this extraordinary figure, the core of Indian culture would be gone forever.[26]

The forms assumed by Nanabush in *Dry Lips* are those of women spoken about in the course of the action, although often grotesquely distorted. Highway merges in a provocative but consistent fashion the 'spirituality' of Nanabush as a mythical figure with the icons of Western culture. Nanabush's 'perch' is, for example, a jukebox, on which a female figure depicted by Nanabush gives birth in a drunken stupor; the jukebox is later transformed into a toilet, on which Nana-bush is found answering the call of nature as an iconographic parody of the Christian god ('He/she is dressed in an old man's white beard and wig, but also wearing sexy, elegant women's high-heeled pumps');[27] in another scene Nanabush performs a strip (see Plate 11); in another he/she is an over-weight teenage girl with an over-large artificial rear-end ('prosthetic bum'). This list makes clear that for Highway the sphere of corporeality is central to Nanabush as a stage figure. Since these appearances are mostly in the form of flashbacks, the bizarre body images are to be understood as distorted projections of male imagination and memory. At the same time the accumulation of scatalogical and obscene images can be seen as a theatrical counter-model to the folkloristic and idealized-romantic notions of Indian spirituality so dear to popular culture. If the mythological creature Nanabush is to survive as a contemporary and culturally

---

[26] Highway, *Dry Lips Oughta Move to Kapuskasing*, 12 f.   [27] Ibid. 117.

appropriate stage figure, then he/she (this seems to be one of High-way's messages in the play) will have to adapt to and assume images deriving from popular mass culture, which are an integral part of present-day Native experience.[28]

The comparison of four different theatre movements from as many countries serves to demonstrate that visual body signs, quite independently of their kinaesthetic qualities, form an important textual vehicle for indigenous theatre artists. The body and its transformation into various shapes and forms was always an important part of traditional cultural performances. Therefore it is only logical that writers and directors seek to make use of this existing repertoire while avoiding the pitfalls of reverting back to romanticized images associated with folkloric and touristic performances. Related to this difficult semiotic area is the next section of this chapter, in which the masked body—it too a favourite object of primitivist aesthetics—will be discussed.

The Masked Body

The strategies of corporeal performance outlined above can be considered unique to syncretic theatre. Masking, however, while being a striking feature of syncretic theatre texts, is also subject to double encoding. Dramatists can draw on traditional forms of masking, but also on modernist approaches to masks, explored by many Western theatre artists. The status of mask use in Western theatre is controversial. It oscillates between vehement rejection and passionate advocacy. The absence of masks from mainstream theatre is, of course, linked to the dominance of psychological drama, while their reappearance in theory and practice at the beginning of this century is motivated by dissatisfaction with precisely this tradition. It provides one of the foundations for Edward Gordon Craig's Theatre of the Future[29] and

[28] See Highway's commentary on the modern manifestations of Nanabush-Weesa-gechak in his article 'On Native Mythology', 29 f.: 'he also takes strolls down Yonge Street, drinks beer, sometimes passes out at the Silver Dollar and goes shopping at the Eaton Centre. You should have seen him when he first encountered a telephone, an electric typewriter, a toaster, an automobile. I was there.'

[29] See Edward Gordon Craig, 'I should say that the face of Irving was the connecting link between that spasmodic and ridiculous expression of the human face as used by the theatres of the last few centuries, and the masks which will be used in place of the human face in the near future.' 'The Artists of the Theatre of the Future', in *On the Art of the Theatre* (London: Heinemann, 1911), 12–13. See also Craig's essay 'A Note on Masks', in *The Theatre Advancing* (London: Constable, 1921), 60–125.

represents for Vsevolod Meyerhold in the middle phase of his work a 'symbol of theatre' itself.[30] Among leading contemporary directors there is similar dissent. On the one hand, we find advocates such as Giorgio Strehler and Ariane Mnouchkine, who seek to draw on the tradition of masking in popular culture.[31] On the other, there is Peter Brook's sceptical attitude to reintroducing to 'Western art theatre' what he calls the morbid mask.[32] Brook's standpoint is representative of a widespread view that Western culture has lost any kind of functional masking tradition. As Susan Smith puts it: 'The modern Western world is mask-poor. The areas where masks retain their cultural and religious meanings are all outside the boundaries of Western tradition.'[33] The art historian Herbert Cole comes to a similar conclusion in connection with his notes on ritual-transformational functions of African masks: 'Spirit transformations are complex phenomena, especially when compared to the minor and vestigial roles played by masks and masking in the modern Western world.'[34]

In comparison to this 'minor and vestigial' function in Western culture, masking is still an integral part of ritual and ceremonial life in many post-colonial cultures. Despite the inroads and influences of industrialization, Western-style education, and imported religions such as Christianity and Islam, scholars such as Cole conclude that the cult significance and practice of masks is still intact 'in much of Africa'.[35] In such cultures masks are not just a theatrical device but represent a link to the parallel world of spirits, gods, and ancestors. In this context masks and their performative display are cultural texts, precisely encoded and decipherable for the initiated. This masking tradition can be grouped under the broad rubric of *cult*

[30] See his essay 'Balagan' (1912), in *Meyerhold on Theatre*, tr. Edward Braun (London: Methuen, 1969). The rediscovery of masking by the anti-naturalistic theatre movement is the subject of a study by Susan Valeria Harris Smith, *Masks in Modern Drama* (Berkeley: University of California Press, 1984). Smith begins in 1896 with Alfred Jarry and includes in her survey a great number of dramatists, directors, and theatre-reformers who have experimented with masks such as Yeats, Brecht, Genet, Cocteau, O'Neill, Pirandello, Ionesco, Craig, Meyerhold, and Artaud.
[31] See the essays by Giorgio Strehler and Ariane Mnouchkine in the informative volume Odette Aslan and Denis Bablet (eds.), *Le Masque: Du rite au théâtre* (Paris: Éditions du CNRS, 1985).
[32] This is not to say that Brook has not used masks in his own work; see Peter Brook's essay 'The Mask—Coming out of our Shell', in *The Shifting Point: Forty Years of Theatrical Exploration 1946–1987* (London: Methuen, 1988).
[33] Smith, *Masks in Modern Drama*, 3.
[34] Herbert M. Cole (ed.), *I am not Myself: The Art of African Masquerade* (Los Angeles: Museum of Cultural History, 1985), 19. [35] Ibid.

masks. Another tradition, which is of a more secular nature, can be termed *ceremonial masks*. These include masks used in various carnival traditions, where the original ritual or cult function has been forfeited, but new ones such as satire have been created. A third type is the *theatrical mask*. This category is primarily aesthetic and includes both the Western and oriental traditions. The use of masks in syncretic theatre is predicated on the interaction between the first two categories with the third.

Before embarking on a closer study of particular texts and performances, it is necessary to place masking in a wider performative context than that usually associated with it in Western theatre. The use of full-body masks in West African masking traditions such as *egungun* particularly underlines the necessity to view masking as part of a semiotics of the performing body. African masks have been perceived in the West almost entirely as exhibitive objects, a form of sculpture divorced from its kinaesthetic performative context. In contrast to Western aesthetics, however, African sculptural traditions are closely tied to the performing arts. Many art objects, above all masks, have a precisely defined ritual or ceremonial function whose aesthetic effect is dependent on display through dance. A mask or masked costume is 'Art in Motion', as Robert Farris Thompson entitles his seminal study of African plastic and performance arts.[36] At the centre of Thompson's thesis is a set of, for the European mind, apparent antinomies: 'Icon and Act', 'Art in Motion', 'Danced Art'. According to Thompson it is necessary to overcome dichotomous Western aesthetic categories in order to arrive at an understanding of African art in its broadest sense. This view is echoed by the French scholar Jean Laude, who perceives a connection between the outer form of a mask and its kinaesthetic performance: '[The mask] is in fact conceived as varying with movement in a three-dimensional space, to which it is thus related [. . .] Hence the masks used in the liveliest dances present a more angular aspect and are made up of more clearly separated planes than the masks worn in less complicated slower figures.'[37]

The importance of the *egungun* masks in Wole Soyinka's work, particularly in *The Road* and *Death and the King's Horseman*, has

---

[36] Thompson, *African Art in Motion*.
[37] Jean Laude, *Les Arts d'Afrique noire* (Paris: Le Livre de Poche 1966); cited in Graham-White, *The Drama of Black Africa*, 40.

already been mentioned in the discussion of ritual. Traditional Yoruba performance is perhaps best encapsulated by the *egungun* masqueraders.[38] The masked *egungun* dancer with his whirling display of line and colour, and his direct connection with the metaphysical world, could be considered the central icon in Soyinka's performance aesthetics, in addition to the multifaceted deity Ogun, whom Soyinka explicitly acknowledges as the embodiment of his wider aesthetic creed. The *egungun* masquerader is a recurrent figure and metaphor in his writing. In his autobiography, *Aké: The Years of Childhood*, Soyinka writes of the fear and trepidation accompanying the appearance of masqueraders in his town—and this despite his strict Christian upbringing. In a characteristic act of mental syncretism, the child Soyinka merges the saints depicted on the stained-glass windows of the church with the colourful garb of the masked dancers.[39] They were the messengers of a sacred world coexistent to the one the child inhabited, yet their theatrical antics—both destructive and entertaining—represented an attitude to the sacred that was entirely absent in Christianity: the comic and the tragic, violence and entertainment, alternated and existed side by side. The fact that the masqueraders are actually supposed to embody gods or ancestors and not just represent them adds a further dimension to performative communication entirely absent in Western theatre.

Soyinka's syncretistic merging of masqueraders and saints finds concrete expression in the icons used in the costumes of the dancers. The costumes themselves are an elaborate patchwork of materials and colours, visual *bricolage*, while the masks are often clearly recognizable iconic representations of animals, gods, or even ethnic groups, including Europeans. A masquerader has no difficulty in perching a pith helmet on top of a headdress to represent a British colonial officer, which demonstrates in visual terms that 'attitude of

[38] There is a considerable corpus of ethnographical literature on *egungun*. See the special number of *African Arts*, 11/3 (1978). In his introduction to this issue Drewal defines *egungun* in its broadest sense as 'any masquerade or masked figure. At the basis of this definition is the belief in the presence of some supernatural force.' He then goes on to distinguish *egungun* as a separate tradition attributed to the Oyo Yoruba 'and associated with the honoring of ancestors'. Henry John Drewal, 'The Arts of Egungun among Yoruba Peoples', 18. This area is the one from which Soyinka himself comes and is the tradition with which he is clearly most familiar. The distinction is, however, an ethno-geographical one and not of concern for this study.

[39] Wole Soyinka, *Aké: The Years of Childhood* (London: Rex Collings, 1981), 31–2.

philosophic accommodation'[40] that Soyinka considers to be a vital characteristic of the African world-view.[41]

In one of his earliest syncretic works, *A Dance of the Forests*, Soyinka experimented with a number of masking functions. The central idea of the play, the action of humans and ancestors, is itself predicated on a basic notion of *egungun* masking, which 'stages', as it were, in a ritual function this very interaction. When the three human characters, Demoke, Rola, and Adenebi, put on masks they become possessed; for Eshuoro and his fool, however, the masks serve to conceal their identities. In this way Soyinka mixes cult and theatrical mask functions in such a way that it is often difficult to separate them out.[42] In *The Road* the mask becomes an object of dispute between competing belief systems: Ogun worship, represented by the drivers, and Western-Christian metaphysics embodied by the Professor.

In *Death and the King's Horseman* Soyinka experiments again with the theatrical possibilities of the *egungun* mask, particularly in the second scene, which is set in the bungalow of the District Officer, Pilkings. Structurally, this scene revolves around three different types of text—verbal, visual, and acoustic—and the difficulties of intercultural communication they can provoke. The first text is visual: the appearance of Pilkings and his wife dancing a tango in *egungun* costumes and the reactions this performance evokes in the two African witnesses.[43] Throughout the scene it becomes clear, even to a spectator without knowledge of Yoruba culture, that the Pilkingses' 'fancy dress costume' is, for Sergeant Amusa and the houseboy, Joseph, a cultural text; it is an ensemble of signs which change according to the wearer of the dress and according to the context in which it

[40] Soyinka, *Myth, Literature and the African World*, 54.
[41] According to Joachim Fiebach, the openness, flexibility, and accommodative attitude of contemporary African theatre towards Western theatre forms is something observable in the communicative structures of traditional performance forms and points to a continuity in theatrical aesthetics from pre- to post-colonial times. Joachim Fiebach, 'Offenheit und Beweglichkeit theatralischer Kommunikation in Afrika. Kulturelle Identitäten und internationale Aspekte', in Breitinger (ed.), *Drama and Theatre in Africa*, 42 f.
[42] The functions of the masks are, like most elements in this play, extremely complicated; for a clear delineation of the various masks and their dramaturgical functions, see Götrick, *Apidan Theatre and Modern Drama*, 155–6.
[43] 'Costume' is not really a culturally appropriate term because of its specific associations with theatre and fancy dress; 'dress' is perhaps a more neutral term. Drewal, 'The Arts of Egungun among Yoruba Peoples', 18, defines *egungun* masquerades as 'elaborate ensembles of cloth and other media', although he also uses the term 'costume'.

is worn. The messages this text conveys can thus have radically different, existentially important meanings. The functionalization of the potentially highly dangerous *egungun* dress (traditionally it is thought to be dangerous, even fatal, to touch an *egungun*) as fancy dress is not just an expression of ignorance on the part of the Pilkings, but a visual concretization of the colonial policy to break up and destroy the *egungun* cults. The masks and costumes have been confiscated after just such an action and the cult members arrested. The changing attitude of the Yoruba is also reflected by the different ways in which Amusa and Joseph 'read' the highly confusing semiotic situation. In Amusa's case Soyinka differentiates very subtly in the opening of the scene:

He peeps through and observes the dancing couple, reacting with what is obviously a long-standing bewilderment. He stiffens suddenly, his expression changes to one of disbelief and horror. In his excitement he upsets a flower-pot and attracts the attention of the couple. They stop dancing.[44]

The phrase 'long-standing bewilderment' clearly refers to his normal perplexity regarding the recreational activities of his commanding officer. At this point he can only perceive shadowy figures. The change to 'disbelief and horror' signals that he has recognized that they are wearing *egungun* dress. It is important to be aware, firstly, that the costume totally conceals the wearer: Amusa is confronted with two *egungun* in the 'sacred' space of the colonial bungalow, an entirely Western cultural space, and hence with a bewildering conflation of signs; and, secondly, that only a month before Amusa had arrested *egungun* cult members. Their 'reappearance' then, in the house of the District Officer, possibly signals an act of retribution on the part of the cult. Pilkings's ensuing perplexity and irritation at what he considers to be an inexplicable reaction of a Muslim underlines the overly schematized European concepts regarding religion: 'Come on Amusa, you don't believe in all that nonsense do you? I thought you were a good Moslem.' However, conversion in an African context did not always mean the radical exclusion of indigenous belief, but resulted often in the coexistence of belief systems, or even in syncretization in many cases. Amusa's identification of cult mask and wearer shows that, Muslim or no, he is fully cognizant of

[44] Soyinka, *Six Plays*, 163.

the implications of the costume: 'Is not good for man like you to touch that cloth.' And his refusal to report on Elesin's impending suicide in the presence of the mask is entirely logical within the framework of traditional Yoruba culture, since the ritual and the *egungun* society are part of one and the same cultural system: 'Sir, it is a matter of death. How can man talk against death to person in uniform of death. Is like talking against government to person in uniform of police.'[45]

The houseboy, Joseph, reads the mask somewhat differently. For him, 'it has no power'[46] and because Pilkings is a 'good Christian. Black man juju can't touch master.'[47] The differing reactions of the two men point to disparate processes of conversion that Islam and Christianity effected on the Yoruba. Whereas Islam frequently resulted in a rearrangement and realignment of beliefs with indigenous practices, Christianity, in the early period of its missionary zeal, actively combated traditional beliefs and created a situation of mutual exclusivity and, in many cases, equally ferocious missionary zeal on the part of the new adherents.[48]

In summary, it can be seen that the *egungun* mask is a highly complex sign and cultural text. It is capable of transmitting a bundle of conflicting and contradictory messages because of the different receptive codes and their contexts. It is, in Peircean terms, at once iconic, symbolic, and indexical—in itself not usual. The more interesting question concerns which sign type is dominant here. In terms of its iconicity it is, of course, a theatrical sign, a necessarily recognizable imitation of an *egungun* masquerader to those spectators familiar with that model. Within the fiction of the play, the iconic function is intact for all characters. Of course the ideas the icon evokes in the minds of the beholders are, however, highly disparate, as has been demonstrated. For spectators with no knowledge whatsoever of Yoruba culture, the appearance of the *egungun* dancers cannot be linked to any clearly defined model. Their semiosis of the situation thus takes place primarily on the level of symbol (in a Peircean sense); that is, the scene can be read only on a conventionalized level and will

[45] Soyinka, *Six Plays*, 164 f.   [46] Ibid. 167.   [47] Ibid. 168.
[48] For a comparison of the two religions in Africa, see Ali A. Mazrui, *The Africans: A Triple Heritage* (London: Guild Publishing, 1988), ch. 7: 'Africa at Prayer: New Gods': 'Islam has appeared to be more accommodating to the wider culture of Africa, more ready to compromise with African ancestral customs and usages' (p. 141). For the specific case of the Yoruba between Christianity and Islam, see p. 137.

remain so until more collateral information has been gathered, and which, indeed, is provided in the course of the scene. The mask is also an indexical sign to the extent that a certain contiguity exists between its iconic appearance and its embodiment of supernatural powers, at least to Amusa. For him it is not a *symbol* of dangerous supernatural powers but directly *indicates* that they are there, present. This example demonstrates that it is difficult to isolate a single dominant semiotic function, but that the semiosis is in constant flux, depending on the receiver of the information.

That masks and masklike costumes in a ritual context are not just symbols but may in fact embody supernatural forces indicates a transformative process offering a powerful metaphor for the theatre. In Caribbean syncretic theatre we can detect a tendency to experiment with this metaphor of transformation which is integral to the cult mask and residually present in the ceremonial mask. The strongest living mask tradition in the Caribbean is a ceremonial one, that of carnival culture. Thus it is not surprising that Errol Hill seizes on the visual potential of carnival masks for his vision of a carnival-based syncretic theatre:

Verbal metaphor will be matched by visual symbol. The mask, an ancient theatrical device, which has largely disappeared from the modern theatre, is still a powerful symbol in countries with traditional religious and ritual practices. In Trinidad, through the carnival, masks and masquerades have acquired an urban sophistication that extends their meaning and utility in the theatre.[49]

Hill's comment is representative of a widespread tendency in the Caribbean to extol the virtues of masking on a theoretical or programmatic level without actually using them in concrete dramatical works. One of the reasons for this is suggested implicitly in Hill's comment. What he calls 'urban sophistication' of carnival masking is in fact a change in function from cult to festival and ceremony. The link with 'traditional religious and ritual practices'—Hill is referring here presumably to West African religion—is in the Caribbean a tenuous one as far as masking is concerned. The retentions of West African masking traditions are present only in a secularized form in carnival. Another reason why masks have not become a standard element in Caribbean theatre, as Hill perhaps envisaged, is that

---

[49] Hill, *The Trinidad Carnival*, 116.

carnival masks themselves are tied up in a rigid semiotic. Although they are not subject to strict typologies, their representative function and thus their potential for adaptation to another context, i.e. a play, is severely limited: carnival masks indicate primarily carnival masks. The transformative potential of masks that Hill imagines is in the case of carnival somewhat restricted.[50]

One way of getting around this problem is to set the play itself in a carnival or carnival-like situation. An interesting experiment in this direction is Sylvia Wynter's play *Maskarade* (1973).[51] It deals with the Jamaican performance form *jonkunnu*, a type of masquerade that sprang up in Jamaica in the eighteenth century combining elements of African rites, English morris dancing, and French carnival customs. The play itself grew out of a scholarly article by Wynter in which she traces the acculturative elements leading to the creation of an indigenous Jamaican performance tradition.[52] The high point of *jonkunnu* festivals lay in the early nineteenth century, after which it was subject to official repression resulting in steady decline until it practically died out. Its practice today is the result of a folkloric revival.

Wynter's play links both performance traditions, the present and the past. While the action begins in the present, the main plot is set in

---

[50] Hill writes that he does not expect every production of a Caribbean national theatre to use plays with masks, but the theatricality of the device is too 'potent' to be neglected. In what way the meaning of masking has been 'extended' in carnival and how this 'potent' aesthetic potential is to be understood exactly is not stated; ibid.

[51] The play was first produced on television and broadcast by the Jamaica Broadcasting Corporation in 1973. The first stage production took place in 1979 at the Creative Arts Centre of the University of the West Indies, Mona. Since then it has been staged in various versions. A play script was published in Sylvia Wynter, *Maskarade*, in *Plays for Schools*, introd. and notes by Jeanne Wilson, (Kingston: Jamaica Publishing House, 1979).

[52] See Wynter, 'Jonkonnu in Jamaica', 34–48. Wynter pays particular attention to the influence of African mask traditions, pointing out that the concept of mask here refers to the costume as a whole and is of fundamental religious significance. The masks represent a link with the supernatural and are inseparable from their performance in dance (pp. 35 f.). Through this argument Wynter tries to find a basis for the carnivalesque mask of *jonkunnu* in the West African cult mask, particularly in the practice of *egungun* masquerading. She sees in the *jonkunnu* figure of Pitchie-Patchie, who wears a brightly checked costume, an iconographical mixture of Harlequin and an *egungun* dancer. Wynter's article has contributed to an upsurge in interest in *jonkunnu*; see particularly the studies by Judith Bettelheim: 'The Jonkunnu Festival', *Jamaica Journal*, 10/2–4 (1976), and *The Afro-Jamaican Jonkunnu Festival* (New Haven: Yale University Press, 1979); see also her superbly illustrated contribution on *jonkunnu* in John Nunley (ed.), *Caribbean Festival Arts*, (Seattle: Washington University Press, 1988).

1841 in Kingston, the year in which *jonkunnu* masquerades were officially banned. The link between the past and present is provided by an old puppeteer and his apprentice, who stage a *jonkunnu* performance with marionettes in the present. The story narrated and performed by the puppeteers is that of the riots of 1841. On a raised rear stage we begin to see these events acted out by actors, musicians, and masked dancers. These living performers become then an enlarged projection of the puppet play on the front stage.

The main plot is a drama of jealousy that ends with the death of two *jonkunnu* performers. An older performer becomes infatuated with a pretty young actress. The courtship is watched with growing anger by both his wife and the lover of the young lady. As the troupe performs its *jonkunnu* play, the romantic conflict of this play within a play spills over into the growing tension between the performers themselves. This conflict leads to violent clashes between rival *jonkunnu* troupes, which finally provides the authorities with an excuse to ban all troupes from the precincts of Kingston.

The complexity of *Maskarade* results from its dramaturgical structure and its performance aesthetics. The former arises from the action with its three telescoped dramatic stories: the play of the puppeteer; the conflict within the *jonkunnu* troupe; and, finally, the *jonkunnu* play that the troupe itself performs. The performance aesthetics revolve around the spectacular masks and costuming of the *jonkunnu* players and the music and dance of their performances. The masks themselves have a double function: they index the performance genre of *jonkunnu*, but also provide the traditional theatrical function of disguise: at the crucial point in the action, when the play within the play spills over into real violence, neither performers nor spectators know exactly who is concealed behind the masks. The dance of the masks with its own intrinsic aesthetic values—the interplay of music, dance, and colour—is thus merged with the Western notion of masks as an opportunity for concealing identity, familiar above all in the operatic genre. The interest which Wynter's play has aroused is certainly due to the fact that it combines an accessible story, indigenous aesthetic values linked to the Caribbean carnivalesque tradition, and dramaturgical complexity that permit various levels of perception.

The notion that masks in the Caribbean context can transcend the simple convention of disguise that dominates in the Western theatrical tradition has found a number of exponents. The Trinidad director and dramatist Rawle Gibbons has drawn parallels between external facial characteristics resulting from possession and the theatrical mask. In the process whereby the devotee assumes the role of a god, his 'face stiffens into that of a mask [. . .] the mask is not a physical addition, but a transformation that results from a reshaping of the facial muscles'.[53] The link between such 'inner masks', as Gibbons calls them, and cult religion is proof that a theatre that uses masking as an integral part of its stage language is in some way 'spiritual in its reference'.[54] Although he is using a metaphorically extended concept of masking here, for Caribbean cult religions do not use masks, Gibbons has made use of masks in a variety of functions in plays and productions. In his Trinidad production of Dennis Scott's *An Echo in the Bone* the black actors wore white masks to represent white characters.[55] On the one level this device functions as a grotesquely satirical reversal of the Black and White Minstrel shows with their blackface convention. Used in this way the masks serve as an index of racial category similar to Genet's *The Blacks* and effectively obliterate individual characterization. On another level the masks may even help the actor 'to explore the echo in the well of his unconscious', as Victor Questel surmises.[56] How this is to function Questel does not tell us.

Gibbons returns to masking in his own play *I, Lawah* (1986), which is set during carnival and uses carnivalesque performance elements such as dance, music, and masks.[57] As in Sylvia Wynter's *Maskarade*, Gibbons sets his play in the past, in this case in the 1880s, when violent clashes between the colonial police and former slaves occurred during carnival. The context of the Trinidad carnival permits mask use in a variety of forms. Apart from the processional masks, we find two other contexts. In analogy to the device he introduced in his production of *An Echo in the Bone*, the white Chief

[53] Gibbons, 'Traditional Enactments of Trinidad—Towards a Third Theatre', 136.
[54] Ibid. 138.
[55] For a detailed discussion of this production, see Victor Questel's review 'Unlocking the Gates of History'.   [56] Ibid. 12.
[57] The première took place in 1986 at the Jamaica School of Drama under the direction of Trevor Nairne. It was followed by further productions at the Commonwealth Institute, London, and in Barbados. For an analysis of the play, see Elaine Savory Fido, 'Finding a Truer Form: Rawle Gibbons's Carnival Play *I, Lawah*', *Theatre Research International*, 15/3 (1990), 249–59. See also the entry on Gibbons in Martin Banham, Errol Hill, and George Woodyard, *The Cambridge Guide to African and Caribbean Theatre* (Cambridge: Cambridge University Press, 1994).

of Police in *I, Lawah*, played by a black actor, wears a whiteface mask. By de-individualizing the character in this way and restricting its expressive radius to one of race and official function Gibbons is using a mask function congenial to Western theatrical aesthetics and unrelated to the cult mask function he espouses in his theoretical writing. The desire for a spiritual mask theatre is, however, alluded to, if not fully realized, in another scene. The central female character, Thérèse Le Blanc, a creole, discovers in the attic of her house African masks and dances with them. Estranged from her African cultural heritage, she rediscovers this part of herself and, by extension, of large sections of Trinidad's population through contact with the African mask tradition. In this scene masks signify the retentions of African culture in Trinidad. The fact that Thérèse dances with the masks underlines their original function in cult practice, although the function of cult masking is only cited, but in no way renewed.

The connection between African cult masks and carnival masking is a problematic one, but a link that is evidently of great fascination for Caribbean dramatists and directors, as Derek Walcott admits:

The mask, for instance, is not, as it is in metropolitan theatre, a device: it is a totem. In my own experience, I have always been aware of the power of the mask, or mask-like make-up. In contemporary Carnival, masks have been forbidden, but they used to be an essential part of Carnival. The words 'play masks' really mean 'to play with a mask.' It is a pity that the mask has been removed from Carnival, as it affects the power of the costume. If the face is bare, the rest is only rigid and artificial design. When one puts on the mask, one is creating theatre.[58]

In Walcott's two works that most clearly demonstrate syncretic elements, *Ti-Jean and his Brothers* and *Dream on Monkey Mountain*, masks have central but quite different functions. The figure of the Devil in *Ti-Jean*, for example, wears three masks corresponding to the three personae he inhabits: a devil's mask, the mask of an old man, and the mask of a planter. This convention signals immediately an anti-naturalistic, non-psychological theatre form, but also retains links with Caribbean folk culture.[59] The latter is evident in the

[58] Ciccarelli, 'Reflections before and after Carnival: Interview with Derek Walcott', 297.
[59] Walcott points to the influence of Brecht and via him to Noh theatre as well as to the 'Christmas black mass dances of Papa Diable and his Imps' which he experienced as a child growing up in St Lucia. Walcott, 'Derek' s Most West Indian Play', 7.

visualization by masks of the idea that the Devil can manifest himself in many guises. The masks have an emotive function as well, which works on the basis of contrastive effects. The change from devil and planter masks, evoking hate or fear, to that of a kindly old man is central to the visual dramaturgy of the play, but is only fully realizable in production and is not made explicit in the written text. Because Walcott combines various mask functions, it is not possible to speak of a mere 'imitation' of ethnic models, as has been suggested.[60] Although Walcott certainly alludes to Caribbean cultural practices, he does not restrict himself to a simple replication of such practices.

The mask functions in *Dream on Monkey Mountain* are different again. In this work a white mask with black sisal hair is a central image, yet it is not worn but used principally as a hand-held prop. It makes its first appearance at the beginning of the play, when it is found among Makak's possessions after he has been arrested for disorderly conduct. In the course of the play it becomes a potent image and metaphor and also a totem for Makak. The mask as a totem means that it is not just an aesthetic but is a religious cult object of considerable spiritual power for the wearer-possessor. It is at once a totem of his white Goddess, the *diablesse* of St Lucian folk mythology, a diabolic, seductive creature,[61] and the catalyst which spurs him into his spiritual odyssey.

Walcott's description of the mask, especially its black sisal hair, evokes associations with African masks. The African association connects two aspects of masks: it is a sign of their transformative power, for Makak evidently believes it has the power to metamorphose black into white; it also represents a visual anticipation of Makak's imaginary return to Africa, which takes place in the second part of the play. While Makak views the mask as a totem, as Walcott suggests, his friend Moustique views it with ridicule. On its second appearance in scene 1, after Makak has related his vision of the white Goddess to his friend Moustique, the latter discovers the mask, dons

[60] See Smith, *Masks in Modern Drama*, 81, who deals with *Ti-Jean* in her chapter 'Ritual, Myth and Spectacle'. However, she does not make clear exactly which cultural or ethnic models of masking Walcott is imitating in his play.

[61] 'A *diablesse* appears to be a beautiful white woman, one who is capable of enticing a young man to follow her into the woods where he dies or goes mad.' Daniel Crowley, 'Supernatural Beings in St Lucia', *Caribbean*, 8 (1955), 264 f.; cited in Simpson, *Religious Cults of the Caribbean*, 316 f.

it, and dismisses it as 'cheap stupidness Black children putting on? [*He puts it on, wriggles and dances.*]'[62] For Moustique, it has the association of subterfuge and deceit, which is closer to the connotation masking has on the Western stage; it is desacralized and devoid of totemistic power. Moustique also associates the mask with the schizophrenic attitude of the colonized Black towards his own skin colour that Frantz Fanon analyses in his seminal study *Black Skin, White Masks.*[63] In the market scene, after he has been 'unmasked' for impersonating Makak, Moustique holds out the mask and lambasts the villagers for this naivety: 'All I have is this [*shows the mask*], black faces, white masks! I tried like you!'[64] The allusion to Fanon's analysis of black alienation, self-hatred, and racially conditioned role-playing suggests that Moustique embodies the labile, imitative type of black personality of which Fanon speaks, and the mask is a metaphor for this condition.

In the middle of his dream, after his escape from prison, Makak begins to lose confidence in the mask's totemic power:

MAKAK [*holding out the mask*]. I was a king among shadows. Either the shadows were real, and I was no king, or it is my own kingliness that created the shadows. Either way, I am lonely, lost, an old man again.[65]

The mask functions here as a symbol for Makak's self-deception, and as such begins to forfeit its supernatural powers. In the Epilogue, after the action has returned from the dream world to reality, the mask reverts to its status as an everyday object, devoid of totemic force. Makak leaves the jail without the mask and, in so doing, liberates himself both from his nightmares and, it is suggested, from his feeling of racial inferiority. He no longer feels the need to transform himself into a white man.

In *Dream on Monkey Mountain* the mask is situated in a curious liminal space between Caribbean and Western associations. Although it becomes the totem that Walcott speaks of for the central character, Makak, it is also closely linked to the psychological concept of masking with connotations of self-deception and false identity. The intertextual allusion to Fanon's book, which contains in its title a pejorative Western idea of masking, underscores

---

[62] Walcott, *Dream on Monkey Mountain*, 239–40.

[63] Tr. Charles Lam Markmann (New York: Grove Press, 1967); first pub. as *Peau noire, masques blancs* (Paris: Éditions du Seuil, 1952).

[64] Walcott, *Dream on Monkey Mountain*, 271. [65] Ibid. 304.

the secular, psychological concept. Finally, the fact that the mask is not worn, but only held, suggests that this theatrical device has become a problematic one in Walcott's mind. Devoid of a social-cultural basis in Caribbean religious life, its transformative cult function can only be alluded to in a Caribbean context.

Our final example of mask use is taken from the Indian play *Hayavadana* by the Kanarese playwright, actor, and film-maker Girish Karnad (1938–). Originally written in the south Indian language Kannada in 1971, it was successfully performed in that language and was subsequently rendered into English by the author and performed in English a year later. It has been translated into other Indian languages as well.[66] The play is based on the story of the transposed heads from the collection of Sanskrit tales known as the *Kathasaritsagara* and on Thomas Mann's adaptation of the tale in his novella *The Transposed Heads* (*Die vertauschten Köpfe*).

The story, in Karnad's treatment, revolves around two friends, Devadatta and Kapila, who become estranged over their rivalry for Devadatta's young wife Padmini. Devadatta is a brahmin and devoted to intellectual and literary pursuits; Kapila, a blacksmith, is endowed with enviable physical attributes, which exercise a considerable attraction for Padmini. In a fit of jealous despair Devadatta beheads himself while worshipping before the goddess Kali. Kapila follows suit. Padmini reattaches the heads to the wrong bodies and, thus reconstituted, the men begin to quarrel over their respective rights to Padmini. She decides for the best of both worlds and selects the combination Devadatta's head and Kapila's body. Kapila (the head) flees in despair into the forest. The ideal combination, however, begins after a while to decay—the intellectual mind neglects the athletic body—as does the marriage, until Padmini leaves her husband and seeks out Kapila, who has undergone precisely the opposite process. The two rivals kill each other in a duel and Padmini willingly performs suttee, the Hindu custom of a widow's self-immolation. This central story, which in its ironic tone owes a great deal to Thomas Mann's novella, is framed within the story of Hayavadana, a creature half-horse, half-man, who, in analogy to the main action, is also in

---

[66] Other plays in Kannada are *Yayati* (1961) and *Tughlaq* (1980). Karnad also translated *Tughlaq* into English (1971), as well as Bardal Sircar's acclaimed play *Evam Indrajit* (1974). His most recent play is *Naga-Mandala*. *Hayavadana* and *Tughlaq* have been collected in *Three Plays* (Delhi: Oxford University Press, 1994).

search of completeness. He also seeks out Kali, commits an error, and finds himself transformed totally into a horse.

The performance style is heavily influenced by the conventions and theatrical devices of *yakṣāgana*, a traditional form of theatre wide-spread in Karnad's home state.[67] Most important in *Hayavadana* is the use of the Bhagavata, a narrator-figure who functions as an intermediary between the fictional characters and the audience.[68] This form of Indian dance-drama and its related genres *kathakaḷi* and *chau* utilize elaborate headdresses and brightly coloured facial decoration, which create the impression of a masked face. This body sign, together with the colourful costuming, transform the performer into an archetypal character from the Indian mythical-epic tradition. The visual transformation, in combination with highly stylized move-ment, functions to divorce the performer's body almost entirely from the semiotics of everyday appearance and movement.[69]

This semiotic transformation of the body is central to Karnad's play. The author has pointed out that it was not in fact a story or tale that inspired him to write the play, or even a political conviction or thematic complex. It was rather a discussion about the meaning and

[67] 'Yakshagana dance-plays in the state of Mysore take up the same mythological stories as Kathakali; vigorous stick-drumming is similar to Kathakali. Dance style emphasizes footwork; no codified system of hand gestures. Actors deliver extended songs and prose dialogue in Kannada vernacular. Key performer is the narrator who introduces scenes with eloquent descriptive passages.' Brandon, *Brandon's Guide to Theater in Asia*, 42.

[68] 'The key performer in any Yakshagana play is the *bhagavatha*, for it is up to him to keep the performance under control and to express in his singing the changing moods and emotions the story takes. He also joins in the improvised dialogue when the actors first enter and so helps establish each character.' Rea, 'Theatre in India, Part II', 46.

[69] Apart from the explicit debt to *yakṣāgana* dance-drama, there is an unmistakable Brechtian influence apparent in the play. Karnad has stressed in a recent essay the importance of Brecht, not just to himself, but to modern Indian theatre in general, particularly in redirecting the attention of Indian playwrights and directors to the possibilities of the conventions of anti-illusionistic folk theatre: 'To use a phrase from Bertolt Brecht, these conventions then allow for "complex seeing." And it must be admitted that Brecht's influence, received mainly through his writings and without the benefit of his theatrical productions, went some way in making us realize what could be done with the design of traditional theater. The theatrical conventions Brecht was reacting against [. . .] were never part of the traditional Indian theater. There was therefore no question of arriving at an "alienation" effect by using Brechtian artifice. What he did was to sensitize us to the potentialities of nonnaturalistic techniques available in our own theater.' Girish Karnad, 'In Search of a New Theater', Carla M. Borden (ed.), *Contemporary Indian Tradition* (Washington: Smithsonian Institution Press, 1989), 104.

function of masks and music in Indian theatre.[70] These elements immediately identify two dominants in the play's thematic and performative structure, which even a cursory reading of the play will confirm. Karnad's intention was precisely opposed to notions of psychological realism; the play was in fact conceived as a counter-model to the use of masks in Western theatre, where they are very often linked to psychological questions:

Western theatre has developed a contrast between the *face* and the *mask*—the real inner person and the exterior one presents, or wishes to present, to the world outside. But in Indian traditional theatre, the mask is only the face 'writ large'; since a character represents not a complex psychological entity but an ethical archetype, the mask merely presents in enlarged detail its essential moral nature.[71]

This conception of masking is precisely opposed to most functions that we have hitherto encountered, whether they be cult or aesthetic forms. It is in fact closer to the function of theatrical masking used in Greek theatre, where the mask served to project a visual enlargement of a mythical or comic character. At the same time powerful effects could be attained by altering or changing the mask for the same character within a play.[72] The opposition Karnad sets up applies, then, less to Western theatre in general than to modern psychological theatre. In fact, Karnad's use of masks, which could almost be termed a 'play of masks', is more flexible than found in most forms of traditional Indian theatre.

The opening of the play follows more or less exactly the rituals of *yakṣāgana* theatre:

At the beginning of the performance, a mask of Gaṇeśa is brought on stage and kept on the chair. Puja is done. The BHAGAVATA sings verses in praise of Gaṇeśa, accompanied by his musicians.[73]

Puja is performed at the commencement of all traditional Indian theatre: offerings are made and prayers said, asking for a successful performance. The presence of the mask of Gaṇeśa, the one-tusked elephant and protective deity of actors, serves not only to establish links with traditional theatre but also to anticipate the use of masks

[70] Girish Karnad, 'In Search of a New Theater', 102.   [71] Ibid. 103.
[72] For examples of this kind, see Graham Ley, *A Short Introduction to the Ancient Greek Theatre* (Chicago: Chicago University Press, 1991), 18–19.
[73] Girish Karnad, *Hayavadana*, tr. by the author (Calcutta: Oxford University Press, 1975), 1.

in the play and to underline the key thematic complex, the search for completeness.[74]

Karnad specifies that the three central characters wear masks: the two friends Devadatta and Kapila, who cut each other's heads off, and Hayavadana, who wears a horse's mask.[75] The moral riddle at the centre of the play, concerning whether the head or the body constitutes the true nature of an individual, is visualized in the theatrical device of masking. Between the divine and the human realms, the latter represented by Devadatta and Kapila, stands Hayavadana, the human being with the horse's head seeking human wholeness. The masks represent the visual connection between the two levels of reality.

As well as the metaphysical aspects, masks are shown to elicit a variety of responses which can encompass culturally specific conceptions of masking. For instance, on his first appearance the figure of Hayavadana is subjected to ridicule, because his horse's head is understood to be just a mask in a derogatory sense, a 'stupid mask', or 'silly mask', as the narrator-figure, Bhagavata, repeatedly says. He tries to pull the mask off Hayavadana's head until he realizes that it is not a mask at all.[76] Apart from the visual irony of the scene, whereby a mask is declared not to be a mask, it also establishes the pejorative connotation of masking as disguise or deception, which is perhaps the primary semantic field in the Western understanding of the term and practice.

As far as the story of Devadatta and Kapila is concerned, Karnad is not interested primarily in a psychological analysis of his characters, but rather in theatricalizing the philosophical question of the relationship between mind and body, which is central to Eastern and

---

[74] All traditional theatre performances in India begin, according to Karnad, with a short ceremony in honour of the god Ganeśa, who, himself the victim of divine error, is represented in the form of an elephant mask: 'Ganesha's mask then says nothing about his nature. It is a mask, pure and simple. Right at the start of the play, my theory about masks was getting subverted. But the elephant head also questioned the basic assumption behind the original riddle: that the head represents the thinking part of the person, the intellect.' Karnad, 'In Search of a New Theater', 103. This mask, a kind of ritual emblem of Indian theatre, alludes to the relationship between the riddle and the theatrical device of mask.

[75] In an early interview Karnad maintains that the use of masks in his play was initially just a pragmatic solution to the problem of how to represent the exchange of heads on stage. Up to this point he was actually sceptical about using masks. However, once taken, the decision led to the use of *yakṣāgana* and from there to a more complex treatment of the theme of the play. Rajinder Paul, 'Girish Karnad Interviewed by Rajinder Paul', *Enact*, 54 (June 1971), n.p.   [76] Karnad, *Hayavadana*, 6.

Western philosophy alike. The generalized rather than individualized nature of the characters is already evident in their names, which illustrate the same aesthetic principle behind masklike make-up in traditional dance-theatre: 'The heroine is called Padmini after one of the six types into which Vatsyayana classified all women. Her husband is Devadatta, a formal mode of addressing a stranger. His friend is Kapila, simply "the dark one." '[77] The masks worn by the men are correspondingly simple. Devadatta wears a pale, Kapila a dark mask.[78] The transposition of the heads is represented by exchanging the masks. However, even this device, seemingly dictated by the demands of the plot, corresponds to a convention found in Indian dance-drama. Particularly in *kathakaḷi*, there are scenes where characters, either after death or after transformation into another figure, re-enter wearing another mask.[79]

Once the transposition has occurred the play demands a particular kind of acting to represent the physical changes incurred by the new heads on the old bodies. Because of the semiotic rigidity of the mask, all essential changes in character have to be communicated by corporeal signs. Although the highly stylized movement aesthetics of *yakṣāgana* would appear to offer the appropriate performance convention, Karnad does not require a simple reduplication of the traditional form. He opts instead for an ironic refraction, rather than mimetic imitation, of an existing performance mode. The play requires a style of movement that counteracts the signs of the mask. The scholar's head transforms the athletic figure of Kapila into its opposite; the head of the blacksmith turns the delicate figure of the scholar into a muscle-bound body. These transformations are not only central for the story and the moral point, but they serve equally to comment on the relationship between masking and body signs. For the dramaturgical strategies to be communicated in theatrical signs, the performers must create a precise interplay of mask or movement. In the course of this interaction, in which mask and body

---

[77] Karnad, 'In Search of a New Theater', 103.   [78] Karnad, *Hayavadana*, 11.

[79] Phillip B. Zarrilli describes a scene of this nature from the *kathakaḷi* repertoire: 'In *Dakṣa Yaga*, Daksa at the end of the play is beheaded [. . .] Brahma asks Śiva to forgive Dakṣa his oversight and to return him to life so that the sacrifice may be completed. Śiva agrees and has a goat's head placed on Dakṣa's body to restore his life. This transformation is accomplished by having the actor playing Daksa remove his crown and place a carved, wooden goat mask on his face.' Farley P. Richmond, Darius L. Swann, and Phillip B. Zarrilli (eds.), *Indian Theater: Traditions of Performance* (Honolulu: University of Hawaii Press, 1990), 335.

condition one another, a new harmony is found. The process culminates finally and logically in an exchange of actors:

DEVADATTA comes in. He is now completely changed to his original self— that is, the slender actor who came as Devadatta at the beginning of the play comes back again with the Devadatta mask on.[80]

Karnad requires of the performers specific material body signs: a slender physique for the actor playing Devadatta, and a powerfully built body for Kapila. The specification of material body signs under-scores the limits of masking, or more precisely the limits to which masks can transform one's perception of the performing body. The notion that a mask alone can totally alter the spectator's perception of a performer's physical appearance contradicts Karnad's intention of rehabilitating the value of the body compared to that of the head. This value judgement is particularly evident in the reconciliation between Padmina, the woman between the two men, and Kapila. While the latter's head has certainly changed the outer appearance of Devadatta's body, this exterior transformation has not expunged the body's deeper level of experience:

KAPILA. One beats the body into shape, but one can't beat away the memories in it. Isn't that surprising? That the body should have its own ghosts—its own memories? Memories of touch—memories of a touch— memories of a body swaying in these arms, of a warm skin against this palm—memories which one cannot recognise, cannot understand, cannot even name because this head wasn't there when they happened . . .[81]

In this passage the author undertakes a revision of the judgement made in the *Śāstras*, the sacred texts, whereby the head is the dominant part of the body: 'The head is the sign of a man.'[82] The contrast between the interchangeable masks and the immutable bodies provides a visual, theatrical correlative to the significance of the body as an expressive instrument. Read in this way, the play can be viewed as an indirect plea for a theatre that does not restrict itself to psychological introspection, a theatre of talking heads, but rather a theatre utilizing a fuller range of expressive means.

Karnad's subtle 'play of masks' underlines and at the same time transcends the strategy of double encoding that we outlined at the beginning of this chapter. The visual presentation of the body in syncretic theatre is doubly encoded in a special sense in that it

---

[80] Karnad, *Hayavadana*, 50. [81] Ibid. 57 f. [82] Ibid. 36.

involves a dialogue with two performance traditions—the Western and the indigenous—and very often colonial-based discourses relating to specific discursive practices such as primitivism. Karnad's play is particularly complex because he not only syncretizes the Western and the traditional—in this case *yakṣāgana*—but he enters into a debate with traditional Indian thinking on the relationship between mind and body.

In the course of this chapter I have discussed a number of disparate strategies dramatists and directors have employed to integrate the textuality of the body into the syncretization process. These range from questions involving the materiality of the body, and in particular ethnicity, to various ways of writing over the body including full-body masking. The use of full-body masks particularly underlines the necessity to view masking as part of a semiotics of the performing body. It was shown that the use of masks and the masked body is also subject to double encoding. On the one hand, dramatists in Africa, the Caribbean, and India can draw on intact indigenous ritual and performance traditions; on the other, there is usually some attempt to tap into the Western tradition of theatrical modernism and its experimentation with masks. The question was also addressed how indigenous dramatists and directors working in the syncretic mode have taken up the problem of re-presenting a body often hitherto restricted entirely to indigenous performance and folklore with its connotations of being 'untainted' by Western signs. It was argued that by conscious strategies of resemanticization, particularly in Fourth World performance contexts, the complex cultural and aesthetic dynamics of the body as an instrument of performance are highlighted. Such dynamic kinaesthetic effects also include notions of a mythologized body representing the idea that the realms of the mythical and the quotidian are in some way contiguous or coexistent. Although I have stressed the visual appearance of the body in this chapter—its iconography—it has always been apparent that these signs are not static, but in most cases they only achieve their full aesthetic and cultural impact when in motion. The following chapter deals primarily with dance and movement and should thus be read as a continuation of this one.

CHAPTER SIX

Dance and Body Language

IN the previous chapter I looked at the textuality of the body in terms of physical appearance and iconographic display. In this chapter attention will be focused on different aspects of the kinetic body, the body in motion, particularly the textual aspects of dance. This separation into discrete categories of stasis and kinesis is purely a heuristic one. In performance, because bodies are normally perceived in motion, the iconographic aspects of corporeal textuality are usually inseparable from the kinaesthetic effects. Although the emphasis in the following remarks will be on dance, and to a lesser extent its relationship to music, from which dance cannot normally be separated, the chapter will conclude with an analysis of other forms of kinetic communication such as gesture and sign language.

That music and dance play an important role in syncretic theatre is supported by even a cursory glance. On the one hand, there are important developments towards a dominant musical theatre. Examples in Nigeria are the Yoruba Folk Opera and the Concert Parties of Herbert Ogunde. In South Africa there is the tradition of township musicals beginning with Gibson Kente, and now, with the international success of Mbongeni Ngema's productions of *Sarafina!* and *Magic at 4 am*, assuming a new form under the influence of political township theatre. In all these forms music, song, and dance are the dominant theatrical codes. On the other hand, there are many texts which cannot be termed 'musicals' but where music and dance at certain strategic points supersede dialogue as the dominants. The focus in this chapter is primarily on texts and performances which appear to belong to the genre dialogic theatre but where dominant shifts are very apparent. Examples are drawn from South African township theatre, from Aboriginal drama, from a play by the Indian dramatist Asif Currimbhoy, *The Dumb Dancer*, which is based on the theatre code of *kathakaḷi* dance-drama, and from Wole Soyinka's play *Death and the King's Horseman*. Again and again it can be observed that music and dance, but particularly the latter, can take on the status of a counter-discourse to the logocentric tradition of Western dialogue-based drama.

Dancing Meaning

In Western theatre there are certain techniques of physical performance which can be termed 'acculturative', in Eugenio Barba's terminology.[1] Barba means by this term types of gestural and kinaesthetic performance styles which are clearly distinct from everyday movement and can only be mastered after specialist training. These genres include various types of dance-theatre and pantomime. Both are now perceived as being aesthetically distinct from spoken theatre: either as autonomous theatrical forms such as ballet, dance-theatre, and pantomime, or as clearly demarcated components of a mixed genre such as the dance and ballet sections found in opera, operetta, and the American musical. While the history of Western theatre is a history of increasing specialization and of an ever-widening gap between the dancer and the actor, syncretic theatre shows the opposite development. Western dramatic texts in the nineteenth and twentieth centuries dispense almost entirely with dance, whereas there are in fact very few syncretic dramas which do not evidence some form of dancing and music.[2]

One explanation for the predominance of dance in these texts can be sought in the central idea behind theatrical syncretism. If the driving force motivating it is the desire for a culturally appropriate form of theatre which can accommodate indigenous performance forms, then dance, as an almost universal form of performative

[1] Barba differentiates between 'inculturation' and 'acculturation', terms taken from cultural anthropology (although the term here is 'enculturation') but used by Barba in a specific way. Inculturation technique is, for Barba, the application to a performance situation of everyday, 'natural' behaviour; an example of such 'elaborated spontaneity' would be Stanislavskian acting technique. For an explication of both terms, see Eugenio Barba and Nicola Savarese, *The Secret Art of the Performer: A Dictionary of Theatre Anthropology* (London: Routledge, 1991), 189–90.

[2] When dance appears in dramas in the 19th and 20th centuries, it is certainly an exception to the rule. In *fin de siècle* drama there are a number of experiments incorporating dance; however, the exponents are few and are easily named. Besides Strindberg, Wilde, and Yeats the little amount of research that has been carried out into the relationship between dance and drama in the 20th century names Hugo von Hofmannsthal, and in the contemporary period John Arden because of *Sergeant Musgrave's Dance* (1958), and Brian Friel's *Dancing at Llughnasa*.

expression, must find a place in these experiments. It is a common-place of Western theatre history since Aristotle that dance, or more specifically Greek dithyrambic performance, is one of its major 'sources'. Despite this generic connection between dance and drama, the two forms have in the course of history become in a sense so polarized that a structural reintegration seems scarcely possible. Therefore, the main artistic and dramaturgical problem facing post-colonial dramatists working in the syncretic mode was and is to overcome or ignore this formal dichotomy inherited from the Western tradition and test new ways of reintegrating the two performative codes.

An early example of just such a new dramaturgical structure is Asif Currimbhoy's 'dance-play' *The Dumb Dancer*.[3] Until relatively recently Currimbhoy (1928–) was considered to be one of India's most prolific unperformed English-language playwrights. *The Dumb Dancer*, written around 1961 and first performed in 1965 in New York at La Mama Theatre and in London as part of the British Drama League festival, has apparently not had a major production in India.[4] Nevertheless, it has attracted a great deal of critical atten-tion, an interest which is certainly due to Currimbhoy's attempt to combine the theatrical code of *kathakaḷi* with Western dramatic form.[5]

---

[3] The generic term 'dance-drama' is a Western label for those Indian theatrical forms which are neither strictly dance nor drama but contain elements of both. This classification has, however, gained currency among Indian scholars as well; see the chapter 'Dance-Dramas and Dramatic Dances', in Richmond *et al.* (eds.), *Indian Theatre*, (1990) 307–14. There have also been attempts to create new forms of dance-drama in this century. Rabindranath Tagore created a new genre in the 1930s which he called 'dance-drama'. According to Sujit Mukherjee, dance was supposed to occupy the dominant position: 'dance substitutes action'. *Passage to America*, 144.

[4] Until 1970 Currimbhoy was performed chiefly abroad. For a detailed production history of Currimbhoy's plays until 1975, see Asif Currimbhoy, *This Alien . . . Native Land* (Calcutta: Writers Workshop, 1975), following title-page. See P. Bayapa Reddy, 'Asif Currimbhoy's "Goa": A Study', *Ariel*, 14/4 (1973), 77–86; and K. R. Srinivasa Iyengar, 'The Dramatic Art of Asif Currimbhoy', in K. K. Sharma (ed.), *Indo-English Literature: A Collection of Critical Essays* (Ghaziabad: Vimal Prakashan, 1977), 243–56. He lists twenty-nine plays written between 1959 and 1975.

[5] As well as the article by Srinivasa Iyengar 'The Dramatic Art of Asif Currimbhoy' commentary on *The Dumb Dancer* can be found in Verghese, *Problems of the Indian Creative Writer in English*, 165–7; M. K. Naik, 'The Achievement of Indian Drama in English', in M. K. Naik and S. Mokashi-Punekar (eds.), *Perspectives on Indian Drama in English* (Madras: Oxford University Press, 1977), 182; Murli Das Melwani, 'Indo-Anglian Plays: A Survey', *Enact*, 123–4 (Mar.–Apr. 1977), n.p. Krishna S. Bhatta, *Indian English Drama: A Critical Study* (New Delhi: Sterling Publishers, 1987).

The play is set in a psychiatric institution and deals with the treatment of a mentally disturbed *kathakaḷi* dancer. During his training the actor-dancer Bhima so internalized his mythological character of the same name from the *Mahabharata* that total identification and severe personality disorder have resulted. In order to perfect his performance technique and in the belief that the removal of one of his sensory organs would lead to the better development of the others, he has cut out his tongue. The action begins with a *kathakaḷi* performance in an operating theatre, which is intended as a kind of psychodramatic therapy. The woman psychiatrist, Prema, who is treating Bhima, believes that her patient's mental disorder is linked to the rigorous *kathakaḷi* training. This opening scene depicts sequences from the episode 'Duryodhana's Slaughter', one of the most brutal, and popular, in the *kathakaḷi* repertoire. The god Bhima cuts out the entrails of his opponent Duryodhana and holds them in his mouth.[6] In the hope that the sight of real entrails will provide a kind of shock therapy, Prema asks another doctor to perform an autopsy on a corpse. Unfortunately, the treatment takes an unexpected turn. Prema's initial idea was to have Bhima experience the actual disembowelment of a corpse, but through a process of transference, in the Freudian sense, she has grown obsessed with her patient. In a fit of jealousy she murders the daughter of the guru with whom Bhima has been studying, disembowelling her. The murder of the girl Śakuntala is at once the ultimate shock therapy and the removal of a putative rival for Bhima's affections.

In terms of its theatrical language Currimbhoy's play alternates between dialogic realism and the dance-drama of *kathakaḷi*. These quite diverse codes are supposed to be in balance, as the author claims in his foreword: 'Both choreography and dramatic art play an equally important part'.[7] For example, Currimbhoy uses a flashback showing Bhima's *kathakaḷi* training to demonstrate the fundamental

---

[6] Phillip B. Zarrilli provides a graphic description of this scene in performance: 'In several kathakaḷi scenes disembowelment of the evil character takes place following a protracted, stylized, and choreographed fight. Cloth entrails are dipped in realistic stage blood. The actor keeps these hidden until, at the final climactic moment as the drummers are creating a din of sound, he dips his hands into the victim's stomach and mimes eating his victim's entrails. The actor raises his head from the victim, displaying to the audience his bloodied hand, with entrails streaming from his mouth'. Richmond et al. (eds.), *Indian Theatre*, 342.

[7] Asif Currimbhoy, *The Doldrummers, The Dumb Dancer and 'Om'* (Bombay: Soraya, 1963), 81.

principles of this theatrical form: massages, the practising of *mudras*, the dance steps and recitation of the stories are all performed on stage. The scene has a didactic function—the audience is 'informed' about *kathakaḷi*—and at the same time it serves to provide psychological motivation for Bhima's behaviour. The scene reveals his pathological perfectionism, which finally ends in self-mutilation. In this sequence dialogue and dance are in a balanced relationship, although not in any way integrated. There is, semiotically speaking, continual code-switching between these two sign systems. From the perspective of normative Western dramaturgy such code-switching is incompatible with the Aristotelian requirements of unity and focus. This is clearly the implicit postulate underlying the criticism of the play levelled by M. K. Naik: 'The playwright's passion for sheer technical virtuosity has led him to neglect the *basic dramatic values* to the detriment of a potentially rich artistic conception'.[8] What these 'basic dramatic values' actually consist of is not elaborated; presumably, they owe a considerable debt to the dramaturgy of Ibsen and George Bernard Shaw. The published text of *The Dumb Dancer* bears testimony to the fact that Currimbhoy is well aware of his transgressions against dramaturgic orthodoxy. In the scene direction to Act 2, scene 2, entitled 'Insane Fantasy', the author specifies: 'Like the first scene of ACT I, the choreographic-values [*sic*] of this scene exceed that of the conversational content which has been minimized'.[9] This is a clear indication of a dominant shift, and as such must be taken into account in any critical assessment.

Whatever criticisms one can level at the play, and there are many, they must take cognizance of this fundamental semiotic process. One can take issue with the crude psychology of the play; with the overriding melodramatic tone and a tendency to overwritten dialogue. Yet, the melodramatic flourish, not only of the dialogue, but of the action as a whole, deserves to be measured against the cultural and aesthetic receptive codes of Indian theatre. On contemporary Indian acting Farley Richmond observes: 'Foreign critics cannot help but notice a slightly melodramatic tone to much of what they see on stage, perhaps because India is a land of sharp extremes in emotional relations. The exaggeration and melodramatic situations of many

---

[8] Naik, *Dimensions of Indian English Literature*, 159; my italics.
[9] Currimbhoy, *The Doldrummers, The Dumb Dancer and 'Om'*, 120.

indigenous plays may also explain the melodramatic tendency of this type of acting'.[10]

Richmond's comment suggests that there may in fact be a symbiotic relationship between writing, acting, and audience expectation. Indigenous modern plays tend to be highly commercial and targeted at meeting and confirming receptive codes, not expanding or questioning them. One must be very circumspect when using the term 'melodrama' at all in relation to Indian performance and theatre. Melodrama is a very problematic term when applied to any kind of intercultural analysis, because it carries with it a considerable ideological baggage in its European usage, where it is entirely pejorative.

Whatever the shortcomings of Currimbhoy's play, they must nevertheless be analysed within the cultural and aesthetic context the author himself defines and is working within. His attempt to create a syncretic dramaturgy falls short of achieving a balanced and organic fusion of the two performance codes. Currimbhoy situates the *kathakaḷi* sequences quite securely within a Western dramaturgical frame. Their function and legitimacy are in a sense dictated by the conventions of post-Expressionist drama. The concrete setting of the psychiatric hospital is the point of departure for all other scenes. The *kathakaḷi* scenes are either therapeutic re-enactments in this setting or they are presented in the form of flashbacks for expository purposes.[11]

The presentation of the published play text reveals some further structural problems related to the incomplete fusion of performance codes. The text is swamped not just by extensive stage directions of Shavian proportions but also by explanatory footnotes on *kathakaḷi* and Hindu mythology. Although published in India, the text seems to have been directed at least partly at a Western reader or director. Currimbhoy even includes twelve photographs of a *kathakaḷi* performance depicting the crucial scene 'Duryodhana's Slaughter'. While the author takes great pains to elucidate the concepts and conven-

---

[10] Richmond also points out that in modern Indian plays realism is the dominant mode in regard to setting and dialogue, although this may be expanded by theatrical devices, songs, and dance segments. Richmond *et al.* (eds.), *Indian Theatre*, 404.

[11] Currimbhoy's reception of such anti-illusionistic devices appears to have come via Eugene O'Neill and Arthur Miller. Paul C. Verghese points to the influence of Arthur Miller's *Death of a Salesman* on Currimbhoy's one-act play *The Clock*, which also features a salesman in dialogue with characters from his past (*Problems of the Indian Creative Writer in English*, 164). Currimbhoy describes a more recent play as 'an O'Neillian effort to probe a deep, and frequently anguished past'. *This Alien . . . Native Land*, n.p.

tions underlying *kathaka̤li* dance-drama, which he terms a 'theatre of the imagination',[12] the action itself hinges on the very Western concept of psychodrama: that psychological disturbances can be treated through actual re-enactment of events linked to it.[13] *Kathaka̤li*, while certainly 'an integral part of the play', as Verghese claims,[14] remains a distinct performance code, performed and permissible only within certain clearly defined contexts. Although Currimbhoy seems to suggest in some of his commentary that the aesthetics of *kathaka̤li* as 'a theatre of the imagination' are analogous in some way to the expressionistic, fluid structure of the play, with its fantasy scenes and flashbacks, this is not realized in the actual dramaturgy.

A different kind of attempt to assimilate dance and drama can be found in Derek Walcott's writings on Caribbean theatre. Walcott is, however, less concerned with creating a new kind of dance-drama than with effecting a convergence of dancing and acting. On the occasion of a new 'folk operetta' premièred in Trinidad in 1966 Walcott outlined a number of fundamental problems inherent in the creation of an indigenous musical theatre. The central problem is, he argues, to find a style which permits a musical and choreographic simulation of indigenous forms of cultural expression without having to interpret and readapt them. As an example Walcott points to the work of Trinidad's Little Carib Dance Company, directed by Beryl McBurnie, and their choreographic representation of possession dances:[15]

The power and validity of folk art, still alive enough in the West Indies, almost resists tampering. Real bongos, shangos or pocomania dances are possessed by the faith of their cultists who are not performing when they dance, but are enacting their belief. The choreographer, therefore, prefers to simulate such possession as closely as possible, a technique that draws the dancer closer to acting, and acting emphasizes dramatic development.[16]

[12] Currimbhoy, *The Doldrummers, The Dumb Dancer and 'Om'*, 82.

[13] Psychodramatic theory, as defined and elaborated by its founder, J. L. Moreno, suggests that, by thus 'acting out' these events, a type of curative catharsis can be achieved, an 'abreaction'. The best introduction to the theory and practice of psychodrama is J. L. Moreno, *Psychodrama*, i, (Beacon, NY: Beacon House, 1946). In some respects, it could be argued, Currimbhoy prefigures Peter Schaffer's play *Equus*.

[14] Verghese, *Problems of the Indian Creative Writer*, 166.

[15] For a description of McBurnie's work and career, see Molly Ahye, *Cradle of Caribbean Dance: Beryl McBurnie and the Little Carib Theatre* (Trinidad: Heritage Culture, 1983). For a more detailed discussion of Walcott's collaboration with her, see King, *Derek Walcott and West Indian Drama* esp. ch. 1 and 2.

[16] Walcott, 'Patterns to Forget', 5.

Walcott makes an interesting distinction here between cult dancing and the theatrical imitation of cult dancing, which is in fact a kind of acting. The dancer as actor, and vice versa the actor as dancer, are central requirements for a new autochthonous Caribbean theatre. One of the models is the stylized movement of kabuki theatre, which is located mid-way between dancing and acting.[17] Walcott draws attention to the fact that the local dance forms familiar to all the actors in his group, the Trinidad Theatre Workshop, also constitute a movement style which is nearer to acting: 'All of these actors move well. They don't dance in the ballet or modern idiom; they are not abstract dancers. They can do dances which are spontaneous yet precise and have more to do with acting than with dance'.[18] His goal is a highly physicalized theatre of movement reflecting the variety of kinaesthetic influences—Chinese, Indian, African—which Caribbean culture has absorbed, and combining them in a process of syncretization—Walcott speaks of 'cross-fertilization'—in order to produce 'a true and terrifying West Indian theatre'.[19]

The demand for an actor-dancer and a fusion of dance and dramatic form is one of the leitmotifs in Walcott's theoretical writings. In an article with the programmatic title 'Mixing the Dance and Drama', Walcott uses his review of another Trinidad dance company, Astor Johnson's Repertory Dance Theatre, to return to the topic six years later: 'It was a piece like this which again indicates how much nearer we are getting to a spontaneous fusion of drama and dance without patterning ourselves on the old-fashioned American musical that still cramps our concept of form'.[20] The 'old-fashioned American musical' represents for Walcott the fragmentation of theatrical language endemic to Western theatre.

Opposition to this kind of fragmentation and in particular the division of performance into specialist areas such as acting, dancing, and singing, is one of the central tenets of Errol Hill's projected theatre based on carnival. Hill regards this kind of specialization as an 'imported tradition', ill suited to Caribbean theatre, and requiring counter-action in the area of performer training: 'actors will need to

---

[17] See Earle Ernst's characterization of the Japanese performer: 'As a generalization it can be fairly said that all Kabuki movement shows the qualities of dance movement'. Earle Ernst, *The Kabuki Theatre* (New York: Grove Press 1956), 168 f.

[18] Walcott, 'Meanings', 49.   [19] Ibid.

[20] Derek Walcott, 'Mixing the Dance and Drama', *Trinidad Guardian*, 6 Dec. 1972, 5.

be trained as dancers, singers and possibly as musicians'.[21] Although Walcott and Hill were sharply opposed to one another on a number of issues, in this point their respective visions converge. The common ground for both is the recognition that dance is an eminently important expressive form in Caribbean culture. Thus any kind of genuinely autochthonous Caribbean theatre seeking to find a broad audience will have to make adequate allowance for dance in its new aesthetic.

The central importance of dance in Caribbean performance culture can, of course, be traced back across the middle passage to its African origins. It is therefore not surprising that the earliest experiments with syncretic theatre in African countries include dance. A major difficulty in speaking about African dance arises when we seek a culturally appropriate terminology, a question that has been addressed by the art historian Robert Farris Thompson in his book *African Art in Motion* (1974). Thompson elaborates a set of aesthetic categories for plastic and performative arts from an intrinsic perspective. This means that, although the actual categories stem from him, the information they are based on has been gleaned entirely from indigenous commentators. Thus the study also tries to fix African traditions and categories of artistic criticism.[22] Some of these categories are particularly applicable to an analysis of syncretic theatre. For example, 'ephebism', the cult of youth: 'People in Africa, regardless of their actual age, return to strong, youthful pattern whenever they move within the streams of energy which flow from drums or other sources of percussion'.[23] 'Vital aliveness': this means that the various parts of the body are employed with equal percussive strength—'the remarkable process of infusing, democratically, equal life to different bodily parts'.[24] 'The get-down quality': melody, sculpture, and dance all stress a descending movement, towards the earth. Linked to this is the concept of 'vividness cast into equilibrium'. In both danced and plastic art there is a striving to achieve personal (physical) and representational balance. In African dance the main idea is to keep the feet set flat on the earth, as

---

[21] Hill, *The Trinidad Carnival*, 116.
[22] Thompson carried out his fieldwork primarily amongst the Yoruba people in West Africa. However, with the use of video-recordings of dances and other performances, he was able to replay them in front of people from quite different ethnic and cultural backgrounds and elicit their critical comments on the taped performances.
[23] Thompson, *African Art in Motion*, 7.   [24] Ibid. 9.

opposed to the Western ideal of going up on the toes. Representational balance means that 'African connoisseurs savor moderation of resemblance, avoiding puzzling abstractions or glaring realism'.[25] 'Call-and-response': the relationship between leader and chorus in African performance mirrors the politics of the community. The choral response is a 'direct expression of public sanction and opinion'.[26] The most important result of Thompson's study is that he convincingly demonstrates the interrelatedness of African performing arts with all other cultural forms of the community supporting it.

Thompson's study shows also that in Africa dance is a 'primary art', as the dance scholar and choreographer Peggy Harper has put it.[27] As early as 1965 she drew attention to Nigerian syncretic theatre as a medium for integrating and adapting African dances. Interestingly enough even dancers and choreographers such as Harper regard the dramatic form as a legitimate way of theatricalizing indigenous dance traditions. Harper argues that the staging of traditional dances as dances often means uprooting them from their ritual or ceremonial context and turning them into folkloristic entertainment. Dramas, on the other hand, because of their fictional frame, provide a more appropriate context for the adaptation of indigenous dances. 'In Africa', Harper writes, 'there has not been the specialization of theatre techniques into separate compartments of ballet, mime, opera, literary theatre and orchestral music'.[28] To illustrate her thesis she draws attention to the work of Soyinka and to the Yoruba 'folk opera' of Duro Ladipo and Kola Ogunmola.[29]

The integration of dance into African drama had, however, begun much earlier. The plays of H. I. E. Dhlomo, written in the 1930s, which are concerned primarily with nineteenth-century South African history, or more precisely a black perspective on it,[30] make extensive use of dance in ceremonial and ritual contexts. However, Dhlomo's

---

[25] Thompson, *African Art in Motion*, 26.   [26] Ibid. 27.

[27] Peggy Harper, 'New Roles for the Dance', *New African* (Sept. 1965), 158. Harper is a South African who moved to Nigeria in the 1960s, where she taught at the University of Ibadan. Recently she has worked in Zimbabwe with the National Dance Company.   [28] Ibid.

[29] As far as choreography is concerned Harper saw the future in the production of new 'dance-dramas'. She choreographed a number of such works in the 1960s at the University of Ibadan.

[30] These are *The Girl Who Killed to Save*, *Ntsikana*, *Dingane*, *Cetshwayo*, and *Moshoeshoe*, all reprinted in H. I. E. Dhlomo's *Collected Works*, ed. Nick Visser and Tim Couzens (Johannesburg: Raven Press, 1985).

didascalia are somewhat laconic; he refers simply to 'dancing' or 'singing and dancing', mostly without further generic specification. Although the dances cannot be linked to identifiable cultural texts, dance is intended to have a mimetic function serving as an index of historical and cultural authenticity. A similar function for dance can be detected in Ola Rotimi's historical drama *Kurunmi*, which is based on events from Yoruba history in the late nineteenth century. As in Dhlomo's plays, dance is one of the indicators of traditional culture. For this reason Rotimi places particular emphasis on authenticity. He requires for the performance of war dances 'expert choreography'.[31] This means that for Rotimi, and the same can be said for Dhlomo, the primary objective is to retain the original semantics of such dances. There is no attempt, however, to use dance for more complex dramaturgical or even ideological tasks. Dance is not yet seen as a means to construct a counter-discourse to Western theatrical aesthetics.

That dance can be seen and used as a performative counter-discourse is demonstrated by the Kenyan writer Ngugi wa Thiong'o in comments on his play *Ngaahika Ndeenda*, which he first wrote in Gĩkũyũ together with Ngugi wa Mirii and the participants of a collective theatre project. It was then translated into English as *I will Marry when I Want*.[32] 'Song and dance are not just decorations, they are an integral part of that conversation, that drinking session, that ritual, that ceremony. In *Ngaahika Ndeenda* we too tried to incorporate song and dance as part of the structure and movement of the actors.'[33] The short list ('that conversation, that drinking session . . .') makes very clear that dance is an important element of various spheres of everyday activity. One of the striking characteristics of *I will Marry when I Want* is that dance and song are a feature not just of ritual and ceremony, as in the case of Dhlomo and Rotimi, but also of the quotidian. This reinforces

---

[31] Rotimi, *Kurunmi*, 62.

[32] The play was performed in 1979 at the Kamĩrĩĩthũ Cultural Centre in Limuru, Kenya, as part of a community project, which was closed down for political reasons by government authorities. The production process is described by Ngugi wa Thiong'o in his book *Decolonizing the Mind*. A Gĩkũyũ version was published in 1980. The project has already attracted a great deal of critical and scholarly commentary which has set up an interesting discursive field. While Ngugi stresses the regional significance of the project as an example of local cultural production, his international reputation as a writer and the political controversy caused by the project have led to an internationalization of the project's principles.   [33] Ibid. 45.

the necessity of making dance a structural component of the actors' movement rather than it being a generically discrete specialized activity. Within the overall structure of the play dance and dialogue are in a balanced relationship. However, when examined more closely the dance sequences reveal a dramaturgical as well as a cultural-mimetic function. One of these functions is that of kinaesthetic memory. A few dance steps by the main character Kĩgũũnda serve, for example, to signal a flashback showing how, as a young man, he courted his future wife with the same steps:

He starts the Mũcũng'wa. In his head he begins to see the vision of how they used to dance the Mũcũng'wa. Actual DANCERS now appear on stage led by Kĩgũũnda and his wife.[34]

As with all other dances in the play, this one possesses a complex referentiality. Apart from the personal and emotional perspective, the dance has a political and historical dimension: it is also Kĩgũũnda's reminiscence of the period preceding Kenya's state of emergency (1952–62). And finally Ngugi underscores with the dance the notion of collectivity, essential for African dance aesthetics, for Ngugi's political agenda, and for the theatrical context of a community play. So that the dance can be presented in its culturally appropriate form, the couple on stage are joined by a group of dancers. The dance Mũcũng'wa is only one of several dances that Ngugi specifies. It is by no means a choreographic invention of the authors or directors, but an identifiable cultural text, which is, however, not simply reproduced mimetically but embedded in a many-layered semiotic field linking aesthetics, politics, and the concrete context of performance.[35]

As has been demonstrated, music and dance are integral moments of traditional African performance aesthetics. Wole Soyinka's *Death and the King's Horseman* is a work which achieves an astounding fusion of this aesthetic within the framework of a Western-style dramaturgy. Soyinka's prefatory note to his play states unequivocally that conventional Western theatrical patterns of communication are not applicable. He writes that the paramount problem of the director

[34] Ngugi wa Thiong'o and Ngugi wa Miri, *I will Marry when I Want* (London: Heinemann 1982), 11.

[35] According to Ngugi the local participants of the project were instrumental in selecting and shaping the songs and dances; see interview in Hansel Ndumbe Eyoh (ed.), *Beyond the Theatre* (Bonn: Deutsche Stiftung für Internationale Entwicklung, 1991), 147.

is not to focus on the outworn notion of 'culture clash' but is 'the far more difficult and risky task of eliciting the play's threnodic essence'.[36] 'Threnodic essence' indicates the centrality of music and its link with Yoruba ritual, which is, as has already been noted, one of the key precepts of 'The Fourth Stage'. The function of music as one of the dominants in the play's structure of communication is restated in the final sentence: '*Death and the King's Horseman* can be fully realized only through an evocation of music from the abyss of transition'.[37] In concrete terms, this means that an understanding of the musical and dance forms of the Yoruba is crucial to comprehend fully the play's meaning.

The play begins with the entrance of Elesin, the chief counsellor of the recently deceased Yoruba king and preordained to take his own life within the next few hours in order to accompany his king into the next world. He is 'pursued by his drummers and praise-singers. He is a man of enormous vitality, speaks, dances and sings with that infectious enjoyment of life which accompanies all his actions'.[38] His entrance is marked by music and dance: a man of very high station presents himself dancing. This alone signals the paramount importance of kinesic signs in which rhythmic movement has a very high status, not just for the young, but also for mature and high-ranking personages. But 'that infectious enjoyment of life' may seem a peculiar state of mind for someone preparing for his own death.

Dance and music (the two are mostly so intertwined that they must be examined together as interdependent forms of expression) are also in this context synonymous with death. Dancing is the vehicle by which one joins the ancestors (see Soyinka's dedication of the play to his deceased father: 'who lately danced, and joined the Ancestors'[39]). Elesin intends to celebrate with the women of the market as he wills himself to death: 'This night I'll touch feet with their feet in a dance that is no longer of this earth'.[40] Throughout the opening exchange between Elesin and his Praise-Singer it is necessary to imagine continual movement as the Praise-Singer steers Elesin on his path towards death, strengthening his resolve, warning him of pitfalls, pointing out his duties. It is a balanced verbal and kinesic debate: arguments are posited, discussed, and accepted by means of dance, word, and incantation. This rhythmic to-and-fro is interrupted when

[36] Soyinka, *Six Plays*, 144.   [37] Ibid. 145.   [38] Ibid. 147.
[39] Ibid. 143.   [40] Ibid. 148.

Elesin introduces the story of the Not-I bird, which, as it is a tale centring on the refusal to accept death, is obviously not seen as part of the exchange: 'PRAISE-SINGER [*stopped in his lyric stride*]. The Not-I bird, Elesin?'[41] The stage direction 'stopped in his lyric stride' is an expressively laconic summation of the performance style of this scene, encapsulating as it does both the musicality of the verbal exchanges and the rhythm of the movement.

A visual equivalent to this mood is provided in the next sequence, in which Elesin feigns 'insult', yet only wishes to be garbed in rich clothing, with which the women hasten to adorn him: 'Elesin stands resplendent in rich clothes, cap, shawl, etc. His sash is of a bright red alari cloth. The women dance around him'.[42] The scene serves to underline Elesin's vanity and his universally understandable desire to delay his own death somewhat. Elesin's weakness for profane pleasures, expressed most clearly in his demand for a young bride, is communicated here with visual signs which also set up the connotative field of death and burial.

The overall impact of scene 1 is based on a complete shift in the normal organization of Western theatre. The scene is verbally, musically, gesturally, and philosophically an encounter with the Yoruba world commmunicated in its performance aesthetics. For all the colourful evocation of a bygone age, there is no trace of idealization or of a folkloristic transposition of cultural texts; the integrated performance forms have been refashioned into a fictional ensemble which gives expression to the impending conflict and tragedy.

The transition to scene 2, the verandah of District Officer Pilkings's bungalow, is constructed around a contrapuntal strategy. It is important to remember that Soyinka demands 'rapid scene changes'[43] so that the drumming of scene 1 is almost abruptly interrupted by tango music, 'playing from an old hand-cranked gramophone'.[44] The juxtaposition of two culturally different musical codes carries a variety of connotative associations. The Yoruba *bata* music is performed live and embodies a flexible, changing, and vital element of Yoruba culture: it contributes to the preparation and execution of a communally important ritual. The tango music, on the other hand, is a musical expression of the fundamental incongruities characteristic of and accompanying the colonial presence. It

[41] Soyinka, *Six Plays*, 149.   [42] Ibid. 156.   [43] Ibid. 146.
[44] Ibid. 163.

is mechanically (badly) reproduced Argentinian dance music for English colonials in Africa. The dance itself expresses precisely the same set of incongruities.

Another cultural text that figures predominantly in the scene is the offstage drumming. It too conveys culturally specific and, for the various listeners, contradictory and conflicting information. The drumming can be semioticized on a number of levels. Firstly, it conveys quite literally verbal, or more specifically, paralinguistic, information. The Yoruba 'talking drum' is capable of imitating the tonal patterns of the language and thus communicates iconically as well as symbolically subtle and differentiated messages. For a Western audience, the drumming is probably semioticized on a conventional level not entirely dissimilar to Jane Pilkings's ironical, teasing comment: 'I thought all bush drumming sounded the same'.[45] This is a well-worn cliché deriving from countless Hollywood films in which white explorers are surrounded at night by ominous drumming preceding an onslaught by the 'natives'. Soyinka refers directly to this media-created association when Pilkings asks the houseboy, Joseph, to interpret the message: 'let's ask our native guide. Joseph!'[46] Joseph himself is confused, however, because he hears contradictory messages: 'It sounds like the death of a great chief and then, it sounds like the wedding of a great chief. It really mix me up'.[47] What Joseph hears, of course, is entirely coherent, if the events of scene 1 are borne in mind. From the direction of Osugbo, the sacred cult place of the Yoruba, he hears the announcement that the king's horseman will soon die, whereas from the market-place he presumably hears the drums of Elesin's retinue heralding his wedding.

This acoustic confusion is not insignificant for the tragic events that ensue. Pilkings's action in arresting Elesin and preventing him from carrying out the ritual is partially based on a misunderstanding of Sergeant Amusa's written message: 'the Elesin Oba is to commit death tonight as a result of native custom'.[48] Pilkings interprets the phrase 'commit death' to mean ritual murder. Although this misunderstanding is subsequently corrected, the message itself underlines the potential for cultural misunderstanding inherent in the system of English colonial administration, which relied on indirect rule and the 'native' interpretation of information to carry out decisions. The confusing verbal and acoustic messages, both of which are received

---

[45] Ibid. 167.   [46] Ibid. 170.   [47] Ibid.   [48] Ibid. 165 f.

second-hand, provide the basis for Pilkings's decision to take action and meddle in the affairs of the Yoruba.

Scene 3 contains probably the most striking demonstration of Soyinka's African theatrical poetics. Most of the key precepts enumerated in his theoretical writings can be found in this scene, which is dominated completely by kinesic signs. Here we find African art in motion even more fully expressed than in scene 1. At the same time the spoken word still plays an important role: the market girls' verbal humiliation of the police officers and Elesin's rhetorical *tour de force*, as he wills himself to death, highlight different aspects of verbal dexterity. Yet, this dexterity is matched and aided by kinesic signs. Soyinka specifies precisely defined patterns of movement: the fluid, changing, taunting movements of the women contrast with the stiffness of the policemen, who struggle to retain their status and their dignity (Plate 15). With their departure, the last trace of European-derived rigidity disappears and the African aesthetic signs dominate completely. The change is heralded by the womens' 'song and dance of euphoria',[49] for which Soyinka provides a precise scenario, and consolidated with the appearance of Elesin, who interrupts the festivities to present the bloodstained bridal sheet. He then launches into a long speech, which leads into his trance-dance. He repeatedly refers to the audible drumming, and there are various references to it in the stage directions. It is significant that in this scene, in contrast to the previous scene with its contradictions and confusions, the drumming provides a completely coherent text, which Elesin reads and which guides him in his actions. Here we see, then, the importance of semiotic communication within a unified cultural sphere where all codes and signs cohere and make sense.

The trance-dance itself is a well-known performance form associated with Yoruba religion. The trance-dancer, or, in Soyinka's formulation in 'The Fourth Stage', 'the possessed lyricist',[50] is the mouthpiece of Yoruba tragic drama and the medium between the worlds of the living and the ancestors: 'his somnabulist "improvisations"—a simultaneity of musical and poetic forms—are not representations of the ancestor, recognitions of the living or unborn, but of the no man's land of transition between and around these temporal definitions of experience'.[51] Although Soyinka examined the inherent

---

[49] Soyinka, *Six Plays* 180.
[50] Soyinka, *Myth, Literature and the African World*, 148.   [51] Ibid.

theatricality of spirit possession in earlier plays *Kongi's Harvest* and *The Trials of Brother Jero* in a clearly satirical vein,[52] and also in *The Road*, Elesin's trance-dance is the most prolonged and serious example of possession in Soyinka's work.

It is significant that the central metaphor in Elesin's long speech is equestrian. Not only is he the king's horseman, but the notions of horsemanship, riding, and being 'mounted' by a spirit are integral to Yoruba spirit possession. Expressions such as 'make my limbs strike earth like a thoroughbred' or 'the stallion will ride in triumph on the back of man'[53] abound and not only refer to the notion of the possessed person being 'ridden' by the spirit, but also reflect aesthetic principles. Thompson devotes a whole chapter in his book to sculptures of horse and rider, a theme which is particularly prevalent among the Yoruba.[54] He notes in these sculptural traditions 'suggestions of incarnation and mystical union' and an almost exclusive connection with kings, rulers, or important persons. Soyinka's exact description of Elesin's movement reflect culturally defined aesthetic principles: 'His dance is one of solemn, regal motions, each gesture of the body is made with a solemn finality. The WOMEN join him, their steps a somewhat more fluid version of his'.[55] This short passage contains a number of the aesthetic categories established by Thompson such as 'vital aliveness' ('the dancer must import equal life, equal autonomy, to every dancing portion of his frame')[56] and 'call-and-response', in this case a harmonious relationship between leader and chorus. The scene closes with another allusion to aesthetic categories: 'Elesin's dance does not lose its elasticity but his gestures become, if possible, even more weighty'.[57] The notion of elasticity is also described by Thompson under the heading 'flexibility' ('Les trésors de souplesse'), the ultimate compliment for a dancer being that he has no bones.[58]

The opening stage direction of the next scene consists of two words: 'A Masque'. Both the spelling and the laconism are intentionally anachronistic and redolent of didascalia found in Elizabethan or Jacobean drama. The fancy dress ball in the residency 'of a far flung

---

[52] See here Dapo Adelugba, 'Trance and Theatre: The Nigerian Experience', in Ogunbiyi (ed.), *Drama and Theatre in Nigeria*, 203–18. Adelugba suggests that *Kongi's Harvest* as a whole 'may be seen as a sustained Bori rite with all the entranced characters acting in consonance with the spirit they are possessed by' (p. 208).

[53] Soyinka, *Six Plays*, 181 f.   [54] Thompson, *African Art in Motion*, 73 ff.
[55] Soyinka, *Six Plays*, 182.   [56] Thompson, *African Art in Motion*, 9.
[57] Soyinka, *Six Plays*, 186.   [58] Thompson, *African Art in Motion*, 9.

but key imperial frontier'[59] is supposed to establish associations with
the courtly interludes of early seventeenth-century theatre. It is thus
not by chance that the guest of honour, the Prince of Wales, and his
companions 'are dressed in seventeenth century European
costume'.[60] As a genre, the court masque was, as the name suggests,
exclusively the preserve of royalty and frequently adulatory towards
the royal personages in the audience. Elements such as masks,
disguises, dance, and flamboyant opulence all reappear in varying
degrees of realization in the fancy dress ball. The 'ritual of introduc-
tions'[61] is the debased European response to the dynamic trance-
dance of Elesin, who is literally dancing himself to death for the good
of his community. Pilkings and his wife show off their *egungun*
costumes: They 'demonstrate the dance steps and the guttural sounds
made by the *egungun*, harass other dancers in the hall, MRS PILKINGS
playing "the restrainer" to PILKINGS' manic darts'.[62] Here the
egungun in all its signifying functions is degraded. Not only the dress
itself but also the sounds and movements, both of which are sacred
and express the divine embodiment of the dancer, are blasphemed and
become little more than an exotic curiosity.

Similarly complex dramaturgical functions can be found in the
dance scenes in the plays of Jack Davis, although dance does not
achieve the dominant position found in Soyinka's play. Davis's plays
feature almost without exception Aboriginal dancer-figures who
tend to remain aloof from the realistic action. They represent in
terms of their physical appearance and stylized movement a link
with the traditional past. In addition to these figures there are also
dance scenes involving the realistic characters. On both levels dance
as a non-verbal form of expression is able to achieve types of
signification beyond the scope of spoken language. In *The Dreamers*, for example, Davis's second play, the author specifies the
acculturated movement style of traditional dance: 'in stylized rhythmic steps [he] searches for a straight stick [. . .] striking the *mirrolgah* stance[63] against a dramatic sunset as the music climaxes and
cuts'.[64] The problem of dance and tradition is represented in a
completely different way as well. At the end of Act 1, scene 4,
the old character Worru tries to demonstrate to the 'young fellas' a

---

[59] Soyinka, *Six Plays*, 186.   [60] Ibid.   [61] Ibid. 187.   [62] Ibid.
[63] According to Davis the *mirrolgah* stance has two meanings: it can indicate the
body in balance or the act of throwing a spear. Davis, *Kullark (Home) / The Dreamers*,
144.   [64] Ibid. 99.

traditional dance. The stage direction deserves to be cited in full because Davis describes a movement scenario in which various kinds of dance are juxtaposed and their cultural significations highlighted:

ELI. Go on, Pop, git up an' show 'im a real *middar*. Go on, oldy, a real dinkum *yahllarah*.
WORRU. Awright, awright, I'll show you fellas, me an Nindal we danced for the Prince of New South Wales.

> [WORRU *rises and begins a drunken stumbling version of a half-remembered tribal dance.* PETER *turns the volume up and continues his own disco dance.* WORRU *pushes him aside and dances to the amusement of* ELI *and* ROY, *until his feet tangle and he falls heavily.*
>
> *The scene freezes, the light changes, and the radio cuts abruptly to heavy rhythmic didjiridoo and clap sticks. An intricately painted* DANCER *appears on the escarpment against a dramatic red sky, dances down and across in front of them, pounding his feet into the stage. Finally, he dances back up the ramp where he poses for a moment before the light snaps out on the last note of music.*][65]

Dance as an Aboriginal cultural text reflects in this sequence three phases of cultural breakdown. The end of the development is represented by the figure of young Eli. While he still knows the names of the traditional dances (*middar, yahllarah*), he much prefers his 'disco dance' (phase 3). In fact, his 'gaze' is a folkloristic one, not unlike that of the colonial audience for whom Worru danced as a young man. The actual point of enculturative breakdown is the drunken staggering figure of Worru himself (phase 2). The stage direction 'half-remembered' suggests that while Worru was certainly a recipient of traditional cultural knowledge, he is incapable of passing it down to future generations. The appearance of the dancer, finally, who completes Worru's fragmentary dance points back to the pre-colonial or even mythic time (phase 1), when enculturation processes still functioned. Helen Gilbert contrasts the two sets of movement—Worru and the dancer—and interprets them as an expression of a double Aboriginal identity: 'Here, the interrelationships of the two sets of movements produce an Aboriginal identity that reflects contemporary black reality, but which is, at the same time, also mythic, and therefore resistant to the dominant normalizing

[65] Ibid. 86.

impulses of that reality'.[66] Complex images of this kind that contain both social criticism and a level of mythic reality are scarcely communicable by means of language alone. Traditional dance with its origins in ritual performances is used here to communicate a complexity of experience which is beyond the aesthetics of 'kitchen-sink' realism. The polysemic expressivity of this scene is also a result of the proxemic aspects of the dance. The physical juxtaposition of two dancing bodies—the painted Aboriginal dancer with his controlled stylized movement beside the old man lying on the floor in singlet and trousers—creates a dimension of meaning linked to movement and space, the special domain of the aesthetics of dance.

Davis shows in this scene how colonialism has destroyed almost the last remnants of traditional culture among contemporary urban Aborigines. The beginnings of this process is the subject of Bob Maza's play *The Keepers*, (1988) which traces the fortunes of an Aboriginal family from South Australia belonging to the Boandik people, and a Scottish missionary family in the middle of the nineteenth century. Their first (colonial?) encounter is presented in the form of three contrasting dances. The first meeting between the two main characters, the Aboriginal woman Mirnat and the missionary Elizabeth, takes place in the stylized form of a dance. The one woman is dressed in black leotards, the other in white. Each performs a dance from their respective cultures ('a dance of the home of the Boandik', 'a dance of Scotland'); these are followed by a 'courting dance', and finally by a dance symbolizing birth.[67] The whole sequence is one of balanced cultural reciprocity: cultural differences are presented without establishing cultural hierarchies. The scene implies that the semiotic system dance, like music, offers a way of encountering another culture which is not available to language.[68] However, the play does not try to create an idealized notion of cultural harmony; on the contrary, in the course of the play the relentless destruction of Boandik culture is depicted. Against this background the opening

---

[66] Helen Gilbert, 'The Dance as Text in Contemporary Australian Drama: Movement and Resistance Politics', *Ariel*, 23/1 (Jan. 1992), 142.

[67] Bob Maza, *The Keepers*, in J. Saunders (ed.), *Plays from Black Australia* (Sydney: Currency Press, 1989), 171.

[68] The fact that the dance is performed by women underscores the gender aspect of this encounter; see Gilbert, 'The Dance as Text in Contemporary Australian Drama', 139 f.

scene functions as a utopian image of intercultural communication
before the word.

The Signing Body

The kinetic art of syncretic theatre is by no means exclusively danced
art. There are numerous other forms of body language and kinetic
expression which are culturally coded and incorporated into theatrical
texts. In the second section of this chapter I shall look at the kinetic
codes of South African township theatre, which combine dance, gesture, and sign language in various and rapidly changing combinations.
The final example is sign language, as used in Aboriginal theatre. Here
we find a traditional cultural text being refashioned for the urban
stage.

Anyone who has witnessed a performance of township theatre can
testify to the crucial importance of non-verbal performance devices.
At times it seems as if the language generated by the actors with their
bodies is equally if not more communicative than the actual words
spoken. Percy Mtwa has stressed the central importance of the actor's
body in their form of 'poor theatre': 'you are using your body as the
only instrument you have, and that body which you have can be
anything, can be a piece of sculpture, it can sing, it can be a song,
it can be movement, can be sound, can be anything, that body'.[69]
Mtwa, one of the co-creators of *Woza Albert!*, articulates here how
the actor's body functions as a dominant sign vehicle for the performance. In the context of the Western hierarchy of theatrical devices
we can speak of a shift in dominant function in township theatre to
privilege kinesic codes. The kinesic codes can range from sign language, to mime, to dance, to stylized, sculptured movement. On the
basis of photographs taken during a performance of *Bopha!* we can
illustrate three general, recurrent categories of kinesic codes found in
township theatre.

Plate 12 shows the opening of the play with a dance or a mixture
of music and movement. Dance is a constitutive component of the

---

[69] Eckhard Breitinger, 'I've been an Entertainer throughout my life', Interview with
Percy Mtwa, *Matatu. Zeitschrift für afrikanische Kultur und Gesellschaft*, 3–4 (1988),
170.

theatre form and one of the most important elements which illustrate the syncretic nature of these plays, in which traditional African performance forms can be integrated. Here the physical training routines of the police academies are transformed into a Zulu dance, where the dance is not just an interlude but through the transition from the drill routines retains a clear connection with the action and theme of the play: the predicament of black policemen in the apartheid regime.

In plate 13 a police band playing the South African national anthem is being mimed. The same device is used in the opening image of *Woza Albert!* This is just one instance of the extensive use of mime, but one which is actually drawn from the actors' experience of growing up in the townships. Percy Mtwa describes how as teenagers he and a group of friends created a rock band without instruments:

And then, somebody—just during that moment—started playing a song that was popular at that time—it was called Mr. Bull, it was very popular. And then he started miming it, playing the bass guitar with his lips and his voice and then another person started coming in with the drums, miming them as well and then, all of a sudden, there we were, miming this song and what came out was something very beautiful. We went home. We started arranging it, putting it together and we performed throughout the school.[70]

In Plate 14 physical action approximates cinematic-photographic techniques. The photograph is taken from scene 13, the funeral scene, where the procession turns into a massacre as the police gun down the mourners-protestors. The action and movement is slowed down to resemble a slow-motion or freeze-frame sequence in a film, a technique often used to depict scenes of violence and death. Such use of stylized movement reinforces the intention of township theatre-makers to create strong, vivid images within the episodic structure. Percy Mtwa again: 'These images that I present there on that stage, it is like a photographer—pah!—and it is there.'[71] Mtwa illustrates with this example the productive reception of other media codes: the lived experience of black people is replayed to them via other media and this experience is refashioned in a theatrical equivalent on stage.

The use of sign language in contemporary Aboriginal plays reveals

---

[70] Eckhard Breitinger, 'I've been an Entertainer throughout my life', 160.
[71] Ibid. 174.

a conscious strategy to incorporate a traditional communicative code into the conventions of Western theatrical realism. As early as the nineteenth century ethnographers drew attention to the phenomenon of Aboriginal sign languages.[72] They constitute one of the few examples of fully developed, completely non-verbal sign languages with systemic character.[73] This means that the Aboriginal sign languages are neither language-supportive in the way most gesture is, nor limited in terms of their vocabulary. On the contrary, they are characterized by complete semantic openness independent of linguistic signs, meaning that they can generate a potentially infinite number of messages.[74] Research carried out by the ethnolinguist Adam Kendon, who has studied the sign language of women from the Walpiri tribe in central Australia, shows that this form of communication is still alive and is passed on by enculturation.[75] By drawing a comparison with a written language, Kendon characterizes the individual gestural signs as 'a gestural rendition of the semantic units the words in the language refer to'.[76]

In the culture of present-day urbanized Aborigines only a few relics of this form of communication seem to have survived. Even if these relics no longer possess systemic character and thus the attribute of semantic openness, sign language is nevertheless used and would appear to be part of the enculturation of urbanized Aborigines. This is confirmed in the plays of Jack Davis, where sign language is utilized in the context of everyday communication. The examples he specifies make it clear that the gestures belong to a culturally specific sign language with fixed

---

[72] The best overview is to be found in the recent study by Adam Kendon, *Sign Languages of Aboriginal Australia: Cultural, Semiotic and Communicative Perspectives* (Cambridge: Cambridge University Press, 1988); see also Kendon's article 'Some Reasons for Studying Gesture', *Semiotica*, 62/1–2 (1986), 13–28.

[73] The other well-known example of a 'natural' sign language with systemic character is that of the North American Plains Indians; see Thomas A. Sebeok, 'Aboriginal Sign "Languages" from a Semiotic Point of View', in *The Sign and its Masters* (Austin: University of Texas Press, 1979), 128–67. Examples of artificial sign languages are the various sign languages for the deaf as well as sign languages of certain monastic orders.

[74] Because Aboriginal sign languages are closely linked to, but by no means dependent on, the semantics of the spoken language they are not very suitable as a means of interlingual communication as is the case with the sign language of the Plains Indians. See ibid.

[75] 'Among these people it is the custom for a woman, when bereaved of spouse or child, to remain silent for a long period as a mark of mourning—in many cases several months, in traditional times for as long as a year or more. There is no other restriction on their communication, however, and as a result a complex sign language has been developed which makes it possible for those who know it to engage fully in conversation'. Kendon, 'Some Reasons for Studying Gesture', 24.   [76] Ibid.

autonomous signs and are not just language-supporting gestures. For example, in a stage direction in *The Dreamers* we read: 'DOLLY gives the Nyoongah gesture for running off'.[77] Davis does not deem it necessary to indicate what this gesture is because the sign is conventionalized and at least for an Aboriginal audience decodable. This is due to its emblematic character.[78] The sign is clearly part of a sign language vocabulary. There are other examples of sign language used in Davis's plays where it accompanies English linguistic signs and is more easily understood by a non-Aboriginal audience. Occasionally sign language is used in combination with Aboriginal expressions, with the result that there is a duplication of indigenous signs:

ELI. [*miming handcuffs*]. I thought you was *woonana* [behind bars].[79]

Sign language is also frequently used deictically: the gestural sign illustrates emblematically what is meant in combination with demonstrative pronouns:

WORRU. Who's 'ome?
DOLLY. Oh, just our lot, they all sittin' around like that. [DOLLY *indicates they are broke, by making a circle with her thumb and index finger.*][80]

This example creates a connection between indigenous signs and the linguistic sign system of Western culture. While the replacement of the linguistic sign 'broke' by a circular gesture formed by the index finger and thumb is as an act indigenous, the emblem, on the other hand, the iconic imitation of a zero in this case, is derived from the Western scriptural system.

Davis specifies quite a number of gestural signs that indicate Western concepts or things. The complex police–arrest–incarceration is frequently indicated and commented on by means of sign language. In a stage direction in *No Sugar* Davis specifies exactly how this complex is depicted by means of gestural signs. The Aborigine Jimmy explains to the white man Frank how his people are subjected to sanctions and police harassment:

---

[77] Davis, *Kullark (Home)/The Dreamers*, 128.
[78] Emblems are a category of gestural signs which are culturally specific, are codifiable independently of language, and possess clearly defined semantics. The term was coined by David Efron in his pioneering comparative study of culturally specific gesture: *Gesture, Race and Culture* (1941; The Hague: Mouton, 1972). Efron's typology of gesture has been developed further by Ekman and Friesen, 'The Repertoire of Nonverbal Behavior'.   [79] Davis, *Kullark (Home)/The Dreamers*, 78.
[80] Ibid. 81.

JIMMY. You allowed to walk down the street after sundown? Eh?

FRANK. Yeah, don't see why not.

JIMMY. Well I'm not. None of us are; you know we're not allowed in town, not allowed to go down the soak, not allowed to march . . . ? [*He mimes handcuffs and gaol by first putting his wrists together and then placing a hand downwards over his forehead with the fingers spread over his eyes.*] *Manatj* grab us like that. Bastards . . .

FRANK. Who?

GRAN. Politjmans.[81]

Frank's question 'who?' indicates that neither Jimmy's sign language nor his term for policeman are comprehensible to him. That these signs are by no means an invention of Jack Davis is demonstrated in Adam Kendon's research, who documents similar signs among the central Australian Aborigines when 'talking' about their experiences with the white justice system.[82]

Sign language is used in Aboriginal plays not only in the form of individual signs but also as an independent communication device analogous to natural language. The most extensive example can be found in Bob Maza's drama *The Keepers*. The action revolves around the relationship between Mirnat, the Aboriginal woman, and Elizabeth Campbell, the Scottish missionary's wife. An important indication of this deepening relationship can be seen in their mutual efforts to learn each others' languages. In the case of Elizabeth she finds the sign language of the Boandik tribe easier to learn than the spoken language. That complex messages can be generated by this sign language is demonstrated when Elizabeth tries to explain to Mirnat where her husband has gone:

She [ELIZABETH] attempts to explain in very poor Boandik, but at last reverts to the easier Boandik hand and sign language, translating to herself in English: JAMES HAS GONE BY BOAT TO SEND SOME STORES TO SHEEP FARMS ON THE COAST.[83]

A similar scene takes place between the husbands of the women, James Campbell and Koonawar.[84] Here as well the message is translated simultaneously into English. This is done primarily for the sake of the theatre audience, for it goes without saying that this sign

---

[81] Davis, *No Sugar*, 28 f.

[82] According to Kendon, the sign for police or policeman was represented by crossed arms to depict handcuffs. *Sign Languages of Aboriginal Australia*, 108.

[83] Maza, *The Keepers*, 185 f.   [84] Ibid. 192.

language is too complex to be understood by a non-indigenous audience without the help of such conventions. The act of translating in fact draws attention to this very complexity.

Above and beyond its function as a means of communication the sign language takes on another signifying function. It stands here metonymically for several larger complexes. The signifier 'sign language' has several referents. On the one hand, it refers to the destruction of the cultural system of this tribe through colonization: the loss of sign language which is incomprehensible to the spectator without the help of translation is only one element of this system. On the other hand, the preferential selection of sign language by the characters as a means of intercultural communication can be understood as a counter-discourse to the privileging of natural languages in the Western system of values. A third referent is the demonstration of the complexity of Aboriginal sign languages to a wider public, knowledge hitherto restricted to Aborigines themselves and a few ethnolinguists.

Although sign language as a sign vehicle never becomes a dominant code in Aboriginal plays, it is, nevertheless, together with songs, dance, orality, and body-painting, one of the cultural texts on which Aboriginal dramatists can and do draw to create a syncretic dramatic form. It is important to stress that sign language, because by definition it depends on the body, draws attention to the body as a semiotic instrument. This foregrounding of the body as a cultural text is even more evident in the use of body-painting described in the previous chapter. Here it was seen how a cultural tradition has been adapted to the stage in two quite different ways. Also, cultural forms such as orality were shown to be a performance code which relies heavily on gestural and kinaesthetic signs, even when incorporated into a contemporary play. This semiotic perspective, with its emphasis on individual sign systems and performance codes, helps to sharpen an awareness of how syncretic drama functions and communicates over and above the dialogic level.

CHAPTER SEVEN

Spaces and Spectators

> We heard of the existence of a National Theatre and ran to it
> full of joy and anticipation. We discovered that there was no
> theatre, there was nothing beyond a precious, attractive building
> in the town centre [. . .] it was disconcerting to find a miniature
> replica of a British provincial theatre.
>
> (Wole Soyinka, 'Towards a True Theatre')

Wole Soyinka's disappointment on discovering that the newly opened
Ugandan National Theatre was little more than a copy of the colonial
model is symptomatic of the attitude held by a whole generation of
dramatists and directors, who sought to accelerate the process of
theatrical decolonization in all spheres of the theatre in their newly
independent countries. There existed general agreement that the form
of the proscenium stage was inappropriate for new dramaturgical
ideas. Soyinka articulates the general design of such ideas when in
the same article he calls for 'the new adaptable space where actor and
audience may liberate their imagination.'[1] Although there was nothing particularly new about this demand in 1962—Soyinka was echo-
ing a critique of the picture frame stage going back to the turn of the
century—the new departure that became evident in the following
decades in post-colonial countries was motivated by experiments to
incorporate indigenous spatial concepts into the requirements of a
syncretic dramaturgy.

  This chapter analyses two different strategies for creating new spatial
forms. The one strategy attempts to create different *physical performance conditions* in keeping with indigenous spatial concepts. The
other is a *dramaturgical* strategy which can be realized on a Western
proscenium stage. Examples of radically different spatial arrangements
for syncretic theatre productions are numerous and can be documented

---

[1] Wole Soyinka, 'Towards a True Theatre', *Nigeria Magazine*, 75 (Dec. 1962), 58–
60; cited in Wole Soyinka, *Art, Dialogue and Outrage: Essays on Literature and
Culture* (Ibadan: New Horn Press, 1988), 4.

in a number of post-colonial countries. The common factor uniting
such culturally disparate experiments is the requirement that heterogeneous spatial concepts are recombined in new forms.

Cultural Spaces

The fusion of disparate cultural spatial concepts implies that not just
the physical forms but also the different behaviours associated with
them are brought together. This means that cultural spaces can
seldom be reconfigured without friction and conflict because they
never purely abstract. Besides natural language, space is one of the
crucial texts of a culture which help define it as a *semiosphere*. A
semiosphere, a concept introduced by Yuri Lotman and defined by
him as the totality of all sign-users, texts, and codes of a culture, is
'the result and the condition for the development of culture'.[2] Central
to Lotman's concept is the notion that space and borders are integral
elements of cultural definition.[3] Although Lotman is clearly speaking
of space in a very broad, almost metaphorical sense, the idea can also
be applied in a pragmatic way. The very act of constructing a building
for the performance of theatre is questionable in the light of indigenous spatial practices. When a British-style theatre building is
reproduced in Uganda, it suggests that it is out of place, a culturally
inappropriate element in the local semiosphere. This example is by
no means unique. All over Africa theatres were built in the post-
colonial period which more or less exhibited unashamedly their conceptual origin in a Western semiosphere. Twenty years after Soyinka
published his critical remarks, two British scholars working in
Nigeria (one a drama lecturer, the other an architect) concluded

---

[2] Yuri M. Lotman, *The Universe of the Mind: A Semiotic Theory of Culture*, tr. Ann
Shukman (London: I. B. Tauris, 1990), 125. Lotman developed this concept in the
1980s in analogy to the notion of a biosphere. However, his cultural semiotics always
had a strong spatial emphasis. In the famous 'Theses' (1. 2. 4) the opposition 'culture–
extracultural space' is defined as 'the minimal unit of the mechanism of culture at any
given level'. Van der Eng and Grygar (eds.), *Structure of Texts and Semiotics of
Culture*, 4.

[3] According to Lotman, semiospheres are characterized by borders or boundaries
which enable cultures to define and exclude elements: 'One of the primary mechanisms
of semiotic individuation is the boundary, and the boundary can be defined as the outer
limit of a first-person form. This space is "ours", "my own", "it is cultured", "safe",
"harmoniously organized", and so on. By contrast, their "space" is "other", "hostile",
"dangerous", "chaotic".' Lotman, *The Universe of the Mind*. 131.

that the not insignificant number of new theatres constructed in that country owed much more to an international Western style than to spatial concepts rooted in indigenous performance forms.[4] In a similar vein is the criticism levelled by Ngugi wa Thiong'o against the Kenyan National Theatre in Nairobi. Until the 1970s this institution was in an architectural sense a Western icon and in terms of its repertoire, administration, and direction a colonial semiosphere. In a sarcastic tone Ngugi asks the rhetorical question regarding the causes of this neocolonial orientation: 'Was it just a building? Was it the location? Was it the kind of plays presented there? Or was it simply the skin colour of the director and the administrative staff?'[5] The answer is that the sum total and fusion of all these elements contributed to the perpetuation of a neocolonial structure of this kind.

Ngugi's question touches on a central concern of the theoretical discussion of theatrical space, which is primarily concerned with expanding the concept itself. Although there exists no unified terminology to describe the various forms of theatrical and dramatic space, there seems to be a general consensus that three categories have to be differentiated: *theatre* space usually refers to architecturally related features, *stage* space designates the stage itself and set design, *dramatic* space refers to the spatial semantics indicated by the dramatic text.[6] Besides architectural aspects, questions raised include spatial semantics, spectator–performer relationships, as well as the wider context of the interface between performance space and surrounding environment. In this expanded sense, theatrical space can include forms such as street theatre. Understood in this way it is more sensible

[4] Michael Etherton and Peter Magyer, 'Full Streets and Empty Theatres: The Need to Relate the Forms of Drama to a Developing Society', *Black Orpheus*, 4/1 (1981), 46–60. This article contains a number of interesting ideas for creating theatrical spaces based on indigenous architectural forms.

[5] Ngugi, *Decolonizing the Mind*, 40. In another book Ngugi draws attention to the colonialistic beginnings of Kenya's national theatre: 'In 1952 the colonial regime in concert with the British Council started the British Kenya National Theatre. Here an annual school's English drama festival was started, with the British Council as the main donor of prizes for deserving African children.' *Detained: A Writer's Prison Diary* (London: Heinemann, 1981), 67.

[6] See Issacharoff, 'Space and Reference in drama'. The same categories are used by Hanna Scolnicov, who differentiates between theatre space (encompassing theatre and stage space) and theatrical space (meaning dramatic space). 'Theatre Space, Theatrical Space, and the Theatrical Space Without', in James Redmond (ed.), *The Theatrical Space* (Cambridge: Cambridge University Press, 1987), 15. See also Patrice Pavis, who also differentiates between concepts such as gestural, textual and inner space (visions, dreams, etc.). *Dictionnaire du théâtre* (Paris: Messidor and Éditions Sociales, 1987), 146 ff.

to speak of 'performance space' or of 'ludic space', as Marvin Carlson suggests.[7] Carlson describes the interrelationship between space, work, and performance as a semiotic process: 'places of performances generate social and cultural meanings of their own which in turn help to structure the meaning of the entire theatre experience'.[8] According to this definition, even specially constructed theatre buildings generate a whole spectrum of connotative meanings in addition to their functional level of signification. These connotative semantic dimensions depend on other cultural codes, for a theatre building is part of the cognitive cartography of a town or city. Thus a place of performance is determined by its integration into the wider referential system of the urban environment. This position in the urban system influences in turn the construction of receptive codes, with the result that any discussion of theatrical or performance space must take cognizance of questions regarding audience and theatrical reception.

Interesting examples of the relationship between performance space and audience reception can be found in productions which are shown in different cultures. It is particularly evident in South African township theatre, which has been able to negotiate successfully between the townships and Western metropolitan centres. The success of these plays in such disparate cultural spheres suggests that the discussion of theatrical space cannot be reduced to the simple dichotomy of the proscenium stage versus theatre-in-the-round or other architectural forms. Since the townships themselves do not as a rule have specialized theatre buildings, plays were performed in churches or school halls. Because of this situation works such as *Woza Albert!*, *Asinamali!*, and *Bopha!* were conceived for an empty and thus multifunctional stage space. In the townships they could be performed on a proscenium-type stage without engendering undue problems for the participatory behaviour of township audiences.[9]

---

[7] 'A permanently or temporarily created ludic space, a ground for the encounter of spectator and performer.' Marvin Carlson, *Places of Performance: The Semiotics of Theatre Architecture* (Ithaca: Cornell University Press, 1989), 6.   [8] Ibid. 2.

[9] The actor Thami Cele from the *Asinamali!* troupe reports on audience response in the townships: 'When we played in the townships, it seemed as if the whole hall was on the stage. By the end of the show, you couldn't differentiate. Every hall had become a stage. Everybody was participating, whistling, ululating, singing'; cited in Sher, 'Apartheid on Tour', 60. Interestingly enough Cele does not cite similar responses during performances in the Johannesburg Market Theatre, or in international metropolitan centres. For a discussion of township performances in an international context, see Loren Kruger, 'Apartheid on Display: South Africa Performs for New York', *Diaspora*, 1/2 (1991), 1–18.

To what extent the place of performance can actually affect the cultural and aesthetic perceptions of spectators can be illustrated with reference to Australia's first Aboriginal theatre. It was established in the Sydney suburb of Redfern in the early 1970s, an inner-city quarter which has become synonymous with the negative aspects of Aboriginal urban life. By setting up a theatre and cultural centre in such a place, spectators attending performances were forced to confront the living conditions of the people being dealt with in the plays themselves. The Aboriginal writer and director Gerry Bostock has described how the interaction of place and play during performances of Robert Merrit's drama *The Cake Man*[10] created levels of meaning and experience which decisively influenced the reception of the piece:

> The audience who'd never been to black theatre and had never been to the ghetto, had to go through the ghetto to get to the theatre, and that in itself was a great psychological advantage to the play, because people were coming there for the first time. [. . .] The thing with *The Cake Man* was that in that environment, in Redfern, you were confronting people not only with what was in the play, but what was in the street outside, so that had a dynamic sort of effect on all the audience.[11]

Although the play itself cannot really be considered an example of syncretic theatre, the actual performance of the work underscores the basic principle that the surroundings in which a theatre space is located can help to structure meaning. A theatre space is not an autonomous aesthetic realm, sealed off from the surrounding culture once the doors close and the lights go out. There is in fact a large degree of osmosis between a theatre space and the cultural signs of the semiosphere in which it is located.

Theatre Spaces

Turning now to the more concrete question of architectural forms that post-colonial theatre should and can take, one can discern a tendency to reject quadratic in favour of circular spatial conceptions. This applies generally to post-colonial writing on theatrical and performance space. It encompasses suggestions for theatre reform,

---

[10] *The Cake Man* was first performed on 12 Jan. 1975 at the Black Theatre Arts and Culture Centre, Sydney, directed by Bob Maza. It was published in 1978 by Currency Press, Sydney.   [11] Bostock, 'Black Theatre', 72.

actual productions, but also scholarly writing on traditional performance, particularly African, where the circle or arena is for African
masquerades and ritual performances the favoured spatial emblem. In
fact the opposition square versus circle has become almost a metaphor for the dichotomy between colonial and indigenous spatial
structures.[12]

The mythical symbolism of the circle is not restricted to the
African continent alone. Forms of arena staging have also been
propagated in the Caribbean as culturally appropriate theatre spaces.
In his manifesto for a carnival-based national theatre Errol Hill
identifies the proscenium stage as a crucial barrier for the audience
participation he desires.[13] A form of arena stage was outlined by
Hill's compatriot Rawle Gibbons in 1979 in his thesis 'Traditional
Enactments of Trinidad—Towards a Third Theatre'. The design,
however, owes its inspiration less to carnival than to the rituals of
Caribbean syncretic cults such as voodoo, *shango*, or the Spiritual
Baptists. Some years earlier Gibbons had stressed the insufficiencies
of proscenium stages for indigenous performances when reviewing a
performance entitled *Black Destiny*:

I feel the production would probably be more successful if done in the round.
In the first place such a location would be more consistent with the traditional theatre of the African peoples. The community was the circle—round a
fire, story-teller or the elders. The inherent restraints of the European stage—
audience division do not allow for the sort of audience participation as fully
as the nature of ritual drama requires.[14]

[12] An example of a circular stage for ritual performances is given by J. N. Amankulor in his analysis of the Ekpe festival of the Igbo in eastern Nigeria: 'The only
staging device of *Ekpe* is the "Arena Staging" in its most traditional form. There is no
raised platform for the chief actor or the drummers. Everybody is on the same level
including the spectators.' J. Ndakaku Amankulor, 'Ekpe Festival as Religious Ritual
and Dance Drama', in Ogunbiyi (ed.), *Drama and Theatre in Nigeria*, 119. This arena
consists of concentric circles in which the protagonists, the chorus, and the spectators
are gathered around a sacrificial altar, the focal point of the ritual.

[13] However, Hill is certainly aware that the introduction of an arena stage will not
automatically abolish the psychological barrier between performers and spectators:
'Even when an arena stage is employed, the audience, though brought closer to the
actors, remains a docile partner in the theatrical experience.' Hill, *The Trinidad
Carnival*, 117.

[14] 'When is a Play not a Play?', *Daily Gleaner* (Kingston), 1 Nov. 1972, 6. This
production staged by the Harambee Theatre called itself 'An African Religious Ritual'
and consisted of a blend of Rastafarian litany, *kumina* drumming and dancing, and
West African invocations.

The basic ideas outlined in the review reappear in Gibbons's thesis. In a chapter laconically entitled 'Place' he brings together theoretical justifications and practical suggestions for an arena stage, which he subsumes under the concept 'ritual of place'. This ritualized spatial conception forms in fact the basis of his wider theatre concept fusing indigenous performance and Western theatre. Indigenous spatial forms can be found in a number of performance spaces already existing in popular culture. He lists these as 'The Yard', 'The Tent', 'The Temple', and the 'Crossroads'. A yard refers to the back-yards of urban slums which form a gathering-place for the local people.[15] The interaction which takes place there is characterized by a high degree of theatricality that is absent in the intercourse of wealthier sections of the population: 'Interaction even at the simplest level assumed a theatricality markedly absent from that of the established classes.'[16] Somewhat less clearly defined is the term 'tent'. Included here are, on the one hand, the well-known performing areas of the Trinidad carnival and, on the other hand, the 'temples' of the *shango* worshippers. In addition to special constructions of this kind, Gibbons views the streets as an important place of performance for popular culture. The streets are the arena where carnival and other ceremonial processions such as the Muslim Hosein festival unfold, and they form therefore almost the quintessential place of encounter and performance. The streets or street corners are also the setting for the singing, hand-clapping, and bell-ringing that accompany the religious services of the Spiritual Baptists, which evidence, according to Gibbons, a high degree of theatricality. Finally Gibbons underlines the special significance of crossroads for Caribbean performance culture. They form the gathering-place for 'limers', young men engaged in public contests of a verbal nature. These verbal displays are 'highly performative' and constitute for the participants a kind of rite of passage.[17] Crossroads possess as well a mythical significance

---

[15] Gibbons borrows the term from Marina Maxwell, whose concept of a 'Yard theatre' was briefly introduced in Ch. 1. In her article 'Toward a Revolution in the Arts' Maxwell outlines how the Yard theatre could become a place of interaction and improvisation for anyone: 'It is an attempt to place West Indian theatre in the life of the people—it is free, it is open to the street where people can stand and hear, come in or leave. It is an attempt to find West Indian theatre, and to find it in the yards where people live and are.' *Savacou*, 2 (1970), 30.

[16] Gibbons, 'Traditional Enactments of Trinidad—Towards a Third Theatre', 7.

[17] Ibid. 34. For a detailed discussion of liming and the verbal art of the streets in the Caribbean, see Abrahams, *The Man-of-Words in the West Indies*; see also the section on orality in the Caribbean in Ch. 4.

in cult religion as 'the junction between mankind and the spirit world'.[18]

The spatial synthesis of these diverse influences is a type of theatre-in-the-round reflecting elements of a number of Caribbean cultural texts (Figure 1). The basic circular form is supposed to reflect the idea of the traditional storyteller with his or her audience gathered around. An inner and an outer performance space permit a flexible spatial arrangement incorporating rather than separating the audience. The musicians' podium placed in the middle of the inner circle alludes to the spirit pole used in voodoo ritual. The 'cardinal points of entry' are not fixed, but can be defined anew for each production and should be decorated with significant colours. In keeping with the practice of *shango* temples Gibbons specifies a hard, earthern floor, which enhances the effect of traditional instruments such as drums.

The sketch reproduced in Figure 1 is, however, not to be taken as an immutable norm. Gibbons views his concept as a model to be expanded and refashioned by other directors and designers providing they take account of the 'significant points of place' characteristic of Caribbean ritual. Gibbons is conscious of the problems inherent in transposing ritually significant spatial signs out of a functioning cultural system into a theatrical one:

They must be transferred from their native domains to the theatre. They must become rituals of the theatre. A new drama will be written, a new theatre produced. Playwright and director must learn in this theatre the ritual of place, the audience must be taught how character corresponds with place, the designer must explore earth design, the use of the earth medium in communicating sound, the whole pattern of existence as plotted in Baptist architecture needs to be closely examined in the theatre.[19]

The basic tenets of this theatre concept are familiar from Chapter 2. Gibbons's particular emphasis is, however, on space and place as the core experience determining all other theatrical elements such as direction, dramaturgy, scenography, and audience response.

What Gibbons advocates is a process whereby elements of indigenous performance spaces are selected and recombined as a counter-model to the Western stage. On closer inspection it becomes clear that he is unashamedly eclectic in his selection criteria. The only common factor linking the various cultural texts is their origin in

---

[18]   Gibbons, 'Traditional Enactments of Trinidad—Towards a Third Theatre', 42.
[19]   Ibid. 46.

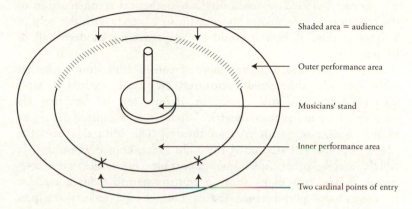

Shaded area = audience

Outer performance area

Musicians' stand

Inner performance area

Two cardinal points of entry

FIG. 1. Model for the arena stage; from Rawle Gibbons, 'Traditional Enactments of Trinidad towards a Third Theatre', 1979

popular culture. Otherwise they belong to different cultural forms: cult religion, street gatherings, and carnival processions are separate activities, which, although they may be attended by the same people, are governed by specific codes of spatial behaviour. Although Gibbons's model has remained unrealized, it still deserves recognition as a significant contribution to a theory of syncretic theatre space.

To find a model of syncretic theatre space that was in fact realized, it is necessary to shift attention to South Africa. In 1973 and 1974 the Zulu writer Credo Mutwa published two programmatic articles in the short-lived theatre magazine *S'ketsh'*. In these articles he argues that there existed in precolonial times a forgotten form of African theatre known as *umlinganiso*, which he translates as 'The Living Imitation'.[20] Mutwa suggests that traditional performance forms included a much broader repertoire of mimetic-theatrical genres than just singing and dancing: 'from simple but highly skilled and highly organized STORYTELLING by an expert storyteller, to actual ENACTMENT of stories by trained players of both sexes, which was performed on sacred occasions in times of peace'.[21] The directors of these performances were the *inyanga*, the medicine men, who exercised a conservative power over

[20] Credo Mutwa, 'On the Theatre of Africa', *S'ketsh'*, 3 (Summer 1973), 38–9; 'Umlinganiso . . . The Living Imitation', *S'ketsh'*, 4 (Summer 1974–5), 30–2.
[21] Mutwa, 'On the Theatre of Africa', 38.

the people.[22] As well as outlining a hypothetical reconstruction of the traditional performance space, Mutwa suggests with the help of a diagram (Fig. 2) how it could be adapted for a modern hall or theatre.

Leaving aside the fact that there is considerable doubt whether such 'specially constructed enclosures' ever really existed,[23] Mutwa's two plans are still significant, if only for the fact that his concept of an indigenous theatrical space was a radical departure in the context of South African theatre. The cultural space that Mutwa's model is based on is the Zulu kraal, known as *isibaya*, in which, among other functions, important ceremonies were celebrated.[24] The two plans show a transformation from a circular to a quadratic performance space. This change reflects the perceived need to adapt a traditional cultural space to the exigencies of Western architecture. Circle and square are in this case less irreconcilable oppositions than adaptable variations of the same spatial principle. The quadratic-shaped outline forms the ground plan for a production of Mutwa's play *uNosilimela*, which was staged in 1973 in Soweto more or less in accordance with the published sketch. In order to realize Mutwa's spatial concept the interior of a hall had to be considerably rebuilt so that a new kind of spatial and participatory relationship between audience and

---

[22] Mutwa writes: 'In this form of storytelling many people used to take part, each person representing a particular character in the story, walking, speaking and even behaving as that particular character is supposed to speak, walk and behave. This form of storytelling had been in existence amongst the Black people for thousands of years and was quite suitable for the purpose for which the INYANGAS now began to use it, which was to keep the people frightened and united and to prevent them from forgetting the unwritten scriptures of the religion of their forebears.' 'Umlinganiso . . . The Living Imitation', 32.

[23] Mutwa does not try to substantiate his assertions. As far as his concept of *umlinganiso* is concerned, there appears to be little evidence in support of his theory: see e.g. Fuchs, 'Re-Creation: One Aspect of Oral Tradition and the Theatre in South Africa', 33; Peter Larlham terms Mutwa's theory of traditional performance space 'purely conjectural'. *Black Theater, Dance, and Ritual in South Africa* (Ann Arbor: University of Michigan Research Press, 1985), 85. Robert Kavanagh, on the other hand, supports the thesis and draws a parallel with H. I. E. Dhlomo's writings on traditional performance forms: *Theatre and Cultural Struggle in South Africa* (London: Zed Books, 1985), 44.

[24] For this reading, see Robert McClaren Mshengu, 'South Africa: Where Mvelinqangi still Limps (The Experimental Theatre of Workshop '71)', *Yale Theatre*, 8/1 (Fall 1976), 41; see also the comments on the kraal as a dramatic space in H. I. E. Dhlomo's plays to be discussed below.

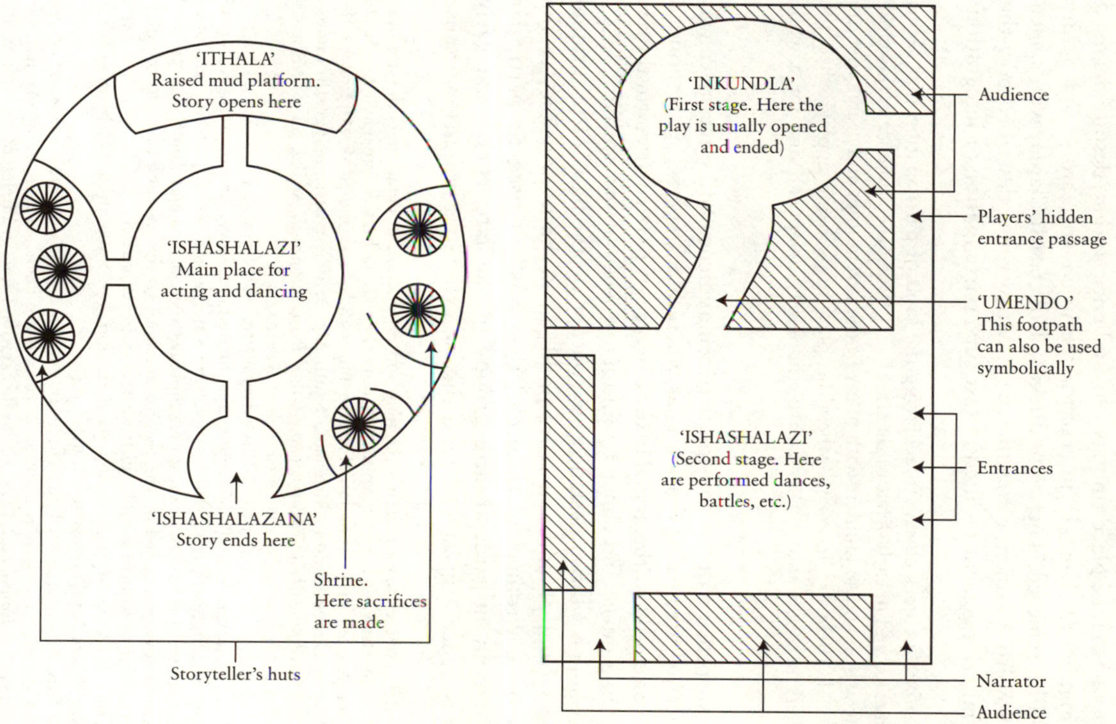

'ITHALA'
Raised mud platform.
Story opens here
'ISHASHALAZI'
Main place for
acting and dancing
'ISHASHALAZANA'
Story ends here
Shrine.
Here sacrifices
are made
Storyteller's huts
'INKUNDLA'
(First stage. Here the
play is usually opened
and ended)
Audience
Players' hidden
entrance passage
'UMENDO'
This footpath
can also be used
symbolically
'ISHASHALAZI'
(Second stage. Here
are performed dances,
battles, etc.)
Entrances
Narrator
Audience

FIG. 2. Zulu kraal as performance space (left) and stage plan for *uNosilimela* (right); after Credo Mutwa, 'On Theatre in Africa', 1973

performer could be established.[25] In *uNosilimela* it is not just songs and dances that require audience participation. The action itself is supposed to take place amongst the audience so that, despite the fixed seating, more dynamic interaction between spectators and actors could be achieved. The white director Robert McClaren, who staged the Soweto production together with Mutwa, has described how the spatial arrangement resulted in just such participation or integration:

> *uNosilimela* comes closest to achieving the kind of participation that seems to have existed in early African theatre. [. . .] When the audience is this close to the action and so familiar with many of the ceremonies and events that are depicted, there are moments when the play stops being a play, when the barriers between audience and cast completely disappear, and for a while you have real life.[26]

The suspension of the division between audience and stage space was especially effective in those scenes where black spectators responded spontaneously to the appellative structure of particular cultural texts involving music and dance by joining in without prompting.[27]

Although Mutwa designed his concept on the basis of traditional Zulu spatial practices, it corresponds in its basic principles to the idea of 'environmental theatre'[28] that was practised by particular Western avant-garde theatre groups in the late 1960s and early 1970s. Since Mutwa was not a theatre artist in a professional sense

[25] It is unnecessary to discuss the play and production in detail as both have been dealt with elsewhere. The play text is published in Robert Kavanagh (ed.), *South African People's Plays* (London: Heinemann, 1981); a thorough description of the production can be found in Mshengu, 'South Africa: Where Mvelinqangi still Limps'; see also Larlham, *Black Theater, Dance, and Ritual in South Africa*, 84–5. Mshengu has also published under the name Robert Kavanagh.

[26] Mshengu, 'South Africa: Where Mvelinqangi still Limps', 43.

[27] As a concrete example Mshengu cites the wedding scene. An important feature of Soweto weddings are competitions involving singing and dancing, which are often characterized by ethnic rivalries, for example between Sothos and Zulus. This cultural behaviour was transposed by the Soweto audience to the wedding scene in the play: 'Occasionally a woman would run from the audience, *lizilela* (howl), do a few steps, and rush back again. This wasn't participation, but integration.' Mshengu, 'South Africa: Where Mvelinqangi still Limps', 44.

[28] This is the term Richard Schechner gave to a phase of Euro-American experimental theatre. The spatial concept is certainly influenced by Antonin Artaud. See Schechner, *Environmental Theater*, for background and examples of 'environmental theatre'. Schechner first published his ideas in 1968. The connection between *uNosilimela* and the experiments of the avant-garde is also indicated by Joachim Fiebach, *Die Toten als die Macht der Lebenden. Zur Theorie und Geschichte von Theater in Afrika* (Berlin: Henschelverlag, 1986), 339.

and this remained his only major theatrical experiment, it is highly unlikely that the idea arose in response to Western ideas. It is much more a genuine syncretic theatre concept merging autochthonous and Western concepts and practices.

The interrelationship between spatial design and audience response demonstrated in the performances of *uNosilimela* can also be illustrated with reference to Maori theatre in New Zealand, although manifested in different ways. Where the South African production remained an isolated experiment, Maori theatre is an example of an institutionalized (spatial) theatrical concept. The basic ideas behind the concept have been outlined in Chapters 2 and 3: the refunctioning of ceremonial gatherings, the *hui*, into theatrical performances in the spatial frame of the ritual place known as the *marae*. The theatrical nature of *hui* gatherings is particularly evident in their spatial organization. The symbolism of the *marae* and meeting-house reflect in their spatial semantics the crucial distinction between virtual (aesthetic–symbolic) and actual (audience) space. Just as the Western stage and performance spaces have traditionally made some kind of distinction between left and right, whether it be inside and outside world or market-place and outside world, so too is the meeting-house divided into a right (*tapu*) and left (*noa*) side; the *tapu–noa* (sacred–common) distinction also determines the spatial arrangement of men and women, visitors and guests.

The meeting-house and the courtyard in front of it (the *marae ātea*) constitute a *templum*, to use Cassirer's concept of a sacred, demarcated space, set aside from the everyday world.[29] A major trend in contemporary Maori theatre has been to experiment with the possibilities of this *templum*: either by actually performing in a *marae*, or by transforming the performance area into a *marae*-like space. In 1990 the Depot Theatre in Wellington, an alternative theatre devoted entirely to performing New Zealand drama, was for the duration of the New Zealand International Festival of the Arts (3–24 March

---

[29] Cassirer argues that the consecration of space begins by separating off a certain section from everyday space as a whole and defining it as religious or sacred. The notion of religious sacrality, which implies also spatial delimitation, is contained in the etymology of the word 'temple'. It goes back to the term *templum* (Greek τεμενος) and the root, τεμ, meaning 'to cut'. Ernst Cassirer, *The Philosophy of Symbolic Forms*, ii: *Mythical Thought*, tr. Ralph Mannheim (New Haven: Yale University Press, 1955), 100.

1990) consecrated as a *marae*. The concept was outlined in the festival programme:

> The Depot Theatre will become a Maori Marae for five weeks over the Festival. The marae's name [Te Rakau Hua O Te Wao Tapu], given by Harata Solomon, means 'The Blossoming Tree of Our Sacred Grove'. The theatre and foyer will be used in the afternoon and evening in a range of activities, becoming a living space for artists and audience. [. . .] The theatre itself will be transformed into a Wharenui, the focus of the marae. It is in this Theatre/Marae setting that the plays will be performed.[30]

The very notion of consecration raises a number of interesting questions, the implication being that the accepted Western dichotomy of theatrical, aesthetic space as a phenomenologically separate entity from sacred, religious space no longer holds. Whether, however, such a dichotomy really exists in this case is more than debatable. Its consecration as a *marae* in no way limits or cancels out the Depot's function as a theatre, or turns it into a place of worship. This ritual act rather adds to it an aura of Maoriness, a place where Maori people are particularly welcome and feel at ease. It should be noted that the Depot did not just present 'plays' as such, but became a forum for a whole range of traditional and contemporary Maori art forms.

An institution such as the Taki Rua/Depot Theatre, as it is now known, raises a number of interesting questions regarding the spatial semiotics of a syncretic form combining the function of a theatre with the ritual significance of a *marae*. Because of its spatial proximity to other theatres, restaurants, and cinemas the Taki Rua/Depot Theatre is part of the entertainment area centred around Courtney Place and thus integrated into the urban system of New Zealand's capital city. In contrast to the Aboriginal cultural centre in Sydney, there is no obvious link to Maori suburbs or other signifiers of Maori culture. In terms of its architectural structure the building itself offers no striking analogies to Maori culture. Housed on the second floor of a commercial building located in a small side-street, the Taki Rua/Depot is not even immediately recognizable as a theatre from the outside. And apart from decorative Maori emblems inside, this theatre resembles any other small private theatre in Wellington. In other

---

[30] *New Zealand International Festival of the Arts: Programme* (Wellington: Agenda Communications, 1989), 19. The transformation was not just limited to the duration of the festival but continued until Taki Rua had to vacate the building.

words, there is no iconic similarity with the architectural and spatial codes of a *marae*. The cultural function of theatrical space in the Western sense is retained as the dominant code; but an additional form of spatial coding, that of Maori culture, is added to it so that the two codes appear to coexist in a productive symbiosis that is characteristic of any form of functioning syncretism.

Present theatrical practice at this theatre suggests that questions of spatial semiotics play only a subordinate role in the dramaturgy of the plays written and performed there. Although the majority of Maori plays make use of indigenous cultural texts, only in very few cases are the spatial possibilities of the *marae* utilized.[31] This was different at the beginning of the Maori theatre movement. In a number of early plays writers attempted to achieve a kind of iconic identity between dramatic space and performance space. Iconic identity means that objects, people, or spaces are not imitated but actually brought on stage.[32] The implications of this strategy will be discussed with reference to Hone Tuwhare's play *In the Wilderness without a Hat* and to two collective productions by the bicultural group the Theatre of the Eighth Day.

As has already been outlined in Chapter 2, the decoration of a new meeting-house forms the physical and thematic framework of *In the Wilderness without a Hat*. As Tuwhare notes: 'In this meeting house the naming of ancestral figures has long ago been determined, but through an oversight they have not been "written in", their names forgotten and almost beyond retrieval. This is a basis for concern, and is a potent complementary current along which the play progresses.'[33] Tuwhare appends to his play text a diagram detailing the spatial arrangement of his meeting-house (Figure 3).

The stage area represents in fact one end of the meeting-house; the edge of the stage is quite literally a fourth wall, where the unnamed and unseen carvings are located. They are an integral part and

[31] In the last few years, however, there has been a change in focus on the part of Maori writers and directors. The term *marae*-theatre is still much used, but in practice it often means little more than the execution of a few rites and ceremonial practices before and after a performance. In 1992 only the group Te Rakau Hua O Te Wao Tapu still propagated *marae*-theatre in spatial terms by performing mainly in and on *marae*.
[32] This term was introduced by Keir Elam, *The Semiotics of Theatre and Drama*, 22 f. An example of iconic identity would be an actor claiming to play himself. On the question of iconic identity and theatre space, see the chapter 'The Iconic Stage' in Marvin Carlson's *Theater Semiotics: Signs of Life*, (Bloomington: Indiana University Press, 1990).   [33] Tuwhare, *In the Wilderness without a Hat*, 57.

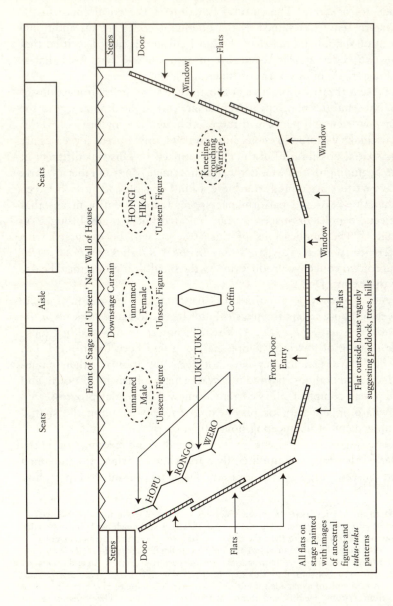

FIG. 3. Author's stage plan; from Hone Tuwhare, *In the Wilderness without a Hat*, 1977

frequent reference-point of the action. The stage represents, then, only part of the building; the other half is formed by the auditorium, through which all the characters must enter when approaching the 'doors' of the meeting-house. In the first production at the New Independent Theatre in Auckland, the entire auditorium was decorated in the fashion of a meeting-house so that in effect spectators and performers were unified in a spatially coherent performance space.[34] The setting and the dramaturgical device of the talking carvings both underline in theatrical terms the complex symbolic nature of the meeting-house and especially its central function of representing in architectural form the affiliations of the tribe, its place in history, and its mythology.[35] The meeting-house is the most palpable concretization of the concept of *turangawaewae*, which means literally a standing-place for the feet. This place to stand gives to the individual Maori a sense of belonging, both tribally and geographically, and is a cornerstone of contemporary Maori culture.

While Tuwhare clearly conceived his play to be staged on a conventional proscenium stage, with the traditional spatial separation of performer and spectator being suspended to a certain degree by the transformation of the performance spaces into replicas of meeting-houses, actual productions of the play have followed a different strategy. Directors have either staged the play in real meeting-houses or have refashioned performance spaces to create the ambience of a meeting-house, as was the case in the Auckland première. Both approaches reveal an attempt to create a form of spatial iconic identity. This strategy, while certainly not unknown in Western theatre, is unusual and not unproblematic because it is located in an uneasy semiotic field between absolute naturalism and a use of space

[34] In his review of this production Robert Leek wrote: 'the theatre had virtually been converted into the replica of a meeting house, with many attractive panel carvings lining the walls, and suggestions of *pukiore* work in between.' *New Zealand Times*, 21 Apr. 1985. The theatrical implications of this structure were noted by Helen White in her review of the Wellington season of the production: 'In the mounting of such a set in the Newtown Community Centre, with the ribs of the building and its decoration continued into the body of the hall, there was a strong sense of inclusion of the audience in the play's community: reason for celebration and enjoyment in anybody's terms.' *ACT: Theatre in New Zealand*, 11/3 (June 1985), 29.

[35] The architecture of a meeting-house has a very complex symbolism. Each house represents a specific ancestor and is named after him or her or an event. The actual structure represents in its terminology the parts of the body. For example, the ridge pole is called *tahuhu*, meaning spine; the rafters are called *heke*, meaning ribs. Cf. Salmond, *Hui*, 39.

which is no longer strictly theatrical. Spatial iconic identity can be problematic for Maori theatre too, although for different reasons. As the discussion of breaches of *tapu* in Chapter 2 showed, the staging of the work in the sacred space of a meeting-house tended to exacerbate an already difficult semiotic situation for some Maori spectators. Tuwhare's original idea of theatricalizing the meeting-house by reproducing it on a proscenium stage would presumably have defused this problem to some extent.

Experimentation with spatial iconic identity was taken a step further by the Theatre of the Eighth Day, a multiracial, semi-professional group based in Wellington (formerly known as Amamus) and now no longer functioning. Under the leadership of a white director, Paul Maunder, the group was, since the late 1960s, in the forefront of theatrical experiment, forging links between the aesthetics of political docudrama, the work of Grotowski, and New Zealand's specific cultural and historical situation. During the early 1980s Maunder and his group focused their attention on bringing the results of this experimental work to bear on the forgotten or ignored chapters of New Zealand history, principally those involving interracial conflict. The purpose here was very much to rewrite and retell these events from the point of view of the Maori people, using their knowledge and their oral and performance traditions, combined with certain techniques of documentary drama and Grotowskian theatre aesthetics.[36]

Thematically and formally the plays represent a synthesis of the theatrical currents Maunder had been experimenting with since the early 1970s. The influence of documentary theatre is evident in the choice of subject-matter: both works rely heavily on documentary material in their portrayal of the historical incidents which form one layer of the action. Grotowski's teachings are particularly palpable in the emphasis on conceptual spaces, in the extreme stylized acting Maunder demands, and in the exploration of ritual and ritualized performance. The focus on ritual and spatial arrangements indicate

[36] For an account of the history of this group and its director, Paul Maunder, see Balme, 'New Maori Theatre'. The productions were *Te Tutakitanga i Te Puna (Encounter at Te Puna)*, first performed in Nov. 1984 at the Depot Theatre; *Ngati Pakeha: He Korero Whakapapa*, premièred on 15 Nov. 1985 at the Depot Theatre; a third work, *Ko Te Kimihanga*, dealing with the life of the Maori queen Te Puea, was never performed because of resistance on the part of the tribe involved. This experience effectively put an end to this phase of Maunder's work. He is now involved in community theatre.

that Maunder, together with his multiracial cast, was especially intent on welding the European aesthetic and Maori ritual traditions into a new kind of theatrical experience.[37] In his notes to the performance text of *Te Tutakitanga i Te Puna*, Maunder specifies that the two performance traditions and cultural ways of seeing should coalesce:

The play takes place within a meeting house. The space can be actual or a theatrical metaphor. In the original production calico screens formed the space of the house. The pillars were representative of cultural transition—colonial/Greek columns, to ship's planking, to kaponga trunks. The characters initially stood or sat against these pillars, as ancestor figures, joining the action as appropriate. The audience sat on mattresses along both sides of the house.[38]

A number of elements in this description are reminiscent of *In the Wilderness without a Hat*. The performance space is a meeting-house, either real or re-created. Here too the characters and carved figures form part of the building and are able to intervene in the action. Finally, the placing of spectators on mattresses around the walls corresponds to *marae* practice, where guests usually spend the night on mattresses.

The action centres on the early missionary Thomas Kendall, who helped establish the first mission station in New Zealand in the Bay of Islands in 1814 and accompanied the famous Maori chief Hongi Hika to England to meet George IV. This 'tragic, Faustian figure', as the historian Keith Sinclair terms Kendall,[39] disintegrated morally

[37] The question whether the productions of the group were in fact Maori theatre, given the dominant position of Maunder in the group, is a difficult one. Maori themes formed the focus of the group's work during this period and Maori performers made crucial contributions to the content of the productions, which were shown on *marae* to Maori audiences. The Maori writer and director Roma Potiki, who was involved in the first production, comments: 'If I was asked to try and draw a definite line, I would say it was Pakeha theatre with a Maori involvement, and that Paul himself had made a genuine attempt from his own background to involve some sort of Maori ritual and get some depth. At the same time, there is always some alienation of the Maori audience, because in the work there comes through a suspicion as to who is in control. [. . .] With the Theatre of the Eighth Day, Paul tried for a high degree of Maori involvement. He tried towards a bi-cultural form but I still think that he had an intellectualized Pakeha form that used Maori motifs, ritual concepts, politics. But it still wasn't a Maori form. You see, to me to find a Maori form, a Maori has to find it. That's the simple definition.' Balme, 'It is Political if it Can be Passed on', Interview with Roma Potiki, 37.
[38] Paul Maunder and the Theatre of the Eighth Day, 'Te Tutakitanga i Te Puna' (Encounter at Te Puna), play script, 1985.
[39] Sinclair, *A History of New Zealand*, 37.

and spiritually in his struggle to understand the Maori world and convert the 'heathen'. An adulterous relationship with a Maori girl finally led to his dismissal ten years later. The play's perspective is not, however, an entirely historical one. The spectators assemble in a re-created, or actual, meeting-house, depending on the place of performance, and are greeted by a young Maori woman, Elisabeth, for a 'journey into the past; a past of fact and imagination'.[40] Maunder uses the decline and fall of Kendall to exemplify his central concern: the spiritual and cultural disintegration of Maori and *pakeha* and even, it seems, of modern man in general. The image of separation and disintegration is introduced by Elisabeth in her opening speech: 'We have been separated into so many pieces, hard now to even dream a time when things were whole.'[41] It is alluded to again a little later, when the Maori actors chant the separation myth of Rangi and Papa (the prising apart of Heaven and Earth is the beginning of the Maori creation myth). This theme is concretized in the context of Maori culture and theology by the meeting-house setting, which by its very structure and architectural terminology symbolizes a lost state of grace when Gods and men were unified. The European exemplification of the idea is seen in Kendall's estrangement from his own culture under the influence of an alien one, and also on an emotional level as his relationship to his wife deteriorates until she takes a lover from among the European workmen. The double focus of the piece— the beginnings of cultural breakdown among the Maori under the influence of European contact; and Kendall as an exemplar of Western alienation—makes it a very bleak depiction of cultural encounter.

The group's next work, *Ngati Pakeha* (subtitled *He Korero Whakapapa*: literally, a discussion about the ancestors or genealogy), continues the themes and formal experiments of the previous play. The historical events of the piece took place in the 1860s in the province of Taranaki. Here the local Maoris under the leadership of a prophet, Te Whiti, practised a form of passive resistance against the authorities. Again an arch of continuity between the present and the past is spanned. The audience is welcomed into the theatrical space by the central character, Irirangi, as if entering a *marae*. He uses a *pōwhiri*, a chant of invitation. Again Maunder

[40] Paul Maunder and the Theatre of the Eighth Day, 'Te Tutakitanga i Te Puna', 1.
[41] Ibid.

stresses the formalistic nature of the representation: 'Much of the movement requires a formality. It is after all representative of historical events. It is, then, almost dance. The historical events take place in Irirangi's mind, yet have an objective reality as well.'[42] The spatial organization is even more complex. A diagram is appended to the play text in which 'conceptual spaces' are demarcated (Figure 4). The audience is grouped at the Maori end of the space so that it may experience the action from the point of view of the Maori family (*whanau*) at the centre of the action. The action of the play, the journey into the past, is set in motion by a question from Irirangi's grandson: 'How did the pakeha blood first come into the family koro?'[43] Irirangi enters the 'space of the past' and the world of Maori myth. The transition is represented scenically by his traditional chant and trancelike state, and by his movement to the stage area representing the Maori past. The initial action involves a continual movement to and from the past and present. During these transitions the family gathered around him gradually comes into focus. The Maori present is omnipresent and forms the filter through which history is experienced; we see then in turn how this historical experience refracts on the present.

The second half of the play is, however, more clearly focused on the historical events. The play ends with Irirangi's family reflecting on the need to resist the *pakeha* system and especially to regain misappropriated land. More important, though, seems to be the notion that reflection on the past, the memory of the tribe, will form the gathering-point for any future action. Despite the manifest litany of injustices and calls for resistance, the final image is one of racial reconciliation. The crucial spatial factor of this arrangement is that the audience is forced to view events from the Maori perspective. The stage direction for the second half reads: 'The cast return, the Whanau has merged into Te Maunga o Rongo, the Village of Peace, the inhabitants of which occupy the audience end of the acting space. At the other end a Victorian drawing room is symbolized.'[44] That the spatial experience was not just intended but actually achieved is amply confirmed in reviews. The Maori actor and critic Keri Kaa

---

[42] Paul Maunder and the Theatre of the Eighth Day, 'Ngati Pakeha: He Korero Whakapapa', play script, 1986, p. i.   [43] Ibid. 1.
[44] Ibid. 65.

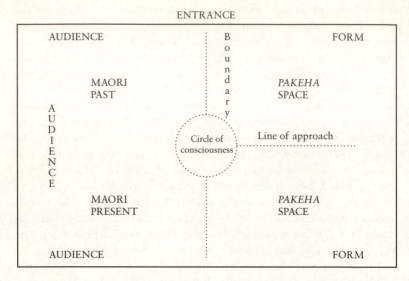

FIG. 4. Spatial conceptions of the stage plan after Paul Maunder; fom the Theatre of the Eighth Day, *Ngati Pakeha*, 1985

associated performance space and style with the oral tradition of her childhood, when she listened to the stories of the elders in the meeting-house.[45] A *pakeha* critic stressed the 'special atmosphere created' and a 'magic' that transcended what is normally possible in the theatre. This was due to the performative and spatial frame of the *marae*:

From the beginning when the audience was guided through the opening in the barricade surrounding the acting area a quietness was palpable. The opening waiatas of the play further confirmed that the amalgam of theatre and whare whakairo of the marae had been achieved. Within this special space the audience enjoyed a privileged position on the ranked seating and cushions

[45] 'Long sessions in meeting-houses listening to story-telling grandparents, parents, aunts and uncles, strengthen one's ears and one's capacity to listen and sift through information.' She also draws attention to the spatial organization of the production: 'The actual setting of the play was unusual but appropriate for the style of the production. The Whanau were grouped around the fire near the audience so that we identified with them.' 'Ngati Pakeha', *ACT: Theatre in New Zealand*, 10/6 (Dec. 1985), 70.

SPACES AND SPECTATORS   249

at the rear of the area. We looked past the action of the tribe in the foreground to the far end and the activities of the pakeha.[46]

Both reviewers document the same production, in Wellington's Depot
Theatre. Both productions toured the country, however, and performed mainly in Maori communities, on *marae*. In such a performance context the setting takes on added significance and emotional
import. On the *marae* the traditional Western theatrical contract, the
purchase of a ticket, was suspended. Instead entry was by *koha*, a gift
that visitors always bring when attending a *hui*. Here the concept of
iconic identity takes on its maximum signifying potential. The significance of spatial dimension of these plays is revealed in a unique
interaction between cultural and performance space, between spectators and actors of both races and between Maori and European
culture. In such examples one can sense that space provides one of
the most powerful arenas of syncretic theatre.

Spatial Dramaturgy and Scenography

A distinguishing feature of Maori theatre is, as has been shown, the
attempt to merge the aesthetic space of theatre with the cultural space
of the *marae*. In addition Maori plays reveal a congruence between
theme and performance space, even if specific productions have not
always realized this equation fully. Often, however, the calls for a
reform of theatrical space, particularly in architectural terms, which
have been voiced in most post-colonial theatre cultures have remained
in the realm of programmatic theory. Most frequently dramatists have
had no other choice than to consign their works to performances on
what Wole Soyinka has termed 'those mind-constrictors', the Western
proscenium stage.[47] In other words, the examples of Maori theatre
and the South African play *uNosilimela* are exceptions in terms of
their experimentation with alternative theatre spaces. However, even

[46] Maurice Halder, 'Towards a New Identity: *Ngati Pakeha* at the Depot', *Illusions*
(Wellington), 1 (Summer 1986), 32. Another *pakeha* reviewer reacted to the same
arrangement but perhaps with a hint of unease: 'Pakeha people will find it uncompro-
mising in its charting of colonization. Some will also be disturbed at being seated along
with the whanau and looking to the far end of the acting space where the new white
migrant tribe arrives with their alien ways.' Philip Tremewan, 'Tribal Squabbles in
Taranaki', *New Zealand Times*, 1 Dec. 1985, n.p.
[47] 'As a decidedly anti-proscenium stage artist, I hope to see fewer and fewer of
those mind-constrictors left in the world.' Soyinka, *Art, Dialogue and Outrage*, 116.

if dramatists are forced, or indeed want, to work within the spatial code of the picture frame stage, there are still opportunities for incorporating indigenous spatial concepts into the dramaturgical and scenographic design of the play. In this case we are dealing with a spatial structure that has been integrated into the theatrical text itself and corresponds to what is usually known as *dramatic*, as opposed to theatrical, space.

Dramatic space can be divided into two broad subcategories: *mimetic* and *diegetic* space. Mimetic space refers to space depicted on stage and visible to the spectator, while diegetic space is only described or referred to by characters in the play.[48] Mimetic space can also include space evoked by acoustic signs such as off-stage noises, but is mainly connected with scenography and the visual design of a stage space. Indigenous cultural texts can be incorporated in all three spatial categories: scenographically, diegetically, and through mimetic–acoustic signs.

The dramaturgical spatial strategies of syncretic plays are based on the premiss that there is no such thing as a culturally neutral space. Both interior and exterior spaces are an integral part of a culturally specific cognitive cartography. Thus even an apparently neutral spatial notion such as a living room as a place of encounter is a highly problematic phenomenon, as the Indian dramatist and director Girish Karnad has argued. The living room is the quintessential space of Western realistic drama and as such it was adopted by Indian dramatists working in the realistic mode as the setting for their plays:

From Ibsen to Albee, the living room has symbolized all that is valuable to the Western bourgeoisie. It is one's refuge from the sociopolitical forces raging in the world outside, as well as the battleground where values essential to one's individuality are fought out and defended. But nothing of consequence ever happens or is supposed to happen in an Indian living room! It is the no-mans-land, the empty, almost defensive front the family presents to the world outside.[49]

---

[48] This distinction has been suggested by Michael Issacharoff, see 'Stage Codes', in Michael Issacharoff and Robin F. Jones (eds.), *Performing Texts*, (Philadelphia: University of Pennsylvania Press, 1988), 215. It corresponds to the differentiation suggested by Hanna Scolnicov of 'perceived space' (dramatic) and 'conceived space' (diegetic). 'Theatre Space, Theatrical Space, and the Theatrical Space Without', 15.

[49] In a traditional Indian house caste and social status determine which parts of a house are accessible: 'And it is in the interior of the house, in the kitchen, in the room where the gods are kept, or in the backyard, where family problems are tackled, or allowed to fester, and where the women can have a say.' Karnad, 'In Search of a New Theater', 100.

The fact that Indian dramatists continued to set their social-critical plays in living rooms, despite the evident discrepancy in cultural spatial conventions, is for Karnad symptomatic of a tendency amongst colonial and post-colonial dramatists to use imported aesthetic tools without adapting them sufficiently to local conditions.[50]

Spatial conceptions prescribed by the dramaturgy of a play revolve around three recurring notions. One is the requirement of an *empty* stage. This is a result, on the one hand, of the reception of a Western theatrical aesthetic associated with the work of Jerzy Grotowski and Peter Brook: South African township theatre, for example, owes an explicit debt to these writings and the search for a flexible, polyfunctional performance space. On the other hand, the empty stage can correspond to indigenous concepts of performance space. This is the case in traditional Indian theatre and can be found in syncretic Indian plays by Tagore and Karnad. A second strategy can be termed *substitution*. The point of departure is the recognition that the living room, the 'sacred space' of Western bourgeois drama, is of little relevance to other cultures. Here dramatists take pains to create significant alternative spaces which represent for their various cultures places of encounter. A third scenographical strategy, *contiguity*, is evident in those works which thematize situations of cultural encounter. In these works the staging requirements call for a clear contrast between cultural spaces. A well-known example is the alternation of spaces in Soyinka's *Death and the King's Horseman* between the Yoruba market place and colonial spaces such as the District Officer's bungalow or the colonial residency. A comparable visual strategy is evident in Jack Davis's plays, where there is almost invariably some kind of spatial contiguity between the kitchen-sink reality of his urban Aboriginal characters and the desert landscape of traditional Aboriginal life. Similar examples of contiguity between the quotidian and mythical worlds and spaces can be found in Tomson Highway's plays.

Girish Karnad's rejection of the Western bourgeois living room as the privileged space of dramatic conflict for an Indian context implies that a strategy of substitution must be adopted. The search for

---

[50] 'It may also be said that the refusal to go beyond the living room exactly mirrored the reluctance of these Westernized, upper-caste writers to go to the heart of the issues they were presenting.' Ibid. 101.

culturally relevant dramatic spaces as alternatives to the Western realist mode can already be detected in H. I. E. Dhlomo's historical dramas of the 1930s, which thematize the lives of important black leaders of the nineteenth century.[51] The most frequently used setting in these plays is the open compound or kraal. It is the scene of all important gatherings and cultural performances (rituals, singing, and dancing), which are so characteristic of Dhlomo's plays. For Dhlomo the kraal is the space of political representation of the once-powerful Zulu nation, symbol of a still-intact and politically potent culture. It is at the same time the historically documented performance space in which the Zulu chiefs Shaka and Dingane received the first European visitors with spectacular displays of dancing and singing.[52] Apart from the dramaturgical significance of the kraal scenes, they also dominate the plays in purely quantitative terms. The few scenes set in huts, i.e. interior settings, focus on the more intimate psychological dimension of the plays, in contrast to the public character of the kraal scenes.[53]

A similar spatial structure can be found in Ola Rotimi's historical drama *Kurunmi*, which deals with the Yoruba kingdom at the end of the nineteenth century. In a 'Note for the Producer' the author suggests dispensing with concrete settings in order better to depict the episodic action of the play. The only scenographic fixture that Rotimi requires is a shrine for the god of war, Ogun. Nevertheless the first stage direction of the play specifies a concrete setting, the *agbo'le*, or courtyard, of the Yoruba king, for which Rotimi provides a kind of ethnographic commentary: 'The play opens on Kurunmi's "agbo'le", the closest English term for which is "compound". Even

---

[51] For a discussion of these plays, see Elmar Lehmann, 'Colonial to Post-Colonial South African-Style: The Plays of H. I. E. Dhlomo', in Maria T. Bindella and Geoffrey Davis (eds.), *Imagination and the Creative Impulse in the New Literatures in English* (Amsterdam: Rodopi, 1993), 109–22.

[52] The first visitors to King Shaka in 1824 tell of a reception in the royal cattle kraal measuring two miles in circumference, in which 80,000 people were gathered. For this report and other descriptions of other performances in the kraals of the Zulu kings, see Peter Larlham, *Black Theater, Dance, and Ritual in South Africa* (Ann Arbor: University of Michigan Research Press, 1985), 2–5.

[53] Other favoured settings are the forest and river bank, which point up Dhlomo's penchant for the bucolic mode. For example, in the play *Ntsikana* (1936), which deals with the life of the eponymous Xhosa prophet, there is a bathing scene, in which the queen of the Ndlambe tribe is attended by four girls on the river bank, who rub her body with ointment, and dress and decorate her. Dhlomo, *Collected Works*, 54.

this term falls miserably short in portraying the *sacred pictorial essence* of what an "agbo'le" really is. In this particular "agbo'le", for instance, the gods of the tribe are present in varying images of earth, granite and wood.'[54] In addition to its explicit religious function the *agbo'le* space has a public character analogous to the kraal in Dhlomo's plays. It is an arena for dance, song, discussion, and prayer, whereby these activities are frequently interrelated in terms of their cultural function. In the *agbo'le* all major performative cultural texts of the Yoruba can interact and thus provide the most obvious demonstration of theatrical syncretism. On the one hand, the exterior spaces of *agbo'le* and kraal fulfil the function of providing a counter-model to the Western living room. But because they also represent authentic spaces for significant *cultural performances*, this strategy of spatial substitution means that performance forms such as dances and songs can be deployed in an organic relationship to the performance space.

As the scenographic requirements laid out by Dhlomo and Rotimi can be read as spatial counter-models to the restrictive spatial semantics of Western realist drama, in a similar sense experiments with the aesthetics of the empty space—the second strategy of spatial dramaturgy—can be seen on one level as a reactive counter-discourse in theatrical terms. But it can also be regarded as an approximation of the spatial semantics of indigenous performance forms. In South African township theatre the empty stage is a crucial dramaturgical device, and not just a form of stage decoration. Township theatre employs a multifunctional spatial concept, which is linked neither to a culturally coded performance space nor to particular living space. In *Woza Albert!*, for example, the decor consists of two tea chests, a cloth, and a few items of clothing. In *Bopha!* the actors make do with a clothes-stand and three chairs; the scenography of *Asinamali!* consists only of a few chairs. It hardly needs repeating that the episodic structure of these plays means that the action moves swiftly among various settings. These can be living areas, train compartments, a helicopter, or a prison cell. The iconic–mimetic spatial signs are evoked using either off-stage noises or spatial references in the dialogue. Also the few props on stage are utilized multifunctionally. In an endless chain of transmutations, the actors transform everyday objects into new signs and

<hr/>

[54] Rotimi, *Kurunmi*, 11; my italics.

spaces.[55] The device whereby actors on an empty stage create new dramatic spaces by means of internal recoding is certainly one reason why the code of township theatre is internationally accessible. However, apart from this iconic-mimetic function the empty stage also generates a more complex referential message which is only fully comprehensible by means of external recoding of factors outside the fictional world of the play. The empty stage is thus more than just a kind of intertextual reference to the theatre aesthetic of Jerzy Grotowski and Peter Brook. It also carries a political statement about the state of theatre for Blacks in South Africa: in the townships 'poor' theatre is not a self-determined aesthetic credo, but an existential necessity for theatre artists. It is linked both to the lack of specialized performance spaces in the townships and to the need for mobility on the part of the groups performing.[56]

An alternative strategy of 'empty staging' can be found in Girish Karnad's play *Hayavadana*. Here the use of the empty stage as a spatial concept is based on questions of theatrical aesthetics. For his contemporary play Karnad makes use of the spatial code of traditional Indian dance-theatre. According to the Indian theatre scholar Suresh Awasthi, there are a number of factors determining the nature of its scenography. These include a 'nonrealistic and metaphysical treatment of time and place', and a playing area consisting of a neutral, unlocalized space, 'easily manipulated by the actor and capable of serving the basic requirement of traditional theatre—multiplicity of locales and simultaneity of action'. The actor is therefore a key determining factor in the audience's perception of the scenography: 'with stylized and symbolic make-up, gorgeous cos-

---

[55] The influence of Grotowski is very evident in this aesthetic of transformation: 'By his controlled use of gesture the actor transforms the floor into a sea, a table into a confessional, a piece of iron into an animate partner, etc.'. Jerzy Grotowski, *Towards a Poor Theatre* (London: Methuen, 1969), 21. On the influence of Grotowski on township theatre, see the interview with Percy Mtwa, who explains the same principle: 'This transformation, as Grotowski describes it, this transformation is when one thing gives birth to another. It is like a bucket with which you fetch water, but in winter you bore holes in it and use it as an oven to warm yourself.' Breitinger, 'I've been an Entertainer throughout my Life', Interview with Percy Mtwa, 172 f.

[56] For an outline of the crassly inequitable distribution of resources for Blacks and Whites in South Africa under apartheid, see Fuchs, *Playing the Market*, ch. 1. This is already beginning to change now in the post-apartheid era. For an example of the restructuring of the previously white Performing Arts Councils, which received the lion's share of state subsidies, see Thomas Riccio's article '*Emandulo*: Process and Performance in a Changing South Africa', *Theatre Research International*, 19/3 (1994), 238–61.

tumes, and a huge and fantastic headdress, he stands on a bare stage disengaged from any kind of decor and creates a vivid *mise en scène* with his own dynamic presence. The scenic effect is strengthened by the actor's codified gait, choreographic acting, and symbolic hand-gestures.'[57] A number of these stage conventions recur in *Hayava-dana*. When, with the exception of a chair and table for the musicians, Karnad specifies an empty stage, this corresponds to both the scenographic conventions of *yakṣāgana* as well as to his own requirement for dramaturgical spatial semantics that are free from the dictates of Western conventions. As the play certainly demands a 'metaphysical treatment of time and place', a multiplicity of settings, and a neutral background allowing the play of masks to achieve its full scenic effect, then the choice of an empty space appears to be justified mainly in terms of the traditional aesthetics of Indian dance-theatre.

By working within the conventions of the empty stage of Indian dance-theatre Karnad followed a path which had already been prepared in the theatrical texts and productions of Rabindranath Tagore. Tagore's use of theatrical space was influenced by both classical Sanskrit drama and *jatra*, the folk theatre of Bengal.[58] While Tagore remained fundamentally opposed to the picture frame stage throughout his career, his dramaturgical and directorial practice reveals a development towards *rapprochement* between the bare Indian stage and a stylized, anti-naturalistic scenography developed by the European avant-garde. A shift from the austere stage of, say, *Chitra* to experiments with European scenographic elements becomes apparent in *The Cycle of Spring* (1917). Written and performed in Bengali (*Phālguni*) in 1916, this work defies easy generic classification in Western terms. In *The Cycle of Spring* dialogic structures play a relatively minor role compared to the extensive use of songs and dynamic scenography. The long prologue to *The Cycle of Spring* contains a discussion between the King and the Poet on theatre and staging, a convention which Tagore borrowed from classical Sanskrit drama, and which is still practised in traditional theatre forms such as

---

[57] See Awasthi, 'The Scenography of the Traditional Theatre of India', 38.

[58] In the words of M. K. Naik, this form of theatre is 'totally free from the conventions of the "well-made" play and has a fluid form and minimal stage props, and makes ample use of myth and legend, symbol and allegory'. Naik, *Dimensions of Indian English Literature*, 173. For additional comments on Tagore's relationship to *jatra* and its influence on his play *Chitra*, see Ch. 3.

yakṣāgana.[59] The poet points out the generic indeterminancy of the piece about to be performed: 'Whether it is a drama, or a poem, or a play, or a masque, I cannot say.'[60] And recapitulates the precepts of traditional Indian scenography, which has no need of painted canvas scenery: 'Our only background is the mind. On that we shall summon up a picture with the magic wand of music.'[61] 'The magic wand of music' establishes a musical dominant which was not only suggested by the published text but realized by the actual production.[62] The stage directions and the lighting effects indicate possibly a proscenium stage. Tagore requires a stage on two levels, the higher level to be used exclusively for the song preludes preceding each act and 'concealed by a purple curtain'.[63] The lower level is at the same time the King's court and a neutral playing space. In the course of the play Tagore calls for quite precise lighting effects: darkened playing areas, sudden disclosures, contrastive effects, and emotionally coded colour: 'the light on the main stage is dimmed to the heavy purple blackness of mourning'.[64] At the same time he expressly forbids actual changes of scenery, 'this being left to the imagination of the audience'.[65] Tagore showed an explicit distaste for 'the elaborate stage decor' in Western theatre, with its naturalistic aesthetics and laborious scene changes.[66] The stage directions quoted above indicate that Tagore's mental or actual stage would seem to require the inventiveness and stage technology of an Inigo Jones combined with the dynamic lighting of Adolphe Appia or Edward Gordon Craig.

Tagore's response to the anti-naturalistic theatre movement is

[59] See e.g. the prologue to Kalidasa's *Śākuntala*, perhaps the most famous Sanskrit play, in which the Stage-Manager and Actress discuss the play about to be performed. 'It [the prologue] usually sets the tone for the opening scene and thus is vital to the work. It serves as a bridge between the world of the audience and the world of the play [. . .] the two worlds are linked, making the theatre event special and distinct from everyday life.' Richmond *et al.* (eds.), *Indian Theatre*, 65.
[60] Tagore, *Collected Poems and Plays*, 350. [61] Ibid. 352.
[62] On the function of songs in Tagore's plays, Balwant Gargi observes: 'songs are an integral part of the action. While the singer comments on the play in song, the action is carried on without words at times. [. . .] The singer's function as Tagore uses him is to generalize on the particular scene being enacted and this adds another dimension to the characters and the situation.' 'The Plays of Tagore', in Mahendra Kulasrestha (ed.), *Tagore Centenary Volume* (Hoshiarpur: Vishveshvarand, 1961), 105. For an account of the original Bengali production, see P. Guha-Thakurta, 'Tagore's *Phālguni*: An Interpretation', *Visva-Bharati Quarterly*, 7/2 (1929), 274.
[63] Tagore, *Collected Poems and Plays*, 333. [64] Ibid. 387.
[65] Ibid. 368. [66] Sanyal, 'The Plays of Rabindranath Tagore', 242.

made clear in the following eyewitness account of a production of his drama *Visarjan* (*Sacrifice*) staged in Calcutta in 1923 and in which the author played the main role:

The stage was draped throughout in different shades of dark blue, deepening as they receded into the background. There was no changing of scene; the blood-stained temple steps, designed Cubist fashion, dominated the eye throughout; a lurid red light marked the entrance to the Temple itself [. . .] The other stage accessories, requisitioned to assist in the interpretation, were colour schemes of the costumes in combination with changing light effects against the dark blue of the hangings, symbolic of the play of *samsāra* on the continuum of *Mahākāla*.[67]

The scenographic aesthetics described here would, of course, have been proud to grace any avant-garde European stage of the time. They also suggest that the staging Tagore envisaged in *The Cycle of Spring*, and which is indicated in the stage directions, was in fact realized in practical terms. The passages also show quite clearly that Tagore was no longer working within the conventions of traditional Indian scenography, but was engaged in a productive reception of those elements of European *mise-en-scène* which now corresponded to his own unique and quite distinctive theatrico-aesthetic sensibility.[68]

The third dramaturgical and scenographic category, contiguity, takes into account the thematic treatment of intercultural encounters. This means that the post-colonial condition of cultural coexistence, conflict, and interchange, where disparate semiospheres exist in promiscuous contact, finds expression in spatial signs. One of the first dramatists consciously to use a dramaturgy of spatial contiguity was Wole Soyinka, a question which he also reflects on in his theoretical writings.[69] Spatial semantics are clearly, for Soyinka, one of the keys to understanding both traditional ritual performance as well as 'all

[67] Anon., 'The Staging of Rabindranath's *Visarjan*', *Visva-Bharati Quarterly*, 1/3 (1923), 309.
[68] His writing and directing (the scenography was usually designed and executed by his nephews Abanindranath and Gaganendranath, who were established artists in their own right) led him to create a 'distinctive stage that is now associated with his name, evolving an altogether new tradition in theatrical production'. Sanyal, 'The Plays of Rabindranath Tagore', 239.
[69] The most extensive discussion of theatrical and dramatic space can be found in Soyinka's essay 'Drama and the African World View', first published in Rowland Smith (ed.), *Exile and Tradition* (London: Longman, 1976), 173–90; repr. in Soyinka, *Myth, Literature and the African World*. All quotations are from the latter.

profound drama.'[70] A ritualized sense of space is one of the crucial reflections of a society's world-view and is defined precisely 'through a process of interruption':

In theatrical terms, this interruption is effected principally by the human apparatus. Sound, light, motion, even smell, can all be used just as validly to define space, and ritual theatre uses all these instruments of definition to control and render concrete, to parallel (this is perhaps the best description of the process) the experiences or intuitions of man in that far more disturbing environment which he defines variously as void, emptiness or infinity.[71]

Although Soyinka makes no explicit reference to cultural semiotics, the above definition of ritual space as an existential necessity to demarcate and define culture from non-cultural space parallels closely some of the fundamental tenets of cultural semiotics as outlined by the Russian school of Yuri Lotman and B. A. Uspenskij in their famous 'Theses on the Semiotic Study of Cultures'. The concept of 'interruption' as a means of delimiting and semantically defining space is not dissimilar to the notion of discrete and non-discrete texts, one of the key differentiations in the typology of cultural texts elaborated in the theses. Verbal signs are discrete, i.e. separate and demarcated, while iconic signs are mainly non-discrete, communicating as an entirety. Soyinka's trope of the human performer as an 'interrupter' of space as well as the various non-human instruments of interruption—'Sound, light, motion, even smell'—all of which find application in theatre, encapsulates an essential feature of the semiotics of theatre. The interaction of these various sign systems forms a basic model of semiotic communication in performance.

Soyinka goes on to contrast performance in such ritualistic space—what he calls the 'basic adventure of man's metaphysical self'—with modern theatre technology and its deconsecrated, secular semantics: 'the spatial vision of theatre has become steadily contracted into purely physical acting areas on a stage as opposed to a symbolic arena for metaphysical contests'.[72] The second major idea regarding space pertains to the intrinsic dramatic space of a play: in Soyinka's terminology, the 'spatial architecture' of a work which creates 'an internal cogency impervious to accident of time and place'.[73] The

[70] Soyinka, *Myth, Literature and the African World*, 50.   [71] Ibid. 39 f.
[72] Ibid. 40.   [73] Ibid. 50.

internal spatial aesthetics of *Hamlet* or *King Lear*, or indeed of modern plays by Synge, Lorca, or Wedekind (these are Soyinka's examples), can correspond to whatever world the audience inhabits: their greatness results directly from this ability to evoke a spatial universe capable of striking responsive chords anywhere. The two examples of successful contemporary African tragedies that Soyinka cites—J. P. Clark's *Song of a Goat* and Duro Ladipo's *Oba Koso*—whatever other shortcomings they may have, are capable of striking such universally responsive chords, despite the culturally specific spatial semantics of their respective settings.[74]

If we turn now to Soyinka's plays, and particularly to *The Road* and *Death and the King's Horseman*, the two works which reveal most clearly elements of theatrical syncretism, we can detect a tension between settings of local specificity and their place in larger cultural contexts. In both plays the contiguity of cultures and cultural practices is foregrounded in spatial as well as in other sign systems. Although the two works use different scenographic techniques—*The Road* relies on just one setting, while *Death and the King's Horseman* switches between four different scenes—both are structured around an opposition between significant spaces. In *The Road* these spaces are described and specified in the didascalic text:

Dawn is barely breaking on a road-side shack, a ragged fence and a corner of a church with a closed stained-glass window. Above this a cross-surmounted steeple tapers out of sight. Thrusting downstage from a corner of the shack is the back of a 'bolekaja' (mammy waggon), lop-sided and minus its wheels. It bears the inscription AKSIDENT STORE ALL PART AVAILEBUL. In the opposite corner, a few benches and empty beer cases used as stools. Downstage to one side, a table and chair, placed in contrasting tidiness.[75]

---

[74] The achievement of such universality was, Soyinka argues, particularly intriguing in the case of *Oba Koso*, which was performed entirely in Yoruba. The key to its ability to communicate to international audiences lay in what Soyinka terms 'a rich and persuasive evocation achieved through the felicitous plurality of the dramatic media [. . .] A code of meanings is established through rhythm, movement and tonal-specific harmonies.' Ibid. 56. This analysis restates once again Soyinka's questioning of the traditional Western semiotic hierarchy of theatrical codes. While Soyinka's own plays rely heavily on dialogic communication, those works which attempt 'ritual transformation' in some way draw equally for their effect on precisely those non-verbal elements that Soyinka finds so successfully employed in *Oba Koso* and which are the central communicative idioms of traditional Yoruba performance: music, dance, and poetry.

[75] Soyinka, *Collected Plays*, 151.

The division between the spheres of the shack and church is demarcated by the 'ragged fence'.[76] The shack represents the space of a
society in transition from a traditional to a Western way of life. The
problematic and even destructive course that such a transition takes is
represented by the half-demolished 'mammy waggon' that dominates
one side of the shack and the verbal inscription it bears. In striking
contrast to this chaos are the chairs and table on which the Professor
will later carry out his business. African and Western signs are placed
in a less than harmonious contiguity in the semiosphere of the shack.
It will become the site and setting for traditional rites and corrupt
business deals. The church in the background, on the other hand, is
an iconographic representation of a purely Western semiosphere; as a
sign of spiritual and political power, it is located on the margins of
the action, but exerts its influence none the less. It never becomes,
however, a mimetic–dramatic space, but manifests itself acoustically
and visually. This acoustic spatial presence makes itself felt in the
scene in Act 2 in which the Professor enacts a palm wine ritual for the
assembled 'layabouts', while in the church a religious service is being
conducted. The ritual in the shack is dominated acoustically by the
Christian service until the Professor gives the order to drown out the
church organ by Yoruba music.[77]

In *Death and the King's Horseman* a similar structure of spatial
contrasts can be seen. In this case there is contiguity of Yoruba and
British colonial presence. That Soyinka utilizes a contrastive dramaturgy by alternating between the two cultural spaces has already been
pointed out in the remarks on dance. The opening scene of the play is
set in a market, an open-air space with quite specific semantic connotations. It is an important place of communication; it is, perhaps,
in Yoruba and African culture the quintessential public arena, and
not just a place of commerce.[78] It is into this public and female-
dominated space that Elesin, the deceased king's counsellor, enters as
he prepares himself for ritual suicide.

[76] On this division, see Moody, 'The Steeple and the Palm-Wine Shack', 99. Moody
sees the fence as 'the "hybrid" margin itself, separating the power of the churchyard,
with all its magical threat, from the equally potent world of the palm-wine shack'.

[77] Soyinka, *Collected Plays*, 223.

[78] On the significance of the market square, Bakary Traoré comments: 'it is there
that the collective consciousness of the community takes concrete form through the
medium of theatre. The square symbolizes the village and the entire country.' *The Black
African Theatre and its Social Functions* tr. Dapo Adelugba, (Ibadan: Ibadan University
Press, 1972), 24.

The spatial transition to scene 2, the verandah of District Officer Pilkings's bungalow, follows the same contrapuntal strategy suggested by the music, which changes from African drumming to gramophone-produced tango rhythms. The performance space of the market is characterized by circularity, fluidity, and constantly changing arrangements created by Elesin, his retinue, and the market women. In scene 2, however, the perspective alters significantly. The audience is confronted with a frontal, linear perspective. They are outside the house, looking through the windows into the interior space, observing the officer and wife at their recreation. In a sense, Soyinka establishes a fifth wall between the audience and the action, instead of creating a conventional living room scene. This scenographic device places the audience in the position of the Yoruba subjects of colonial domination. Like the policeman Amusa, the spectators do not get past the verandah. This contrast of two types of theatre space has almost a programmatic function: the circularity, the multifunctionality, of African theatre is contrasted with the fixed structures of Western proscenium staging, which places the spectators in a position resembling that of a voyeur.[79]

The transition from scene 3, set once again in the market and which demonstrates Yoruba performance aesthetics in their ritual context, to the next (the fancy dress ball in the residency) is effected with precisely the same intentional jarring contrast as that from scene 1 to scene 2. Again there is a severe contrast on all signifying levels: visually, acoustically, and kinesically. It is, however, not so much a 'clash' of cultures that is presented here in theatrical terms as a juxtaposition of two cultures occupying the same geographical space but inhabiting radically different cultural semiospheres. Through a whole series of incongruities in which signifier and referent are kept deliberately apart Soyinka demonstrates the hetereogeneous, incongruous mixture of aesthetic and cultural elements that constitute European culture, at least in the Nigerian setting. A British monarch in seventeenth-century costume dances to Viennese waltz music badly

---

[79] See e.g. Roland Barthes on the semiotics of the Western stage as a place of artifice and deception: 'The Italian-style stage is the space of this lie: everything takes place in an interior which is surreptitiously opened, surprised, spied upon, savored by a spectator hidden in the shadow. This space is theological, a space of Guilt.' 'On Bunraku/The Written Face', *Drama Review*, 15/3 (T50) (1971), 79. Soyinka indeed places the spectator, if not in the position of a voyeur, then perhaps in something akin to that of a theatrical ethnographer.

played by African musicians led by a white conductor. This deliberate highlighting of incongruities is a form of *Verfremdung* and enables Soyinka to create for the audience an ethnographic perspective not unlike that of the Yoruba outside, who witness such curious behaviour on a daily basis. This perspective is enhanced by the spatial drama-turgy of the setting because, by setting the scene in a corridor, Soyinka draws a dividing line between the spectators and the ballroom.[80]

The setting of the final scene in the cellar of the residency sets up a very complex semiotic field. We are told that it was once used to hold slaves awaiting transportation. Thus Elesin's incarceration not only represents colonial intervention into and interference with indigenous life and ritual, but endows the spatial field with historical signifiers as well. His predicament is linked iconically with the historical back-ground to European presence in Africa: his particular situation is not just an *individual* predicament, but indivisibly chained to the whole historical complex of economic exploitation and slavery. The fact that he is literally *chained* underlines Soyinka's intention to establish a visual connection with the historical background to European colonial policy.

The concept of spatial contiguity is one that can be applied to the dramaturgical and scenographic strategies of plays by authors from the Fourth World. Particularly in Australia and Canada, the spatial experience of the indigenous people is characterized by both separa-tion and contiguity.[81] The separation brought about by the system of reserves is itself an ambivalent one.[82] The contiguity of Western and

---

[80] The stage direction reads: 'The front side of the stage is part of a wide corridor around the great hall of the Residency extending beyond vision into the rear and wings.' Soyinka, *Six Plays*, 186.

[81] For a discussion of the reserve system in Canada, see Geoffrey York, *The Dis-possessed: Life and Death in Native Canada*, foreword by Tomson Highway (London: Vintage Books, 1990), ch. 3: 'Inside the Reserves': 'The reserves were created to remove Indians from the path of white settlement and to assimilate them by transforming them into farmers. [. . .] In the end, most of the reserves were too small and infertile to permit any significant amount of farming. [. . .] Less than 0.2 percent of Canada's total area is reserved for Indians, while in the United States the proportion set aside for Indians is twenty times larger' (pp. 57 f).

[82] The reserves in Australia are mostly situated in the traditional areas of the tribes concerned. This is a cultural necessity because the whole basis of Aboriginal culture, particularly the notion of the dreamtime, is tied to particular geographical spaces. The loss of these spaces would effectively mean the destruction of the basis of their non-material culture. Needless to say, this has already happened wherever Whites have settled or established farms. It is still happening in the case of mining projects. For a discussion of the link between religion and space, see Kenneth Maddock, 'The Founda-tions of Aboriginal Religious Life', introd. to Max Charlesworth, Howard Morphy,

indigenous spatial concepts is evident in the urban context, where many of the plays of Fourth World authors are set.

The plays of Jack Davis are set in and around Perth, the capital city of Western Australia. By the middle of the nineteenth century the Aborigines had been expelled from the area by British settlers and their traditional culture and language largely destroyed.[83] The trilogy *No Sugar*, *The Dreamers*, and *Barungin* traces the history of an Aboriginal family from the 1930s to the 1980s. The spatial dramaturgy of these works employs two methods to depict the past in both its historical (in the Western sense) and its mythical dimensions.[84] In *The Dreamers* and *Barungin*, which are set in the early 1970s and the mid-1980s respectively, the contiguity of urban life, on the one hand, and the historical or mythical past, on the other, is realized with one setting divided into two discrete areas. The focal point of the action in both plays is the living room of the Wallitch family. In the original Perth production of *The Dreamers* there was situated behind the downstage living area a raised area or 'escarpment' suggesting a desert landscape. This part of the stage was the preserve of the tribal family and the Aboriginal dancer. As well as this clear opposition between living room and desert landscape the stage was covered in sand in order to evoke an association between the urban setting and its Aboriginal past. The director of the original production, Andrew Ross, explains the implications of this scenography:

It definitely reminds you all the time that the house in the city is on land that was once occupied in a very different way. And that that history is not going to go away. That it is part of the whole being of people and living there. And in a way the thing was designed with this in mind. [. . .] On the stage was an expanse of sand. The set was just the house floor sitting on top of that.[85]

Diane Bell, and Kenneth Maddock (eds.), *Religion in Aboriginal Australia: An Anthology* (St Lucia: University of Queensland Press, 1984), 26. On the connection between ritual performance and space, see the case-study by Richard Moyle 'Songs, Ceremonies and Sites: The Agharringa Case', in Nicola Peterson and Maria Langton (eds.), *Aborigines, Land and Landrights* (Canberra: Australian Institute of Aboriginal Studies, 1983), 66–93.

[83] The story of these initial 'encounters' is depicted in the first play by Jack Davis, *Kullark*.

[84] The following remarks on scenography draw on the published texts, which themselves are based in the main on the first productions.

[85] Balme, Interview with Andrew Ross, Perth 16 Mar. 1991; cited in Balme, 'Strategien des synkretischen Theaters', 400.

The setting, the principles of which were replicated in *Barungin* (see Plate 9), forms a place of encounter for two cultures that are still in a state of tension. The presence of the dancer and his movement through this space points to the spatial-historical connection of colonialization and the destruction of Aboriginal culture.

In order to conform to the practical exigencies of a touring production the scenography of *The Dreamers* had to be adapted and modified. In his autobiography Jack Davis describes how the Aboriginal artist Shane Pickett transferred motives of his painting onto gauze backdrops. In the style of what is now the internationally famous Aboriginal art, Pickett depicted the dreamtime myth of the creation of the local landscape around Perth. With the help of lighting effects a similar alternation between the past and present was achieved.[86]

A completely different scenographic design was created by Davis and Ross for the historical play *No Sugar*, which deals with the forced resettlement of an Aboriginal family during the 1930s. As the mythic aspect of Aboriginal culture plays a less important role here, staging considerations were focused primarily on the spatial experience of resettlement and being uprooted. Ross explains that Davis, who cooperated closely on the original production, wanted to combine two aspects: the immediacy of everyday life with the more abstract historical and political factors affecting this life. It was decided to use what Ross calls 'promenade staging', with locations or settings in different rooms. This spatial design forced audience and actors to 'wander', and in a sense experience for themselves dislocation. This approach helped also to create a visual structure for the play's various themes and levels of meaning:

Physically, we had intimacy on the one hand and then a sense of vastness and landscape on the other. It also meant that you could have two or three disparate worlds and locations occurring simultaneously, so you got the sense of these things going on at the same time. So, you looked at history saying— well, there is political history and social history and that political history could be over there and social history could be over here and they could be

---

[86] 'Clever lighting effects accentuated the beauty of Shane's work and allowed an interplay between the past, which could emerge from a shadow behind the gauze to become a reality, and the present.' Chesson, with Davis, *Jack Davis*, 200. See also the reaction of the theatre critic Peter Kemeny: 'This [the new set design] enabled director Andrew Ross to develop the dream sequences before the beautiful gauze backdrop of genuine Aboriginal motifs. These incorporate the extended metropolitan area [of Perth], based on Shane Pickett's drawings and joined to reality by Steve Nolan's design.' 'Bigger Stage Benefits Play', *West Australian*, 16 July 1983, 14.

there together. The fact that they could occupy the same time on stage had to be a useful tool for us.[87]

That these ideas achieved the intended effect is suggested by the critical reaction to the production.[88] The audience's movement between settings was placed in relation to the fate of the Aboriginal family whose story was being told.[89]

No Sugar has also been successfully produced on a proscenium stage, on a 'dispersed setting on an open stage', as Davis specifies in a note to the published text.[90] In a new production of the play in Perth in 1990 the stage was covered in sand with the different settings either following successively or shown contiguously to one another. The sand formed a palpable scenographic signifier of the different cultural processes at work in the play. This semiotic potential was reinforced by the (re)arrangement of scenes. In contrast to the published text the corroboree (examined in Chapter 6) was followed by the entrance of the Chief Protector of Aborigines, Neville, who holds a speech on 'our Aboriginal and coloured folk'.[91] The white civil servant, clad in a suit and leather shoes, occupies and alters the performance space of the previous scene; his footsteps desecrate what the Aboriginal performers had designed as a kind of *templum*.[92] This spatial device also

---

[87] Balme, Interview with Andrew Ross, Perth 16 Mar. 1991; cited in Balme, 'Strategien des synkretischen Theaters', 398–9.

[88] *No Sugar* was first performed on 18 Feb. 1985 in Perth in a former brewery. In May 1986 it was restaged for the World Theatre Festival in Vancouver and performed in the National Arts Centre, Ottawa. This Canadian tour was followed by several performances in Melbourne. In June 1988 *No Sugar* was staged in the Riverside Studios, London, as part of Australia's bicentennial celebrations.

[89] The London production of *No Sugar* was reviewed by both the local and national press. Peter Kemp, 20 June 1988, in the *Independent*: 'No Sugar makes you go walkabout. In a way very appropriate to this story of dislocation and resettlement, you're kept moving back and forth between different settings in the Riverside's two studios.' Betty Caplan in the *New Statesman*, 24 June 1988: 'The two-arena arrangement allows us to physically accompany the Marli Biyol troupe on their laborious journey to the Moore River settlement.' Malcolm Hay in the June edition of *Time Out*: 'Thanks to Steve Nolan's splendidly designed set, this absorbing production by Andrew Ross conveys an overpowering sense of locale [. . .] This is no theatrical gimmick but instead a subtle reinforcement of Davis's restrained and moving account of his own people's mistreatment and displacement.'   [90] Davis, *No Sugar*, 14.

[91] Ibid. 85.

[92] I am indebted to Helen Gilbert for this example. She stresses the incongruity of Neville's presence: 'As Auber Octavius Neville, Chief Protector of Aborigines, walked tentatively across this ground in his three-piece suit to deliver a speech that situated Aborigines firmly within White historical discourse, traces of the *corroboree* marked his presence as incongruous, invasive, and ultimately illegitimate.' 'The Dance as Text in Contemporary Australian Drama', 141.

highlights the fact that two different performance forms proffering accounts of history occupy the same space: Aboriginal orality and European speech-making.

In contrast to the plays of Jack Davis, Tomson Highway's 'Rez' dramas are firmly located in an indigenous semiosphere, the fictional reserve of Wasaychigan Hill on Manitoulin Island in the province of Ontario. But analogous to Davis's dramaturgy Highway also creates a dramatic space in which several cultural spaces are contiguous. In *The Rez Sisters* the spatial effect is evoked by the tension between mimetic and diegetic space; in *Dry Lips Oughta Move to Kapuskasing* Highway works with strong visual contrasts in the set design. Cultural spaces are for Highway not just actual empirical places, but also spaces of consciousness that his characters evoke and dwell in and which underline the stark contrast between the material misery of reserve life and the imaginative richness of Native American spirituality.

The female characters in *The Rez Sisters* seem to have only one wish: to escape their life on the reserve and take part in the 'Biggest Bingo in the World' in Toronto. The metropolitan centre Toronto is in this play primarily a diegetic space, which is repeatedly evoked in allusion to the Moscow yearnings of Chekhov's *Three Sisters*. In the opening sentence of the play we hear the name Toronto. 'I wanna go to Toronto,' says Pelajia Patchnose, who is repairing tiles on the roof of her house.[93] From this vantage-point, in a manner not unlike the opening of a Greek tragedy, she proceeds to describe both visible and invisible spaces, from the rubbish tip behind Big Joey's 'dumpy little house' to the CN-Tower in Toronto, which she can only see in her imagination. In deceptively simple exchanges Highway unfolds his multi-layered spatial concept, which is rooted, however, in traditional cultural space:

PELAJIA. I'm tired, Philomena, tired of this place. There's days I wanna leave so bad.
PHILOMENA. But you were born here. All your poop's on this reserve.[94]

The women do indeed leave, take part in the bingo game, and then return. There are in fact three discrete mimetic spaces: the reserve, the road to Toronto, and the 'Bingo Palace'. The indigenous semiosphere of the scenes on the reserve stand in stark contrast to the Western

[93] Highway, *The Rez Sisters*, 2.   [94] Ibid. 3.

semiosphere of the bingo scene. The linking element is the road to Toronto. It is a liminal space belonging to neither cultural sphere. Within this semanticization of space it is little wonder that Toronto is only visible in the dreamlike fantasy world of the Bingo Palace. For the visual presentation of this Western cultural and dramatic space Highway specifies a mixture of glitter, illusion, and Christian iconography:

The house lights go out. And the only lights now are on the bingo balls bouncing around in the bingo machine—an eery, surreal sort of glow—and on the seven women who are now playing bingo with a vengeance on center-stage, behind the BINGO MASTER, where a long bingo table has magically appeared with ZHABOONIGAN at the table's center banging a crucifix Veronique has brought along for good luck. The scene is lit so that it looks like 'The Last Supper.'[95]

The iconographical juxtaposition of antithetical elements such as bingo and Christianity is a consciously intended shock effect for Western spectators. The scenographic specification suggests that in Highway's view both icons—the surreal glow of the 'bingo machine' and the symbolism of the crucifix—are part and parcel of the same cultural space. Both exert a seductive and destructive influence on Native peoples.

Although the arrangement of cultural spaces in *The Rez Sisters* is primarily linear, the principle of juxtaposition used in the bingo scene becomes the dominant device in *Dry Lips Oughta Move to Kapus-kasing*. In a prefatory note to the play Highway provides a detailed description of the stage design used in the first production and stresses 'certain elements which I think are essential to the play'.[96] The set design consisted of a lower and upper level. On the lower level were located stage left and right the living rooms of Big Joey and the 'Newborn Christian' Spooky Lacroix. Centre-stage front was a space covered with Teflon serving both as an ice hockey rink and as a forest clearing. The upper area, whose focal point was a brightly lit juke-box, represented 'the realm of Nanabush'.[97] This area was made visible only in certain scenes: 'the effect sought after here is of this magical mystical jukebox hanging in the night air, like a haunting and persistent memory, high up over the village of Wasaychigan Hill'.[98] Analogous to the bingo machine in *The Rez Sisters*, Highway

[95] Ibid. 102.   [96] Highway, *Dry Lips Oughta Move to Kapuskasing*, 9.
[97] Ibid. 10.   [98] Ibid.

attributes to the jukebox, an object from the world of popular culture, the aura of magic and spirituality by linking it to Nanabush. To
a much greater extent than in *The Rez Sisters* the spatial semantics of
Dry Lips are structured around ideas of mixture and overlap. The
Teflon area as a forest clearing is defined as a place of cultural
rejuvenation: it is here that young Simon Starblanket, brandishing a
feather bustle, performs traditional dances. In its function as an ice
hockey arena this area becomes a place of mass culture, which probably exerts a much stronger influence on the inhabitants of Wasaychigan Hill reserve than Simon Starblanket's dances.[99] By overlaying a
defined space with another, seemingly disparate, even antithetical,
activity, Highway can point up links between them which would
probably not occur to the spectator. The same principle lies behind
the simultaneous visual contrast of contiguous spaces. Highway contrasts, for example, Spooky Lacroix's living room with its Christian
iconography[100] and Simon Starblanket's traditional dance in the
forest: 'he is dancing and chanting in a forest made of light and
shadows'.[101] (See Plate 16)

Highway's plays show very clearly that space is an arena of cultural
embattlement, where cultural forces vie for control over peoples,
especially Native peoples living as a minority among an economically
dominant majority. What is in everyday life a disturbing problem can
offer for the theatrical artist a possibility to depict the complexities
of cultural exchange.

This chapter on theatrical and dramatical space concludes our
survey of strategies of syncretism in post-colonial theatre and drama.
The strategies treated have been wide-ranging, covering experiments
in new forms of theatre architecture and staging as well as reassess-
ments of dramaturgical approaches to space. The apparently simple
question of where plays are set and how setting can reflect culturally
specific understandings of space and place focuses ultimately on the
larger and much more complex issue of cultural space in a political
and historical context. Questions of theatrical space engage directly

[99] The comical figure Pierre St Pierre refers in a derogatory sense to Simon
Starblanket as 'that drum-bangin' young whipperschnapper'. Ibid. 31.

[100] For a characterization of this space, see Highway's didascalic description: 'The
place is covered with knitted doodads: knitted doilies, tea cozy, a tacky picture of "The
Last Supper" with knitted frame and, on the wall, as subtly conspicuous as possible, a
crucifix with pale blue knitted baby booties covering each of its four extremities.' Ibid.
35 f.   [101] Ibid. 38

or indirectly with the fact that post-colonialism is finally a debate about the contestation of occupied space. It results directly from the occupied geographical space of imperialism which led to the occupation of cultural space by colonialism, and now, in the infinite variety of decolonization processes, the reoccupation and redefinition of cultural and geographical spaces will be a dominant topic of debate and agenda for action. Perhaps the stage may be able to provide a contribution to elucidating the problems involved.

Conclusion

> As we move towards global cross-fertilization or *métissage* of
> cultures and languages, writers and other rhetors are inevitably
> drawn by and engaged in an overall search for a third code. The
> 'Third World,' as the site of this third code, may well turn out to
> be the privileged site for the artful co-existence of post-colonial
> syncretism.
>
> (Chantal Zabus, *The African Palimpsest*)

The vision expressed in the above quotation of the Third World as a
privileged space for the 'artful co-existence of post-colonial syncretism' is one shared by this book. What Chantal Zabus articulates here
is the (perhaps utopian) desire for a fundamental reformulation of
aesthetic and ideological hierarchies, in which *métissage*, the third
code, becomes increasingly the norm and not the marginalized infer-
ior product. While this study of syncretic theatre as one manifestation
of this third code has tended to stress the aesthetic implications and
processes of *métissage*, they are naturally part of a wider ideological
discursive field. The topic under discussion is situated at the interface
of two highly politicized debates: interculturalism and post-colonialism. Although the research and discussion surrounding these two
discourses have informed in one way or another this study throughout, I feel it may be necessary to restate more clearly how and where
these debates are relevant.

Interculturalism and forms of intercultural theatre in particular
have attracted a great deal of attention in recent years. The growth in
aesthetic phenomena appearing to correspond to any one of several
broad definitions of the term has gone hand in hand with an equally
large body of critical and scholarly commentary on the subject. Much
of this writing focuses on what has been termed the 'politics of
representation' and explores the ideological implications of work in
which directors such as Peter Brook, Ariane Mnouchkine, and
Eugenio Barba, to name only the most famous exponents, have

transferred and reworked foreign, mostly Asian, performance traditions for their diverse directorial purposes. Ultimately their experiments engage directly with the question of representing and perceiving the Other. While syncretic post-colonial theatre as it has been broadly defined here is certainly in formal terms a branch of intercultural theatre, the ideological issues involved are different ones. The essential difference lies in the fact that the processes of mixing take place on different political ground. Indigenous theatre artists are concerned with writing and staging their own stories using their own cultural and performative material. While even the most serious Western experiments in intercultural theatre are never entirely free of the scent of theatrical exoticism or orientalism (in Said's sense of the term), exponents of syncretic theatre are by definition situated at the other end of the power continuum. While Brook and Mnouchkine, by sheer fact of their location in a neocolonial metropolitan centre, are always implicated in a long tradition of exploitative theatrical representation, dramatists and directors working in post-colonial countries on the other hand, are involved, on one level at least, in writing and performing back to that tradition.

The trope of writing or performing back to the centre brings us, of course, to a discussion of post-colonialism, the second major debate. Although this study has focused primarily on theatre and drama in terms of its formal stage language, the works discussed are situated in a historical and political context which has been subsumed under the very problematic term 'post-colonialism'. The common foundation of the very disparate cultures discussed is the colonial experience. Theatrical syncretism is a direct result of this experience and the decolonization processes ensuing from it. It is thus an artistic expression of some of the most important historical, political, and social processes of the second half of this century. Theatrical syncretism is both embedded in these wider decolonization processes as well as embodying a reflection on them. Many, if not most, of the texts discussed here engage in some way with political debates. In the case of South African township theatre the broad frame of political reference is clear; the specificity of reference is often not. The engagement of these works with local problems, whether they be political, cultural, or aesthetic, or any combination of these, is, however, but one level of their implication in what one could term the formal response of post-colonial aesthetic processes. This whole study is predicated on two assumptions: firstly, that formal response is more readily comparable across cultures, whereas thematic response usually is not; and secondly, that formal response is itself implicated in the wider ideological issues of post-colonialism and decolonization, that the choice of form on the part of an artist is a political act, and that every modification and indigenization of, in this case, the theatrical form implies an ideological standpoint. This book set itself the task to explore in detail and from a cross-cultural comparative perspective these strategies of formal response. It may be useful to recapitulate briefly these points once again before ending on what I see as a further direction for research in this field.

The first step was to debate the applicability of the term 'syncretism' as a means to describe the processes of mixing and amalgamating Western and indigenous performance forms. The pejorative use of the term in religious studies was a useful starting-point to discuss the wider epistemological implications of mixing in Western humanistic discourse. The strong tendency in Western thinking, particularly since the early nineteenth century, to keep categories 'pure' is diametrically opposed to the fundamental dynamic of syncretism in whatever form it may manifest itself. A survey of recent applications of the term in comparative religion, cultural anthropology, and literary and theatre studies demonstrated that a decisive paradigmatic shift has taken place in Western scholarly discourse, which can now far better accommodate notions such as 'syncretism', 'hybridity', or 'creolization'. Of these terms, all of which describe processes of cultural mixing and amalgamation, 'syncretism' seemed the one which had a conceptual framework best lending itself to application to the theatre. 'Syncretism' designates a process of cultural exchange based on mutual respect and sympathy for the cultural signs and symbols being adopted. The important difference compared to the syncretic processes observable in religious phenomena lies in the programmatic nature of syncretic theatre, where cultural mixing is propagated as an aesthetic credo. Applied to the theatre, this means that theatrical syncretism proceeds from a perspective predicated on the bridging of cultural dichotomies. Liberated from aesthetics and normative rules, performance traditions are viewed as cultural raw material from which new works can emerge.

Among the many dichotomies in need of bridging, or, perhaps better, dissolving, belong oppositions such as Western versus traditional or European versus indigenous. Just as the cultural products of the West are increasingly difficult to categorize along conceptual lines defined by ideas of national culture, so too is the concept of tradition within indigenous cultures a problematic one. This does not mean, however, that such cultures are to be categorized as Westernized or 'diluted'. It does mean, however, that the borders between semio-spheres are becoming increasingly porous, permitting a growing exchange and redefinition of cultural texts. In a time where very few cultures can completely withdraw from the global circulation of cultural and technical products, cultural difference delineates itself through the *selection* and specific redefinition of these products.

Cultural and aesthetic redefinition perhaps best summarizes the formal processes at work in syncretic theatre. For this reason, this study opted for an approach which illuminated a restricted number of formal strategies described and analysed in the vocabulary of theatre semiotics. It was argued that semiotics, whatever disadvantages it might have in terms of its erstwhile scientist allures and esoteric terminology, has at least developed a vocabulary that enables cultural and aesthetic comparisons on relatively neutral ground. A central concept for this approach was that of 'cultural text', defining as it does an almost unlimited number of expressive forms in a culture, which are capable of being integrated into the framework of a thea-trical performance. This definition established the parameters for analysis. Elements of plays and performances were examined which could be identified as indigenous cultural texts such as rites, oral forms, the textuality of the body, dance, and spatial conceptions. This approach differs fundamentally from previous criticism of post-colonial drama, which has tended to be thematically orientated. This also applies to the analysis of language, which focused on per-formance-related problems such as multilingualism and theatrical translation.

It is difficult to arrive at any kind of satisfactory summation of the importance of syncretic theatre, either on a local or on an interna-tional level. Such value judgements, once so constitutive and characteristic of literary and dramatic criticism, are contingent on so many factors, and can receive equally convincing and contradictory answers, depending on local, national, and international viewpoints, that they have become practically redundant. Because this study has tried to approach this phenomenon from a comparative perspective, it is perhaps relevant, however, to raise a final question concerning the transposition and production of syncretic theatrical texts between cultures. This does not imply any kind of value judgement, though.

That the plays examined here evidence a very special relation between
text and *mise-en-scène* results from the fact that syncretic theatrical
texts are highly dependent on culturally specific signs and codes. By
being rooted in a particular culture these works often appear to be
restricted to production and reception within a national or even
regional context, and that access to a cross-cultural, international
theatrical discourse is thereby severely curtailed. Quite apart from
the question whether the theatre artists concerned are actually
interested in international reception, it is evident that syncretic texts
have already reached audiences outside the countries of their genesis.
The modes of production and reception are, however, quite different.
South African township theatre represents the most striking example
of syncretic theatre that has found an international audience. These
plays are shown abroad both in their original South African productions as well as in productions by other directors in other languages.
Peter Brook's Paris production of *Woza Albert!* with francophone
West African actors is probably the most prominent example of the
latter. The text withstood the process of linguistic translation and
theatrical adaptation without forfeiting its identity as township
theatre. More problematic texts are Wole Soyinka's syncretic plays.
When the English director Phyllida Lloyd staged *Death and the King's
Horseman* in 1990 at Manchester's Royal Exchange Theatre, she
required the assistance of a Yoruba adviser, Yoruba musicians, and a
number of West African performers, presumably to ensure cultural
authenticity.[1] This example points up an interesting dilemma for
Western theatre. The putative search for 'authenticity', if it can,
indeed, be imputed in this case, implies a desire bordering on rigidity
to retain such texts in a state of Otherness. While syncretic theatre
texts themselves are almost without exception based on semiospheres
in a state of flux, their production in a Western context may seek to
hold on to a rigid concept of 'authentic Otherness'. This is a very
problematic concept because, as was repeatedly pointed out in the
course of this book, any attempt to freeze cultural forms within a
matrix of authenticity results very quickly in the folklorization of
cultural texts. This notion of authenticity is not just restricted to
practical exigencies of performing songs and dances; it also concerns

---

[1] For an account of this production, see Martin Rohmer's article 'Wole Soyinka's
Death and the King's Horseman, Royal Exchange Theatre, Manchester', *New Theatre
Quarterly*, 10/37 (1994), 57–69.

questions of ethnicity and corporeal textuality. As Peter Brook's production proves, an international audience may certainly be prepared to accept West African francophone actors in the roles of South African Blacks. But whether such an audience, or any other for that matter, will or wants to have the opportunity to see white actors in such roles depends largely on conventions which, in contrast to Western theatre's usually extremely flexible semiotics, makes casting contingent on ethnicity.

The point here is that the difficulties facing a production of a syncretic theatre text outside its original performative context are determined largely by receptive codes and their estimation on the part of prospective directors. Receptive codes will determine how syncretized cultural texts are understood, whether as theatre or as folklore. This means that the performability of syncretic theatre is not a question of aesthetics alone. It concerns directly the complex of cultural prejudices and categories of alterity that govern the reception of theatre in any cross-cultural situation. It is perhaps this very difficulty, and (it is hoped) the growing number of productions of these plays, that will demonstrate the importance of syncretic theatre in the crucial processes of cross-cultural communication and understanding. For this process to grow and continue, we need an increasing number of productions of syncretic plays, accompanied by informed scholarly and critical debate.

Bibliography

ABRAHAMS, ROGER D., 'Patterns of Performance in the British West-Indies', in Whitten and Szwed (eds.), *Afro-American Anthropology*, 163–79.

—— *The Man-of-Words in the West Indies: Performance and Emergence of Creole Culture* (Baltimore: Johns Hopkins University Press, 1983).

ADEDEJI, J. A., 'The Place of Drama in Yoruba Religious Observance', *Odù: University of Ifę Journal of African Studies*, 3/1 (1966), 88–94.

—— 'Form and Function of Satire in Yoruba Drama', *Odù: University of Ifę Journal of African Studies*, 4/1 (1968), 61–72.

—— 'Aesthetics of Soyinka's Theatre', in Adelugba (ed.), *Before our Very Eyes*, 104–31.

ADELUGBA, DAPO, 'Language and Drama: Ama Ata Aidoo', *African Literature Today*, 8 (1976), 72–84.

—— 'Trance and Theatre: The Nigerian Experience', in Ogunbiyi (ed.), *Drama and Theatre in Nigeria*, 203–18.

—— (ed.), *Before our Very Eyes: Tribute to Wole Soyinka* (Ibadan: Spectrum Books, 1987).

AIDOO, AMA ATA, *Two Plays: The Dilemma of a Ghost; Anowa* (1965; Harlow: Longman African Classics, 1989).

AKERMAN, ANTHONY, 'Why Must these Shows Go On? A Critique of Black Musicals Made for White Audiences', *Theatre Quarterly*, 8/28 (Winter 1977–8), 67–9.

AMANKULOR, J. NDAKAKU, 'Ekpe Festival as Religious Ritual and Dance Drama', in Ogunbiyi (ed.), *Drama and Theatre in Nigeria*, 113–29.

—— 'The Condition of Ritual in Theatre: An Intercultural Perspective', *Performing Arts Journal*, 33/4 (1989), 45–58.

ANDERSON, MICHELLE, 'Authentic Voodoo is Synthetic', *Drama Review*, 26/2 (1982), 89–110.

ARCHIE, CAROL, 'Every *marae* is a Theatre', *Listener and TV Times* (Wellington), 26 Aug. 1991, 48.

ARMSTRONG, ROBERT PLANT, 'Tragedy—Greek and Yoruba: A Cross-Cultural Perspective', *Research in African Literature*, 7 (1976), 23–43.

ARTAUD, ANTONIN, *The Theatre and its Double*, tr. Victor Corti (London: Calder & Boyars, 1970).

ASAD, TALAL (ed.), *Anthropology and the Colonial Encounter* (Ithaca: Cornell University Press, 1973).

—— 'The Concept of Cultural Translation in British Social Anthropology', in Clifford and Marcus (eds.), *Writing Culture* (Berkeley and Los Angeles: University of California Press, 1986), 141–64.

ASHCROFT, BILL, GARETH GRIFFITHS, and HELEN TIFFIN, *The Empire Writes Back: Theory and Practice in Post-Colonial Literatures* (London: Routledge, 1989).

ASHTON, ELAINE, and GEORGE SAVONA, *Theatre as Sign-System: A Semiotics of Text and Performance* (London: Routledge, 1992).

ASHTON, MARTHA B., 'Yakshagana', *Drama Review*, 13/3 (Spring 1969), 148–55.

ASLAN, ODETTE, and DENIS BABLET (eds.), *Le Masque: Du rite au théâtre* (Paris: Éditions du CNRS, 1985).

AUSLANDER, PHILIP, 'Embodiment: The Politics of Postmodern Dance', *Drama Review*, 32/4 (Winter 1988), 7–23.

AWASTHI, SURESH, 'The Scenography of the Traditional Theatre of India', *Drama Review*, 18/4 (T-64) (1974), 36–46.

—— '"Theatre of Roots": Encounter with Tradition', *Drama Review*, 33/4 (1989), 48–69.

BADEJO, DEIDRE L., 'Unmasking the Gods: Of Egungun and Demagogues in Three Works by Wole Soyinka', *Theatre Journal*, 39/2 (1987), 204–14.

BAKER, DONALD, 'A Structural Theory of Theatre', *Yale/Theatre*, 8/1 (Fall 1976), 55–61.

BAKHTIN, M. M., *The Dialogic Imagination: Four Essays*, ed. Michael Holquist, tr. Caryl Emerson and Michael Holquist (Austin: University of Texas Press, 1981).

BALME, CHRISTOPHER, 'The Aboriginal Theatre of Jack Davis: Prolegomena to a Theory of Syncretic Theatre', in Geoffrey V. Davis and Hena Maes-Jelenik (eds.), *Crisis and Conflict in the New Literatures in English* (Rodopi: Amsterdam, 1989), 401–17.

—— 'New Maori Theatre in New Zealand', *Australasian Drama Studies*, 15–16 (1989–90), 149–66.

—— 'A Place to Stand: Concepts of Space and Ceremony in Contemporary Maori Theatre', in Claude Schumacher and Derek Fogg (eds.), *Small is Beautiful: Small Countries Theatre Conference* (Glasgow: Theatre Studies Publications, 1991), 192–202.

—— 'The Caribbean Theatre of Ritual', in Anna Rutherford (ed.), *From Commonwealth to Post-Colonial* (Sydney: Dangaroo Press, 1992), 181–96.

—— 'Between Separation and Integration: Contemporary Maori Theatre', *CRNLE Reviews Journal* 1 (1993), 41–8.

—— 'Interview with Andrew Ross', Perth, 16 Mar. 1991, in 'Strategien des synkretischen Theaters', University of Munich Habilitation thesis, 398–402.

—— Interview with Tomson Highway (1991), in 'Strategien des synkretischen Theaters', 394–7.

—— 'It is Political if it Can be Passed On', Interview with Roma Potiki, *CRNLE Reviews Journal*, 1 (1993), 35–40.

—— 'Strategien des synkretischen Theaters. Studien zu einer postkolonialen Theaterform im anglophonen Raum', University of Munich Habilitation thesis, 1993.

—— 'The Performance Aesthetics of Township Theatre: Frames and Codes', in Geoffrey V. Davis and Anne Fuchs (eds.), *Theatre and Change in South Africa*, Contemporary Theatre Studies, 12 (Amsterdam: Harwood, 1996), 65–84.

BANHAM, MARTIN, 'Ola Rotimi: "Humanity as my Tribesman"', *Modern Drama*, 32/1 (Mar. 1990), 67–81.

—— ERROL HILL, and GEORGE WOODYARD, *The Cambridge Guide to African and Caribbean Theatre* (Cambridge: Cambridge University Press, 1994).

BARBA, EUGENIO, and NICOLA SAVARESE, *The Secret Art of the Performer: A Dictionary of Theatre Anthropology* (London: Routledge, 1991).

BARBER, KARIN, 'Radical Conservatism in Yoruba Popular Plays', in Eckhard Breitinger (ed.), *Drama and Theatre in Africa*, Bayreuth African Studies (Bayreuth: Bayreuth University, 1986), 5–32.

BARFOOT, C.C., and COBI BORDEWIJK (eds.), *Theatre Intercontinental: Forms, Functions, Correspondences*, Studies in Comparative Literature, 1 (Amsterdam: Rodopi, 1993).

BARTHES, ROLAND, 'On Bunraku/The Written Face', *Drama Review*, 15/3 (T50) (1971), 76–82.

BAUGH, EDWARD, 'Derek Walcott on West Indian Literature and Theatre: An Interview' *Jamaica Journal*, 21/2 (May–July 1988), 50–2.

BAUMANN, RICHARD, *Story, Performance, and Event: Contextual Studies in Oral Narrative*, Cambridge Studies in Oral and Literate Culture, 10 (Cambridge: Cambridge University Press, 1986).

BEATTIE, JOHN, and JOHN MIDDLETON (eds.), *Spirit Mediumship and Society in Africa* (London: Routledge & Kegan Paul, 1969).

BEIER, ULLI, 'The *Egungun* Cult', *Nigeria Magazine*, 51 (1956), 380–92.

—— 'The Agbegijo Masqueraders', *Nigeria Magazine*, 82 (Sept. 1964), 189–99.

—— (comp. and ed.), *Yoruba Poetry: An Anthology of Traditional Poems* (Cambridge: Cambridge University Press, 1970).

—— *Yoruba. Das Überleben einer westafrikanischen Kultur*, Exhibition Catalogue, Schriften des Historischen Museums Bamberg, 21 (Bamberg: Historisches Museum, 1991).

BENDER, WOLFGANG, *Kolonialismus, Bewusstsein und Literatur in Afrika. Zur Veränderung des Bewusstseins der Yoruba in Westnigeria durch den Kolonialismus von 1850 bis heute. Aufgezeigt an literarischen Dokumenten insbesonders an Beispielen aus der Oralliteratur*, Bremer Afrika-Archiv, 10, ser. F (Bremen: Übersee-Museum, 1980).

BENJAMIN, WALTER, 'The Task of the Translator', in *Illuminations*, tr. Harry Zohn (New York: Shocken Books, 1969).

BERNDT, RONALD M., and CATHERINE H. BERNDT, *The World of the First Australians: Aboriginal Traditional Life: Past and Present* (Canberra: Aboriginal Studies Press, 1988).

BETTELHEIM, JUDITH, 'The Jonkunnu Festival', *Jamaica Journal*, 10/2–4 (1976).

—— *The Afro-Jamaican Jonkunnu Festival* (New Haven: Yale University Press, 1979).

—— 'Jonkunnu' in John Nunley (ed.), *Caribbean Festival Arts* (Seattle: Washington University Press, 1988).

BHABHA, K. HOMI, *The Location of Culture* (London: Routledge, 1994).

BHARUCHA, RUSTOM, *The Theatre and the World: Performance and the Politics of Culture* (London: Routledge, 1993).

BHATTA, S. KRISHNA, *Indian English Drama: A Critical Study* (New Delhi: Sterling Publishers, 1987).

BIGGS, BRUCE (ed.), *English–Maori Maori–English Dictionary* (Auckland: Auckland University Press, 1990).

BOSTOCK, GERRY, 'Black Theatre', in Davis and Hodge (eds.), *Aboriginal Writing Today* (Canberra: Australian Institute of Aboriginal Studies, 1985), 63–73.

BOURGUIGNON, ERIKA, 'World Distribution and Patterns of Possession States', in Prince (ed.), *Trance and Possession States*, 3–34.

—— 'Ritual Dissociation and Possession Belief in Caribbean Negro Religion', in Whitten and Szwed (eds.), *Afro-American Anthropology* (New York: Free Press, 1970), 87–101.

BRANDON, JAMES, *Brandon's Guide to Theater in Asia* (Honolulu: Hawaii University Press, 1976).

BRASK, PER, and WILLIAM MORGAN (eds.), *Aboriginal Voices: Amerindian, Inuit, and Sami Theater* (Baltimore: Johns Hopkins University Press, 1992).

BRATHWAITE, EDWARD KAMAU, 'The Love-Axe: Developing a Caribbean Aesthetic', in H. A. Baker (ed.), *Reading Black: Essays in the Criticism of African, Caribbean and Black American Literature* (Ithaca: Cornell University Press, 1976).

—— 'Caliban, Ariel, and Unprospero in the Conflict of Creolization: A Study of the Slave Revolt in Jamaica in 1831–32', Vera Rubin and Arthur

Tuden (eds.), *Comparative Perspectives on Slavery in New World Planta-tion Societies* (New York: New York Academy of Sciences, 1977), 41–62.

BREITINGER, ECKHARD (ed.), *Drama and Theatre in Africa*, Bayreuth African Studies, 7 (Bayreuth: Bayreuth University, 1986).

—— 'I've been an Entertainer throughout my Life', Interview with Percy Mtwa, *Matatu. Zeitschrift für afrikanische Kultur und Gesellschaft*, 3–4(1988), 160–75.

—— (ed.), *Theatre and Performance in Africa: Intercultural Perspectives*, Bayreuth African Studies, 31; (Bayreuth: Bayreuth University, 1994).

BROOK, PETER, *The Shifting Point: Forty Years of Theatrical Exploration 1946–1987* (London: Methuen, 1988).

BROUGHTON, JOHN, *Te Hokinga Mai (The Return Home)* (Dunedin: Aoraki Productions, 1990).

BROWN, JENNIFER, and ROBERT BRIGHTMAN, *'The Orders of the Dreamed': George Nelson on Cree and Northern Ojibwa Religion and Myth 1823* (Winnipeg: Manitoba University Press, 1988).

BULLER, EDWARD, *Indigenous Performing and Ceremonial Arts in Canada: A Bibliography* (Toronto: Association for Native Development in the Performing and Visual Arts, 1981).

CARLSON, MARVIN, *Places of Performance: The Semiotics of Theatre Archi-tecture* (Ithaca: Cornell University Press, 1989).

—— *Theater Semiotics: Signs of Life* (Bloomington: Indiana University Press, 1990).

CASSIDY, F. G., and R. B. LE PAGE, *Dictionary of Jamaican English*, 2nd edn. (Cambridge: Cambridge University Press, 1980).

CASSIRER, ERNST, *The Philosophy of Symbolic Forms*, ii: *Mythical Thought*, tr. Ralph Mannheim (New Haven: Yale University Press, 1955).

CHESSON, KEITH, with JACK DAVIS, *Jack Davis: A Life-Story* (Melbourne: Dent, 1988).

CICCARELLI, SHARON, 'Reflections before and after Carnival: Interview with Derek Walcott' in Michael S. Harper and Robert B. Stepto (eds.), *The Chant of Saints: A Gathering of Afro-American Literature, Art, and Scholarship* (Urbana: University of Illinois Press, 1979), 296–309.

CLARK, EBUN, *Herbert Ogunde: The Making of Nigerian Theatre* (Oxford: Oxford University Press, 1979).

CLARK, J. P., 'Aspects of Nigerian Drama', in G. D. Killam *African Writers on African Writing* (ed.), (1966; London: Heinemann, 1973), 19–32.

CLIFFORD, JAMES, *The Predicament of Culture: Twentieth Century Ethno-graphy, Literature, and Art* (Cambridge Mass: Harvard University Press, 1988).

—— GEORGE E. MARCUS (eds.), *Writing Culture: The Poetics and Politics of Ethnography* (Berkeley and Los Angeles: University of California Press, 1986).

COBHAM, RHONDA, '"Wha Kind a Pen Dis?" The Function of Ritual Frameworks in Sistren's *Bellywoman Bangarang'*, *Theatre Research International*, 15/3 (1990), 233–49.

COKE, LLOYD, 'Walcott's Mad Innocents', *Savacou*, 5 (June 1971), 121–4.

COLE, HERBERT M. (ed.), *I am not Myself: The Art of African Masquerade* (Los Angeles: Museum of Cultural History, 1985).

COLPE, CARSTEN, 'Die Vereinbarkeit historischer und struktureller Bestimmungen des Synkretismus', in Albert Dietrich (ed.), *Synkretismus im syrisch-persischen Kulturgebiet. Bericht über ein Symposion in Reinhausen bei Göttingen in der Zeit vom 4. bis 8. Oktober 1971* (Göttingen: Vandenhoeck & Ruprecht, 1975), 15–37.

—— 'Synkretismus, Renaissance, Säkularisation und Neubildung von Religionen in der Gegenwart', in J. P. Asmussen and J. Laessøe in Verbindung mit Carsten Colpe, (eds.), *Handbuch der Religionsgeschichte*, 3, (Göttingen: Vandenhoeck & Ruprecht, 1975), 441–523.

—— 'Syncretism', in Mircea Eliade (ed.), *The Encyclopedia of Religion*, xiv (New York: Macmillan, 1987), 218–27.

CONOLOGUE, RAY, 'Mixing Spirits, Bingo and Genius', *Globe and Mail* (Toronto), 21 Nov. 1987, C5.

CONRADIE, P. J., 'Syncretism in Wole Soyinka's Play *The Bacchae of Euripides'*, *South African Theatre Journal*, 4/1 (1990), 61–74.

COPLAN, DAVID B., *In Township Tonight! South Africa's Black City Music and Theatre* (London: Longman, 1985).

CORNEVIN, ROBERT, *Le Théâtre haïtien des origines à nos jours*, Collections Caraïbes (Montreal: Leméac, 1973).

COUZENS, TIM, *The New African: A Study of the Life and Work of H. I. E. Dhlomo* (Johannesburg: Raven Press, 1985).

CRAIG, EDWARD GORDON, 'The Artists of the Theatre of the Future', in *On the Art of the Theatre* (London: Heinemann, 1911), 1–53.

—— 'A Note on Masks', in *The Theatre Advancing* (London: Constable, 1921), 60–125.

CROW, BRIAN, and CHRIS BANFIELD, *An Introduction to Post-Colonial Theatre*, Cambridge Studies in Modern Theatre (Cambridge: Cambridge University Press, 1996).

CURRIMBHOY, ASIF, *The Doldrummers, The Dumb Dancer and 'Om'* (Bombay: Soraya, 1963).

—— *This Alien . . . Native Land* (Calcutta: Writers Workshop, 1975).

CURTIN, PHILIP D., *The Image of Africa: British Ideas and Actions* (Madison: University of Wisconsin, 1964).

—— (ed.), *Africa and the West: Intellectual Responses to European Culture* (Madison: University of Wisconsin, 1972).

DANSEY, HARRY, *Te Raukura: The Feathers of the Albatross: A Narrative Play in Two Acts* (Auckland: Longman Paul, 1974).

DASS, VEENA NOBLE, *Modern Indian Drama in English Translation* (Hyderabad: Noble Dass, 1988).

DATHORNE, O. R., *The Black Mind: A History of African Literature* (Minneapolis: University of Minnesota Press, 1974).

DAVIS, ANN B., 'Dramatic Theory of Wole Soyinka', in James Gibbs (ed.), *Critical Perspectives on Wole Soyinka* (Washington: Three Continents Press, 1981), 139–46.

DAVIS, JACK, *Kullark (Home)/The Dreamers* (Sydney: Currency Press, 1982).

—— *No Sugar* (Sydney: Currency Press, 1986).

—— *Barungin (Smell the Wind)*, introd. Mudrooroo Narogin and Bob Hodge (Sydney: Currency Press, 1989).

—— and BOB HODGE (ed.), *Aboriginal Writing Today,* Papers from the First National Conference of Aboriginal Writers, Perth, Western Australia, 1983 (Canberra: Australian Institute of Aboriginal Studies, 1985).

DEBENDAM, DIANE, 'Native People in Contemporary Canadian Drama', *Canadian Drama*, 14/2 (1988), 137–58.

DE GRAFT, J. C., 'Roots in African Drama and Theatre', *African Literature Today,* 8 (1976), 1–25.

DHLOMO, H. I. E., *Literary Theory and Criticism of H. I. E. Dhlomo*, ed. Nick Visser, *English in Africa*, Special Issue, 4/2 (1977).

—— *Collected Works*, ed. Nick Visser and Tim Couzens (Johannesburg: Raven Press, 1985).

DREWAL, HENRY JOHN, 'The Arts of Egungun among Yoruba Peoples', *African Arts,* 11/3 (1978), 18–19.

DREWAL, MARGARET THOMPSON, 'The State of Research on Performance in Africa', *African Studies Review*, 34/3 (1991), 1–64.

DROOGERS, ANDRÉ, 'Syncretism: The Problem of Definition', in Jerald Gort, Hendrick Vroom, Rein Fernhout, and Anton Wessels (eds.), *Dialogue and Syncretism: An Interdisciplinary Approach* (Grand Rapids, Mich: William B. Eerdmans; Amsterdam: Rodopi, 1989).

DUERDEN, DENNIS, and COSMO PIETERSE (eds.), *African Writers Talking: A Collection of Radio Interviews* (London: Heinemann, 1972).

DUTT, UTPAL, *Towards a Revolutionary Theatre* (Calcutta: Sarcar & Sons, 1982).

ECHERUO, M. J. C., 'The Dramatic Limits of Igbo Ritual', *Research in African Literature*, 4 (1973), 21–31.

EFRON, DAVID, *Gesture, Race and Culture* (1941; The Hague: Mouton, 1972).

EKMAN, PAUL, and WALLACE V. FRIESEN, 'The Repertoire of Nonverbal Behavior: Categories, Origins, Usage and Coding', *Semiotica*, 1 (1969), 49–98.

ELAM, KEIR, *The Semiotics of Theatre and Drama* (London: Methuen, 1980).

ENEKWE, OSSIE, 'Myth, Ritual and Drama in Igboland', in Ogunbiyi (ed.), *Drama and Theatre in Nigeria*, 149–63.

ERNST, EARLE, *The Kabuki Theatre* (New York: Grove Press, 1956).

ESSLIN, MARTIN, 'Two Nigerian Playwrights', in Ulli Beier (ed.), *Introduction to African Literature: An Anthology of Critical Writing* (1966; London: Longman, 1979).

ETHERTON, MICHAEL, *The Development of African Drama* (London: Hutchinson, 1982).

—— and PETER MAGYER, 'Full Streets and Empty Theatres: The Need to Relate the Forms of Drama to a Developing Society', *Black Orpheus*, 4/1 (1981), 46–60.

EYOH, HANSEL NDUMBE (ed.), *Beyond the Theatre* (Bonn: Deutsche Stiftung für Internationale Entwicklung, 1991).

FERNANDEZ, JAMES W., 'Fang Representations under Acculturation', in Curtin (ed.), *Africa and the West*, 3–48.

FIDO, ELAINE SAVORY, 'Finding a Truer Form: Rawle Gibbons's Carnival Play *I, Lawah*', *Theatre Research International*, 15/3 (1990), 249–59.

FIEBACH, JOACHIM, *Die Toten als die Macht der Lebenden. Zur Theorie und Geschichte von Theater in Afrika* (Berlin: Henschelverlag, 1986).

—— 'Offenheit und Beweglichkeit theatralischer Kommunikation in Afrika. Kulturelle Identitäten und internationale Aspekte', in Breitinger (ed.), *Drama and Theatre in Africa*, 33–64.

—— 'Theater as Cultural Performance: Anthropology, Ethnography and Studies in Performing Arts', in Willmar Sauter (ed.), *Nordic Theatre Studies*, Special International Issue (Stockholm: Munksgaard, 1990), 144–51.

FINNEGAN, RUTH, *Oral Literature in Africa* (London: Clarendon Press, 1970).

FISCHER-LICHTE, ERIKA, *The Semiotics of Theater*, tr. Jeremy Gaines and Doris L. Jones (Bloomington: Indiana University Press, 1992).

—— MICHAEL GISSENWEHRER, and JOSEPHINE RILEY (eds.), *The Dramatic Touch of Difference: Theatre, Own and Foreign* (Tübingen: Narr, 1990).

FLAVEL, FLOYD, 'The Theatre of Orphans/Native Languages on Stage', *Canadian Theatre Review*, 75 (Summer 1993), 8–11.

FLEISHMAN, MARK, 'Workshop Theatre as Oppositional Form', Paper delivered at the conference 'Theatre and Politics in South Africa', Bad Boll, Germany, 13 Dec. 1989.

FUCHS, ANNE, 'Re-Creation: One Aspect of Oral Tradition and the Theatre in South Africa', *Commonwealth: Essays and Studies*, 9/2 (Spring 1987), 32–40.

—— *Playing the Market: The Market Theatre Johannesburg 1976–1986*, Contemporary Theatre Studies, 1 (Chur: Harwood, 1990).

FUGARD, ATHOL, 'Sizwe Bansi is Dead', in Ronald Harwood (ed.), *A Night at the Theatre* (London: Methuen, 1983), 26–32.

—— JOHN KANI, and WINSTON NTSHONA, *Statements: Two Workshop Productions devised by Athol Fugard, John Kani, and Winston Ntshona* (Oxford: Oxford University Press, 1974).

GARGI, BALWANT, 'The Plays of Tagore', in Mahendra Kulasrestha (ed.), *Tagore Centenary Volume* (Hoshiarpur: Vishveshvarand, 1961).

GEE, DEBBIE, 'Theatre-*marae*: Welcome Change', *On Film* (Wellington), 7/1 1989), 44–5.

GEERTZ, CLIFFORD, *The Interpretation of Cultures: Selected Essays* (New York: Basic Books, 1973).

—— 'Blurred Genres: The Refiguration of Social Thought', *American Scholar*, 49/2 (1980), 165–79.

GEIOGAMAH, HANAY, *New Native American Drama: Three Plays*, introd. Jeffrey Huntsman (Norman: Oklahoma University Press, 1980).

—— 'Indian Theatre in the United States, 1991: An Assessment', *Canadian Theatre Review*, 68 (Fall 1991), 12–14.

GIBBONS, RAWLE, 'Traditional Enactments of Trinidad—Towards a Third Theatre', University of the West Indies, St Augustine, M.Phil. thesis, 1979.

GIBBS, JAMES (ed.), *Critical Perspectives on Wole Soyinka* (Washington: Three Continents Press, 1981).

—— *Wole Soyinka*, Macmillan Modern Dramatists (London: Macmillan, 1986).

GILBERT, HELEN, 'The Dance as Text in Contemporary Australian Drama: Movement and Resistance Politics', *Ariel*, 23:1 (Jan. 1992), 133–47.

—— and JOANNE TOMPKINS, *Post-Colonial Drama: Theory, Practice, Politics* (London: Routledge, 1996).

GÖTRICK, KACKE, *Apidan Theatre and Modern Drama: A Study in a Traditional Yoruba Theatre and its Influence on Modern Drama by Yoruba Playwrights* (Stockholm: Almqvist & Wiksell, 1984).

—— 'Soyinka and *Death and the King's Horseman*; or, How Does our Knowledge—Or Lack of Knowledge—of Yoruba Culture Affect our Interpretation?', *African Literature Association Bulletin*, 16/1 (1990), 1–9.

GOFFMAN, ERVING, *Frame Analysis: An Essay on the Organisation of Experience* (Cambridge, Mass.: Harvard University Press, 1974).

GOPALE, S., 'Playwright in Perspective', *Enact*, 54 (June 1971), n.p.

GRABURN, NELSON H. H. (ed.), *Tourist and Ethnic Arts: Cultural Expressions from the Fourth World* (Berkeley and Los Angeles: University of California Press, 1976).

—— '1, 2, 3, 4 . . . Anthropology and the Fourth World', *Culture*, 1/1 (1981), 66–70.

GRAHAM-WHITE, ANTHONY, *The Drama of Black Africa* (New York: Samuel French, 1974).

—— '"Ritual" in Contemporary Theatre and Criticism', *Educational Theater Journal*, 28 (1976), 318–24.

GROSSE PERDEKAMP, GABRIELE, 'Junction Avenue Theatre Company mit *Tooth and Nail*. Kontrapunkt-Montage als theatrale Momentaufnahme des südafrikanischen Interregnums', University of Munich MA thesis 1992.

—— 'Junction Avenue Theatre Company's *Tooth & Nail*: The State of 'Interregnum' and New Theatre Forms in South Africa', in Breitinger (ed.), *Theatre and Performance in Africa*, 161–165.

GROTOWSKI, JERZY, *Towards a Poor Theatre* (London: Methuen, 1969).

GUHA-THAKURTA, P., 'Tagore's *Phalguni*: An Interpretation', *Visva-Bharati Quarterly*, 7/2 (1929), 272–8.

HALDER, MAURICE, 'Towards a New Identity: *Ngati Pakeha* at the Depot', *Illusions* (Wellington), 1 (Summer 1986), 32.

HALLE, MORRIS *et al* (eds.), *Semiosis: Semiotics and the History of Culture, in Honorem Georgii Lotman*, Michigan Slavic Contributions, 10 (Ann Arbor: University of Michigan, 1984).

HAMNER, ROBERT, 'Derek Walcott's Theater of Assimilation', *West Virginia University Philological Papers*, 25 (Feb. 1979), 86–93.

—— *Derek Walcott*, Twaynes World Author series (Boston: Twayne, 1981).

HANNERZ, ULF, 'The World in Creolization', *Africa*, 57/4 (1987), 546–59.

HAPIPI, RORE, *Death of the Land*, in Simon Garrett (ed.), *He Reo Hou: 5 Plays by Maori Playwrights* (Wellington: Playmarket, 1991).

HARDISON, O. B., *Christian Rite and Christian Drama in the Middle Ages*, (Baltimore: Johns Hopkins University Press, 1965).

HARPER, PEGGY, 'New Roles for the Dance', *New African* (Sept. 1965), 158.

HARRIS, WILSON, 'Oedipus and the Middle Passage', *Landfall*, 43/2 (June 1989), 198–208.

HAUPTFLEISCH, TEMPLE, 'Beyond Street Theatre and Festival: The Forms of South African Theatre', *Maske und Kothurn*, 33/1–2 (1987), 175–88.

—— 'Citytalk, Theatretalk: Dialect, Dialogue and Multilingual Theatre in South Africa', *English in Africa*, 16/1 (May 1989), 71–92.

HERSKOVITS, MELVILLE J., 'Dramatic Expression among Primitive Peoples', *Yale Review*, 33 (1943–4), 683–98.

—— *Man and his Works: The Science of Cultural Anthropology* (New York: Alfred A. Knopf, 1956).

HIGHWAY, TOMSON, 'On Native Mythology', *Theatrum: A Theatre Journal*, 6 (Spring 1987), 29–31.

—— *The Rez Sisters* (Saskatoon: Fifth House, 1988).

—— *Dry Lips Oughta Move to Kapuskasing* (Saskatoon: Fifth House, 1989).

HILL, ERROL, *The Trinidad Carnival: a Mandate for a National Theatre* (Austin: University of Texas, 1972).

—— 'The Emergence of a National Drama in the West Indies', *Caribbean Quarterly*, 18/4 (1974), 9–40.

—— *Shakespeare in Sable: A History of Black Shakespearean Actors* (Amherst: Massachusetts University Press, 1984).

—— (ed.), *Plays for Today* (1974; London: Longmans Caribbean, 1985).

HIRSCH, EDWARD, 'An Interview with Derek Walcott', *Contemporary Literature*, 20/3 (1979), 279–92.

HONZL, JINŘICH, 'The Hierarchy of Dramatic Devices', in Matejka and Titunik (eds.), *Semiotics of Art* (1943; Cambridge, Mass: MIT Press, 1976), 118–27.

HORN, ANDREW, 'Ritual Drama and the Theatrical: The Case of *Bori* Spirit Mediumship', in Ogunbiyi (ed.), *Drama and Theatre in Nigeria*, 181–202.

HORTON, ROBIN, 'New Year in the Delta: A Traditional and a Modern Festival', *Nigeria Magazine*, 67 (1960), 256–97.

HUET, MICHEL, *The Dance, Art and Ritual of Africa* (London: Collins, 1978).

HUGGAN, GRAHAM, 'Opting out of the (Critical) Common Market: Creolization and the Post-Colonial Text', *Kunapipi*, 9/1 (1989), 27–40.

HYMES, DELL (ed.), *Pidginization and Creolization of Languages* (Cambridge: Cambridge University Press, 1971).

—— *'In vain I tried to tell you': Essays in Native American Ethnopoetics*, Studies in Native American Literature, 1 (Philadelphia: University of Pennsylvania Press, 1981).

INNES, CHRISTOPHER, *Holy Theatre: Ritual and the Avant Garde* (Cambridge: Cambridge University Press, 1981).

ISSACHAROFF, MICHAEL, 'Space and Reference in Drama', *Poetics Today*, 2/3 (Spring 1981), 211–24.

—— 'Texte théâtral et didascalecture', *Modern Language Notes*, 96/4 (1981), 809–23.

—— 'Stage Codes', in Michael Issacharoff and Robin F. Jones (eds.), *Performing Texts*, (Philadelphia: University of Pennsylvania Press, 1988), 61–74.

IZEBAYE, D. S., 'Language and Meaning in Soyinka's *The Road*', in Gibbs (ed.), *Critical Perspectives on Wole Soyinka* (Washington: Three Continents Press, 1981), 90–103.

JAKOBSON, ROMAN, 'The Dominant', in Ladislav Matějka and Krystyna Pomorska (eds.), *Readings in Russian Poetics: Formalist and Structuralist Views* (Cambridge, Mass.: MIT Press, 1971), 82–7.

JEYIFO, BIODUN, 'The Reinvention of Theatrical Tradition: Critical Discourses on Interculturalism in the African Theatre', in Erika Fischer-Lichte, Michael Gissenwehrer, and Josephine Riley (eds.), *The Dramatic Touch of Difference: Theatre, Own and Foreign* (Tübingen: Narr, 1990), 239–51.

—— *The Truthful Lie: Essays in a Sociology of African Drama* (London: New Beacon Books, 1985).

JOHNSON, COLIN, 'White Forms, Aboriginal Content', Davis and Hodge (eds.), *Aboriginal Writing Today* (Canberra: Australian Institute of Aboriginal Studies, 1983), 21–34.

JOHNSON, EVA, *Murras*, in *Plays from Black Australia* (Sydney: Currency Press, 1989).

JOHNSTON, DENIS W., 'Lines and Circles: The "Rez" Plays of Tomson Highway', *Canadian Literature*, 124–5 (1990), 254–64.

JUNCTION AVENUE THEATRE COMPANY, *Sophiatown* (Cape Town: David Philip, 1988).

JUNEJA, RENU, 'Recalling the Dead in Dennis Scott's *An Echo in the Bone*', *Ariel*, 23 (Jan. 1992), 97–114.

KARNAD, GIRISH, *Hayavadana*, tr. by the author (Calcutta: Oxford University Press, 1975).

—— 'In Search of a New Theater', Carla M. Borden (ed.), *Contemporary Indian Tradition* (Washington: Smithsonian Institution Press, 1989), 93–105.

—— *Naga-Mandala, Hayavadana and Tughlaq*, in *Three Plays* (Delhi: Oxford University Press, 1994).

PAUL RAJINDER, 'Girish Karnad Interviewed by Rajinder Paul', *Enact*, 54 (June 1971), n.p.

KATRAK, KETU H., *Wole Soyinka and Modern Tragedy: A Study of Dramatic Theory and Practice*, Contributions in Afro-American and African Studies, 96 (Westport, Conn.: Greenwood Press, 1986).

KAVANAGH, ROBERT (ed.), *South African People's Plays* (London: Heinemann, 1981).

—— 'Political Theatre in South Africa and the Work of Athol Fugard', *Theatre Research International*, 7/3 (1982), 160–79.

—— *Theatre and Cultural Struggle in South Africa* (London: Zed Books, 1985).

KENDON, ADAM, 'Some Reasons for Studying Gesture', *Semiotica*, 62/1–2 (1986), 3–28.

—— *Sign Languages of Aboriginal Australia: Cultural, Semiotic and Communicative Perspectives* (Cambridge: Cambridge University Press, 1988).

KING, BRUCE (ed.), *Post-Colonial English Drama: Commonwealth Drama since 1960* (New York: St Martin's Press, 1992).

—— *Derek Walcott and West Indian Drama: 'Not Only a Playwright but a Company': The Trinidad Theatre Workshop* (Oxford: Clarendon Press, 1995).

KRUGER, LOREN, 'Apartheid on Display: South Africa Performs for New York', *Diaspora*, 1/2 (1991), 191–208.

—— *The National Stage: Theatre and Cultural Legitimation in England, France and America* (Chicago: University of Chicago Press, 1992).

LAL, P[URUSHOTTAM], *Transcreation: Two Essays* (Calcutta: Writers Workshop, 1972).

LARLHAM, PETER, *Black Theater, Dance, and Ritual in South Africa* (Ann Arbor: University of Michigan Research Press, 1985).

LEHMANN, ELMAR, 'Colonial to Post-Colonial South African-Style: The Plays of H. I. E. Dhlomo', in Maria T. Bindella and Geoffrey Davis (eds.), *Imagination and the Creative Impulse in the New Literatures in English* (Amsterdam: Rodopi, 1993), 109–22.

LEIRIS, MICHEL, 'Martinique, Guadeloupe, Haiti', *Les Temps modernes*, 5/52 (1950), 1345–68.

—— *La Possession et ses aspects théâtraux chez les Éthiopiens de Gondar* (1958; Paris: Le Sycomore, 1980).

LEVY, SHIMON, 'Maori Theatre in Pakeha Masks', in Claude Schumacher and Derek Fogg (eds.), *Small is Beautiful: Small Countries Theatre Conference* (Glasgow: Theatre Studies Publications, 1991), 203–12.

LEWIS, MAUREEN WARNER, *The Nkuyu: Spirit Messengers of the Kumina* (Mona: Savacou Publications, 1977).

LORD, ALBERT B., *The Singer of Tales* (Cambridge, Mass.: Harvard University Press, 1960).

LOTMAN, YURI M., *Universe of the Mind: A Semiotic Theory of Culture*, tr. Ann Shukman (London: I. B. Tauris, 1990).

—— *The Semiotics of Russian Culture*, ed. Ann Shukman, Michigan Slavic Contributions, 11 (Ann Arbor: Michigan Slavic Publications, 1984).

—— and B. A. USPENSKY, 'On the Semiotic Mechanism of Culture,' *New Literary History*, 9/2 (1978), 211–32.

LYN, DIANA, 'The Concept of the Mulatto in Some Works of Derek Walcott', *Caribbean Quarterly*, 26 (1980), 49–69.

MACALOON, JOHN J. (ed.), *Rite, Drama, Festival, Spectacle: Rehearsals toward a Theory of Cultural Performance* (Philadelphia: Institute for the Study of Human Issues, 1984).

MADDOCK, KENNETH, 'The Foundations of Aboriginal Religious Life', introd. to Max Charlesworth, Howard Morphy, Diane Bell, and Kenneth Maddock (eds.), *Religion in Aboriginal Australia: An Anthology* (St Lucia: University of Queensland Press, 1984), 1–27.

MANUEL, GEORGE, and M. POSLUMS, *The Fourth World: An Indian Reality* (New York: Free Press, 1974).

MATEJKA, LADISLAV, and IRWIN R. TITNUK (EDS.), *Semiotics of Art: Prague School Contributions* (Cambridge, Mass.: MIT Press, 1976).

MAUNDER, PAUL, and THE THEATRE OF THE EIGHTH DAY, 'Te Tutakitanga i Te Puna (Encounter at Te Puna)', playscript, 1984.

—— —— 'Ngati Pakeha: He Korero Whakapapa', playscript, 1985.

MAXWELL, MARINA, 'Toward a Revolution in the Arts', *Savacou*, 2 (1970), 19–32.

MAZA, BOB, *The Keepers*, in J. Saunders (ed.), *Plays from Black Australia* (Sydney: Currency Press, 1989).

MAZRUI, ALI A., *The Africans: A Triple Heritage* (London: Guild Publishing, 1988).

MELWANI, MURLI DAS, 'Indo-Anglian Plays: A Survey', *Enact*, 123–4 (Mar.–Apr. 1977), n.p.

MESNIL, MARIANNE, 'The Masked Festival: Disguise or Affirmation?', *Cultures*, 3/2 (1976), 11–29.

MÉTRAUX, ALFRED, *Voodoo in Haiti* (New York: Oxford University Press, 1959).

MEYERHOLD, W. S., 'Balagan' (1912), in *Meyerhold on Theatre*, tr. Edward Braun (London: Methuen, 1969).

MOJICA, MONIQUE, 'In the Mother Tongue: Issues of Language and Voice: Excerpts from a Conversation with Billy Merasty', *Canadian Theatre Review*, 68 (Fall 1991), 39–43.

MOODY, DAVID, 'The Steeple and the Palm-Wine Shack: Wole Soyinka and Crossing the Inter-Cultural Fence', *Kunapipi*, 11/3 (1989), 98–107.

MORENO, J. L., *Psychodrama*, i (Beacon, NY: Beacon House, 1946).

MOYLE, RICHARD, 'Songs, Ceremonies and Sites: The Agharringa Case', in Nicola Peterson and Maria Langton (eds.), *Aborigines, Land and Land-rights* (Canberra: Australian Institute of Aboriginal Studies, 1983), 66–93.

MSHENGU, ROBERT MCCLAREN, 'South Africa: Where Mvelinqangi still Limps (The Experimental Theatre of Workshop '71)', *Yale Theatre*, 8/1 (Fall 1976), 38–48.

MTWA, PERCY, *Bopha!*, in Ndlovu (ed.), *Woza Afrika!*, 229–57.

—— MBONGENI NGEMA, and BARNEY SIMON, *Woza Albert!* (first pub. 1983), in *Woza Afrika!*

MUECKE, STEPHEN, 'Ideology Reiterated: The Uses of Aboriginal Oral Narrative', *Southern Review*, (Adelaide) 16 (1983), 86–101.

—— 'Body, Inscription, Epistemology: Knowing Aboriginal Texts', in Emmanuel S. Nelson (eds.), *Connections: Essays on Black Literatures* (Canberra: Aboriginal Studies Press, 1986), 41–52.

MUKHERJEE, SUJIT, *Passage to America: The Reception of Rabindranath Tagore in the United States 1912–1941* (Calcutta: Bookland, 1964).

—— *Translation as Discovery and Other Essays on Indian Literature in English Translation* (New Delhi: Allied Publishers, 1981).

MUNN, NANCY D., *Walbiri Iconography: Graphic Representation and Cultural Symbolism in a Central Australian Society* (Ithaca: Cornell University Press, 1973),

MUTWA, CREDO, 'On the Theatre of Africa', *S'ketsh'*, 3 (Summer 1973), 38–9.

—— 'Umlinganiso . . . The Living Imitation', *S'ketsh'*, 4 (Summer 1974–5), 30–2.

—— *uNosilimela!*, in Kavanagh (ed.), *South African People's Plays* (London: Heinemann, 1973), 5–61.

NAIK, M. K., 'The Achievement of Indian Drama in English', in M. K. Naik and S. Mokashi-Punekar (eds.), *Perspectives on Indian Drama in English* (Madras: Oxford University Press, 1977), 180–94.

—— *Dimensions of Indian English Literature* (New Delhi: Sterling, 1984).

NAIPAUL, V. S., *The Middle Passage: Impressions of Five Societies—British, French and Dutch—in the West Indies and South America* (New York: Vintage Books, 1962).

NAROGIN, MUDROOROO, 'Black Reality', in Davis, *Barungin (Smell the Wind)*.

—— 'Towards a New Black Theatre', *New Theatre Australia* (Mar.–Apr. 1989), 16–17.

—— 'Review of Jack Davis' *Kullark/The Dreamers*, *No Sugar*, and *The Honey Spot*', *Australasian Drama Studies*, 15/16 (1989–90), 187–9.

NDLOVU, DUMA (ed.), *Woza Afrika! An Anthology of South African Plays* (New York: George Braziller, 1986).

NGEMA, MBONGENI, *Asinamali!*, in Ndlovu (ed.), *Woza Afrika!*, 181–224.

NGUGI, WA THIONG'O, *Detained: A Writer's Prison Diary* (London: Heinemann, 1981).

—— *Decolonizing the Mind: The Politics of Language in African Literature* (London: James Currey and Heinemann, 1986).

—— and NGUGI WA MIRI, *I will Marry when I Want*, (African Writers Series, 246 (London: Heinemann, 1982).

OGUNBA, OYIN, 'The Agemo Cult', *Nigeria Magazine*, 86 (1965), 176–86.

OGUNBIYI, YEMI (ed.), *Drama and Theatre in Nigeria: A Critical Source Book* (Lagos: Nigeria Magazine, 1981).

OKPEWHO, ISIDORE, *African Oral Literature: Backgrounds, Character, and Continuity* (Bloomington: Indiana University Press, 1992).

OLANIYAN, TEJUMOLA, 'Dramatizing Postcoloniality: Wole Soyinka and Derek Walcott', *Theatre Journal*, 44 (1992), 485–99.

OMOTOSO, KOLE, *The Theatrical into Theatre: A Study of the Drama and Theatre of the English-Speaking Caribbean* (London: New Beacon Books, 1982).

ONG, WALTER, *Orality and Literacy: The Technologizing of the Word* (London: Methuen, 1982).

ORKIN, MARTIN, *Drama and the South African State* (Manchester: Manchester University Press, 1991).

OWOMOYELA, OYEKAN, 'Yoruba Folk Opera: A Cross-Cultural Flowering', in Rutherford (ed.), *From Commonwealth to Post-Colonial* (Sydney: Dangaroo Press, 1992), 160–80.

OXFORD, GILLIAN, 'The Purple Everlasting: The Aboriginal Cultural Heritage in Australia', *Theatre Quarterly*, 8/26 (Summer 1977), 88–98.

PAVIS, PATRICE, *Dictionnaire du théâtre* (Paris: Messidor and Éditions Sociales, 1987).

—— 'Approaches to Theatre Studies', *Assaph C*, 6 (1990), 23–42.

—— *Theatre at the Crossroads of Culture* (London: Routledge, 1992).

—— (ed.), *The Intercultural Performance Reader* (London: Routledge, 1996).

PETERS, HELEN, 'The Aboriginal Presence in Canadian Theatre and the Evolution of Being Canadian', *Theatre Research International*, 18/3 (1993), 197–205.

PFISTER, MANFRED, *The Theory and Analysis of Drama*, tr. John Halliday (Cambridge: Cambridge University Press, 1988).

POTIKI, ROMA, 'Introduction', in Simon Garrett (ed.), *He Reo Hou: 5 Plays by Maori Playwrights* (Wellington: Playmarket, 1991), 9–13.

—— 'A Maori Point of View: The Journey from Anxiety to Confidence', *Australasian Drama Studies*, 18 (Apr. 1991), 57–63.

—— 'Confirming Identity and Telling the Stories: A Woman's Perspective on Maori Theatre', in Rosemary Du Plessis (ed.), *Feminist Voices: Woman's Studies Texts for Aotearoa/New Zealand* (Auckland: Oxford University Press, 1992), 153–62.

PRESTON, JENNIFER, 'Weesagechak Begins to Dance: Native Earth Performing Arts Inc.' *The Drama Review*, 36/1 (T133) (1992), 135–59.

PRESTON, RICHARD J., *Cree Narrative: Expressing the Personal Meanings of Events*, Canadian Ethnology Service Paper No. 30 (Ottawa: National Museum of Man, 1975).

PRINCE, RAYMOND (ed.), *Trance and Possession States: Proceedings of the Second Annual Conference of the R. M. Bucke Memorial Society* (Montreal: R. M. Bucke Memorial Society, 1968).

PRONKO, LEONARD C., *Theatre East and West* (Berkeley: University of California Press, 1967).

QUESTEL, VICTOR, 'Unlocking the Gates of History', *Tapia* (Trinidad) 19 Dec. 1976, 12–13.

REA, KENNETH, 'Theatre in India: The Old and the New, Part I', *Theatre Quarterly*, 8/30 (1978), 9–23.

—— 'Theatre in India: The Old and the New, Part II', *Theatre Quarterly*, 8/31 (1978), 45–60.

—— 'Theatre in India: The Old and the New, Part III', *Theatre Quarterly*, 8/32 (1979), 47–66.

REDDY, P. BAYAPA, 'Asif Currimbhoy's "Goa": A Study', *Ariel*, 14/4 (1973), 77–86.

RICCIO, THOMAS, '*Emandulo*: Process and Performance in a Changing South Africa', *Theatre Research International*, 19/3 (1994), 238–61.

RICHARDS, DAVID, 'Òwe l'esin òrò: Proverbs like Horses: Wole Soyinka's *Death and the King's Horseman*', *Journal of Commonwealth Literature*, 19/1 (1984), 86–97.

RICHMOND, FARLEY P., DARIUS L. SWANN, and PHILLIP B. ZARRILLI (eds.), *Indian Theatre: Traditions of Performance* (Honolulu: University of Hawaii Press, 1990).

ROHMER, MARTIN, 'Wole Soyinka's *Death and the King's Horseman*, Royal Exchange Theatre, Manchester', *New Theatre Quarterly*, 10/37 (1994), 57–69.

ROTIMI, OLA, 'The Drama in African Ritual Display', *Nigeria Magazine*, 99 (1968), 329–30.

—— *The Gods are not to Blame* (Oxford: Oxford University Press, 1971).

—— *Kurunmi* (Ibadan: Ibadan University Press, 1971).

—— 'Traditional Nigerian Drama', in Bruce King (ed.), *Introduction to Nigerian Literature* (Lagos: Lagos University Press, 1971), 36–49.

—— *If: A Tragedy of the Ruled* (Ibadan: Heinemann, 1983).

—— *Hopes of the Living Dead: A Drama of Struggle* (Ibadan: Spectrum Books, 1988).

RUTHERFORD, ANNA (ed.), *From Commonwealth to Post-Colonial* (Sydney: Dangaroo Press, 1992).

SAID, EDWARD W., *Orientalism* (New York: Vintage Books, 1978).

—— *Culture and Imperialism* (London: Vintage Books, 1993).

SALMOND, ANNE, *Hui: A Study of Maori Ceremonial Gatherings* (Wellington: Reed and Methuen, 1975).

SANYAL, HIRANKUMAR, 'The Plays of Rabindranath Tagore', in *Rabindra-nath Tagore: A Centenary Volume (1861–1961)*, ed. Mahendra Kulastetha (New Delhi: Sahitya Akademi, 1961), 233–42.

SARANG, VILAS, 'Self-Translators', *Journal of South Asian Literature*, 16/2 (1981), 33–8.

SAUNDERS, JUSTINE (ed.), *Plays from Black Australia* (Sydney: Currency Press, 1989).

SAVARESE, NICOLA, *Teatro e spettacolo fra Oriente e Occidente* (Bari: Editori Laterza, 1992).

SAVORY, ELAINE, 'Strategies for Survival: Anti-Imperialist Theatrical Forms in the Anglophone Caribbean', J. Ellen Gainor (ed.), *Imperialism and Theatre: Essays on World Theatre, Drama and Performance* (New York: Routledge, 1995).

SCHECHNER, RICHARD, 'Drama, Script, Theater and Performance', *Drama Review*, 17/3 (1973), 3–36.

SCHECHNER, RICHARD, *Environmental Theater* (New York: Hawthorn Books, 1973).

—— 'Introduction: Towards a Field Theory of Performance', *Drama Review*, 23/2 (June 1979), 2.

—— 'Intercultural Performance', *Drama Review* (T94), 26/2 (Summer 1982), 3.

—— *Performance Theory*, 2nd edn. (London: Routledge, 1988).

SCHEUB, HAROLD, *The Xhosa Ntsomi* (Oxford: Oxford University Press, 1975).

—— 'Body and Image in Oral Narrative Performance', *New Literary History*, 8/3 (1977), 345–67.

SCHIPPER, MINEKE, *Theatre and Society in Africa*, tr. from the Dutch by Ampie Coetzee (Johannesburg: Raven Press, 1982).

SCOLNICOV, HANNA, 'Theatre Space, Theatrical Space, and the Theatrical Space Without', in James Redmond (ed.), *The Theatrical Space*, Themes in Drama, 9, (Cambridge: Cambridge University Press, 1987) 11–26.

SCOTT, DENNIS, 'Walcott on Walcott, Interviewed by Dennis Scott', *Caribbean Quarterly*, 14/1–2 (1968), 77–82.

—— *An Echo in the Bone*, in Hill (ed.), *Plays for Today*, 73–138.

SEAGA, EDWARD, *Revival Cults in Jamaika: Notes towards a Sociology of Religion*, (Special Issue of *Jamaica Journal*, 3/2 (June 1969) Kingston: Institute of Jamaica, 1982).

SEBEOK, THOMAS A., 'Aboriginal Sign "Languages" from a Semiotic Point of View', in *The Sign and its Masters* (Austin: University of Texas Press, 1979), 128–67.

SENELICK, LAURENCE (ed.), *Performance in Gender: The Presentation of Difference in the Performing Arts* (Hanover: New England University Press, 1992).

SHENNAN, JENNIFER, *The Maori Action Song*, Studies in Education, 36 (Wellington: New Zealand Council for Educational Research, 1984).

SHER, EMIL, 'Apartheid on Tour', *Canadian Theatre Review*, 50 (Spring 1987), 59–62.

SIMPSON, GEORGE E., *Religious Cults of the Caribbean: Trinidad, Jamaica and Haiti*, 3rd edn. (Rio Piedras: Institute of Caribbean Studies, University of Puerto Rico, 1980).

SINCLAIR, KEITH, *A History of New Zealand*, 3rd edn. (Harmondsworth: Penguin, 1980).

SIRCAR, BARDAL, *The Third Theatre* (Calcutta: Bardal Sircar, 1978).

—— 'The Changing Language of Theatre', *Enact*, 183–4 (1982), n.p.

SMITH, SUSAN VALERIA HARRIS, *Masks in Modern Drama* (Berkeley: University of California Press, 1984).

SOTTO, WIVECA, *The Rounded Rite: A Study of Wole Soyinka's Play 'The Bacchae of Euripides'* (Lund: C. W. K. Gleerup, 1985).

SOYINKA, WOLE, *Collected Plays*, i (Oxford: Oxford University Press, 1973).

—— *The Bacchae of Euripides* (London: Methuen, 1973).

—— 'Drama and the Revolutionary Ideal', in Karen L. Morell (ed.), *In Person: Achebe, Awoonor and Soyinka at the University of Washington* (Seattle: University of Washington Press, 1975), 61–88.

—— *Myth, Literature and the African World* (Cambridge: Cambridge University Press, 1976).

—— *Aké: The Years of Childhood* (London: Rex Collings, 1981).

—— *Six Plays* (London: Methuen, 1984).

—— *Art, Dialogue and Outrage: Essays on Literature and Culture* (Ibadan: New Horn Press, 1988).

SRINIVASA IYENGAR, K. R., *Drama in Modern India and the Writer's Responsibility in a Rapidly Changing World*, Symposia at the Fourth PEN All-India Writers' Conference, Baroda, 1957 (Bombay: PEN All-India Centre, 1961).

—— 'The Dramatic Art of Asif Currimbhoy', in K. K. Sharma (ed.), *Indo-English Literature: A Collection of Critical Essays* (Ghaziabad: Vimal Prakashan, 1977), 243–56.

SZONDI, PETER, *Schriften*, vol. i (1956; Frankfurt-on-Main: Suhrkamp, 1978).

TAGORE, RABINDRANATH, 'The Stage', tr. from the Bengali by Surendranath Tagore, *Modern Review*, 14/6 (1913), 543–5.

—— *Collected Poems and Plays* (1936; New York: Macmillan, 1941).

TAYLOR, COLIN, 'Seeing Soyinka', *Theatrum: A Theatre Journal*, 10 (1988), 35–8.

THOMPSON, EDWARD, *Rabindranath Tagore: Poet and Dramatist* (London: Oxford University Press, 1926).

THOMPSON, ROBERT FARRIS, *African Art in Motion: Icon and Act* (Berkeley and Los Angeles: University of California Press, 1974).

TODD, LORETO, 'The English Language in West Africa', in R.W. Bailey and M. Görlach (eds.), *English as a World Language* (Ann Arbor: Michigan University Press, 1982), 303–22.

TOMASELLI, KEYAN G., 'The Semiotics of Alternative Theatre in South Africa', *Critical Arts*, 2/1 (1981), 14–33.

TRAORÉ, BAKARY, *The Black African Theatre and its Social Functions*, tr. Dapo Adelugba (Ibadan: Ibadan University Press, 1972).

TREMEWAN, PHILIP, 'Tribal Squabbles in Taranaki', *New Zealand Times*, 1 Dec. 1985, n.p.

TRIVEDI, HARISH, *Colonial Transactions: English Literature and India* (Manchester: Manchester University Press, 1995).

TURNER, VICTOR, 'Betwixt and Between: The Liminal Period in *Rites de Passage*', in J. Helms (ed.), *Proceedings of the American Ethnological Society for 1964* (Seattle: University of Washington, 1964), 4–20.

TURNER, VICTOR, *Forest of Symbols: Aspects of Ndembu Ritual* (Ithaca: Cornell University Press, 1967).

—— *The Ritual Process: Structure and Anti-Structure* (Chicago: Aldine, 1969).

—— *Dramas, Fields, and Metaphors: Symbolic Action in Human Society* (Ithaca: Cornell University Press, 1974).

—— *From Ritual to Theatre: The Human Seriousness of Play* (New York: Performing Arts Journal Publications, 1982).

—— *The Anthropology of Performance* (New York: Performing Arts Journal Publications, 1987).

TUWHARE, HONE, *On Ilkla Moor B'aht 'at (In the Wilderness without a Hat)*, in Simon Garrett (ed.), *He Reo Hou: 5 Plays by Maori Playwrights* (1977; Wellington: Playmarket, 1991).

URBAN, GREG, and JANET WALL HENDRICKS, 'Signal Functions of Masking in Amerindian Brasil', *Semiotica*, 47 (1983), 181–216.

VAN DER ENG, JAN, and MOJMÍR GRYGAR (eds.), *Structure of Texts and Semiotics of Culture* (The Hague: Mouton, 1973).

VATSYAYAN, KAPILA, *Traditional Indian Theatre: Multiple Strands* (New Delhi: National Book Trust, 1980).

VERGHESE, C. PAUL, *Problems of the Indian Creative Writer in English* (Bombay: Somaiya Publications, 1971).

VOGEL, SUSAN M., *African Aesthetics: The Carlo Monzino Collection* (New York: Center for African Art, 1986).

WALCOTT, DEREK, 'Carnival: The Theatre of the Streets', *Sunday Guardian* (Trinidad), 9 Feb. 1964, 4.

—— 'The Kabuki . . . Something to Give to our Theatre', *Sunday Guardian* (Trinidad), 16 Feb. 1964, 14.

—— 'Opening the Road', *Sunday Guardian* (Trinidad), 23 Oct. 1966, 6.

—— 'Patterns to Forget', *Trinidad Guardian*, 13 July 1966, 5.

—— 'Why is our Theatre so Tame?', *Sunday Guardian* (Trinidad), 30 Apr. 1967, 8.

—— 'Soyinka—a Poet not Content with Genius', *Sunday Guardian* (Trinidad), 12 Jan. 1969, 13.

——*Dream on Monkey Mountain and Other Plays* (New York: Farrar, Straus & Giroux, 1970).

—— 'Derek's Most West Indian Play, *Ti-Jean and his Brothers*', *Sunday Guardian Magazine* (Trinidad), 21 June 1970, 7.

—— 'Meanings', *Savacou*, 2 (1970), 45–51.

—— 'What the Twilight Says: An Overture', in *Dream on Monkey Mountain and Other Plays*, 3–40.

—— 'Mixing the Dance and Drama', *Trinidad Guardian*, 6 Dec. 1972, 5.

—— 'The Caribbean, Culture or Mimicry?', *Journal of Interamerican Studies and World Affairs*, 16/1 (Feb. 1974), 3–13.

—— 'Theatre and the Tents in Trinidad', *Tapia*, 9 Jan. 1976, 6–7.

—— 'Conversation with Derek Walcott (Robert Hamner)', *World Literature Written in English*, 16/2 (Nov. 1977), 409–20.

—— *The Joker of Seville and O Babylon!* (New York: Farrar, Straus & Giroux, 1978).

WHALEY, GEORGE, 'A City's Place of Dreaming: Black Theatre in Sydney', *Theatre Quarterly*, 8/26 (Summer 1977), 98–100.

WHITAKER, BEN (ed.), *The Fourth World: Eight Reports from the Minority Rights Group* (London: Sidgwick & Jackson, 1972).

WHITTEN, NORMAN E., JOHN F. SZWED (eds.), *Afro-American Anthropology: Contemporary Perspectives* (New York: Free Press, 1970).

WILLIAMS, NANCY, 'Australian Aboriginal Art at Yirrkala: Introduction and Development of Marketing', in Graburn (ed.), *Tourist and Ethnic Arts*, 266–284.

WINNER, IRENE PORTIS, 'Some Comments upon Lotman's Concept of Semiotics of Culture: Implications for the Study of Ethnic Culture Texts', in Morris Halle *et al.*, *Semiosis: Semiotics and the History of Culture*, 28–36.

—— and THOMAS WINNER, 'The Semiotics of Cultural Texts', *Semiotica*, 18/2 (1976), 101–56.

WYNTER, SYLVIA, 'Jonkonnu in Jamaica: Towards the Interpretation of Folk Dance as a Cultural Process', *Jamaica Journal* (June 1970), 34–48.

—— *Maskarade*, in *Plays for Schools*, introd. and notes by Jeanne Wilson (Kingston: Jamaica Publishing House, 1979).

YAJNIK, R. K., *The Indian Theatre: Its Origins and its Later Developments under European Influence with Special Reference to Western India* (1934; New York: Hashel House Reprint, 1970).

YORK, GEOFFREY, *The Dispossessed: Life and Death in Native Canada*, foreword by Tomson Highway (London: Vintage Books, 1990).

YOUNG, ROBERT J.C., *Colonial Desire: Hybridity in Theory, Culture and Race* (London: Routledge, 1995).

ZABUS, CHANTAL, *The African Palimpsest: Indigenization of Language in the West African Europhone Novel*, Cross/Cultures, 4 (Amsterdam: Rodopi, 1991).

—— 'Under the Palimpsest and Beyond: The "Original" in the West African Europhone Novel', in Geoffrey V. Davis and Hena Maes-Jelinek (eds.), *Crisis and Creativity in the New Literatures in English*, Cross/Cultures, 1 (Amsterdam: Rodopi, 1990), 103–21.

Index

creolization 10, 272
cultural text 3–4, 5, 23, 57, 74, 81,
    104, 134, 148
Currimbhoy, Asif 204, 207
    The Dumb Dancer 201, 203, 205,
    206
    The Clock 206 n.
Dansey, Harry 122–3
    *Te Raukura: The Feathers of the
    Albatross* 72 n., 121–3
Dathorne, O. R. 32 n.
Davis, Jack 60–2, 160–1, 164–5, 175,
    176, 218, 223, 251
    Barungin (Smell the Wind) 164 n.,
    173, 174–5, 263
    The Dreamers 173, 174–5, 218–20,
    224, 263–4
    No Sugar 162–4, 164–6, 172–3,
    224–5, 263, 264–5
Debendam, Diane 59 n.
Decamp, David 111 n.
Depot Theatre, *see* Taki Rua/Depot
    Theatre
Dhlomo, Herbert I. E. 25, 30–40, 147,
    210–11, 252, 253
    Cetshwayo 210 n.
    Dingane 210 n.
    The Girl Who Killed to Save 32,
    210 n.
    Ntsikana 210 n.
    Moshoeshoe 210 n.
    on *ingoma* 37
    on orality 36–7
    on rhythm 33–5
Dingane 40, 152, 252
Dogon 68
Dos Passos, John, *see* Group Theatre
Drewal, John 183 n., 184 n.
Droogers, André 11 n.
Dutt, Utpal 20

Echeruo, M. J. C. 41
Efron, David 224 n.
egungun 42, 80, 85, 86, 87, 167, 182–7
Ekman, Paul 164–5, 224 n.
Eliot, T. S. 51
Esslin, Martin 126
Evans-Pritchard, E. 9

Fanon, Frantz 193
Fiebach, Joachim 17, 184 n.
Filewod, Denis 59 n.
Fischer-Lichte, Erika 147 n.

Fleishman, Mark 150
Foucault, Michel 167
Fourth Stage, The 42, 216
Fourth World 2 n., 20–2, 55, 168, 171,
    173, 262
frame analysis, *see* Goffman, Erving
Frazer, J. G.:
    The Golden Bough 41
Freud, Sigmund 102, 204
Friel, Brian:
    Dancing at Llughnasa 202 n.
Friesen, Wallace V., *see* Ekman, Paul
Fuchs, Anne 117 n.
Fuchs, Georg 16
Fugard, Athol:
    Sizwe Bansi is Dead 38 n., 151–2

Gargi, Balwant 256 n.
Geiogamah, Hanay 55 n., 56 n., 57 n.
    Body Indian 57 n.
    Foghorn 57 n.
    49 57 n.
Genet, Jean 82, 181 n.
    The Blacks 48, 190
George IV. 245
Gibbons, Rawle 91 n., 160 n., 190,
    232–3, 235
    I, Lawah 190–1
Gibbs, James 82 n.
Gilbert, Helen 219, 265 n.
Gilkes, Michael 91 n.
Goethe, J. Wolfgang von 51
Goffman, Erving 63, 69–70, 73
Götrick, Kacke 68 n., 88 n., 184 n.
Graburn, Nelson H. H. 20–1
Graham-White, Anthony 68
Griaule, Marcel 68 n.
Grotowski, Jerzy 82, 151, 169, 244,
    251, 254
Group Theatre 39 n.

Haiti 9
Hamner, Robert 50
Hannerz, Ulf 10, 11
Hapipi, Rore:
    Death of the Land 72 n., 176
Harlem Theatre, *see* Teer, Barbara Ann
Harper, Peggy 210
Hauptfleisch, Temple 14, 115–16, 120,
    152
Herskovits, Melville J. 9, 92 n.
Highway, Thomson 58–9, 129, 177–8,
    180 n.